A Julio Ortega
con agradecimiento
y amistad lezamiana

César Salgado
Austin 2002

From Modernism
to Neobaroque

The Bucknell Studies in Latin American Literature and Theory

General Editor: Aníbal González, *Pennsylvania State University*

The literature of Latin America, with its intensely critical, self-questioning, and experimental impulses, is currently one of the most influential in the world. In its earlier phases, this literary tradition produced major writers, such as Bartolomé de las Casas, Bernal Diaz del Castillo, the Inca Garcilaso, Sor Juana Inés de la Cruz, Andrés Bello, Gertrudis Gómez de Avellaneda, Domingo F. Sarmiento, José Marti, and Rubén Dario. More recently, writers from the U.S. to China, from Britain to Africa and India, and of course from the Iberian Peninsula, have felt the impact of the fiction and the poetry of such contemporary Latin American writers as Borges, Cortázar, Garcia Márquez, Guimaraes Rosa, Lezama Lima, Neruda, Vargas Llosa, Paz, Poniatowska, and Lispector, among many others. Dealing with far-reaching questions of history and modernity, language and selfhood, and power and ethics, Latin American literature sheds light on the many-faceted nature of Latin American life, as well as on the human condition as a whole.

The aim of this series of books is to provide a forum for the best criticism on Latin American literature in a wide range of critical approaches, with an emphasis on works that productively combine scholarship with theory. Acknowledging the historical links and cultural affinities between Latin American and Iberian literatures, the series welcomes consideration of Spanish and Portuguese texts and topics, while also providing a space of convergence for scholars working in Romance studies, comparative literature, cultural studies, and literary theory.

Titles in Series

César Augusto Salgado, *From Modernism to Neobaroque: Joyce and Lezama Lima*

Robert Ignacio Diaz, *Unhomely Rooms: Foreign Tongues and Spanish American Literature*

Mario Santana, *Foreigners in the Homeland: The Latin American New Novel in Spain, 1962–1974*

http://www.departments.bucknell.edu/univ_press

From Modernism to Neobaroque

Joyce and Lezama Lima

César Augusto Salgado

Lewisburg
Bucknell University Press
London: Associated University Presses

Associated University Presses
440 Forsgate Drive
Cranbury, NJ 08512

Associated University Presses
16 Barter Street
London WC1A 2AH, England

Associated University Presses
P.O. Box 338, Port Credit
Mississauga, Ontario
Canada L5G 4L8

The paper used in this publication meets the requirements of the American National Standard for Permanence of Paper for Printed Library Materials Z39.48-1984.

Pages 63–70 and 77–93 from the article "*Barroco* Joyce: Jorge Luis Borges's and José Lezama Lima's Antagonistic Readings," which first appeared in Karen Lawrence, ed., *Transcultural Joyce* (Cambridge University Press, 1998), are reprinted with the permission of Cambridge University Press. All quotations from Gregory Rabassa's translation of *Paradiso* are reprinted with permission of the Dalkey Archive Press.

Library of Congress Cataloging-in-Publication Data

Salgado, César Augusto.
    From modernism to neobaroque : Joyce and Lezama Lima / César Augusto Salgado.
        p.   cm.—(The Bucknell studies in Latin American literature and theory)
    Includes bibliographical references and index.
    ISBN 0-8387-5420-1 (alk. paper)
    1. Lezama Lima, José—Criticism and interpretation.   2. Joyce, James, 1882–1941—Criticism and interpretation.   3. Joyce, James, 1882–1941—Influence.   I. Title.   II. Series.
PQ7389.L49 Z85   2001
861'.62—dc21   00-028930

PRINTED IN THE UNITED STATES OF AMERICA

*This book is for Ana Teresa
and for my children.*

Contents

Preface   9
Acknowledgments   11

Lezama's Joyce: An Introduction   15
1. Joyce and the Eschatology of the Novel: Jorge Luis
   Borges's and José Lezama Lima's Antagonistic Readings   33
2. Incarnating the Word: Poetry, Adolescence, and
   Aesthetic Theory in *A Portrait of the Artist as a Young
   Man* and *Paradiso*   48
3. Orphic Odysseus: Mythical Method and Narrative
   "Technology" in *Paradiso* and *Ulysses*   88
4. Oppianos Wake: Vico, Resurrection, and Neologisms in
   Finnegans Wake and *Oppiano Licario*   132
5. Joyce Wars, Lezama Wars: The Scandals of *Ulysses* and
   Paradiso as "Corrected" Texts   181

Notes   207
Bibliography   249
Index   262

Preface

FROM MODERNISM TO NEOBAROQUE: JOYCE AND LEZAMA LIMA EXAMINES the historical and intertextual relationship between the "difficult" aesthetics of European modernism and contemporary neobaroque Latin American literature by means of a comparative analysis of the works of José Lezama Lima and James Joyce (with emphasis on *A Portrait of the Artist as a Young Man, Ulysses, Finnegans Wake, Paradiso*, and *Oppiano Licario*). Revising concepts such as influence, imitation, and appropriation, it portrays "modernism" as a postcolonial "world" aesthetic rather than as a European-centered movement through an archival reading of the dissemination and reception of Joyce's work in Hispanic fiction, articles, reviews, journals, letters, and other documents related to Lezama's intellectual biography. Contrasting Lezama Lima's reading of Joyce to those by Borges, Pound, Eliot, Stuart Gilbert, and other exegetes, it studies the systematic "refraction" of principles taken from Joyce— aesthetic epiphany, stasis, the use of neologisms, the "technic of the labyrinth," the "mythical method," and the fictional interpretation of Vico's *New Science*—in Lezama's neobaroque novels. Each chapter discusses a different issue in Hispanic cultural history that influences Lezama's reading of Joyce: José Ortega y Gasset's and Jorge Luis Borges' positions in the debate on the "death" of the novel; the role of the 1927 revival of Góngora in the "neobaroque" Hispanic interpretation of Joyce's work and in Dámaso Alonso's translation of *A Portrait of the Artist*; the influence of Alfonso Reyes' neo-Hellenistic scholarship of the 1940s on the *Ulysses*-like mythical framework of *Paradiso*; the Joyce-like use of Fernando Ortiz's Viconian study *El huracán* in Lezama's *Oppiano Licario*. The book also details how a period of Joycean "enthusiasm" that arose in Hispanic American letters around the time of the publication of *Ulysses'* first Spanish translation in 1945 influenced Lezama's reading of Joyce, and discusses intriguing similarities in the ways *Ulysses* and *Paradiso* have been read and critically evaluated, focusing on the "scandals" prompted by the novels' challenge to sexual taboos, the heated debates inspired by attempts to "correct" the text

9

in new editions, and their powerful iconization as definitive twentieth-century masterpieces in their respective languages. *From Modernism to Neobaroque: Joyce and Lezama Lima* studies how Lezama
Lima's principal works ponder and reformulate in a new light some
central Joycean themes—the interplay between the Homeric and
the Orphic, orthodoxy and heterodoxy, death and resurrection.

Acknowledgments

Writing comparative criticism on James Joyce and José Lezama Lima cannot but be a collaborative enterprise. The notion of one scholar coping single-handedly with the weight of such monumental legacies is, of course, a convenient fiction. I would like to acknowledge here the support of The University of Texas at Austin Institute of Latin American Studies (ILAS) which, in 1993, awarded me a Mellon Research Grant to travel to Cuba for the first time. During this trip, I was able to consult the "Fondo Lezama Lima" collection at the Biblioteca Nacional José Martí and became acquainted both with Lezama's grand Havana and the crumbling post-revolutionary city now tittering on the brink of the millennium. First-hand knowledge of Cuba helped add a crucial experiential dimension as well as bibliographical authority to this book. I thank the 1993 staff of the Biblioteca Nacional—director Marta Terry, ace bibliographer Araceli García-Carranza, and librarian Nancy Machado—for facilitating my access to Lezama's papers and manuscripts during the worse summer of Cuba's "special period." My thanks go as well to the old staff of now-defunct Pablo Milanés Foundation and to Cintio Vitier, José Prats Sariol, and Annie Ambrosio of the still-operating "Casa José Lezama Lima" museum for organizing the events that gave shape to my next two visits to Havana: the 1994 International Conference on *Orígenes* and the 1996 Anniversary Conference on *Paradiso* deepened my engagement with Lezama studies in ways I still have to fathom. Thanks go as well to Madeline Sutherland, chair of UT Austin Department of Spanish and Portuguese, and to Nicolas Shumway, current ILAS director, for their continuous encouragement and institutional support.

I also wish to express my gratitude to those eminent scholars of Lezama who have overseen my project, inspiring me with the rigor of their writing and the gift of their insight. My mentor and dissertation advisor Robert González-Echevarría introduced me both to Lezama Lima and neobaroque studies. Among many things, he taught me to be assertive about the merits of comparative literature

12 ACKNOWLEDGMENTS

projects involving Latin American literary figures. I owe special
thanks to Enrico Mario Santí for enthusiastically endorsing my
work during its last stages and for carefully reading and annotating
the final version of the manuscript. Julio Ortega, whose interest in
my Lezama scholarship has been a constant source of satisfaction
and ideas, provided this book's final title. My conversations with
Irlemar Chiampi—in Havana conferences and during her generous
participation in our 1996 MLA panel "The Scandals of Paradiso"—
tremendously increased my critical understanding of the current
state of Lezama studies in Cuba and abroad. I am thankful as well
to those professors that taught me to regard Joyce both as a modernist phenomenon and as just another Latin American writer.
Christine Froula and Mark Wollaeger made the close study of Ulysses a watershed event for me in their seminar and lecture courses
at Yale. Thanks go to Karen Lawrence who thought enough about
my work to invite me to contribute to Transcultural Joyce. Today I
have the fortune of counting on Charles Rossman as a colleague
and friend at UT. His willingness to share his expertise on all things
Joycean has given a lot to this book, particularly to its last chapter.
I also thank colleague Andrew Hurley and soon-to-be colleague
Gloria Díaz Rinks for reading the full manuscript and offering valuable editorial suggestions. I am also personally indebted to editors
Aníbal González-Pérez and Greg Clingham and the staff at Associated University Presses for their trust and Job-like patience.

My appreciation goes as well to a whole generation of fellow lezamistas toiling in U.S. academia; their ideas, gregariously shared in
LASA, MLA, CRI and other conferences, inflect many instances of
this book. To Ben Heller, Alina Camacho Gingerich, Arnaldo Cruz
Malavé, Orlando José Hernández, Brett Levinson, Gustavo Pellón,
and Patrick O'Connor: may our dialogue continue and flourish.
Many amigos lezamianos from Cuba have broadened my knowledge of Lezama and Cuban history and literature with their erudition, literary abnegation, and intellectual integrity: Víctor Fowler,
Jorge Luis Arcos, Alberto Garrandés, Rafael Almanza, Jesús Bar-
quet, Francisco Morán, and Rafael Rojas. A heartfelt thank you to
those friends whose faith, moral support, and tactful advise helped
me overcome racking self-doubt during key moments of production: Emilio H. Kourí, Sonia Labrador-Rodríguez, and Alan West.
My parents' spirituality infuses even the most agnostic of these
pages; when I think of Lezama's fineza, I think of them. Ana Teresa
Irizarry, my wife and companion, bears equal responsibility for the
existence of this book. Her love has been the true sustenance of
this project. Para ella, el mayor abrazo.

From Modernism
to Neobaroque

Lezama's Joyce: An Introduction

I

THIRTY YEARS AGO, IN AN ARTICLE THAT HELPED FOCUS INTERNATIONAL attention on the work of Cuban poet and novelist José Lezama Lima (1910–1976), the Argentine writer Julio Cortázar anticipated that, although it would take time for most readers to overcome their initial bafflement when confronting Lezama's difficult poetry and prose, Lezama would come to be considered, with Jorge Luis Borges and Octavio Paz, among the greatest Latin American literary figures of the twentieth century.[1] In 1998, despite the objections and condescension of those who misunderstood or were intimidated by Lezama's achievement, this prediction seems to have come true. Lezama Lima has reached a canonical status in today's Cuba that has surpassed that formerly held in the Revolution by novelist Alejo Carpentier and poet Nicolás Guillen. After a slow beginning, the critical bibliography on his work is growing rapidly while that on other contemporary Cuban writers appears static in comparison.[2] Specialists on Lezama's work have emerged in all parts of Latin America and Spain. Mexican, Argentine, Venezuelan, and Peruvian scholars have devoted whole books to Lezama's work, and scholars from Brazil, France, and Italy are reading Lezama in an inquisitive, resourceful, and devoted fashion. Lezama's literary universe—his baroque poetry, his poetic fiction, and his ambitious cultural theory—is attracting a wealth of critical approaches of a theoretical and exegetical sophistication comparable to that which James Joyce's work has inspired in the English language. As in Joyce's case, this critical surge shows few signs of abating.

The visibility and respect that Lezama's work has achieved in the Romance languages have not occurred, however, in the institutions of English literary studies. Octavio Paz described in a letter to Lezama his reaction to the publication of the latter's first novel, *Paradiso*, in 1966:

Leo *Paradiso* poco a poco, con creciente asombro y deslumbramiento. Un edificio verbal de riqueza increíble; mejor dicho, no un edificio sino

15

un mundo de arquitecturas en continua metamorfosis y, también, un mundo de signos—rumores que se configuran en significaciones, archipiélagos del sentido que se hace y se deshace . . . es la comprobación de lo que unos pocos adivinamos al conocer por primera vez su poesía y su crítica. Una obra en la que Ud. cumple la promesa que le hicieron al español de América Sor Juana, Lugones y otros cuantos más.

[I read *Paradiso* slowly, with increasing amazement and stupefaction. A verbal edifice of incredible richness; better still, not an edifice, but a world of architectures in constant morphing, a world of signs as well—rumors reconfigure into significations, archipelagoes of meaning come together and then drift apart . . . it is the confirmation of what a few of us anticipated when we first knew your poetry and criticism. With this novel you fulfill the promise Sor Juana, Lugones, and a few more made to the Spanish language in America.][3]

Yet Paz's sense of wonderment has been difficult to replicate in translation. Although there is an important cadre of North American critics who have written illuminating analyses in English on Lezama—Raymond Souza, Emilio Bejel, Gustavo Pellón, Brett Levinson, and Ben Heller are among the best of these—such work has yet to make a dent in favor of a greater appreciation of Lezama in the English establishment. One is tempted to speculate that there are just too many culturally specific, tenaciously idiosyncratic elements in Lezama that do not allow for the easy conveyance in a non-Romance tongue of the dazzling poetic utterances and the pliant, syncretistic world view that sustain his work. The fact that Lezama's poetic and narrative lexicon is drawn mostly from the baroque idiom of Spanish Golden Age literature and the rich, refined metaphors of French symbolism probably make him a less appreciable author in English translation than the revered Jorge Luis Borges. (Unlike Lezama, Borges considered English his childhood language and allowed his prose to be influenced by many of its formal, lexical, and syntactical qualities.) Lezama's so-called "transcendental" Catholic cosmology—despite its many doctrinal fissures and contradictions—may also seem unpalatably naive to Anglo readers. And the rich, suggestive nature of Lezama's brilliant opacity—which some critics consider a "tropical" variety of hermetic mysticism while others regard it as a postmodern form of dissemination—has generated little enthusiasm. Lezama clearly has not had the success in English other Latin American novelists of the "boom" period have had. While English language editions of García Márquez proliferate and translations of Carpentier remain ever in stock, Gregory Rabassa's version of *Paradiso* is currently out of print. Except for some poems, none of Lezama's other works—including his essays, which have been so influential across Latin America in the recent reappraisal and reinvigoration of baroque aesthetics—has been rendered in English. Cuban writers who often have portrayed themselves as admirers, even "disciples" of Lezama (like Guillermo Cabrera Infante, Reinaldo Arenas, and Severo Sarduy) have had much better luck than their *maestro* crossing over to the English-speaking establishment.

This oversight of Lezama and his works is regrettable since in great measure Lezama's exceptionality as a Cuban and Latin American writer lies in his persistent quest for "universality." Despite his affirmative, protective vision of marginal autochtonous cultures, Lezama wrote in order to be considered and appreciated in the wider context of world literature, a context which Lezama believed was grounded on—although not limited to—the Western canon. As in the case of Carpentier and other noted novelists of the so-called Latin American literary "boom" of the 1960s, Lezama's literary dialogue was not just with an insular or peninsular Hispanic tradition but with the totality of European and American writing. As Cortázar first pointed out, this exchange was often plagued with misquotations, misreadings, and misunderstandings since it was held from a peripheral, "ab-original" perspective that refracted and distorted First World paradigms in unexpected, fascinating ways. In any case, the desire for a transcultural universality is clear from the beginnings of Lezama's poetry. The complex, ramifying system of allusions in Lezama's first major poem, "Muerte de Narciso" [Death of Narcissus] of 1936, is not restricted to quotations from Luis de Góngora, Sor Juana Inés de la Cruz, or Rubén Darío, but also addresses works by Stéphane Mallarmé and Paul Valéry. In Lezama's later poetic and prose works, we can glimpse Dante and Goethe seated next to the French symbolists, the Spanish baroques, and the Hispanic colonial poets. Nevertheless, in the period when Lezama was writing his novels *Paradiso* (1949–1966) and *Oppiano Licario* (begun around 1967 and posthumously published in 1977), Lezama's intertextual dialogue addressed crucial issues of contemporary European modernist fiction as much as of the great European past against which modernism stood. A glance at the subjects of Lezama's critical writings and editorial work during the time would suffice to prove this point. Lezama wrote searching essays on Thomas Mann, Marcel Proust, André Gide, Hermann Hesse, and Joyce; nevertheless, his debate with modernism is better gauged in the tables of content of *Orígenes,* the journal

Lezama edited from 1944 until 1956. *Orígenes*' aesthetic agenda clearly reflected that of high modernism, and the journal paid special attention to the Anglo-American branch of the movement by featuring numerous translations of and/or articles on T. S. Eliot, Ezra Pound, Stephen Spender, D. H. Lawrence, William Carlos Williams, Wallace Stevens, and, of course, James Joyce.

Part of the scant critical consideration of Lezama's relationship with high modernism of the "Anglo-American" type—and, thus, of the little attention Lezama has been accorded in the English establishment—stems from the lack of systematic comparative studies that highlight Lezama's place in a global conception of modernism. Most works of criticism on Lezama either study how Lezama's poetic theory is reflected by his verse and fiction or how Lezama incorporates seventeenth-century baroque rhetorical and tropological strategies in his texts. So far, *lezamistas* have practiced a linguistically endogenous criticism that sets its concerns and methods within the historical, philological, and bibliographical parameters of the Romance languages. Despite notable attempts to situate Lezama in a wider context (the work of Pellón, Levinson, and Heller should be mentioned here), studies that explore systematically Lezama's relation to his non-Spanish "sources" are scarce. This book is, of course, an attempt to fill this vacuum by demonstrating Lezama's proximity to who is arguably the most important modern and postmodern writer of the English language: James Joyce.

What I propose to do here will surely be met with a number of caveats. Major *lezamistas* in Cuba and distinguished Joyceans in the states have been reluctant to read Lezama and Joyce jointly and have justified their resistance with the following rationalizations.

1. *Lezama's connection to English language writers should not be overemphasized since Lezama visibly preferred the French canon. After all, Lezama did not know English well enough to be truly influenced by any of its major writers, Joyce least of all.* According to this logic, it is Mallarmé's influence which prevails in Lezama's poetry and Proust's in Lezama's novels. Thus, the English version of Severo Sarduy's first piece on Lezama was titled "A Cuban Proust" and the few cross-linguistic comparative essays on Lezama invariably discuss how *Paradiso* echoes many strategies and affectations of *A la Recherche*.[4] To this I respond that Lezama did master English enough to quote *Ulysses* when no complete Spanish translation was available, and, that, in the end, even if Lezama did

come to read Joyce in depth in French or Spanish translation, this fact does not lessen in any degree the influence of a linguistically mediated Joyce on his work.

2. *Lezama should be considered fundamentally a poet and, at most, only an amateur novelist who used fiction for the exclusive reason of exploring and illustrating his poetic notions. The ornate, lyrical imagery and metaphorical complexity of Lezama's prose should not be associated with the experimental, mostly naturalistic, and essentially unpoetic narrative technique of Joyce. Inversely, the fact that Joyce did not share Lezama's veneration for the expressive and epistemological faculties of poetry invalidates any proposal to study them together in a systematic fashion.* This argument forgets Joyce's beginnings as a poet and the many deliberations about poets and poetry in his criticism and his fiction up to the publication of *Finnegans Wake*. It disregards the way many critics read Joyce's works as a fusion of poetry and narrative that is very reminiscent of Lezama. It also underestimates the great familiarity with novelistic form and narrative method that Lezama demonstrates in his criticism as well as in *Paradiso* and *Oppiano Licario*.

3. *Joyce was a great rebel, exile, and egotist who turned his back on Irish culture and nationalism, ridiculed Catholicism, and even denigrated his family with exhibitionistic crudity in his fiction. He was an ironist: a comic novelist who abhorred sentimentalization and deflated with relentless parody any epic or mythical grandeur that could be attributed to the modern period. Lezama, on the other hand, was a pious poet who created a celebratory, heroic vision of nationhood and cubanía (Cubanness) with which he nostalgically idealized his family roots and unabashedly apologized for Catholicism.* This interpretation is blind to the many instances in Joyce and Lezama's work in which the oppositions between belief and disbelief, nationalism and universality, and orphanhood and filiality are questioned or dissolved. It disregards Joyce's paradoxical, steadfast loyalty to Ireland and the Church, and cannot account for the affirmative, romantic "yes" that concludes *Ulysses*. It also neglects the important comic and parodic ingredients in Lezama's style as well as his critical vision of the moral squalor, political conformism, and cultural stagnation of Havana during the first half of the century.

These objections are somehow summarized in Raymond Souza's assessment in 1976 criticizing "the mistaken proclivity of some to consider Lezama Lima as the Cuban answer to James Joyce. The works of both authors are complex, and Lezama Lima and Joyce reflect an amazing ability to use language in unusual and unexpected manners, but the essence of their art is different. Lezama Lima's work is as much an affirmation of one cultural context as Joyce's is a denial of another."[5] Several critics have already wisely disputed Souza's assumptions; still, their work has not gone as far as exploring Lezama's indebtness to Joyce as it could. Responding to Souza in his article "Joyce and the Contemporary Cuban Novel" (1992), Leonard Orr considers Lezama's *Paradiso* and Guillermo Cabrera Infante's *Tres tristes tigres* [*Three Trapped Tigers*] as examples of Joycean novels in Latin America, but circumscribes *Paradiso* within the modernist stylistic and aesthetic orbit of *A Portrait of the Artist* and the first part of *Ulysses* while associating *Three Trapped Tigers* with the postmodern elements present in the second half of *Ulysses* and all of *Finnegans Wake*.[6] Orr writes: "Lezama Lima seems to share the modernist elements of Joyce, that which we might associate with *Portrait* and the Telemachus, Nestor, and Proteus chapters of *Ulysses*, and the general modernist concerns for structuring, verbal patterns, the use of myth, and order and coherence" (18). Nevertheless, by drawing Lezama away from the characteristics of high or post- modernism—parody, pastiche, discontinuity, wordplay, babelization—he bolsters the mistaken notion that Lezama only read *A Portrait of the Artist* productively and either ignored or did not understand Joyce's later works. Orr does not take into consideration how aware Lezama was of *Ulysses* and *Finnegans Wake,* and how, as critics like Enrico Mario Santí, Irlemar Chiampi, and Brett Levinson have demonstrated, postmodern elements of dissemination, language-games, and fragmentation are very much present in Lezama.

In a thoroughly researched chapter of his book *José Lezama Lima's Joyful Vision* (1989), Gustavo Pellón comes closer to the mark by pointing out the correlations between the literary and aesthetic explorations of "epiphanies"—experiences of revelation borne out from everyday trivial occurrences—in both Lezama and Joyce's work.[7] Speaking of Lezama's "creative assimilation" of Joyce's theory of epiphany, Pellón writes: "If Cemí discovers his mirror image in Goethe's *Wilhelm Meister,* Lezama himself also finds his in the work of Joyce" (76), a statement I will subscribe to throughout this book. Still, Pellón's qualifications about how "fundamental poetical and philosophical differences" in the end make Lezama and Joyce's epiphanies antithetical in nature tend to dim rather than brighten the affinities between these authors. Pellón believes that Lezama endorses in his fiction the transcendental definition of epiphany espoused by Aquinas and St. Augustine, while Joyce divests the concept of its religious dimension to make it an exclusively secular aesthetic category : "The unbelieving Irish author looks upon epiphany as a surrogate for religious revelation. Literary knowledge and religious knowledge are irreconcilable, competing systems for Joyce, while for Lezama they are complementary [. . .]. Lezama adopts not only the structural pattern of the epiphany but also its traditional ideological content" (78). I feel Pellón here is too categorical about Lezama's creed and Joyce's lack thereof. Heretics and heresy play as important a part in Lezama's worldview as they do in Joyce's, and Lezama misreads and manipulates scholasticism as much as Joyce did, to the point of proposing in *Paradiso* a "heterodox Aquinas" at the end of chapter 9. Lezama's eccentric interpretation of Catholicism, broadened by grafted elements from pagan, judaical, and non-Western cosmologies, recalls, if not Joyce's attitude, certainly the latter's heterogeneous presentation of Church doctrine. By emphasizing "fundamental differences," Pellón ends up supporting Souza's assertion; by privileging in his discussion Stephen-qua-poet and the topos of epiphany, Pellón implies with Orr that Lezama's work can only be associated with that of the early Joyce. Lezama, I will argue, is just as close to the later Joyce as is Cabrera Infante, although, unlike Infante, he does not mimic Joycean verbal procedures in any visible, derivative fashion.

Ironically, the most engaging observations I have found on Lezama's relation to Joyce do not come from a *lezamista* but from a prominent Joycean, and it predates the commentaries of both Orr and Pellón. In *Afterjoyce: Studies in Fiction After Ulysses* (1977), a important study about Joyce's literary legacy, the "polyphlusboious richness" of *Paradiso* encourages Robert Martin Adams to declare Lezama a Joycean "counterpart" next to an Anglo novelist as prominent as Thomas Pynchon.[8] Remarking on the "arabesques" in Lezama's prose—the "multidirectional, anti-narrative, static" forms of reading it inspires (169)—Adams's appreciation of Lezama's Joycean elements moves in a direction opposite to that of Souza, Orr, or Pellón: "In this liberation of language to its own inner energies, Lezama surely represents the fulfillment of a major Joycean potential, one that we're more likely to associate with the *Wake* than with the *Portrait* . . . there's enough fascination in *Paradiso*, even for a relatively uninformed reader, to give it a major place among the books that have fulfilled and extended lines that Joyce first began to trace" (184).

This book has been written in the spirit of Adams's sentence above, but I want to take his position further beyond. Having read only *Paradiso*, Adams writes that Lezama's relation to Joyce "transcends all questions of influence and even inspiration, but can only be intimated under the loose formula of affinity" (184). My presentiment that Joyce's central role in Lezama's system exceeds "loose" affinity and raises important questions about inspiration and influence in a global conception of modernism, is encouraged by a cursory reading of Lezama's criticism. In *La expresión americana* [The American Expression] (1957), an immensely erudite and ambitious essay that scrutinizes Old World-New World relations throughout cultural history, Lezama chooses to discuss Joyce as the most significant literary figure of twentienth-century literature over Proust, Mann, Rilke, and other writers with whom Lezama was supposedly better acquainted.[9] In the first chapter, titled "Mito y cansancio clásico" [Classical Myth and Exhaustion], Lezama makes an exalted statement about Joyce's novels that tacitly proposes Joyce as a model for a new, invigorated literary agenda that could overcome the creative exhaustion of the modern age. When confronted with Joyce's novels, writes Lezama, "la crítica asomó sus perplejos, se encontró sofocada por la elemental cuestión de los géneros, de una realismo que creaba su propia realidad, de una filología manejada por la sanguínea reventazón de una gigantomaquia primitiva" [critics were dumbfounded and perplexed by their basic questioning of genre, a realism capable of generating its own "reality," and its manipulations of philology through the sanguine eruption of a primitive gigantomachy] (56). Joyce reappears in the essay's concluding chapter, "Sumas críticas del americano" [Summa Critica of American Culture], as one of Lezama's paradigms for renewed literary creation during modernism, one that rather than break with tradition was inspired by it in new, surprising fashions. With Picasso and Stravinsky, Joyce represents:

> el surgimiento de una nueva manifestación del hombre con su lucha con la forma. Era un tipo de creador, que podía ser al terminar su primera formación, nutrido por todo el aporte de la cultura antigua, que lejos de fatigarlo, exacerbaba sus facultades creadoras, haciéndolas terriblemente sorpresivas . . . Las grandes figuras del arte contemporáneo, han descubierto regiones que parecían sumergidas, formas de expresión o conocimiento que se habían desusado, permaneciendo creadoras. El conocimiento de Joyce del neotomismo, siquiera sea como diletante, no era un eco tardío de la escolástica, sino un mundo medieval, que al ponerse en contacto con él se volvía extrañamente creador. (160–61)

[the emergence of a new manifestation of man in his struggle with form, a kind of creator able to complete his initial training nourished by the entire contribution of ancient culture, which, far from exhausting him, incited his creative faculties, rendering them remarkably surprising. . . . The great figures of contemporary art have discovered regions that seemed to be submerged, forms of expression or knowledge that, though once misread, continued to be creative. Joyce's knowledge of neoThomism, even as a dilettante, was not a late echo of Scholasticism but rather that of a medieval world that, in making contact with him, became oddly creative.][10]

Lezama's peculiar view that Joyce's modernist achievements rested on acts of creative recuperation rather than rupture is revealing. First, it shows how concerned Lezama was with reading Joyce in a probing, documented, contextual and intertextual fashion. Second, it sheds new light on Lezama's "creative assimilation" of Joyce's novelistic practice in *Paradiso* and *Oppiano Licario*. In this book, I will explore how the idea of Joyce's novelistic practice as a type of creative appropriation of many cultural traditions—as a "modern/medieval" summa—was a constant concern for Lezama throughout his career. Still as late as 1964, in a colloquium on Julio Cortázar's 1963 novel *Rayuela* in which Lezama objects to Roberto Fernández Retamar's assessment of *Rayuela* as a Hispanic "equivalent" to Joyce's *Ulysses*,[11] Lezama grandly describes Joyce's work as a "colossal synthesis" in which many past traditions—the "Greco-Roman tradition," the "Irish medieval," the "Jesuit tradition," "Renaissance English expression," and the nineteenth-century novel in Europe—are put side by side with the innovations of modernism. By refusing any equivalence between Joyce and Cortázar, Lezama implies that this level of achievement is still to be matched in the Latin American novel:

Aparte de un conocimiento, muy directo e innovador, de Flaubert, de Chejov, de la novela rusa y de la novela francesa; aparte de su enorme gigantismo de raíz irlandesa; aparte de su sentido grotesco que le viene de Rabelais; aparte de esos inmensos materiales que recibe, Joyce es un hombre que lleva la novela a nuevas posibilidades. Es decir, destruye casi lo que en la novela eran tipos, caracteres, etc. Y llega a una forma de novela teogónica, donde caben todas las cosas. (56)

[Besides having a direct and very original acquaintance with Flaubert, Chejov, with the Russian and the French novel, besides his enormous gigantism of Irish extraction, besides the great materials he inherits, Joyce is a man that takes the novel to unforeseen possibilities. He destroys almost all which in the novel were stolid types, characters, etc.

And he inaugurates a new type of theogonical novel, in which all things can fit.]

Lezama's reference to "a new type of theogonical novel" right at the time when he is in the process of concluding *Paradiso* is enough to inspire a complete study of Lezama's fiction under the light of Joyce. This is what I purport to do in this book. Here I will examine comparatively, historically, and theoretically the poetic, novelistic, and critical writings of James Joyce and José Lezama Lima, placing special emphasis on the former's *A Portrait of the Artist as a Young Man, Ulysses, Finnegans Wake,* and the latter's *Paradiso* and *Oppiano Licario,* with the purpose of tracing a common textual aesthetic. At the core of this investigation is my wish to understand the conditions that allow for such coincidences in their literary projects, and to revise conventional categories of modernist literary history and comparative analysis. In a way, the final objective of this book is to explore in depth the relationship of "influence" that exists between Joycean modernism and contemporary Latin American fiction in the Lezamian, neobaroque mode.

II

Most contemporary Latin American writers have openly recognized their debt to the aesthetics of high modernism, particularly in the field of the novel. Gabriel García Márquez, Carlos Fuentes, and Mario Vargas Llosa, for example, have identified Faulkner, Lowry, Woolf, Mann, Proust, Kafka, and Joyce as intellectual and creative models and as crucial sources for technical innovation. Encouraged by these statements, criticism has adopted, in discussing the connections between the European avant-garde and modern Latin American narrative from 1920 on, a form of conventional literary history that recalls what Franz Boas called the "evolutionary" model of cultural transmission.[12] The application of this model generates, in most cases, an Anglo-, Eurocentric imputation of derivative status to the Latin American "imitator." The model searches for a "single source" of technical innovation and maps the spread of its mechanical adoption (or "appropriation") along temporal and geographical axes. This method can become formulaic: if there is innovation in the Latin American novelistic tradition, an "origin" is located in the history and the "isms" of the Anglo-European avant-garde.

The most extreme accounts of this trickle-down theory of influence consider the appearance of modernist aesthetics in Latin American fiction as the result of literary cannibalism. The prevalence of modernist forms in the Latin American fiction of the last half of the century results thus from an outright simulation of foreign techniques and modes by means of their application in native narratives. Though there might be a potential subversive element in the willful act of appropriation—Caliban storming Prospero's magical bag of tricks—the relationship between Latin American fiction to its modernist "precursors" is still derivative in this account, the underlying assumption being that the modernity of the Latin American novel is a corrupted or "transcultured" European transplant.

According to chronology, the source/derivation, model/imitator, center/periphery formula could be applied taking José Lezama Lima's *Paradiso* as the reflection of James Joyce's work in the Hispanic-American mirror. Lezama's *Paradiso* can be read as a syncretic, "Cubanized" version of *A Portrait of the Artist as a Young Man* and *Ulysses*, with elements from *Dubliners* and *Finnegans Wake* here and there. The parallels between *Paradiso* and *A Portrait* are immediately evident; the connections between *Paradiso* and *Ulysses*, although not as obvious, are equally compelling. Even though *Ulysses* is, storywise, one day in the life of Dublin in the summer of 1904, and *Paradiso*, by contrast, is a family history that spans the early decades of this century in Cuba, both novels adopt the same archetypal plot that recasts the Homeric epic journey into a modern transcendental quest for a father-figure. In both *Paradiso* and *Ulysses*, Telemachus searches for Odysseus in a marginal, (post)colonial city. This instrumental reliance on classical myth is synthesized in the most obviously Joycean element in Lezama's novel: the charged symbolism of the name of its protagonist, José Cemí. Mirroring the Hellenic allusions in the name Dedalus, "Cemí"—a Caribbean, Arawak word signifying "god-image"—also refers to a founding mythology of culture, to a classical antecedent. Its eccentric joining to "José"—like Stephen, a name invested with great Catholic, "saintly" signification—slyly announces the hybrid negotiations between Christian and pagan cosmologies that occur throughout *Paradiso*, a negotiation that is also central in Joyce's narrative poetics. What T. S. Eliot called Joyce's "mythical method" in *Ulysses*—the anti-realist use of the novel to stage a "continuous parallel between antiquity and modernity"—is equally at play in *Paradiso*. *Ulysses'* *homme bourgeois* Leopold Bloom is reflected in the character of Oppiano Licario (although clearly with greater intellectual faculties and for a much shorter portion of the novel), and meets his "spiritual son" in an Ithaca turned Cuban: a Dublinized Havana.

Joyce and Lezama's fictional worlds coincide in their interpretations of literature, culture, history, theology, antiquity, and modernity. Both their oeuvres tackle similar projects with the same ambition. Both break new ground in the subgenres of the novel: the bildungsroman, the kunstleroman, the family novel. Both reappraise naturalist and realist poetics by incorporating marginal, anti-rationalist modes of causation into their narrative systems. Both reassess prevalent theories of the origin, rise, and decline of cultures and civilizations. The encyclopedic scope of Joyce and Lezama's works bear the same dimensions. The genre of the novel provides the architecture that will support the colossal, proto-scholastic scope of Joyce and Lezama's visions. Both *Paradiso* and *Ulysses* present themselves as summations of cultural knowledge that exhaust and renew the possibilities of literary language. In both cases, the project blueprints are taken from the same paradigms—Homer, Thomas Aquinas, Dante, Giordano Bruno, Nicholas of Cusa, Goethe, and Giambattista Vico, just to mention the most obvious—making the relationship between *Paradiso* and Joyce's novels more *meta*-intertextual than merely intertextual.

Lezama's choice of the novel as an expressive vehicle obeys geopolitical principles as well. Like Joyce, Lezama comes from a Catholic "island culture" formed and deformed by colonialism. Both Lezama and Joyce were very self-conscious of the anomaly of this background in the context of mainstream, "continental" literature. In an act of countercolonial self-assertion, Lezama attempts to reinterpret and refashion the poetic and political history of the imperial language, as Joyce did with English, in the space of the novel—the quintessentially European, "continental" form. At the same time, the novel as an urban literary form allows them to represent fully the intricate physiognomy of their port cities: *Paradiso* attempts to map the space and character of Havana as lyrically and precisely as *Ulysses* does with Dublin. Finally, both Joyce and Lezama use the novel to pursue a bold and profound exploration of forbidden sexualities, for which they suffered censorship and scandal.

Yet, whose image is in the mirror? Can we call these common elements the result of "influence"? How and why are Joyce and Lezama's work intertextual? Tracing the use of William Faulkner's techniques in Gabriel García Márquez or of André Breton's in Julio Cortázar yields important insights into the formal aspect of these writers' work, but leaves as many questions unanswered. Why

Faulkner in García Márquez? Why Joyce in Lezama? Why these intertextualities and not others? What conditions must exist for the successful "transmission" of modernist aesthetics in a polyglot, multicultural context? How is influence exercised in Babel, especially when the language discrepancy is complicated by historical and cultural difference, competing traditions, and geographical distance?

At the core of the modernist fictional project shared by Lezama and Joyce is a reconfiguration of *world* knowledge. The crisis of European centralism after the First World War and the expansion of anthropological studies dislocate the hierarchy of center and periphery, high and low, metropolis and margin. Aesthetic forms of knowledge such as the novel participate in this revision regardless of national context, so that modernism becomes a global phenomenon, a poetics exercised simultaneously in areas politically and geographically remote. As part of its critique of the Western mode of thought, European high modernism actively sought to incorporate aspects of foreign cultural traditions drawn from the wealth of information produced by the new anthropological sciences. Surrealists like Artaud and modernists like Lawrence "borrowed" from studies of Mexican folklore; this, in turn, permitted Mexican writers like Octavio Paz the possibility of self-recognition in their works, of finding something of themselves reflected in European literature. Periphery and center, antiquity and modernity, primitive and civilized, colonized and colonizer, are thus engaged in a specular rather than a derivative relationship, a horizontal rather than vertical confrontation, what Boas would call a "diffusionist" scenario of multiple centers and sources, producing a network of enhanced permeability and increasing the possibilities of mutual recognition.

Thus Lezama's relation to Joyce is not that of creative dependence, but of recognition, of *anagnorisis*: it is the margin seeing the margin, the colonized seeing the colonized, the islander the islander. Joyce is in Lezama's mirror; his work *is* the mirror. Joyce's work allows Lezama to undertake a self-reading and contemplate the literary shape of the Cuban condition in the Irishman's text. Although in this study I often use terms that convey the idea of derivation—"assimilation," "appropriation," "absorption," "transmission"—this book uses more frequently the idea of "mirroring," for I see in this term a less hierarchical meaning: the arrogant image in the mirror looks at us eye to eye. The result is a rewriting of Joyce that is at odds with all prevalent interpretations, at odds with Joyce's work itself. This "assimilation" or "transmission" of high modernism is far from being derivative, linear, or unilateral.

When Latin American "appropriation" occurs, a distortion happens. Something is added or subtracted; the reflection is often poor; sometimes it is too perfect; in the best moments it is something altogether different, yet alike. Like a concave mirror, Lezama's adoption of Joyce's aesthetics of difficulty is not a faithful reflection; the mirror breaks up the image, purposefully and accidentally.

The result is a splendorous, enriching refraction. This refractive effect often takes Lezama's narrative in *Paradiso* into oppositional representations whose difference is most manifest in Lezama's counter-manipulation of Greek mythology. In *A Portrait* and *Ulysses*, Stephen Dedalus, like his namesake, ascends into solitary and ascetic exile by flying out the insular labyrinth and dodging the stiffling nets of family, nation, language, and religion. In *Paradiso* and *Oppiano Licario*, Cemí descends like Orpheus in an often infernal voyage down into the ground of Cuban culture, burrowing toward the center of a labyrinth to arrive at a stronger sense of nationhood and *cubanía* [Cuban identity], at a vindicated belief in the resurrection of the soul expounded by Catholicism, and at the filial company of Fronesis, Foción, and Oppiano Licario. In other words, there is in *Paradiso* and *Oppiano Licario* a deliberate refashioning of the motifs that inform Joyce's reconstruction of the mythical quest. The antagonistic polarities of this reconstruction—the conflict between paganism and Catholicism, insularity and continentality, nationalism and cosmopolitanism, ellipsis and profusion—often have their valoration switched (inverted, as through the looking glass) in Lezama's work. Throughout his work, Lezama re-Catholicizes Joyce, annuls his exile, and sacralizes his secular labyrinth. Yet, in the process and under Joyce's influence, Lezama's fiction becomes increasingly heterogeneous, unorthodox, and pluralistic. Lezama's "orthodox" Joyce conversely engenders a highly heretical Lezama.

This book is organized to prove how systematic the refraction of Joyce's textual aesthetics in Lezama Lima's work is. Each of its chapters shows that Lezama and Joyce seek to generate a higher, deeper aesthetic experience of literature through similar strategies of textual complication: multiple symbolic and mythical "schemes" structure the plot; a profusion of erudite allusions requires the reader to search for sources outside the text; literary language is deployed as a highly crafted, semantic puzzle the reader needs to solve; the narrative moves according to an intricate, carefully drawn "labyrinth-like" design. As Gustavo Pellón has argued, Lezama, like Joyce, envisions his texts as harbingers of "epiphanies." The play between structure and particular; the attention paid to preventing the force of any narrative pattern from diluting the independent poetic utterance; the celebration of the virtues of excess and obscurity as vehicles for literary gnosis: these features, in the work of both authors, problematize and enrich the aesthetic experience of reading by creating a "difficulty" that requires attaining a point akin to epiphanic revelation. There the enigma is solved, the semantic knot is untied, and the labyrinth yields the mysteries of its design. Both Joyce and Lezama regard the reading of their work as a form of laborious yet joyous decipherment that can yield new pleasures and new knowledge: an aesthetic of the difficult.

Both Lezama and Joyce consider this complex pleasure is best achieved in the genre of the novel. Chapter 1 thus focuses on the modernist debates concerning the "death" or "agony" of the novel in order to understand what exactly Joyce and Lezama did with the genre. It is argued that Lezama's response to this debate—his unconventional, "optimistic" reading of Joyce in contrast to Jorge Luis Borges's "eschatological" reading—is what creates the basis for his attempt in *Paradiso* to renovate or "resurrect" the novel through poetry. Chapters 2, 3, and 4 study the role each of Joyce's novels plays in the constitution of Lezama's literary system. Chapter 2 studies how poetry is perceived as the "incarnation" of language—the "word made flesh"—in both *A Portrait* and *Paradiso*. It examines how both novels develop an aesthetic theory based on the principle of arrestedness or, in Lezama's terms, *fijeza*. It also postulates a hypothesis about how Joycean textual aesthetics come to be identified with what is known today in Caribbean literary studies as the neobaroque movement. Chapter 3 evaluates the weight canonical criticism on Joyce's novels carries in Lezama's interpretation of *Ulysses*, and analyzes the bold reconfiguration *Ulysses'* "mythical method" undergoes when applied in *Paradiso*. It also documents the reception of *Ulysses* into the Spanish language, arguing that a period of Joycean "enthusiasm" arose in Hispanic-American letters during the forties on the occasion of the appearance of the novel's translation. Chapter 4 attempts to prove that *Finnegans Wake* was a book Lezama bore very much in mind when writing his later works. Rather than compare systematically Joyce's last novel to Lezama's *Oppiano Licario*, it studies the pivotal yet contrasting uses of Vico's *Scienza Nuova* in each. It also analyzes the role of neologism in the elaborate density of their literary discourse and in the context of the accusations of illegibility leveled against their work.

Chapter 5 is not a comparative analysis of Joyce and Lezama's work as the former chapters are, but an investigation of the uncanny similarities shared by the critical industries they have spawned. Reviewing the literary and political history of the so-called "scandals" generated by the publication of *Paradiso* and *Ulysses*, the chapter concentrates on the controversies their "corrected" editions have generated, proposing a theory that may explain the peculiar polysemic, heterodox, polemical quality that both Joyce and Lezama's textualities are able to achieve and the role of error in such textualities. To fully understand the breadth of their achievement and the complexity of their views, analysis is not restricted to Lezama and Joyce's fiction. This book considers their poetry, critical essays, notebooks, diaries, correspondence, and journals as well, regarding their work—novelistic or otherwise—as a unified system: as an aesthetic.

III

To the biographical critic with a touch of the visionary, James Joyce and José Lezama Lima appear to be kindred yet antagonistic spirits, antipodal *doppelgänger*, demonic twins, negative and positive images of the same photographic plate. Not only does their work have comparatively the same revolutionary importance in the history of their respective languages; one's personality and biographical myths resemble and reverse the other's in twisted and eccentric ways. Both writers were cursed by physical ailments that affected the way they created literature. Joyce's diminishing eyesight transformed the very fabric of his fiction, and could have modified his concepts of writing and authorship as he increasingly relied on dictation for his "Work-in-Progress." Lezama considered his asthma a "sacred presence" that influenced his idea of the divine; thus, in a way, it determined the whole of his transcendentalist poetic system. More relevant perhaps is the fact that both Joyce and Lezama confronted their "insular" backgrounds in contrasting yet equally tenacious ways. Joyce lived his whole life in European exile while writing obsessively about his native Ireland. Lezama, on the other hand, treasured greatly his permanent residence in Cuba, but he did not balk from exploring, in his most hermetic and speculative writings, what he called the *eras imaginarias* [imaginary eras] of Greek, Chinese, and Egyptian civilizations.

Both Lezama and Joyce were exposed to powerful traditions of Catholicism that left a definitive mark on their work and on their character. The agnostic Joyce cultivated a Jesuitical casuistry that made him and his literature skeptical, ironic, and self-involved. Lezama the believer celebrated instead the baroque sensuality of Catholic ritual, cultivating a palate that made him perhaps the most corpulent *homme des lettres* in the history of his country. Both inspired a generation of writers and followers. Joyce did this reluctantly, with business-like formality, distance, sometimes disdain. Lezama, on the other hand, practiced the Paulist doctrine of the *ordo caritatis* by strengthening bonds of friendship among the members of his literary circle.

Following Vico's analysis of Pythagoras's notion of the triple function of language discussed in chapter 4, the frequent use in this study of the expression "Lezama's Joyce" is meant to have a "common," a "symbolic," and an "occult" meaning.

Common: "Lezama's Joyce" refers to Lezama's interpretation of Joyce in contrast to the other "Joyces" discussed in this book: that of José Ortega y Gasset, Leopoldo Marechal, Antonio Marichalar, Juan Jacobo Bajarlía, Ezra Pound, Valery Larbaud, T. S. Eliot, Stuart Gilbert, and, most importantly, Jorge Luis Borges. The reading of Joyce in Spain and Latin America set off a war of interpretations, just as it did in Europe. Our polemical claim is that, because of his affirmative recognition of the Joycean baroque *poiesis*, Lezama's Joyce might be a richer Joyce than most.

Symbolic: Lezama's reading of Joyce contradicts what he calls the "crepuscular pessimism" of contemporary criticism in *La expresión americana*. To quote critic Gustavo Pellón, Lezama's transcendental vision of literature is a joyful one. Lezama reads Joyce's work as proof of poetry's "resistance" against the erosion of time and as testimony of an "afterlife" that is not merely literary.

Occult: There must exist a vantage point in some other-worldly, occult history of literature where, despite their systematic discrepancies (or precisely because of them), somehow Lezama *is* Joyce. Somehow their work shares the same destiny in different countries, different languages, different postcolonialities. The new textual forms engineered by these writers irradiate in the same way, beacon with the same power. More work will be needed to fathom how the colonial, religious, and cultural circumstances of Cuba and Ireland generate a set of common themes and symbols that can inspire projects so similar in ambition and aesthetic philosophy. In some divine realm, the mirror could be found that would reconcile rather than refract the images, that would show that Joyce's iconoclastic rebelliousness and Lezama's hallowed splendor are but two sides of one identical coin. I quote from Borges's story, "Los teó-logos" [The Theologians]: "It is more correct to say that in Para-dise, Aurelian learned that, for the unfathomable divinity, he and John of Pannonia (the orthodox believer and the heretic, the ab-horrer and the abhorred, the accuser and the accused) formed one single person."[13]

1

Joyce and the Eschatology of the Novel: Jorge Luis Borges's and José Lezama Lima's Antagonistic Readings

I

FOR JORGE LUIS BORGES AND JOSÉ LEZAMA LIMA, TWO GRAND MASTERS of Latin American literary discourse in this century, reading Joyce both in their formative years and in their maturity meant contemplating the most urgent issues of literary history and pondering the very future of their own writing. The polemics inspired by Joyce's novels in Europe and the United States—the protest against the publication of *Dubliners* and *A Portrait of the Artist As A Young Man*, the trials and censorship of *Ulysses* for obscenity, the controversy regarding *Finnegans Wake*'s unintelligibility—produced in the Latin American "periphery" an anxious anticipation that gave the critical confrontation with Joyce's novels momentous implications. From his 1925 review of *Ulysses* in an Argentine avant-garde magazine to the poems dedicated to James Joyce in *Elogio de la sombra* (1969) [English edition, *In Praise of Darkness*], Borges never ceased to have Joyce as an obsessive topic for literary reflection.[1] Likewise, Lezama Lima was interested in Joyce throughout his life. Early in his literary career he discussed Joyce's work in an article published in 1941 in the Cuban journal *Grafos*; later he included a section contesting T. S. Eliot's interpretation of *Ulysses* in his influential 1957 essay *La expresión americana*; in the last collection of essays to be published during his lifetime, *La cantidad hechizada* [The Measure of Enchantment] (1970), he made various references to *Finnegans Wake*.[2] Borges and Lezama's lifelong critical preoccupation with Joyce should help us explore the peculiar molding quality Joyce's aesthetic had upon their own creative work, and thus illustrate the determining role Joyce has in the very constitution of Latin American literature today, both in its Borgesian fantastic, metaphysical mode and in the neobaroque mode inaugurated by Lezama.

Borges and Lezama's readings of *A Portrait, Ulysses,* and *Finnegans Wake* occurred in the context of the intense theoretical speculations of the twenties, thirties, and early forties about the "exhaustion" of literature brought on by modernist experimentation in the novel. Joyce's experiments in the novel were taken to be the ultimate example of the modernist exhaustion of novelistic discourse; his use of baroque elements that stressed ingenious utterance and rhetoric over narrative and humanistic content seemed to be the "limit" past which literature would cease to be literature. It is my argument that we can read in Lezama and Borges's comments on Joyce's novels a debate in which Borges adopts a position antagonistic to the baroque "monstrosities" of James Joyce's work while Lezama articulates a positive theory of the Joycean novel, reflecting the idiosyncratic incorporation of Joycean principles into his own monumental novel *Paradiso* (1966). Borges reads Joyce's work as the conclusion of a chapter in literary history, an instance of what I will call "genre eschatology," while Lezama reverses Borges's judgment and takes the Joycean textual system as a vibrant resurgence of baroque aesthetics that renovates and invigorates the novel.

II

The earliest Hispanic manifesto of the genre eschatology that Borges develops in his estimation of Joyce's work can be found in José Ortega y Gasset's 1925 essay "Ideas sobre la novela" [Notes on the novel].[3] There Ortega makes a categorical prognostication of the "death" of the novel. In Ortega's cultural historicism, the "objective possibilities" of circumstance limit the "lifespan" of genres. Just as the transition from one cultural period to another requires a transformation of subjectivity, it also demands the replacement of archaic artistic genres by new ones. According to Ortega, the era of post-World War I modernity must necessarily catalyze the decline of the novel, the art form that had flourished in the former epoch. On the threshold of its extinction, Ortega believes that the novel is exaggerating the formal elements that made it the principal genre during the nineteenth century age of realism. Thus, in its final phase—the modernist phase—the novel's increased reliance on "magnified" realist detail rather than on romance or fantasy produces an overburdening—a dehumanized, aesthetically debilitating "infrarealism." The pace of the novel approaches "morosidad" [sluggishness] and "paralysis," and its emphasis on extended psychological introspection ("psicologismo") and atmospheric setting rather than on action gives the novel a hermetic imperviousness ("hermetismo") that defeats its realist poetics.[4] Thus, in modernism, the baroque exaggeration of psychological, descriptive, and atmospheric principles and the recession of the narrative component send the novel into irrevocable decay. The idea of the mortality of the novel as a genre proposed by Ortega and his disciples makes the reviews of modernist novels in Ortega's *Revista de Occidente* read like a kind of death watch, in which great expectations are held for a new, succeeding form of fiction.[5]

Although Borges's antagonism toward most of Ortega's observations on literature is well documented,[6] Ortega's account of the novel's obsolescence in modernity influences Borges's theory of the novel and his later reading of Joyce. Despite their differences, Ortega and Borges are mostly in agreement that the novel is "on its deathbed," and in their analysis both use the same European novelists—Flaubert, Dostoevsky, Proust, and Joyce— as the conclusive evidence of its exhaustion. Commentary on Borges has mistakenly argued that he has a "hopeful" vision of the modernist novel,[7] but in most cases, Borges adopts the guise of Ortega's skeptical critic whose vision of the novel—both in its naturalist-realist and modernist modes—becomes a lament for a disappearing genre. In "Vindicación de *Bouvard et Pécuchet*" [Vindicating *Bouvard et Pécuchet*], a 1957 essay on Flaubert's unfinished work, Borges states that the novel's absurd premise, structural inconsistencies, and temporal lapses are not accidental or frivolous, but aesthetically and paradoxically organic to its form, part of a deliberate, *suicidal* acceleration of the genre's decline: "El hombre que con *Madame Bovary* forjó la novela realista fue fue también el primero en romperla. Chesterton, apenas ayer, escribía: 'La novela bien puede morir con nosotros.' El instinto de Flaubert bien presintió esa muerte, la que está aconteciendo . . ." [The man who, with *Madame Bovary*, forged the realist novel was also the first to break it. Just yesterday, Chesterton wrote: 'the novel could very well die with us.' Flaubert instinctively foresaw this death, which is taking place today . . .][8] The prominence that Joyce's work has in this view is clear in the Borges's postulation of *Ulysses* as the executor of Flaubert's death sentence. At the essay's conclusion, in unambiguous terms, Borges pictures *Ulysses* as the last phase in the dissolution of the genre: "¿no es el *Ulises*, con sus planos y horarios y

precisiones, la espléndida agonía de un género?" [isn't *Ulysses*—
with its charts, itineraries, and precisions—the splendid death rat-
tle of an entire genre?].[9]

Andres Sánchez Robayna has argued convincingly that there are
two opposed visions of Joyce in Borges's work: "Se advierte, en
efecto, en el trato borgesiano de la obra de Joyce dos fases diferen-
ciadas; podría hablarse, también, de dos actitudes contradictorias:
la una es ironía de la otra."[10] [We can detect in the Borgesian treatment of Joyce's work two distinct phases; we could also speak of
two contradictory attitudes: one is the irony of the other.] This
irony could be seen as the result of Borges's well-documented evolution from the expressionist, baroque-oriented, aesthetic ideology
of *ultraísmo* in his youth to the classical, pantheistic view of literature of his mature years.[11] This change of heart motivates the mature Borges's rejection of Joyce's experiments in the novel after the
young Borges had promoted Joyce's work. Critics who have studied
Borges's famous 1925 review "El *Ulises* de Joyce" [Joyce's *Ulysses*],
published in the Argentine avant-garde magazine *Proa* together
with Borges's own translation of the last page of the novel's concluding monologue, have noted its unconditional, celebratory reverence.[12] Borges begins: "Soy el primer aventurero hispánico que
ha arribado al libro de Joyce: país enmarañado y montaraz. . . .
Hablaré de él con la licencia que mi admiración me confiere y con
la vaga intensidad que hubo en los viajeros antiguos, al describir
la tierra que era nueva frente a su asombro errante."[13] [I am the
first Hispanic adventurer who has reached the entangled and rugged landscape of Joyce's book. . . . I will speak of it with the license
my admiration confers and with the vague intensity of the ancient
travelers when describing the new lands before their wandering
awe.] This enthusiasm—and the extravagant prose style—is part
of the baggage Borges wants to leave behind when he decides to
repudiate his avant-garde beginnings as a writer in the Hispanic
ultraísta movement.

Significantly, Borges's rejection of avant-garde poetics coincides
with his disengagement from the revaloration of the Hispanic baroque undertaken by Ortega and the *Revista de Occidente*-influ-
enced "Generation of 1927." The desire for a modernist aesthetic
objectivity and the rejection of the romantic and naturalist models
from the previous century inspired a paradoxical search for precursors among young Hispanic writers. These writers "resurrected"
the works of formerly discredited poets of the Spanish Golden Age,
particularly those who had employed the flamboyant baroque style
abhorred by turn-of-the-century Spanish philology and epitomized

in the work of Luis de Góngora. The Góngora revival reached its zenith in 1927 when the poets and scholars of the *Generación* organized the celebration of the tricentenary of Góngora's death with recitals, avant-garde happenings, and an ambitious plan to publish a new critical edition of his oeuvre and books and articles on unresearched aspects of his work.[14] In that same year Borges published a collection of essays, *El idioma de los argentinos* [The Language of the Argentines], in which he criticizes the festivities' promotion of Góngora's baroque metaphors, verse experimentation, and difficulty as a misguided understanding of the nature of literature. In Borges's words: "Góngora es símbolo de la cuidadosa tecniquería, de la simulación del misterio, de las meras aventuras de la sintaxis. . . . Es decir, de esa melodiosa y perfecta no literatura que he repudiado siempre."[15] [Góngora has become a symbol for meticulous but superfluous games of technique, for the simulation of mystery, for mere adventures in syntax. . . . In other words, for that melodic and perfect non-literature that I have always repudiated.] Given that *ultraísta* poetic manifestos promoted the cultivation of striking, expressionistic metaphors not unlike Góngora's, Borges's attack on the "new Gongorism" can be regarded as a climactic moment in his notorious abjuration of the avant-garde aesthetic ideology of his younger days. Joyce can be included among the writers on Borges's new index, since, from very early in his literary criticism, Borges had postulated a connection between Góngora's specious language and the Joycean novelistic discourse. Thus, in the 1925 conclusion to "El Ulises de Joyce," Borges quotes, in regard to Joyce, the "palabras decentes" [decent words] used by Góngora's contemporary Lope de Vega to describe his love and esteem for Góngora's poetry even in its obscurity, "admirando con veneración lo que no alcanzare a entender" [admiring with veneration even what I cannot fully comprehend] (25). In his 1971 prologue to his translation of Walt Whitman's *Leaves of Grass*, Borges, less encomiastic and more deeply critical, is still associating the two authors: "Hablar de experimentos literarios es hablar de ejercicios que han fracasado de una manera más o menos brillantes, como las *Soledades* de Góngora o la obra de Joyce."[16] [To speak of literary experimentations is to speak of projects that have failed more or less brilliantly, like Góngora's *Soledades* or Joyce's work.]

Jorge Luis Borges's most mordant critique of Joyce's "brilliant failure" occurs after his encounter with the neologisms of the first installments of *Work in Progress*, published from 1934 to 1938 in Eugene Jolas' journal *transition*. In the 1939 article in *Sur* entitled "Joyce y los neologismos" [Joyce and Neologisms], Borges claims that Joyce's compulsive fabrication of compound terms represents the work's main but failed purpose as an experimental novel. From the opening sentence he consistently refers to these puns as "monstruos verbales" [verbal monstrosities] using the same teratological motif employed to describe the excesses of Góngora's poetry in *El idioma de los argentinos*. More impressed by the "lyrical or mournful" sonority and rhythm in *Finnegans Wake*'s discourse than by the semantic complexity of its neologisms, Borges considers Joyce's synthesized words as forced and unaccomplished. Therefore, after listing and explaining a random dozen-and-a-half of these, dictionary-style, Borges writes: "Esos monstruos, así incomunicados y desarmados, resultan más bien melancólicos. Algunos . . . son meros calembours que no excenden las módicas posibilidades de Hollywood."[17] [These monstrosities, thus isolated and disarmed, become somewhat melancholy. Some of them . . . are mere *calembours* that fail to exceed the limited [talents] of Hollywood.]

The few, cautious words of praise in "Joyce y los neologismos" (a Joyce pun can sometimes be, writes Borges, "terrible y majestuoso" [terrible and majestic], 162) have misled some critics to think that Borges's assessment of *Finnegans Wake* is a positive one.[18] The fact is that although Borges adopts the hermeneutic strategy and the "dictionary" format of Stuart Gilbert's introductory article to *Finnegans Wake,* he does not share Gilbert's view of the artistic quality of the Joycean neologism.[19] What Gilbert extols as original, lasting achievements ("a miniature treasury of new-minted words" that could "in course of time pass into general currency," [18]) Borges regards as dubious inventions with little chance for permanence in common or literary language. "El último libro de Joyce" [Joyce's Latest Book], Borges's second review of *Finnegans Wake* written for the popular journal *El Hogar*, expresses more vividly his disappointment with both the encyclopedic dimensions and the aesthetics of the novel. With a demure sense of bafflement, Borges ridicules the pretentiousness of *Finnegans Wake*: *Finnegans Wake*

constituye, nos dicen, el madurado y lúcido fruto de dieciséis enérgicos años de labor literaria. Le he examinado con alguna perplejidad, he descifrado sin encanto nueve o diez *calembours*, y he recorrido los atemorizados elogios que le dedican la N.R.F. y el suplemento literario del *Times*. Los agudos autores de estos aplausos dicen haber descubierto la ley de tan complejo laberinto verbal, pero se abstienen de aplicarla o de formularla. . . . Sospecho que comparten mi preplejidad esencial y mis vislumbres inservibles, parciales.[20]

[represents, so they say, the ripe, lucid harvest of the literary labor of sixteen energetic years. I have examined it with some perplexity, I have deciphered without delight nine or ten *calembours*, and I have reviewed the terrorized words of praise that appear in the *N.R.F.* and the *Times Literary Supplement*. The brilliant authors of these accolades claim to have discovered the principle that rules this overly complex verbal labyrinth, but they abstain from revealing it. . . . I suspect they share my basic perplexity and my few useless and partial insights.]

The article's concluding remarks bear the hint of condescension that will characterize Borges's future references to Joyce's work: "*Finnegans Wake* es una concatenación de retruécanos cometidos en un inglés oníricio y que es difícil no calificar de frustrados e incompetentes. . . . Jules Laforgue y Lewis Carrol han practicado con mejor fortuna ese juego." [*Finnegans Wake* is an amalgamation of puns executed in a dreamlike English, and it is difficult not to describe these as frustrated and incompetent. . . . Jules Laforge and Lewis Caroll have played this game with better luck.]

From here on Borges will insist (with a curious retraction in one of the two poems on Joyce featured in *Elogio de la sombra*[21]) that Joyce's literary achievement is a form of "verbal music"—*ergo* poetic, not novelistic—and that it occurs only in isolated moments of his texts. Rather than celebrate T. S. Eliot's "order of myth" in Joyce's novels, Borges believes that Joyce's linguistic and symbolic experiments leave the genre in shambles. This conviction is best expressed in "Fragmento sobre Joyce" [Fragment on Joyce], an article written for the Argentine journal *Sur* in 1941 on the occasion of Joyce's death, in which Borges makes it clear that he regards the framing symbolic schemes in *Ulysses*—the correspondence of "every one of its eighteen chapters to an hour of the day, a organ of the body, an art, a symbol, a color, a literary technique, and one of the adventures of Ulysses"—as failed conceits rather than as organic narrative principles.[22] Borges spoofs the schema's cerebral convolutions, calling them "imperceptible, laborious congruities," "arduous symmetries and labyrinths," or, more bitingly, "tics voluntarios" [willful mannerisms]. This minimization of the symbolic order in Joyce's experimental novels is masterfully expressed in Borges's curt reference to the Homeric subtext, in which he subtly ridicules Stuart Gilbert's famous 1930 study *James Joyce's Ulysses* for its excessive reliance on the philological arguments made in Victor Bérard's *Les Phéniciens et l'Odyssée*.[23] Borges mocks the elaborateness and academicism of Gilbert's analysis of the Homeric parallel with a brutal, prosaic reduction: "the most acclaimed [mannerisms] are most insignificant: James Joyce's contacts with Homer, or (simply said) with the Senator for the Department [of Jura], M. Victor Bérard" (135). Nor does Borges valorize the novel's alleged intensification of naturalism, by which critics regarded the scatteredness of the interior monologue as a new form of deep psychological exploration with potential scientific accuracy. According to "Fragmento sobre Joyce," the clutter of psychorealist detail in the novel makes it "indecifrablemente caótica" [indecipherably chaotic] to a "lector desprevenido" [unprepared reader] with no access to a study guide.

Borges admires neither Joyce's naturalism nor his symbolism, but does respect his capacity for conveying or simulating a "multitudinous diversity of styles." It is in regard to this Protean virtuosity that Borges makes the often quoted comment that, "like Shakespeare, like Quevedo, like Goethe," Joyce is a "less a man of letters than a literature." Nevertheless, this recognition of the breadth of Joyce's verbal prowess does not mean that Borges regards this "literature" as a wholly accomplished one. According to Borges, Joyce's art lacks "the talent to construct," which I understand as the elementary plot and character structures that can sustain the suspense and consistency necessary for a novel to be a successful narrative unity. (Interestingly, Borges never mentions the names of Stephen Dedalus, Molly, or Leopold Bloom anywhere in his critical writings, perhaps because he does not regard them as archetypal, successful creations that can transcend the incidental text, the way Borges argues, following Miguel de Unamuno, that Don Quixote the character survives beyond Cervantes' novel.) Joyce compensates for this deficiency with a different type of craftmanship, foreign to the realm of the novel: a "verbal" gift for poetic phrasing and prose mimicry which allows for segments of self-enclosed stylistic brilliance amid the novel's chaos. Borges writes: "Lacking the talent to construct (which . . . he was obliged to supplant with arduous symmetries and labyrinths) he was blessed with a verbal knack, a gifted omnipotence of the word" (135). Borges commends not the novelist in Joyce, but rather the polished wordsmith who works and reworks scenes and phrases to improve their cadence and musicality, deftly simulating archaic or contemporary prose styles and capturing their peculiar timbre. It follows that the virtues Borges sees in Joyce vis-á-vis Quevedo and Goethe—"intensidad" [intensity] and "delicadeza" [delicacy]— are more appropriate to the forging of aphoristic, short forms than to the art of the novel. Joyce's genius is for pastiche and for precise, choice phrasing, not for the wide, unruly canvases of novelistic writing. This perspective explains Borges's conviction—implicit in the essay's title—that Joyce's work can only be appreciated through an aesthetic of the fragment: "Like the rest of the world, I have not read all of *Ulysses*, but I happily read and reread some scenes" (135). To further illustrate his point, rather than summarize a chapter or an episode, Borges quotes decontextualized, "well-wrought" sentences that he finds pleasurable or memorable for their syllabic crafting. Borges thus recognizes the excellence of Joyce's verbal art, but he believes such excellence can only happen sporadically, since Joyce's incapacity for real structure in the novel form leads him away from coherence into dissolution. For Borges, *Finnegans Wake*, "no less inconceivable than C. H. Hinton's fourth dimension or the Nicean Creed" (136), is the final evidence of this disintegration.

In a brief section on Joyce in his 1965 *Introducción a la literatura inglesa* [An Introduction to English Literature], Borges reiterates his view of the Joycean novel as an artistic failure: "His greatest work, *Ulysses*, attempts to replace the unity that is lacking with a system of labored and gratuitous symmetries."[24] He goes on to describe Joyce as a writer who "lástima gastó" [lamentably wasted] his "innegable" [undeniable] verbal genius on the novel. He concludes by quoting Virginia Woolf's description of *Ulysses* as "una gloriosa derrota" [a glorious defeat]. The mature Borges portrays Joyce as an ersatz novelist, a closet poet who did not live up to his promise since he failed to realize that the limitations of a declining genre did not suit his talents. Borges seems to suggest that Joyce's inability to achieve true expressiveness in the novel, in spite of his "undeniable" genius, is but one more piece of evidence of the exhaustion—the "death"—of the genre.[25]

III

Lezama's approach to the debate on Joyce and novelistic exhaustion happens in a text which, like Borges's "Fragmento sobre Joyce," is written as a literary obituary. Lezama published "Muerte de Joyce" [Death of Joyce] in March of 1941 in the Havana journal *Grafos*.[26] Like Borges, Lezama's understanding of Joyce is mediated by the lore of European criticism. The essay's eccentric, enigmatic voice succinctly reviews the multiple debates generated by the contending visions of Joyce's work as scandalous or aesthetically revolutionary. Lezama's strategy of allusion in this essay has, however, a peculiar enigmatic density. Rather than summarize biographical information or reproduce other critics' arguments as Borges has done, Lezama's text takes for granted the reader's knowledge of them. Thus, except for the transparent references to the censorship scandal and to Stuart Gilbert's study, the allusions tend to be oblique and riddlelike. The essay begins with the puzzling motif of a journey that can only be decoded through further access to Joyce's work and legend: "Ya sabemos el camino del profesor solitario. Va desde el benedictino en su torre de Sicilia hasta el maestro de Berlitz. . . . Este profesor de la Berlitz muere silenciosamente después de haber vivido en olor de buen escándalo: unos comparándole con Dante, otros considerándolo como una 'curiosidad' " (*OC* 2: 236). [We all have been informed of the schoolteacher's lonely journey from the benediction in the Sicilian tower to the Berlitz classroom. . . . Thus the Berlitz professor dies quietly after having lived through the stench of scandal, while some compared him to Dante and others considered him a mere curiosity.]

With the "benediction in the Sicilian tower" Lezama alludes to the mocking of Catholic ritual at the Martello tower in the first chapter of *Ulysses* (although Lezama does a "misquoting" that is characteristic of his often deliberately erratic erudition: what Mulligan's "black mass" spoofs is the host's consecration in the mass, not its use in the benediction, and British defense structures like the Martello tower were first built in Corsica, not Sicily).[27] Lezama also refers here to Joyce's stints as a Berlitz language instructor in Paris, Pola, and Trieste. Thus, in one sentence, Lezama speaks of Joyce's literary journey through several European languages (foregrounding a special connection with the language of Dante), his journey of exile (from Ireland to France to Italy back to France), and Joyce's "journey" novel, *Ulysses*. Equally enigmatic for a Hispanic reader is Lezama's mention of "el intento y la manera de los isabelinos" [the port and manner of the Elizabethans] among Joyce's literary preferences, which can only be understood if the reader is familiar with the Elizabethan style and spirit of Joyce's first book of poems, *Chamber Music* (inaccessible in Spanish but thoroughly analyzed in Herbert Gorman's biography). Disentangling the full meaning of Lezama's essay requires the reader to consult Lezama's critical sources. By adding the difficulty of unexplained references—very much like the allusive style of Joyce's fiction—the text calls for the reader to investigate and decipher, to penetrate the subject matter in a committed fashion. As in the rest of Lezama's criticism, the oracular erudition in "Muerte de Joyce" requires from the reader an archival effort, implying that, however laborious, the investment in interpreting Joyce will be well repaid. Unlike Borges, Lezama does not minimize Joyce's novelistic achievement; the irony of the essay's mock-pedantic tone is directed against some of Joyce's interpreters but not at Joyce's work.

Lezama's essay can thus be read as a concentrated, revisionist survey, a catalog of the main critical tendencies that surfaced in response to Joyce's work during Lezama's youth, and we could probably identify Wyndham Lewis, Ezra Pound, T. S. Eliot, Valéry Larbaud, Herbert Gorman, Stuart Gilbert, E. R. Curtius, and Borges himself among Lezama's sources.[28] Lezama's main purpose in "Muerte de Joyce" is to contradict prominent critics who have imposed "la complicación de sus preferencias" [their complicated preferences] on Joyce's "para aumentar sus peligros" [in order to heighten the risks taken] in his texts, focusing on the experimental and technical boldness of the scandalous or vanguardist segments:

> Durante mucho tiempo . . . los lectores del cuantioso Ulysses [sic] reclamaban la escena del burdel, los monólogos, abandonando la polémica sobre el *Hamlet* en la Dublin Library, o la bellísima página sobre el color y lo vital. . . . Un tipo especial del lector se obstinaba en crear un Joyce especial, viéndolo hermano mayor del surrealismo, revestido de la muralla del conocimiento de todas las lenguas románicas, babélico, imposible, babilónico, rabelesiano, continuador de simbolistas menores. (*OC* 2: 236–37)

> [For some time the readers of the bulky *Ulysses* praised the brothel scene and the monologues, neglecting the polemic on *Hamlet* at the Dublin Library or the beautiful, poetic page on color and life. . . . A special type of reader obstinately created a special kind of Joyce: Surrealism's big brother, fortified by a great wall of linguistic knowledge: Greek, Latin, and all Romance languages; indecipherable, Babylonian, Rabelaisian; follower of minor symbolists.]

If on the one hand Lezama's concern for the whole of the novel rather than for the technically adventurous episodes strikes against Borges's aestheticization of the fragment in Joyce, on the other hand Lezama agrees with Borges when he argues that these readers' obsession with the novelty of Joycean technique betrays a confused sense of what literature is. Adopting a nonvanguardist approach not unlike the second Borges's, Lezama believes that the merit and permanence of Joyce's work lie in its "unexceptionality," its traditional framework. Despite the newness of its experimentation, Lezama argues, "Hoy vamos viendo que aquella obra se hizo como se hacen todas las obras: la lucha adolescente entre el sexo y el dogma, el ritmo de la voz y cierta heterodoxia superficial que

va en busca de una ortodoxia central" (*OC* 2: 237) [Today we realize that Joyce's work was built as all great works are: out of the
adolescent struggle between sex and dogma, (searching for a
unique) rhythm through voice, and (developing) a sort of superficial heterodoxy in search of a central orthodoxy]. Lezama serenely
recognizes an immanent coherence amidst the chaos in Joyce's
work, a timeless *doxa* (order) rooted in the great theological systems. Thus, Lezama does not necessarily consider the baroque elements in Joyce as examples of modernist or avant-garde
experimentation, but as new, topical applications of time-proven
narrative, stylistic, and figural strategies which Lezama probably
also recognized in the great works of Spanish Golden Age literature
by such baroque writers as Cervantes, Quevedo, and Góngora.

Like the later Borges, Lezama is skeptical of the vagaries of
avant-garde experimentation; unlike Borges, Lezama believes that
Joyce's novels transcend and outlast such vagaries. Lezama concludes his essay by introducing a semimystical, sacrificial concept
of the *afterlife* of the novel by manipulating Joyce's remark to Max
Eastman that he wrote for the ideal reader who would devote his
whole life to the interpretation of his work.[29] "Muerte de Joyce"
reads, in fact, as a summons to this "new type of reader" who will
"reclaim the delight and verity" of Joyce's grounding in tradition.
"Ahora que la marcha de su obra se detine, pidamos el nuevo lector que ya él se había ganado. Si él había afirmado que a su obra
le había dedicado su vida, y que por lo tanto reclamaba que el lector le entregara su vida también, deseémosle ese tercer lector capaz
de jugarse su vida en una lectura . . . que tenga para una sola lectura la presencia y la esencia de todos sus días" (*OC* 2: 238) [Now
that his work is concluded, let us call forth the new reader he has
already earned. If he once declared that he had given his life to his
work, and thus demanded that the reader give over his life in return, let us wish him that third reader capable of staking his life in
his reading . . . may this act of reading have the collected presence
and essence of all his waking days]. With this "new reader," Lezama builds a sequence of images where novel reading and novel
writing are regarded as activities that extend and perpetuate life beyond death. Reading Joyce's work here is a death-defying act since
this reader "se juega la vida" (gambles his life) in the process of
giving himself to the novel by sacrificing his "preferencias" (which
I interpret as giving up the fashionable avant-garde agenda of the
day) to be absorbed into a total, unbiased dedication to the text. In
"Muerte de Joyce," death is thus considered one stop in a journey
to some higher destination, since it is after death that Joyce's nov-

els will reach their apogee, reborn and resurrected through the devoted "new reader." After a lifetime amid the noise of scandal, it is in the author's death that Joyce's work finds the "suficiente silencio" [due share of silence] in which the real reading and appreciation of his novels can begin.

The idea that Joyce's novels have an afterlife explains the cryptic conclusion of Lezama's complex essay, in which he describes the new reader as "el solo y misterioso lector resuelto como un escriba egipcio" (*OC* 2: 238) [the lonely and mysterious reader, as intent as an Egyptian scribe]. This reference to the Egyptian *Book of the Dead*—the king's scribe is hired to produce a guidebook that can orient the pharaoh through the underworld and back to the living[30]—does not portray the pharaoh's mummy as an archaeological relic. The scribe/reader watches over the mummy/novel convinced ("resuelto") that it is bound to be resurrected. *A Portrait, Ulysses, Finnegans Wake*—the concept of the modern baroque novel itself thus becomes a figure for "resurrection" in Lezama's analysis. Lezama's tropological inversion of Borges and Ortega's death motif permeates all of his references to Joyce and defines his vision of the contemporary novel's purpose as a genre. When the narrator in the tongue-in-cheek conclusion of Borges's "Funes el memorioso" [Funes the Memorious] finally sees Funes's face in the light of dawn after their nightlong conversation, he sees him "monumental as bronze, more ancient than Egypt, older than the prophecies and the pyramids."[31] If, according to the symbolic logic of Borges's story, Funes can be thought of as the "mummified" embodiment of Joyce's novelistic enterprise, an archaeological piece bound for the oblivion of museums or academic foundations, in "Muerte de Joyce" Lezama would make Funes the devoted reader of the new novel—"el solo y misterioso lector"—in whom Joyce is reborn.

Lezama's piece on Joyce must be read as a significant statement of Lezama's own brand of literary eschatology. Here death, the "death of the novel" in particular, cannot be equated to extinction but instead represents the guarantee of an afterlife. In "Muerte de Joyce," Lezama manipulates Borges's trope of authorial/textual death to introduce his own nascent ideas of a "sistema poético del mundo" [poetic world system], where the incarnation of poetry in the new baroque novel serves as a confirmation of literature's resistance to time. Lezama extricates literature from finitude: true literature is made of something that survives exhaustion. Writing and reading, genre and discourse, contingency and permanence, poetry and the novel, are thus intricately enmeshed in Lezama's complex notion of the afterlife. The act of reading Joyce is thus a validation of resurrection by what Lezama called the *imagen*.[32] Lezama's short essay on Joyce must not only be read as the rebuttal of the nihilistic, nontranscendental eschatology suggested by Borges, but as the prolegomenon to his own novelistic project. Joyce's work represents not an exhaustion to Lezama, but the beginning of the "other life" of the novel as a renovated genre, a new novel that, like Dante's *Commedia*, is capable of conveying a sense of immortality for which literature, with its capacity for universality and timelessness, stands as some form of annunciation.

Such a positive appraisal of Joyce led Lezama to a strategy of replication and improvement of the Joycean novelistic project in his own work, to his decision, after years of writing his distinctive, hermetic "Gongorist" poetry, to "write novels when the possibilities of the genre [were] at their slimmest,"[33] thus producing *Paradiso* (1966) and the unfinished, posthumously published *Oppiano Licario* (1977). The systematic refraction of Joyce's textual aesthetic in Lezama Lima's novels becomes clear when we realize that elements that differentiate and distinguish *A Portrait, Ulysses,* and *Finnegans Wake* are carefully incorporated and balanced in *Paradiso* and *Oppiano Licario*. By the same token, "Muerte de Joyce" can be read as a prolegomenon to Lezama's novels, an anticipatory description of their principal themes and design. Lezama's list of his "preferences" in "Muerte de Joyce"—the motif of the quest, the debate on Hamlet, the stellar poetry of Ithaca, the music of Joyce's verbal rhythms, the search for a new orthodoxy—marks the points of contact of which *Paradiso* and *Oppiano Licario* mirror (and refract) the content and composition of *Portrait, Ulysses,* and *Finnegans Wake*. *A Portrait* and *Paradiso* both narrate the genesis of poetic consciousness in the young artist, and both develop an aesthetic theory based on the experience of arrestedness in the contemplation of art—Stephen Dedalus calls this stasis in *Portrait,* and José Cemí *fijeza* in *Paradiso*. Both *Paradiso* and *Ulysses* feature scenes of philosophical debate that reenact the Platonic symposium, highlighting the relevance of Socratic dialogism in the constitution of the novel as genre. The "Scylla and Charybdis" debate at the Dublin Library concerning Shakespeare's androgynous creativity in *Hamlet* is picked up in *Paradiso*'s chapter 9, where Cemí and his friends, Foción and Fronesis, debate about poetry, homosexuality, and the myths of androgynous procreation. *Paradiso* features passages of wordplay reminiscent of *Finnegans Wake*—chapter seven, featuring Uncle Alberto's punning letter in which, according to Cemí, "language becomes nature," is the best case in point. Like Joyce's last novel, *Oppiano Licario* is partly constructed upon cosmological notions drawn from Vico's *New Science*. All of these novels explore new discursive rhythms in order to generate a distinctive syntax that can revitalize the language of the contemporary novel. Meanwhile, the Joycean technical novelties or "tecniquerías" that Lezama argues critics have overemphasized—stream-of-consciousness, interior monologue, "deep" psychological naturalism—are notoriously absent in *Paradiso*.

IV

Lezama and Borges's antagonistic readings of the Joycean novels end up generating a "baroque" Joyce not just because they focus on artifice, intricacy, and semantic difficulty, but because they also connect his work with the extreme spiritual obsessions of the baroque ethos: death and resurrection. Borges's linking of Joycean fiction with genre eschatology and Góngora's labored "vacuousness" reflects the dark side of the baroque spirit. Lezama's celebration of the "afterlife" of Joyce's work represents its luxuriant, affirmative side.

2

Incarnating the Word: Poetry, Adolescence, and Aesthetic Theory in *A Portrait of the Artist as a Young Man* and *Paradiso*

I

THE PROMINENCE OF *A PORTRAIT OF THE ARTIST AS A YOUNG MAN* IN JOSÉ Lezama Lima's estimation of the Joycean corpus is one of the most striking features in Lezama's interpretation of Joyce. Spurning the "preferences" of modern critics, Lezama downplays the literary prestige of *Ulysses* and *Finnegans Wake* and takes *A Portrait* to be the textual matrix from which the Joycean system originates. In his essay "Muerte de Joyce," Lezama refutes the common critical premise that Joyce's literary achievement is to be measured mostly by his technical innovations and the experimental nature of his later work.[1] Lezama even parodies the technical orientation of this interpretative tendency—obsessively focused, according to Lezama, on "la física del lenguaje" [the physics of language]—by filling his essay with biting pastiches of the jargon used in such criticism. According to Lezama, Joyce's critics mistakenly overlook the role played by poetry in Joyce's work since they consider poetic language to be "la pervivencia del tipo fonético por la vitalidad interna del gesto vocálico que la integra" (*OC* 2: 238) [the persistence of phonetic type over the internal vitality of the vocal gesture that constitutes it]. Elaborating on the journey motif that opens "Muerte de Joyce," Lezama posits Joyce's first published novel as the key to a new reading that will reveal the full extent to which "lo poético" [the poetic experience] participates in Joyce's work, warning: "¡Cuidado con la filología! Que Joyce fue también por otros caminos pruébalo aquel delicioso *Portrait* en que hay una simultaneidad dentre el Eros y su encarnación y el artista que ve surgir de ese apetito la forma" (*OC* 2: 238) [Beware of philology! That Joyce walked other paths is proven by that delicious *Portrait*

48

where there is a simultaneity between Eros and its incarnation and the artist who sees form emerge from this appetite].

The very language crystalized in Lezama's statement, together with the arguments developed in the rest of his essay, reveal Lezama's keen and intimate knowledge of *Portrait*. In cataloguing what he believes are the fundamental themes of Joyce's oeuvre— "postrimerías, juicio e infierno y el azufre desprendido por el rey de los orgullosos" (*OC* 2: 237) [afterlife, judgment and hell, and the sulfureous stench released by the king of the vain]—Lezama is in fact quoting from the notorious sermons on death, judgment, and hell at the Belvedere College retreat that are the core of *A Portrait*'s chapter 3. In his essay, Lezama refers to the sermons' pivotal discussion of the sin of Luciferine pride, a theological motif that *A Portrait* follows as Stephen's own arrogant spirit struggles between Catholic grace, Satanic fall, and Daedalian flight. The postulations of Lezama's essay—the mapping of Joycean topoi emphasizing Joyce's Jesuit schooling according to Loyola's *Spiritual Exercises* "leído como manual de retórica y como coro de disciplinantes" (*OC* 2: 238) [read as a rhetoric primer and as a chorus for disciplinants]—apply more aptly to the construction of *A Portrait* than to either *Ulysses* or *Finnegans Wake*.

Lezama's comment on the religious orientation of Joyce's work— "aquella obra se hizo como se hacen todas las obras: la lucha adolescente entre el sexo y el dogma, el ritmo de la voz y cierta heterodoxia superficial que va en busca de una ortodoxia central" (*OC* 2: 237) [his work was built as all works are: with the adolescent struggle between sex and dogma, a vocal rhythm, and a sort of superficial heterodoxy in search of a central orthodoxy]—can be read as a systematic, condensed appreciation of the design of Joyce's first novel. The first phrase can be interpreted as a reference to Stephen's discovery of carnal pleasure in chapter 2 and his ensuing dogmatic repentance in chapters 3 and 4. The second phrase speaks to the dawning of Stephen's artistic vocation through the discovery of rhythm as the key to poetry during the seaside epiphany of chapter 4. The last phrase addresses the eventual collapse of Stephen's Catholic faith and his conversion to the new *ortodoxia central* of a Thomistic-inspired aesthetics through the assumption of the priestly role of expatriate poet in chapter 5. Lezama implies that Stephen's renunciation of the Church and adoption of a "theology of art" are motivated by his cultivation of a heretical yet nonblasphemous sensibility, a heterodoxy inspired by the writings of Giordano Bruno which Stephen discusses with Cranly.[2] Bruno is also important in Lezama's own eccentric vision of Catholicism and figures distinctly in the corresponding youthful debates of *Paradiso* and *Oppiano Licario*.[3]

Lezama's fascination with *A Portrait* in "Muerte de Joyce" can be explained given the central role of poetic phenomena in Joyce's novel, a centrality mirrored in Lezama's own literary system. Lezama's insights into the sources and the structure of *A Portrait* in "Muerte de Joyce" suggest the importance of that work as a model for Lezama's novelistic enterprise, and thus provide a key for reading *Paradiso*. Lezamian critics have discussed the messianic figuration of the protagonist in *Paradiso* as thoroughly as Joyceans have analyzed that of Stephen in *A Portrait*,[4] but the scope and ambition of Lezama's novelistic enterprise demonstrate a *literary* messianism as well. Lezama seems to be saying in his essay that, following Joyce's example, poetry should be used to *save* the genre of the novel from its extinction. Complaints made by Julio Cortázar and other critics about the naive, unsophisticated, or non-novelistic nature of *Paradiso*'s narrative (the "softness" of its technical elements, the flawed and irregular third-person narrator, and the excessive privileging of description over narration)[5] are invalidated by Lezama's nuanced critical awareness of the fertile narrative tension inherent when novelistic form addresses poetic experience, as evidenced in both *Paradiso* and his reading of Joyce's *A Portrait*. Lezama himself has argued for this hard-earned narrative sophistication in a reference to the change in narrative voice from Flaubertian *style indirect libre* to the first-person journal notes at the conclusion of *A Portrait*: "Otros rastacueros con desviaciones medulares fingen asombro de clarisas porque comienzo las oraciones en tercera persona y las termino en primera, olvidando que esas mutaciones verbales son, desde Joyce, un hallazgo de la novela contemporánea"[6] [Some perverse show-offs fake gasps of maiden surprise because I begin sentences in the third person and finish them in the first, forgetting that these verbal mutations have, since Joyce, been a discovery of the contemporary novel].

Poetry, Lezama seems to say in his reading of *A Portrait*, mutates the verbal fabric of the novel, invigorating it, "making it new" and contemporary. Lezama sees in the contradictions between poetic language and narrative discourse the source of an energy that can lead to the "rebirth" of novel as genre. Even when "Muerte de Joyce" can be read as a vindication of the "spirit" of poetry over the "technology" of novelistic technique, Lezama's observations on *A Portrait* consistently express the paradoxical necessity for narrative prose to express the poetic experience. This is shown in the very polysemy of Lezama's adjectives. When Lezama describes *A Portrait* as "delicious," he points to the opening of a narrative space that simultaneously identifies a desire—Eros, appetite—and its fulfillment—incarnation, consumption. Critics have noted how poetic gnosis in Lezama arises out of a shift between contrasting states: from fragmentation to cohesion, from kinesis to stasis, from a lower state of definition to a higher one, from sequence to simultaneity, and vice-versa.[7] "La poesía ve lo sucesivo como simultáneo" [Poetry sees sequence as simultaneity], writes Lezama in his *Diario* (80). The careful structure of Joyce's *A Portrait* proves to Lezama that the stasis of aesthetic knowledge is novelistic in form since only through the illusion of a stilled narrative that both makes manifest and suspends temporality can the moment of poetic gnosis be conveyed. Translated into Lezamian terms, Lezama sees the modernist novel, represented by Joyce's *A Portrait*, as a mediating construction between *dispersión* [dispersion] and *fijeza* [stillness].[8] When Lezama speaks of "the simultaneity of Eros and its incarnation" in *A Portrait*, he speaks of an ambiguous but necessary continuity between the flash of aesthetic experience (the poem) and its full account (the novel).[9]

Poetry and the novel thus become variables of the same equation as one genre "emanates" from the other; just as the spectral, transcendental essence of poetry—what Lezama calls *lo invisible* [the invisible]—requires a brief materialization in the poem, the full complexity of aesthetic experience requires yet another incarnation, the bildungsroman of the artist "seeing form emerging from his appetite." As poetry becomes a system in Lezama and a metaphor begins to generate other metaphors in a network binding the *imago*, it tends toward narrative supra- or para-poetic forms (anecdotes, plots, fables) which Lezama associates with the *sobreabundancia* [overabundance] of the novel.[10] The story of the dawning of poetry on the poet is thus a narrative paradox which only the novel as form can convey: the initiation into an alternative form of cognition that, ironically, "had always been there"; a process that seems incremental since it takes a lifetime of maturation but arrives suddenly in the shape of a revelation; a fate accidental in appearance but in fact preordained. The bildungsroman is thus the optimal form, childhood and adolescence the proper sites, for Joyce and Lezama's genre hybridization. In the progressive narrative of character-formation, both *A Portrait* and *Paradiso* allegorize the advancement of poetry toward the novel and of the novel toward poetry.

II

The number of scenes, symbols, motifs, character types, and plot patterns that *Paradiso* shares with *A Portrait* is surprisingly high. Both novels tell the story of the growth of a poet from early childhood through adolescence in urban and insular contexts that are culturally and politically similar. In *A Portrait* and *Paradiso*, turn-of-the-century Dublin and early twentieth-century Havana are represented as the nerve centers of colonial territories burdened with the legacies of foreign imperialism, frustrated nationalism, and parochial Catholicism. In both novels, the young protagonists decide to pursue the art of poetry in order to escape the anomie and stagnation of their urban surroundings. Both novels use classical mythology to produce a peculiar cosmogonical syncretism, where pagan motifs vie with, merge with, and/or displace Judeo-Christian symbols and dogmas. Critics have noted how the unusual name of *Paradiso*'s poet-hero, José Cemí, mimics the complex symbolism of Stephen Dedalus's name by juxtaposing a Christian saint with a Caribbean pagan figure—"cemí" refers to the fetish Cuba's arawak Indians used to venerate gods like Juracán, the hurricane. Both novels use words like *irradiación* [radiance] and *fijeza* [stasis] in passages where the adolescent protagonist wanders the city while developing a personal aesthetic theory. At one point in *Paradiso*, one character (Foción) congratulates Cemí on his ideas about sexuality, resurrection, and creativity saying that they seem to be fashioned by a "Santo Tomás de Aquino heterodoxo" [heterodox St. Thomas Aquinas] (*P* 269/*R* 269), thus recalling Stephen's eccentric use of scholastic doctrine in chapter 5. At another point, this same character visits a 1929 Havana bookstore to ask jokingly for what could be a copy of *A Portrait* but referring to the novel as "el Goethe de James Joyce" [Joyce's book on Goethe], thus making a sly reference to *A Portrait*'s use of *Wilheim Meister* as a model bildungsroman and insinuating *Paradiso*'s parallel reliance on *A Portrait* (*P* 236–37/*R* 232–35).[11] Any fairly astute reader would conclude that *Paradiso* cheerfully cannibalizes *A Portrait*; that, despite its baroque idiosyncracies, Lezama's novel is an inspired palimpsest of Joyce's work.

However, Lezama's portrait of the poet's as *adolescente* is proximate but not identical to that of Joyce's "young man." In *Paradiso*, *adolescencia* is mostly described as a ten-year period of plenitude and of heightened promise in which the complexities of childhood are successfully worked out, an age of "gravedad visible y una embriaguez secreta" [visible sobriety and a secret intoxication], "un paréntesis de horas privilegiadas" (*P* 322/*R* 325–26) [a parenthesis of privileged hours] in which the young poet-to-be "como seducido[s] por algo secreto, alcanzó su medida más alta" [as if seduced by something secret, reached his most generous measure]. In *A Portrait*, Stephen's adolescence is more the brooding and impatient anticipation of the flight that adulthood will bring; it is a period of internal turmoil and humiliation, of sexual confusion and anxiety, of unresolved neuroses and debasements that compromise and threaten any wish to achieve emancipation through the priesthood of art. Thus, despite the remarkable similarities and derivations, Lezama's *adolescencia* and Joyce's "young man" do not quite agree in spiritual and moral content. Dedalus's wings do not carry Stephen as far into artistic maturity as the forces of the hurricane god take Cemí.

This disparity may not result only from Lezama's deliberate revisions of *A Portrait* but from the fact (which I will discuss later) that Lezama works from an affirmative Hispanic reading of *A Portrait* that has prevailed ever since its publication in Spanish. Nevertheless, although Lezama paints a more upbeat, celebratory picture of the young poet's coming of age than Joyce, the echoes and resonances between José Cemí and Stephen Dedalus's lives still ring loudly. This might be so since, while the adolescent Cemí does not exhibit the same resentments nor the same degree of alienation as does Stephen, Cemí the child goes through a series of events and circumstances that are strikingly close to those of Stephen as a boy. Here perhaps lies the secret of the uncanny proximity between Lezama and Joyce's bildungsromane: the prominence accorded to early childhood as the gestation period of artistic inclination, as the real beginning of the poetic vocation. Lezama's fascination with *A Portrait* can be understood given the importance Lezama gave in his cultural theory to explaining the genesis and nature of poetic phenomena, to tapping its primal sources. What Lezama called the *paideuma*—the strong presence of childlike fancifulness and self-withdrawal in the poetic character—is carefully explored in *A Portrait*.[12] It is this careful, measured study of the relevance of childhood experience in an artist's adolescence that gives *Paradiso* and *A Portrait* their fearful symmetry.

I would propose that, in order to illustrate the importance of childhood as the grounds in which poetry becomes "incarnated" in the poet, *Paradiso* and *A Portrait* rely on an archetypical narrative model: the epigenetic story of the child's acquisition of language. To see how this is so it would help to review some theories of infant language-learning in contemporary developmental psychology.

The most modern accounts of infant language learning—the "constructivist" and the "nativist" models—reenact the contradictions between the immediacy of poetry and the gradualism of the novel. According to Piaget's "constructivist" model, arrival at language is gradual since the child progresses by means of his or her phenomenological exchange with the world, from a state of *tabula rasa* through successive stages of linguistic competence and performance.[13] According to "nativist" models, on the other hand—Chomskian transformative grammar and the linguistics of Ferdinand de Saussure—acquisition of language is in fact unnarratable since, arguably, language is preformed, innate, synchronic, and operating since birth like any bodily organ, and any given moment of linguistic acquisition is impossible to pinpoint.[14] Like "Eros and its incarnation," there is a simultaneity between language and its acquisition, between a sentence and its utterance, between *langue* and *parole*: it is impossible to say which precedes the other.

To overcome this paradox, modern psycholinguistics narrates the child's "arrival" at language as a process of increasing complexity where progress is measured as the movement from one period of accumulation of linguistic skills to the next. Such transitions configure a series of climatic moments, a sequence of breaks in continuity that signal the appearance and disappearance of elementary verbal behaviors—babbling as a sensory-motor response, echolalia, first speech acts, single and multiple-word utterances, spatial terms and lexical entry—until polysemy, lexical creativity, idioms, and metalinguistic awareness complete the full functioning of language-thought in the mature child's mind.[15] Psycholinguistics divides this progress into a number of neat age-stages in a young person's life.

Both *Paradiso* and *A Portrait* mirror this narrative design by staging a sequence of select, critical, often traumatic moments of infant experience that represent the transition from one "lower" state of linguistic sophistication to a "higher" one in a proto-Ericksonian cycle of growth. Thus, like *A Portrait*, *Paradiso* is concerned with representing what Joyce described as "the fluid succession of presents, the *development* of an entity of which our actual present is a phase only,"[16] only that the changing nature of these "presents"— the "entity" that differentiates them—is language. At every stage, the protagonist's relationship to language is galvanized and advanced. Thus, in *A Portrait* and *Paradiso*, the poet is not born but made in his experimental interaction with the world throughout. Joyce and Lezama thus would appear to subscribe to Piaget's "constructivist" model of language acquisition (rather than a "nativist" or innate model, like Chomsky's transformative grammar), since both Stephen and Cemí acquire language by means of their experimental exchange with the world, from a state of relative *tabula rasa* through successive stages of linguistic competence and performance.

Given their momentousness, the shifts from one culmination to the next in Joyce and Lezama acquire the mystique of revelations, which would explain why Joyce and Lezama tend to illustrate the turning points of childhood growth as epiphanies. Even when one could question the logic of using the term *epiphany* as the deciding aesthetic category in Joyce and Lezama,[17] what is clear is that both authors draw terms from Catholic theology to figure the child's maturing in language. Thus, sacraments (baptism, confirmation, eucharist), rituals (constriction, sanctification, homily), and liturgical cycles (annunciation, advent, epiphany, Lent, Easter, and Pentecost) serve as metaphors for stages of linguistic growth. Notable are those metaphors related to Marian symbology. Both *A Portrait* and *Paradiso* feature references to the annunciation, the incarnation of the word, the sanctity of the womb, and the mystery of assumption. (Mariology reappears in other moments of their writing, as in the "Scylla and Charibdis" chapter of *Ulysses* and Lezama's *Sonetos a la Virgen* [Sonnets to the Virgin].)[18] The effect of this figural use of theology in both Joyce and Lezama is the relativizing of theology and the sacralization of human experience. Both Lezama and Joyce generate an aesthetic psychology out of the building blocks of Catholic dogma.

As with those from theology, these traces of tenets from developmental psychology in Joyce and Lezama's novels are, nevertheless, strictly symbolic; neither *A Portrait* nor *Paradiso* are concerned with complying with standards of psychological veracity. Ezra Pound and H. G. Wells interpreted *A Portrait*'s technique of moving from simple to complex discourse as cogently mimicking the stages of language acquisition in a child.[19] There is no possibility of charting psychological accuracy in *Paradiso*, since most characters there—whatever their age, sex, or social status—demonstrate a fantastic level of sibylline verbal sophistication that frequently is difficult to distinguish from that of the narrator. The oracular knowledge and oratorical gift of speech displayed by the characters in *Paradiso* have prompted the argument regarding the predominance of figural discourse over narrative and of fancy over realism in the text, as well as the notion that *Paradiso* departs from the conventions of novelistic representation to the point of being a misguided or aberrant instance of the genre.[20] Nevertheless, a parallel claim has been made about *A Portrait*. As Harry Levin and other critics have argued, *A Portrait* does not necessarily concern itself with the naturalistic illustration of infant psychology, but with a process that exceeds the rules of realistic representation and redefines the realist poetics of the novelistic genre.[21] As many critics have shown, the meticulous symbolic structure of *A Portrait* belies any claims to deliberate naturalism.[22] As a rewriting of *A Portrait*, *Paradiso* seeks to correct the reading prevailing in the first decades after the novel's publication which situated *A Portrait* in the tradition of naturalist realism rather than in that of symbolism or modernism reserved for *Ulysses* and *Finnegans Wake*. Lezama thus anticipated in "Muerte de Joyce" the rise of the symbolist reading of *A Portrait* that surfaced in the forties encouraged by Kenneth Burke's study of symbolic order in the novel.[23]

Either way, *Paradiso* and *A Portrait* turn the story of a child's linguistic development into an allegory of poetic initiation. What *Paradiso* and *A Portrait* evidence is a pattern of acquaintance with the extra- (almost para-) psychological materiality of words—a *poetic* materiality different from the merely *reproductive* materiality analyzed by cognitive psychology. Even in its early stages, Stephen and Cemí's language acquisition is not just the acquisition of natural language but of poetic language. This "second" language is not the pragmatic, semiotic function of denoting or signifying the world, but a hermetic world in itself. For both Lezama and Joyce, the artist-child moves through peculiar phases of growth, discovering the treacherous, "wounding" qualities of the "first," "natural" language at certain critical junctures of development. In these junctures, the child associates certain manifestations of language—utterances, admonitions, commands, prayers, inscriptions—with disease, pain, punishment, penance, even death. These experiences lead the poet-child to a dramatic *linguistic* reconfiguration—almost an "alphabetization"—of phenomenal experience. The work of the poet-adolescence is to overcome the perturbations and traumas that result from these junctures through a poetic reinterpretation of the world. Joyce and Lezama narrate an epigenesis of poetic consciousness, with adolescence as the culminating moment, where the child discovers how to use poetic language in order to repair and heal the painful disorder of "natural" language. In Cemí and Stephen's stories, these stages are part of the design of their artistic vocation, just as the stages are preordained in the developmental psychologist or linguist's account of the person's arrival at language.

III

Before dealing with these issues, we need to consider some crucial biographical parallels between José Cemí and Stephen Dedalus's childhoods. First, both children suffer from physical
impairments that constrain their sociability and interaction with
their peers, stimulate their introspective character, and shape their
aesthetic persona. Dedalus's bad eyesight and weakness make him
the target of abusive classmates and motivates his rhythmical and
auditory rather than pictorial or visual appreciation of poetry.[24]
Cemí's asthma is the cause of the most humiliating and traumatic
scenes of his boyhood, and is referred to throughout the novel as a
"divinidad" [diety] that shapes and controls his destiny. Although
the force of visual imagery stimulates the visions of Cemí's imagination, his struggle with asthma inspires his search for a soothing,
serene rhythm (what will be called at the end of the novel the
"ritmo hesicástico" [rhythm of hesychasts]) after bouts of frantic
breathing (associated in the novel with the violent beat of the "estilo sistáltico" [systolic style]).

Second, as children both Cemí and Dedalus are exposed to the
"mature language" of debates at the family table, language with
which family members argue not only over domestic problems and
petty intrigues, but over matters of colonial politics in which they
are deeply embroiled. Many of Stephen's older relatives were members of the Union of Irish Republicans, and his family is torn between maintaining their devotion to the Church and remaining
loyal to Parnell's memory. The mother's side of Cemí's family went
into exile to Jacksonville to flee Spanish persecution after the defeat of the nationalists in the Cuban Ten Year War (1868–78). Like
the Dedaluses, in later years the Cemís will continue to pay homage to a Parnell-like political martyr, José Martí. At one family gathering, the Basque origin of Cemí's father is regarded as a threat
according to Augusta's staunch Cuban patriotism. Thus, in both
Paradiso and *A Portrait*, family history can be read as a chronicle of
the most specific repercussions of a conflictive colonial condition.
(Although we must note that the spirit of these gatherings is strikingly different in each novel. In *Paradiso*, despite fraternal frictions
and jealousies, family reunions tend to end in reconciliations that
exhibit great Cuban charm and grace, which Lezama called *la fineza cubana*, while asperity and angry, resentful emotions characterize political discussions among family members in *A Portrait*.)

Third, the Cemí and Dedalus families can both be described as
middle-class families fallen on hard times, *familias venidas a*

menos.[25] As the novels progress, each family's financial situation grows more precarious. Chapters in *A Portrait* usually begin with the sight of moving vans packing the family furniture, and each change of scenery (the move from Clongowes, Stephen's visit to his Uncle Charles, his enrollment in Belvedere) is another link in a chain of displacements brought on by Simon Dedalus's loss of money and status, a decline summarized wrily and bitterly by Stephen's quips about his father's erratic career (*PA* 93). Nevertheless, Simon Dedalus's professional failure is due not just to his weakness of character, but to the familial fragmentation that resulted from societal change caused by the crisis in Irish nationalist politics after Parnell's death. The Cemís' moves from house to house in Havana are also part of the loss of status of powerful families which, in the wake of the Wars of Independence, gave up their position among the creole ruling class. This loss came about not just as the outcome of a family tragedy—the death of Cemí's father, Colonel Cemí; Alberto Olaya's fatal accident—but as an ironic consequence of the period under the Platt Amendment during the early Cuban Republic in which opportunistic American penetration dissolved the power hold of the old Cuban aristocracy.[26]

Finally, in both *Paradiso* and *A Portrait*, the reader closely follows the protagonists as they are "schooled." Each novel represents, from a critical, caustic perspective, institutional "methods of instruction," particularly the use of violent punishment as a means for "building character." Both texts methodically scrutinize all the levels of formal education to which their protagonists are subject: elementary Jesuit education in Clongowes, intermediate school in Belvedere, and the University College in Stephen Dedalus's case; José Eugenio Cemí's secondary school, Cemí's elementary and secondary school, and "Upsalón"—the sardonic name Lezama gives to the University of Havana—in *Paradiso*. Every single institutional pedadogical experience brings great disappointment to both protagonists and stirs them into an attitude of nonconformity and rebellion. This is best seen in Dedalus's "non serviam" when invited to join the Jesuit order, and in Cemí's collaboration in the Cuban student protest that shut down the University of Havana in September 1930. In both *A Portrait* and *Paradiso*, students take into their own hands the rigors of education, skeptical that any enlightenment might be forthcoming from the institutions. The self-taught Stephen goes on his own to the National Library and sharpens his intellect in his peripatetic discussions with Cranly, but not in the classroom. Cemí holds long, erudite discussions with

Fronesis and Foción as a Socratic compensation for the tendentious lessons he must tolerate in the classroom.

Out of these similar contexts, a pattern of epiphanic development emerges in which the "treacherous" substance of language dawns upon the artist. The stages of childhood provide a crucible for poetry since it is during childhood that words "become flesh" for these Catholic boys, not in the theological sense, but in their capacity to inflict psychic wounds. Innocence in *A Portrait* and *Paradiso* ends with the treason of names, with the discovery that there is more to words than meaning, that a word's suasive, rhetorical dimension has *material*, almost physiological effects, not as a mere "speech act,"[27] but as the perpetrator of trauma, piercing through the safe envelope of perception and the body like a bacterium or a laceration. The chapters that introduce the protagonist in *A Portrait* and *Paradiso* deal with how, in childhood, the denotative or referential function of language is disrupted, the stability of names and naming is thrown into a crisis, and this crisis in turn brings about a breakdown in the body and the self through the experience of sickness or pain. In childhood, this betrayal of language becomes associated with disease, punishment, and death to the point where it is difficult to distinguish utterances, threats, and admonitions from breaking fevers, stings, or blows upon the body, as if words had a physical, pathogenic "magical" force of their own.

Poetic consciousness in *Paradiso* and *A Portrait* appears as a homeopathic remedy, a form of redressing the wounds inflicted by language through a higher form of expression. This double nature of language as *pharmakon* has been analyzed by Kenneth Burke, Jacques Derrida, and Geoffrey Hartman. All agree that the curative power of language lies in its soothing poetic component, but its cure is precarious, since the antidote always carries the strain of new maladies.[28] Because of its therapeutic value, poetry in Joyce and Lezama is associated with corporal wholeness and, thus, with the dogma of incarnation, the notion of the "word made flesh." By combining the epigenetic and physiological narratives of development, Joyce and Lezama argue for a *somatic* basis for the Catholic theology of *logos*, where the word needs to "incarnate" in order to heal and repair the fallen nature of man. The "fall" of the body in Lezama and Joyce is thus physical and metaphysical, real and symbolic. Both *A Portrait* and *Paradiso* begin with the traumatic submersion of the child's body.

The opening episode of *A Portrait* has been interpreted as a calculated encapsulation of the novel's complete design.[29] Through

Stephen's perspective, we are presented with a child playing with fictitious names for himself and reciting nursery rhymes intermingled with sensory references to wetness. The scene ends with Stephen's turning his aunt's admonishments into a rhyme: "Pull out his eyes / Apologize / Apologize / Pull out his eyes" (*PA* 8). Stephen's reflex action exemplifies the function of poetry that is promoted in the rest of the novel. Stephen's "poem" is a suasive remedy to the anxiety generated by the admonishment's implied threat, magnified by the infant's imagination.

The novel's next episode—a day in ten-year-old Stephen's life at the Clongowes's school class of elements—ends the following morning in the infirmary. Following a day of exercise and classes, Stephen falls sick after being thrown into a ditch during a student prank. The episode's prose, filtered again through Stephen's consciousness, interweaves the gradual appearance of the symptoms of Stephen's fever with the growing anxiety induced by Stephen's realization of the unreliability of names, beginning with his own. The taunts of his classmates ("what kind of a name is that?") is a question that Stephen is compelled to methodically apply to all names. Stephen's suspicion about the referential ability of words will increase as he discovers the hoax of nominalism in his ponderings on the slippery, dual nature of names: his schoolmates' nicknames ("Nasty Roche," "stink"), terms for objects and actions ("a belt is a belt but is also a push"), professional titles (Stephen is perplexed by the social importance of the mysterious term "magistrate"), geographical names (which confuse him with their potential infinity and diversity: "America is one but is many"), and God's (whose name changes according to languages but is nevertherless the same). Stephen begins thus to question the correspondence between word and object—between signifier and signified—and begins to regard language as an abnormality, "something queer" (*PA* 11–12). That "suck," an insult, is also the sound of water, or that faucets can be named either "hot" or "cold" are facts that mystify him. Thinking about names induces fever-like symptoms in Stephen ; it "[makes] him very tired . . . it [makes] his head feel very big" (*PA* 16).

In its use of the problematic semantics of the riddle, Joyce's text summarizes the arbitrariness of language that preoccupies Stephen. In the childhood chapters of *A Portrait*, Stephen faces riddles in which language shows its sinister insufficiency by formulating unsolvable aporias which indirectly cause him to have bodily discomfort. Stephen is thrown into the ditch by Wells after the boys tease him about whether he "still kisses his mother or not," a question to which any response appears unsatisfactory (*PA* 13). At the infirmary his roommate makes a riddle out of his name (Athy) which Stephen cannot understand (*PA* 25).

Stephen's first instinctual response to his sickness comes from "poetic" language: Brigid's song and the rhymes from "Doctor Cornwell's spelling book" are the therapeutic means by which he dominates his anxiety (*PA* 24). Some of these words, in turn, betray him, since they inspire new visions of disease ("Canker is a disease of plants, / Cancer one of animals," *PA* 10) and death ("Wolsey died in Leicester Abbey," *PA* 22). Stephen remembers the legend of Little's death and pictures himself in Little's coffin (*PA* 24). The enigmatic, riddle-like quality of words produces a sense of loss and bafflement that in turn demands resolution and compensation through new words. In *A Portrait*—as in most of Joyce's work—water is associated with this dual strain of discourse.[30] Stephen recalls "the cold and slimy" water together with the words of Wells, Rody Kickham, and Nasty Roach; then he confuses the lapping of waves with the sound of voices (*PA* 26). The announcement at the lakeshore of Parnell's death in his reverie produces a final mental image: Stephen's visualization of his own sick, bedridden body as that of the dead Parnell (*PA* 27).

A Portrait thus traces the psychic source of the "magical" wounding quality of words. Marked by the wound, Stephen will obsessively meditate on names, especially his own name, until the day of his vocational epiphany. *Paradiso,* too, begins with a situation that connects language with something beyond the function of referentiality: disease. In *Paradiso*, the complex narrative discourse in the chapters on childhood differs notably from the distilled stylistic directness of *A Portrait*'s first chapter. *Paradiso* is not concerned with textually "performing" the workings of the child's consciousness from within, but with producing diegetically from without a "magical" language that is already confused with substance. In the style of *Paradiso*, the reader confronts a discourse whose polysemic mutations induce a child-like awe and fear, an anxiety of understanding similar to that of *A Portrait*'s child protagonist. The novel opens with a powerful image: As he suffers from an asthma attack, Cemí's five-year-old body is covered with the violent rash of his allergic reaction to ant bites. The language describes Cemí's condition, and multiplies demonstratively, the way the rash grows on Cemí's body. Thus the novel's discourse is linked with the nature of disease. (The novel repeats this association between language and disease later with the description of Rialta's fibroma, as Gustavo Pellón has shown.[31]) Two house servants,

Zoar and Truni, perform a ritual cleansing of Cemí's body that flusters and perturbs him just as riddles and words befuddle Stephen. The servants' incantations suggest to Cemí the magical, curative-yet-potentially-poisonous power of words, and produce in him a sense of anxiety that induces him to wet himself.

Language is presented again as a potential wound and as having the contagious quality of a sickness when, the day after, Cemí's sister tells him a rhyme that carries a punitive admonition very reminiscent of Stephen's aunt's: "Pepito, Pepito / si sigues jugando / te voy a meter / un pellizquito / que te va a doler" [Joey, Joey / stop your game / or I'll give you a pinch / and you will hurt]. The term "pellizquito" is a magical-metaphorical invocation of the skin rash. As in *A Portrait*, the sympathetic connections implied by such utterances carry an immanent sense of danger throughout Cemí's childhood.

The association of language with disease reappears in chapter 4 of *Paradiso*, in which Cemí, like Stephen, undergoes several traumatic submersions. These jolting experiences stimulate morbid hallucinations in which water and language are confused as one substance. Both Lezama and Joyce's texts represent aversion to water as a resistance to the negative, unreliable, fleeting dimensions of language.[32] Attempting to teach Cemí how to swim at age five, his father the colonel has him float while holding on to one of his fingers. Cemí loses his grip, sinks, and has to be rescued. A feeling of dread and foreboding similar to that in *A Portrait* permeates the scene even after the rescue. This "cure by poison," "sink or swim" motif is repeated again in the colonel's attempt to cure Cemí's asthma by forcing him into a bath of ice; this scene echoes the heat and cold patterns of the first section of *A Portrait*. In another scene, Cemí's sister Violante swims across a moat that recalls the ditch in *A Portrait*'s Clongowes Castle. The debris in the foul water pulls Violante in, and she is rescued while Cemí watches transfixed during an asthma attack. As in Stephen's case, these experiences inspire powerful and disturbing visions in Cemí. Deep in his sleep, Cemí stretches his arm to grasp his father's vanished finger. In his dream, Cemí sinks in the pool like his sister, but is saved by his mother who has assumed the form of a fish (P 133–35/R 132–34).[33] Against the eroding, duplicitous, rushing movement of water-language, the *cuerpo resistente* [resistant body] of poetry begins to form, incarnated in the capacity of the fish to overcome the force of the current. The fish, a Christological symbol, appears thus as a central trope for poetic language in Lezama's novel.

As Stephen and Cemí mature, utterances conjure visions in them so extreme that language appears to be a substantial replacement of reality, capable of superseding immediate sensory perception. Spoken words can stimulate Stephen and Cemí's imaginations beyond their referential fields. "His recent monstrous reveries came thronging into [Stephen's] memory . . . sprung up before him, suddenly and furious, out of mere words" (PA 90). To Cemí, words carry a similar hallucinatory force. The phrases "cuando la emigración" [during the emigration] and "allá en Jacksonville" [back there in Jacksonville] stimulate Cemí's imagination like coming from "un tiempo remoto y en un lugar lejano, como si aludiesen a la Orplid o a la Atlántida" (P 43/R 43) [a remote time and in a distant place as if they were referring to Orplid or to Atlantis]. These phrases have the "condición de arca de la alianza resistente en el tiempo" (P 43/R 43) [feeling of the Ark of the Covenant as it resisted time]. The expression "la hija del oidor" [the daughter of a hearer (judge)], in reference to his great-grandmother, has a similar corporeal, sentient quality to Cemí: "era esa palabra de *oidor*, oída y saboreada por José Cemí como la clave imposible de un mundo desconocido" (P 44/R 44) [It was that word 'hearer' heard and savored by José Cemí as the impossible key to an unknown world]. Lezama compares the enchantment of this word with the paradoxical effect erosion has on the face of a statue in the Palazzo Capitolino, a face whose youthfulness is not marred but refined and preserved by time—"rostro que ha permanecido inmutable" (P 44/R 44) [the face has remained unchanged]—in a manner unforeseen by the sculptor. The word, in its magical incandescence, projects on Cemí's mind a dual image: that of a "vieja y sarmentosa, apenas reconstruible" [an old and puckered woman, barely reconstructible] and that of an immortal young lady. The word "ivory" shimmers as well in Stephen's brain, clearer and brighter than the visual image of ivory itself, "than any ivory sawn from the mottled tusks of elephants" (PA179). Like Cemí, Stephen measures the weight, volume, and density of phrases as if they were liquid-like and palatable. In the confessional, "sins trickle from his lips, one by one . . . in shameful drops . . . oozing like a sore" (PA 144).

In A Portrait and Paradiso, poetry seeks to close the wound of an absence opened by the perfidious character of language. Lezama's doctrine of *ausencia* [absence] can here be linked to Derrida's critique of presence in Western logocentric metaphysics.[34] Nevertheless, while in Derrida all signification is loss, in Lezama and Joyce's A Portrait, language becomes its own antidote in the form of poetic expression. In Lezama and Joyce, poetic language can overpower the terror inspired by the void of death. Stephen is terrified by the stories about the ghost that walks Clongowes, a legend that he identifies with the death of Parnell in the first chapter of A Portrait. A similar fear is instilled in Cemí's heart when his grandmother speaks about the corpse of her father which, exhumed after ten years, had become a perfect statue of dust that dissolved instantly when struck by air. This tale provokes new nightmares that mix the invisible with the visible in the mind of the susceptible Cemí. The simulation of death inspires in Cemí a particular anxiety. Cemí is told that the wax statue in the Church "es una santica que está ahí, muerta de verdad" (P 142/R 141) [that's a saint there, a real dead saint]. Confronting this fake corpse brings back the visions provoked by submersion: "El frío amarillo de la piel, semejante al extenderse del agua, penetraba por sus pesadillas" (P 143/ R 142) [The yellowing coldness of the skin similar to the spreading out of water penetrated his nightmares]. When the colonel plays the role of a ghost by hiding behind the door and speaking out "una salmodia funeral" [a funereal dirge], the paradox of this "pretended" absence frightens Cemí (P 144–45/R 143–44).

A comparative reading of A Portrait and Paradiso can thus yield a pattern of corresponding figures of death that each protagonist confronts in the process of developing his poetic vocation: Parnell and the colonel; dead Little and the wax statue; the grandfather and the ghost of Clongowes. When the colonel dies, all the visions of submersion converge before Cemí's mental eye, just as Parnell's death produces a convergence of images in Stephen's mind. In this chaotic moment, Cemí is "saved" by "la fijeza de los ojos" [the stillness in the look] of Oppiano Licario, whose face replaces the disappearing face of the father "que se . . . fueron llevando las olas" (P 157/R 156) [that . . . was then taken away by the waves]. Oppiano's presence at the colonel's death bed is a poetic antidote; it reinstates the fixed resistance of poetry against the "fiero aguarrás" [fierce bleach] of the sealike currents of time. Cemí's therapeutic glimpse of Oppiano Licario thus strengthens the child and foretells the "education" that will teach Cemí how to effectively fill the void of death and resist the flow of time through poetry.

After language's crisis of referentiality, the practice of metaphor appears as a saving grace in both A Portrait and Paradiso. What is first realized as a disease of language—the confusion of names, the incongruity of signs, the disparity between signifier and signified—is rediscovered by accident as a potential redemptive tool: a potens, in Lezama's theoretical language. If name and object do not correspond, then metaphor can take advantage of this difference by ascribing new things to old names, devising new correspondences more illuminating and more "natural" than nominal ones. Cemí stumbles upon "the gift of metaphor" when he confuses two illustrations inscribed as "amolador" [grindstone] and "bachiller" [student]:

> [P]or una irregular acomodación de gesto y voz, creyó que el bach- iller era el amolador. Así que cuando días más tarde su padre le dijo: . . . ¿Qué es un bachiller?—Contestaba con la seguridad de quien ha comprobado sus visiones. —Un bachiller es una rueda que lanza chis- pas, que a medida que la rueda va alcanzando más velocidad, las chis- pas se multiplican hasta aclarar la noche—. En ese momento su padre . . . se extrañó del raro don metafórico de su hijo. De su manera profé- tica y simbólica de entender los oficios. (P 135–36/R 135)

> [[A] warped accommodation of gesture and voice caused him to be- lieve that the student was the grindstone, and the grindstone the stu- dent. Several days later his father asked him . . . "What's a student?," and with the certainty of one whose visions have been proven, he an- swered: "A student is a wheel that gives off sparks, and as the wheel picks up speed the sparks multiply until they light up the night." At that moment his father . . . was startled at his son's rare gift of metaphor, his prophetic and symbolic way of understanding a profession.]

Cemí unwittingly discovers that the linguistic imprecision of meta- phor is the source of a new accuracy. Stephen makes a similar dis- covery through the recitation of litany. The designations of the Virgin in litany perplex Stephen, but when he applies these attri- butes to a secular context, transforming the litany into metaphor, he produces a new, recognizable meaning. "This is what tower of ivory means," Stephen realizes while thinking of Eileen's hands. "Her fair hair had streamed out behind her like gold in the sun. Tower of ivory. House of gold. By thinking things you could under- stand them" (PA 43).

The uncanny power of words to wound and heal increases when transferred to the written mode. Written words, particularly graffiti, exercise a strong hallucinatory spell upon Stephen. While Stephen searches for his father's carved initials at Cork college, the sight of the word "fetus" triggers powerful associations in his mind: "The sudden legend startled his blood: he seemed to feel the absent stu- dents of the college about him and to shrink from their company. A vision of their life, which his father's words had been powerless to evoke, sprang up before him out of the word cut in the desk" (PA 89). As he roams the night, inscriptions all around Dublin appear to dance before Stephen's eyes, and the street and commercial

signs seem to obstruct his way: "He found himself glancing from
one casual word to another on his right or left in stolid wonder that
they had been so silently emptied of instantaneous sense until
every mean shop legend bound his mind like the words of a spell"
(PA 178–79). Graffiti has the same spellbinding power in *Paradiso*,
as in the obscene design scribbled above the urinal in chapter 11.
Cemí's inscriptions in chalk on the wall near a *cuartería* [a poor
Havana neighborhood] in the Vedado stir an altercation in chapter
2.[35]

Writing magnifies the capacity of words to disrupt the body and
cause pain. The problem of writing lies at the center of the punishment episode in *A Portrait*. Father Dolan singles Stephen out because he is not writing the Latin exercises, and Fleming is punished
because of the sloppiness of his notebook which is "stuck with a
wad of ink." Fleming's inkstained hands initiate a compulsive
motif in the symbolic order of the novel: hands in *A Portrait* have a
troublesome synecdochic connection to writing. In *A Portrait*, the
hand is the organ of writing in the way the tongue is colloquially
associated with speech and the eye with reading. The hand is the
very target of punishment as Dolan inflicts upon Stephen's the
word-wound with his whip.

In Lezama, as in Joyce, the hand is the sixth sensory organ. In
Lezama's autobiographical essay "Confluencias" [Confluences],[36]
there is a fantastic discourse on "the hand" and its association to
childhood and poetic language:

> La noche se ha reducido a un punto, que va creciendo de nuevo
> hasta volver a ser la noche. La reducción—que compruebo—es una
> mano. La situación de la mano dentro de la noche, me da un tiempo.
> El tiempo donde eso puede ocurrir. La noche era para mí el territorio
> donde se podía reconocer la mano. Yo me decía, no puede estar la
> mano, no necesita de mi comprobación. Y una voz débil . . . me decía:
> estira tu mano y verás como allí está la noche y su mano desconocida.
> Desconocida porque nunca veía un cuerpo detrás de ella: Vascilante
> por el temor, pues con una decisión inexplicable, iba lentamente ade-
> lantando mi mano, como un ansioso recorrido por un desierto, hasta
> encontrarme la otra mano, lo otro. . . .
>
> Despues supe que en los *Cuadernos* de Rilke estaba también la
> mano, y después supe que estaba en casi todos los niños, en casi todos
> las manuales de psicología infantil.
>   . . .
> Cada palabra era para mí la presencia innumerable de la fijeza de la
> mano nocturna . . . larvas de metáfora, desarrolladas en indetenible
> cadeneta, como una despedida y una nueva visita. (*OC* 2: 1209–211)

[Night has shrunk into a spark, that begins to grow anew until it becomes the night again. This shrinking—I can confirm this—is a hand. The situation of the hand in the night offers me a Time. A Time where such things can happen. Night to me was the region where the hand could be recognized. I told myself, the hand cannot be out there waiting, it doesn't need me to prove its existence. And a faint voice prompted me: stretch out your hand and you will see how night and its unknown hand are there. Unknown because there was never a body behind it. Doubtful with fear, with an inexplicable determination, I slowly advance my hand as though anxiously crossing a desert, until I find the other hand, the Other. . . .

I learned later that the hand is also in Rilke's *Notebooks* and is almost in all children, in almost any textbook on child psychology.

. . .

Each word was to me the incommensurate presence of the stillness of the nocturnal hand . . . larvae of metaphor, developed in an unstoppable chain, like a farewell and a new visitation.]

This is the hand Cemí reaches out to in his sleep: the penlike finger of the colonel drawing a line of safety on the water. This is the hand that replaces Cemí's when, at ten, he begins to scribble with chalk on the *paredón* [standing wall]: "Al fin apoyó la tiza como si conversase con el paredón. La tiza comenzó a manar su blanco. . . . Llegada la prolongada tiza al fin del paredón, cuando la personalidad hasta entonces indiscutida de la tiza fue reemplazada por una mano que la asía y apretaba con exceso, como temiendo que su distracción fuese a fugrase, pues aquella mano comenzaba a exigir precisiones, como si reclamase la mano el cuerpo de una capturada presa" (P 20/R 20). [Finally he put the chalk to the wall. The chalk began to spread out its white. . . . The long chalk came to the wall's end, when its undisputed individuality was usurped by another hand that clutched and held it too tightly, as if fearing that its abstraction would flee; that hand began to make demands, fighting for the captured prey's body.]

The connection between writing and the body is hypostatized in *Paradiso* in Fibo's devilish pen. The association between pain and the instrument of writing could not be more pronounced:

Fibo era el alumno que empuñaba una pluma de hilos de colores, producto único y engendro satánico del barroco carcelario. Terminaba en un punto cruel, afanoso de hundirse en los arenales más blandos del cuerpo. Sus cambios de sitio estaban justificados por la ausencia del libro de lectura. Llegaba a un pupitre, fingiendo el alboroto de una apetencia de saber, subrayaba la necesidad de penetrar en el facistol del otro escriba, y hundía la pluma del tocoloro infernal por la rendija del pupitre anterior, electrizando la glútea por la penetración de aquel punto teñido de la energía del ángel color de uva. (P 82/R 80)

[Fibo was the student who held a pen of colored stripes, the unique product and satanic monster of a jailer of the baroque. It ended in a cruel point, eager to sink itself into the softest sand dunes of the body. His seat changes were justified by the absence of his textbook. He would reach a desk, feigning excitement and eagerness to learn, he would urgently need to get into the other desk, and he would sink the pen with an infernal subtlety through the crack of the desk in front, electrifying the gluteal muscles with the penetration of that point.]

Thus, on one hand, writing has the capacity to degrade, humiliate, and injure. This negative effect needs to be redressed with the balm of poetry. The final and most crucial substantiation of language through writing in *Paradiso* is Uncle Alberto's playful letter to the dentist Demetrio warning against dealing with prostitutes during a trip to Cienfuegos, in which he refers to venereal disease through the fanciful reinvention of fish names and expressions from marine biology (P 170–72/R 169–71). Here writing has a marvelous healing function. When Uncle Demetrio reads the letter to Cemí after the female members of the family have bashfully left the room, the scene represents a sort of ritual initiation since Cemí will hear for the first time "el idioma hecho naturaleza, con todo su artificio de alusiones y cariñosas pedanterías" (P 170/R 169) [language made into nature with all its artifices of allusion and loving pedantry]. Alberto's letter represents a case in which writing displaces and replaces an absence (the letter is read just as Alberto is about to die in a car accident), making the writing more corporeal as the writer becomes more ghostly. The letter thus involves dying but also resurrection in Lezama. The neologistic style of Alberto's letter—whose punning strategy could have drawn from the experimental prose of *Finnegans Wake* and shows that Lezama also had Joyce's later works in mind while writing *Paradiso*—mystifies Cemí. In response, Cemí pictures the poetic effects generated by Alberto's language as that of a body resisting a current. As in Cemí's submersion dream discussed above, its ideal form is that of a fish:

Mientras oía la sucesión de los nombres de las tribus submarinas, en sus recuerdos se iba levantando no tan sólo la clase de preparatoria, cuando estudiaba los peces, sino cómo las palabras iban surgiendo arrancadas de su tierra propia, con su agrupamiento artificial y su movimiento pleno de alegría al penetrar en sus canales oscuros, invisibles e inefables. Al oír ese desfile verbal, tenía la misma sensación que cuando sentado en el muro del Malecón, veía los pescadores extraer sus peces, cómo se retorcían mientras la muerte los acogía fuera de su cámara natural. Pero en la carta, esos extraídos peces verbales se retorcían también, pero era un retorcimiento de alegría jubilar, al formar un nuevo coro, un ejército de océanidas cantando al perderse entre las brumas. (P 172–73/R 171–72)

[As he listened to the succession of the names of submarine tribes his memory not only brought forth his class in secondary school where he studied fish, but the words themselves rose up, lured up out of their won territory, artificially grouped, and their joyous movement was invisible and ineffable as it penetrated its dark channels. Listening to that verbal parade, he had the same feeling as when he sat on the wall of the Malecón and watched fishermen piling in their catch, the fish twisting as death overcome them outside their natural habitat. In the letter those verbal fish had been hauled out twisting, but it was a twisting of jubilation as they formed a new chorus, an army of oceanids singing as it disappeared in the mist.]

It is after their encounters with writing that Cemí and Stephen begin to develop a prophetic and augurial inclination to see the world as a cabbalistic realm of signs and ciphers, and so to interpret sensorial phemomena as a cover or disguise for the true, grammatological order of things. This phenomenology goes beyond the Aristotelean and the Platonic: it is in fact a synthesis of the two cosmologies, in which formal idealism gains objective materiality, where signs are not abstractions but part of the substantial makeup of the world. Following Merleau-Ponty, the world and its perception are revealed to be organized like a language.[37] Stephen uses the lines of the sidewalk to "read" his fate and predict the evaluation of his English compositions. He regards the path of the birds as writing and sees drifting constellations in the symbols and markings of his trigonometry formulas and exercises (PA 191). Cemí sees letters and signs in the figures of the horses during the student riot; letters become animated before his eyes as if they had organic life (P 224–26/R 221–23). In Paradiso, rare inscriptions and signs make uncanny, foreboding apparitions, like the Arabic characters on the red balloon before Farraluque's orgy with the masked man (P 208, 209/R 207, 208). This strange effect might be called stellar or constellatory since the ultimate locus of writing in Paradiso and A Portrait is on the board of the sky that houses the writing of the zodiac. Writing's ultimate stellar quality has a divinatory character—the poet is found reading, in Lezama's words, "la pizarra del cielo" [the heavens' chalkboard].

IV

Paradiso's representation of Cemí's early childhood mirrors the phases in Stephen's acquisition of poetic language. Both novels explore other common childhood problems as well, such as issues of puberty and sexuality. In both *A Portrait* and *Paradiso* there are instances of sexual initiation and ambiguity in the context of schooling. The rumors about "smugging" in Clongowes recall the Figueras incident in *Paradiso*. In both *A Portrait* and *Paradiso* the latrines and showers are the site of punishment and homosexual encounters. In *Paradiso*, Alberto's sordid encounter with the fantastic and vengeful apparition of the goddess Angra Mainyu in the showers (*P* 93–5/*R* 91–5)—which has been exquisitely analyzed by Lezama specialist Irlemar Chiampi[38]—echoes the squalid mystique of water in the "square" in *A Portrait*: "it was all thick slabs of slate and water trickled all out of pinholes and there was a queer smell of stale water there" (*PA* 43). These common themes unfold differently in the narratives of the two novels. In *Paradiso*, the celibate Cemí, for example, does not undergo a sexual rite of passage, nor is he led to question Catholic orthodoxy and stumble into heresy, as Stephen does in *A Portrait*. After their poetic "maturation," Stephen and Cemí will only mirror each other in their concerted attempts to formulate a personal aesthetic. Other dimensions of Stephen's biography in *A Portrait* could be said to undergo a rewriting in *Paradiso*, only that these problematic aspects of Stephen's character are adopted and diffused into the characters of Fronesis and Foción.

Fronesis shares with Stephen the quest for elegance and a sense of orphanhood. Just as Stephen tries to "build a breakwater of order and elegance against the sordid tide of life without him" (*PA* 98), Cemí notes similar affectations in Fronesis's behavior: "Era una de sus características en el trato diario, la uniformidad señorial" (*P* 277/*R* 278) [Lordly consistency was one of his characteristics in everyday dealings]. Nevertheless, Lezama reverses Joyce's ironic treatment of his character's search for a dignified poise. While Stephen is often dirty and dressed in borrowed clothes, Fronesis is picture-perfect, almost sublime. Similarly, while Stephen fantasizes himself an illegitimate or adopted son, "hardly of one blood with [his family] but [standing] to them rather in the mystical kinship of fosterage, fosterchild and fosterbrother" (*PA* 98), Fronesis happens to discover that he is an illegitimate, adopted son (his mother is in fact his aunt). A chiasmatic reversal occurs: while Stephen wishes to build up a fantasy of non-consanguinity, Fronesis becomes spiritually reconnected with his adoptive mother when she acknowledges that he is not her son (*P* 357–64/*R* 362–69). In *A Portrait*, filial ties are severed and made irrelevant by exile, while in *Paradiso* the quest is to restore them. In *Paradiso*, Fronesis shares with Stephen the opportunity of flight and leaves the island for Europe, but this distance serves to reconcile Fronesis with his parents. Finally, both Stephen' and Fronesis's first heterosexual experiences have a highly elaborate, ritualistic character in which the young men need to overcome mysterious forces and resistances.

Foción and Stephen share the Luciferine sin of pride and the will to heresy; both surrender to lower passions and have commerce with prostitutes. Like Stephen in *A Portrait*, Foción walks in circles when he is swept by base, animalistic appetites. In both novels, the lamplight and the circle are used as Dantesque, infernal symbols that draw together the semiotics of the descriptions of Foción and Stephen's vices. "After early nightfall the yellow lamps would light up, there and there, the squalid quarter of the brothels. [Stephen] would follow a devious course up and down the streets, circling always nearer and nearer in a tremor of fear" (*PA* 102). This picture recalls the sordid circle of light projected by the lamp post that demarcates the sacred space of vice in Foción's seduction of the red-haired boy (*P* 290/*R* 291). Though some critics have detected a streak of homoeroticism in Stephen,[39] these apparent inclinations bear little resemblance to Foción's open *bugarronería* (slang for aggressive homosexual behavior in Cuban Spanish). What is similar is how both characters identify with the satanic and heretical without losing their respect for Catholic norm. Foción is attracted to Fronesis's ideal of rectitude in the same way Stephen still obeys the rules of orthodoxy even when he has lost his faith: as Cranly cleverly notes, Stephen still submits to dogma by not wishing to profane the host in his refusal to participate in the Eucharist (*PA* 239–40). Despite a very detached attitude toward sin, Foción's anti-Catholicism, like Stephen's, is still defined by liturgical form. Both characters are the literary descendants of Nicholas of Cusa and Giordano Bruno: portraits of the once-pious fallen from grace.

V

So far we have noted similarities between the development of Stephen Dedalus and José Cemí's susceptibility to the poetic force of language. While the *imprint* of the linguistic upon them follows similar phases, the *appearance* of poetry—the praxis of the poem—is produced differently. While Stephen's movement toward poetic realization is a trek toward increasing isolation from his family and from insular traditions, Cemí's apprehension of poetry is attained in the context of connectedness and companionship, a development that perhaps relates the moral of *Paradiso* more to *Ulysses* than to *A Portrait*. Moreover, though both characters discover poetry as they develop, this does not mean they are both presented as poets. In *A Portrait*, the writing of the first poem happens in a carefully staged scene in chapter 5, in which Stephen writes a villanelle as he wakes up recalling E. M. While this scene provides a glimpse into the process of poetic composition, in which "in the virgin womb of the imagination the word was made flesh" (*PA* 217), we are not to take it as definitive evidence of Stephen's talent. In fact, some critics contend that the weak, Paterian mannerisms of the villanelle make manifest Joyce's ironic treatment of Stephen.[40] *A Portrait* ends with Stephen on his way to becoming a poet, but he is not yet a poet.

In *Paradiso*, the two instances in which a poem is featured in the text bear Cemí's name in the title but not his signature. Their authors, Fronesis and Oppiano Licario, are poets who guide Cemí's search for poetic language. As in *A Portrait*, the culmination of this process—Cemí's poetic maturity—is situated outside the narrative, in the sequel, *Oppiano Licario*. Even when both Cemí and Stephen have arrived at the healing rhythm of poetry, the reader is left waiting for Stephen's poetic maturity and for Cemí's first villanelle.

Nevertheless, even though neither *Künstlerroman* ends with a concrete instance of poetic praxis, both represent their protagonists in similar contemplations about the nature of literary aesthetics. Both *Paradiso* and *A Portrait* depict their protagonists engineering a theory of beauty during similar peripatetic strolls around their cities. In both plots, poetic theory precedes poetic praxis, and this aesthetic theory is in turn reflected in the novel's design and discourse. In both novels, the work of adolescence is to explore the grounds of aesthetic experience: "[t]o speak of these things and to try to understand their nature and, having understood it, to try slowly and humbly and constantly to express . . . an image of the beauty we have come to understand," as Stephen tells Lynch (*PA* 206).

Notwithstanding the argument that the theory does not match the end result (since Stephen's theory of epiphany is not present in the narrative), the aesthetic presented in *A Portrait* bears an important resemblance to the theoretical and speculative component of *Paradiso* and to Lezama's poetic system. *A Portrait* and *Paradiso* not only postulate a theory of poetic epiphany, but highlight the all-important notion of *arrestedness* so dominant in both Stephen and Cemí's aesthetic postulations. Arguably, the prominence of the notion of stasis in the aesthetic theory of the *A Portrait* is an important influence and component in the evolution of the central topos of *fijeza* in Lezama's system. This common theme demonstrates Lezama's profoundly critical examination of *A Portrait*, and a corresponding reelaboration and anamorphosis of the concept of arrestedness in Lezama's work.

Stephen's formulation of his aesthetic comes at the concluding episode of *A Portrait*, the carefully constructed chapter 5. On this day, Stephen wakes up, tolerates his family's banter, meditates about beauty on his way to the university, is late for French class, talks to the dean about his theories while waiting for his physics class to convene, passes through a student rally, talks to Davin during a soccer game, and walks the beaches of Dublin with Lynch, to whom Stephen presents his full aesthetic theory. Structurally, this episode presents in embryonic form what *Ulysses* will attempt on a more ambitious level. As Stephen moves through an urban labyrinth of perceptions, disputing and discussing issues ranging from priesthood and Irish nationalism to British and Russian politics, he obstinately and steadfastly persists in his ascetic analysis of beauty, disregarding all other issues that might distract his thinking. These reflections lead to his decision to expatriate, which he reveals to Cranly and enters into the journal at the end of the chapter.

The core of Stephen's aesthetic theory is drawn from some "key quotations of Aquinas" which, although estranged from their original meaning, become the basis of his own notions of aesthetic experience. Aquinas is first quoted when, encouraged by the dean to elaborate on his theory, Stephen analyzes aesthetic apprehension ("pulchra son que visa placent") and the satisfaction of desire ("bonum est in quod tendit appetitus"). Stephen addresses the issue of stasis in a clever wordplay about the need to extricate the terminology of aesthetics from the "language of the marketplace." Stephen uses the phrase "I hope I am not *detaining* you" to emphasize the difference between the aesthetic meaning he gives the verb "to detain" from its idiomatic usage. Later in his promenade with Lynch, Stephen returns to the subject. Quoting Aquinas tendentiously, Stephen claims that "Beauty awakens an esthetic stasis, an ideal pity or ideal terror, prolonged and at last dissolved by

. . . the rhythm of beauty" (*PA* 205–6). Stephen shows here an equal degree of attention to his use of terms. "You see, I use the word arrest," he tells Lynch, "The feelings excited by improper art are kinetic. The esthetic emotion is therefore static" (*PA* 206).

Using scholastic categories as models, Stephen postpones speaking about the problem of artistic conception, gestation, and reproduction, and refers only to aesthetic apprehension, following Aquinas' dictum, *ad pulcritudinem tria requiruntur, integritas, consonantia, claritas. Integritas* ("integridad" in Dámaso Alonso's translation, which I will discuss later) is thus the first in a series of phases leading to aesthetic apprehension: the visual "grasping" of an object as self-bound and self-contained, independent from context. *Consonantia* ("consonancia" in Alonso's translation) comes after the realization of the object qua object, whose parts constitute a whole among themselves, where the notion of rhythm stems from the relation of its parts within itself. *Claritas* ("luminosidad" in Alonso's translation) is the last phase of aesthetic appreciation, in which a "radiance" coming from the isolated object reaches out to the perceiving subject to exercise an "enchantment of the heart," a nullification of desire, since the viewer does not wish to possess or to act upon the object but solely to behold it in the brief realization of its formal perfection. Since this comes as a type of revelation, some critics have considered this radiance as the equivalent of Joyce's early theory of epiphany, even when he chooses to discard the latter term after revising *Stephen Hero*.[41] Stephen's theory regards aesthetic perception as a form of cognition: even the ugly has an aesthetic potential as long as it can be known as such. The antecedents to this aesthetic theory can be found in Joyce's former writings, as part of a series of topics that obsessed him before writing *Ulysses*.[42] Even when critics disassociate the theory from the result, Stephen's theory *was* the author's theory at some point.

The same can be said of Lezama's aesthetic theory, although in *Paradiso* there is more consistency between the protagonist's speculations and the aesthetic praxis of the novel. Even though Lezama's notes from the thirties and forties address the topic of poetry and not beauty, Lezama's notion of the poetic embraces all art forms and includes terms that are drawn from outside the bounds of verse. Lezama's notion of the *imago* (of metaphors building toward one evolving image) is also an aesthetic formulation, drawn from Aquinas, in which stasis plays an important role. In Lezama there is a great deal of reflection on how aesthetic apprehension leads to revelation and creation. To Lezama artistic production is a component of apprehension given that the poet generates his metaphors as he attempts to "know" and "grasp" the *imago*.

Critics such as Octavio Paz and Severo Sarduy have commented on the crucial role of stasis and arrestedness in the aesthetics of Lezama's prose. "Lezama fija" [Lezama fixes], writes Sarduy; Paz speaks of the "efecto de estalactita" [stalactite effect] in Lezama's writing.[43] Lezama develops his idea of *fijeza* in much of his writing, but specifically in his book of poems titled *La fijeza* (1949), in which Lezama draws from Zenonian paradox to create images of frozen movement. Lezama finds *fijeza* mostly in images of subdued or suspended motion, such as the vibration of a cord or the flight of an arrow: "Entre la flecha y el punto / el insecto bordonea. / El arco del cejijunto / crea paréntesis, crea." [Between the arrow and its target / an insect chirps. / The tightbrowed bow / keeps making parentheses.] (*Poesía* 148)

The *fijeza* in Lezama's poetry is the separation of being from becoming within time's flow by means of a natural accident or ritual experience—"el bosque soplado desprende el colibrí del instante" [struck by the wind, the forest releases the hummingbird of the instant]—or by a slight, almost imperceptible pause. It is poetry's duty to record such pauses, like the fall of a leaf in a snowstorm— "Si interrumpe la amargura / el jardín desarreglado, / la pausa es la hoja impura / entre el soplo y el nevado" [If sorrow breaks / into the dishevelled garden / pause is the soiled leaf / between draft and snowstorm] (*Poesía* 150)—or the breaking of a branch—"el imán entre las hojas / teje una doble corona. / Sólo una rama caída" [the magnet in the thicket / weaves a double halo. / Only one branch is fallen] (*Poesía* 151). Lezama envisions a "frialdad" or stellar coldness where things remain suspended in still, star-like configurations: "Tirando del instantero / dormida abeja ya pace / el árbol de las estrellas." [Pulling out the clock hands / the sleeping bee now feeds / on the heaventree of stars.] (*Poesía* 149) This verse shows the double debt of Lezama's stellar-like notion of *fijeza* to the synthetic, baroque verses of Góngora's *Soledades* ("el rudo robador de Europa / en campos de zafiro / pace estrellas" [Europe's rough abductor / on field of safire / grazes on stars]), and to the impersonal detachment and the "godlike" distance of Joyce's style, especially expressed in *Ulysses*' "Ithaca" chapter, whose poetic language is very close to Lezama's poetic diction. (Consider, for example, the line "The heaven tree of stars hung with humid night-blue fruit," *U* 573/1039, in this context.) This cold, authorial "lejanía" [distance] is regarded as problematic *and* indispensable in Lezama's poetics.

In *Paradiso*, the *fijeza* is evident in both the figural construction of the novel's descriptive passages and in Cemí's meditations on the nature of the poetic. It is in the latter that the debt to the concept of stasis developed in *A Portrait* is most evident. In *Paradiso*'s chapter 11, after a number of peripatetic displacements down the "calle de Obispo" [Bishop Street] similar to Stephen's meanderings in *A Portrait*'s Dublin, after having received Fronesis's poem Cemí finds himself alone reflecting on the nature of aesthetic perception, which he considers that which "en un instante pasa de la visión que ondula a la mirada que se fija" [what in one instant passes from ondulant vision into fixed look] (*P* 351/*R* 356). This section (*P* 350–57/*R* 355–61) can be read as the exposition of Cemí's aesthetic theory the way that chapter 5 of *A Portrait* can be in Stephen's case. Here Cemí engages in a similar exercise of formal Thomistic *quidditas* through the contemplation of some statuettes in a shop window. These figures are subjected to a process of cognitive isolation and analysis, similar to Stephen's explanatory exercise with the basket in *A Portrait*. Cemí's gaze "les dintinguía y aislaba" [distinguished and isolated them]. The practice of the Stephen-cum-Aquinas principle of aesthetic apprehension is reenacted and expanded:

Casi siempre la adquisición del objeto se debía a que ya frente a la vitrina, cuando comenzaban a distinguirse algunos pespuntes coloreados, en el momento en que su mirada lo distinguía y lo aislaba del resto de los objetos, lo adelantaba como una pieza de ajedrez que penetra en un mundo que logra en un instante recomponer todos sus cristales. Sabía que esa pieza que se adelantaba era un punto que lograba una infinita corriente de analogía, corriente que hacía una regia reverencia, como una tritogenia de gran tamaño, que quería mostrarle su rendimiento, su piel para la caricia y el enigma de su permanencia. . . .
Los días que lograba esos agrupamientos donde una corriente de fuerza lograba detenerse en el centro de una composición, Cemí se notaba alegre sin jactancias. . . .
Eso lo llevó a meditar cómo se producían en él esas recomposiciones espaciales, ese ordenamiento de lo invisible, ese sentido de las estalactitas. Pudo precisar que esos agrupamientos eran de raíz temporal, que no tenían nada que ver con los agrupamientos espaciales, que son siempre una naturaleza muerta; para el espectador la fluencia del tiempo convertía esas ciudades espaciales en figuras, por las que el tiempo al pasar y repasar, como los trabajos de las mareas en las plataformas coralinas, formaba como un eterno retorno de las figuras que por estar situadas en la lejanía eran un permanente embrión. (*P* 351–53/*R* 356–58)

[His (purchase) of an object was due, almost always, to the nascent discernment, before a shop window, of some brightly colored back-stitching; the moment his look distinguished it and isolated it from the rest of the objects, he moved it forward like a chess piece that penetrates a world that in an instant succeeds in recomposing all its crystals. He knew that the piece that moved forward was a point that encompassed an infinite current of analogy, a current that made a regal bow, like a Trigtogenia of great size, wanting to show her submissiveness, her skin to be caressed, and the enigma of her permanence. . . .

On the days he achieved those groupings, when a current of strength managed to halt itself in the center of a composition, Cemí seemed happy without arrogance . . .

That brought him to meditate on the manner in which those spatial rearrangements were produced in him, that ordering of the invisible, that feeling for stalactites. He was able to establish that those groupings had temporal roots, had nothing to do with spatial groupings, which are always still-lives; for the viewer, the flow of time converted those spatial cities into figures, through which time, as it passed back and fourth like the labor of the tides on the coral reefs, produced a kind of eternal change of the figures, which by being situated in the distance, were a permanent embryo.]

To Stephen's three steps—*integritas, consonantia,* and *claritas*—Cemí adds a fourth: transcendence. According to Cemí's theory, first the aesthetic object is isolated in its integrity ("moved forward" and separated "like a chesspiece"). The organization of the object's inner components is then reconstituted into a new consonance (like "a world that has recomposed all its crystals"). This reordering releases from the object a quality—a "radiance"—that fascinates and captures the viewer's gaze (the object's "regal bow"). After these phases, an animistic effect occurs in which the object reinvents its relationship to its surroundings. The mirroring of Stephen's theory is clear enough. Cemí's gaze juxtaposes objects to produce new, interesting "radiances" emanating from a brief spell of *fijeza*. On all occasions, a moment of stillness—a *sentido de estalactitas* [feeling for stalactites]—anticipates an animistic movement: objects become suspended before being set newly in motion once again on a higher transcendental plane. Lezama's stasis is a strategic pause between two distinct kinetic states.

Lezama can also be read to parody Joyce in this passage. All of Cemí's visions occur in "marketplaces" while he is window-watching, a practice anathema to the purist Stephen. Lezama also reinjects Aquinas in Stephen's aesthetics, derived from Aquinas yet characteristically un-Aquinian.[44] The radiance of Stephen's *claritas* is non-transcendental: it belongs to the thing-in-itself and to the capacity of the artist to isolate the object in contemplation and to appreciate its secular beauty. Lezama's notion of radiance is linked to the Thomistic concept of the *imago*, the term used in the *Summa Theologica* to describe the mystery of the Trinity. The *imago* is the concept to which the terms *integritas, consonantia* and *claritas* refer. To Joyce, the artistic image is sufficient and meaningful by itself; Lezama reads Aquinas as saying that all images, all artistic objects, and all aesthetic experiences refer to a mystical source, since the world and man are made in God's "imagen y semejanza" [image and likeness]. Beauty is but the recognition of this divine specularity.[45]

VI

The number of tropes and concepts that recur in *A Portrait* and *Paradiso* is impressively high. Both refer to luminosity, stasis, and integrity in passages on aesthetic theory; both use the same liturgical terms to figure human growth; both use water imagery and the trope of disease to allegorize the unstable and potentially destructive nature of language. Finally, both make adolescence the "umbrella-term" embracing the postulates of their project. The reader is tempted to think that *Paradiso* shares *A Portrait*'s idiom, and that, despite its baroque excesses, Lezama's language might be a direct derivation of Joyce's. However, as we noted before, Lezama's *a-dolescente* is approximate but not identical to Joyce's "young man." In *Paradiso*, adolescence is a extended, ten-year period of plenitude and of fulfilled potential, what Jorge Guillén would call "the noon in the day of human existence." This exaltation is manifested in the following description of Fronesis: "entre los quince y los veinticinco años, deteminados seres ofrecen una gravedad visible y una embriaguez secreta," "en ese paréntesis de horas privilegiadas, . . . su gravitación y la fuerza que los hizo vivir como algo secreto, alcanzó su medida más alta" (P 322/R 325–26) ["between the ages of fifteen and twenty-five, certain beings offer a visible sobriety and a secret intoxication," "in that parenthesis of privileged hours . . . their gravitation and the strength that made them live as if seduced by something secret, reached their most generous measure"]. In *A Portrait*, adolescence is the brooding and impatient anticipation of the emancipatory flight that adulthood will bring. Thus, as terms, Lezama's *adolescente* and Joyce's "young man" do not agree either in moral meaning or in time frame.

This disparity may not result from a deliberate distortion, but from a problem of translation. Throughout *Paradiso*, Lezama fixates on the term *adolescencia*, a word absent in *A Portrait* but very much present in Dámaso Alonso's 1926 Spanish translation of *A Portrait of the Artist*, *El artista adolescente. Retrato*,[46] the version Lezama was known to comment and reread frequently. Even though Lezama was acquainted with *Ulysses* before its Spanish translation was published (Lezama probably read the original with the help of the French translation by Larbaud, Gilbert, and Morel), he probably drew the term *adolescencia* and most of his Joycean aesthetic language from Dámaso Alonso's translation. It could be argued that, if *Paradiso* is indeed a rewriting of *A Portrait*, when Lezama drives Joyce toward a transcendental aestheticism and an affirmative vision of adoslecence that Joyce's texts themselves reject, he is only completing a reading initiated by Alonso's generation and already inscribed in the idiom Alonso selected to "incarnate" *A Portrait* in Spanish. The source of this idiom is Don Luis de Góngora, whose poetic language thus stands as another nexus between European modernism and the Caribbean neobaroque.

When Alonso began translating *A Portrait* while studying in Oxford in 1925, the Spanish writer, critic, and poet was an active participant of an avant-garde *minorista* movement that at the time was rediscovering and promoting works by poets of the Spanish Baroque that had been abhorred by nineteenth-century Spanish philology. Alonso's absorption of the work of Joyce occurs in the context of the revaloration of the Baroque done by Ortega y Gasset and the *Revista de Occidente*-influenced *Generación del 27*. The search for aesthetic objectivity in modernity as part of a rejection of the Romantic and Naturalist models of the previous century —a search promoted and analyzed in essays such as Ortega's *The Dehumanization of Art* —inspired a paradoxical search for precursors. The "prophets" and the "antiquity" of modernity's "Renaissance" were found in the discredited Baroque poets of the late sixtenth and early seventeenth centuries. This search for sources recalls the surrealist revival of Lautréamont and Sade and was geared to "rediscover" and vindicate the Baroque epitomized in the work of the neglected and unappreciated Luis de Góngora. Thus, the rise of modernist aesthetic theory in the Hispanic world occurred concurrently with a radical reappraisal of Baroque poetics.[47]

The revival of the Baroque is not exclusive to Spanish and Spanish-American letters of the 1920s. Walter Benjamín's study of the German theater of the high Baroque was a hermeneutic maneuver to analyze contemporary expressionism in a parallel, analogous mode.[48] Such was Ortega y Gassett's circular strategy of period definition when he categorized the "dehumanizing" effect of modern art as a "baroque" effect in his essay "La voluntad del barroco" [The Will to the Baroque], lapsing into an ahistorical, cyclical schema of literary history by postulating a "will to the Baroque" in modernity and writing about the current "vigencia" [relevance] of the plastic arts of the Baroque period.[49]

This tendency would reach its zenith in the Hispanic world in 1927, when the poets of the *Generación del 27*, inspired by Mallarmé's concept of a "pure" aestheticism, organized the celebration of the tricentenary of Góngora's death. A forgotten poet of the repressed past was resurrected and acclaimed by a confrontational new generation. Among these intellectuals, nurtured under the aegis of the *Revista de Occidente,* Góngora became a crucial banner and symbol. The *Revista*'s aristocratic *minorismo* thus embraced Góngora's exclusionary and difficult poetics as his most obscure poems were learned by heart and recited in meetings and, as part of the tricentenary celebration, the *Revista* drew an ambitious plan to publish studies and articles on aspects of Góngora's work.[50] What the nineteenth-century philologists had judged as Góngora's "artificio"—artificial, superfluous, excessive, self-indulgent writing—was now considered "artefacto," a carefully constructed, complex, painstakingly chiselled verbal artifact.

It is no coincidence that Dámaso Alonso translates *A Portrait*, a Künstlerroman in which the artist is regarded as a Daedalus-like artificer, while at the same time preparing a critical edition of Góngora's *Las Soledades*, a project which sought to vindicate Góngora as an "artífice," a rigorous word-crafter of a difficult yet indispensable poetry of the absolute. Alonso thought that the great technical achievement of Góngora's poetry was a "luminous," hard-gained clarity, not the inarticulate, blurred oscurity of which Góngora had formerly been accused.[51] The terms of this controversial reinterpretation of Góngora deeply penetrated Lezama's own diction. Lezama's expressions concerning his "escribir oscuro" [writing darkly] and "escribir claro" [writing brightly][52] are phrases generated by the Gongorist revival of the late twenties and early thirties.

The wish to read, understand, translate, and imitate French symbolists such as Mallarmé and English modernists such as Joyce probably forced progressive Hispanic writers like Alonso to search for linguistic equivalents in the history of the Spanish language. The assimilation of the "obscurity" and "difficulty" of Joyce and Mallarmé and their formulation of the problematic status of the aesthetic object in modernity drove the poets of the *Generación del 27* to seek a "vehicle of translation" in the highly crafted language of the Baroque poets of the late sixtenth and early seventeenth century, especially that of Luis de Góngora. Mallarmé's hermeticism, in fact, inspired influential French critics such as Albert Thibaudet—who the *Generación* and Lezama read with relish and reverence—to make comparisons between Mallarmé's and Góngora's works.[53] The Baroque revival is thus intimately connected with the assimilation of a European aesthetic—the reading and translation of European symbolists and modernists—making this assimiliation a double movement in time, both contemporary and antiquarian, iconoclastic and conservative, bohemian and academic. The label "neobaroque" as an avant-garde term is an oxymoron that illustrates well this polar displacement.[54]

The symbolist-neobaroque vogue, it must be noted, was at first a New World phenomenon. The cult of Góngora was initiated by Latin Americans. The Nicaraguan Ruben Darío's adoption of Góngora's musicality and the Mexican Alfonso Reyes's laborious philological investigations on Góngora were attempts to counterattack the terrible, regressive silence in baroque studies that permeated the work of the last generation of Spanish philologists headed by Marcelino Menéndez Pelayo. Alfonso Reyes's interest in formulating a modernist aesthetics beyond preceptive philology inspired his early essays "Mallarmé entre nosotros" [Mallarmé among us] and "Sobre la estética de Góngora" [Concerning Góngora's aesthetics].[55] Reyes's analysis of Góngora during the teens was unique and solitary; the poets of the *Generación del 27* shaped their understanding of Góngora's poetry under the tutelage of Reyes. Reyes became their critical "mentor" in their reappropriation of Góngora. Thus, the Góngora revival was at odds with the turn-of-the-century Spanish literary tradition in multiple ways. First, it was the justification of an imported aesthetic (Mallarmé); second, it was an affirmation of modernity; third, it was inspired by an American initiative.

Joyce's *A Portrait* and *Ulysses* appear in the Hispanic world in the context of this reappraisal and are absorbed by it, making the association Joyce-Mallarmé-Góngora a frequent formulation in literary commentary during the time. While living in Spain, Alfonso Reyes makes a "Joycean" gesture when commemorating the death of Mallarmé. Organizing a ritual ceremony in Mallarmé's honor among members of the *Revista*, he reports it as an exercise in the Joycean technique of stream of consciousness.[56] Lezama will welcome these associations in his interpretation of *A Portrait* given his partiality toward Mallarméan aesthetics.[57] It is no surprise that the Góngora-Joyce connection is made with a peculiar and conspicuous frequency in Jorge Luis Borges's writing, thus making this association paradigmatic to all writers inspired by Borges's literary thought. As we noted in chapter 1, Borges sustains the association between Joycean aesthetics and Góngora's baroque poetry throughout his writings, before his rejection of Joyce and after: in the last line of his first review of *Ulysses*, in his negative articles on Joyce during the early forties, in his comments on the translation of 1945, and in most references to the novelist in his later writings.

The Góngora-Joyce equation denigrated by Borges was elevated and valorized in the absorption of Joyce by the members of the *Generación del 27*. The verbal extravagance of *Ulysses* prompted the *vanguardia* to read Joyce's former works and find there "a sibling soul." The attempt to trace in Joycean aesthetics a doctrine equivalent to that of the *artefacto gongorista* is crystalized in the fact that the first of Joyce's work translated into Spanish—*A Portrait of the Artist as a Young Man*—is the one in which "pure" aesthetics figure as a central topic. Dámaso Alonso, the foremost Góngora expert of the *Generación*, read *A Portrait* as a confirmation of the objective aesthetics that he read in Góngora's *Soledades*. Stephens's doctrine as expressed in chapter 5 summarized the central principles of the Gongorist doctrine of poetic beauty. By translating "claritas" as "luminosidad" (luminosity), Alonso projected onto Stephen's adoption of Aquinas the notion of "claridad radiante, claridad deslumbrante" [radiant and dazzling clarity] and "luz estética" [aesthetic light] which he discusses in his introductory essay to the 1927 edition of Góngora's poetry, "Claridad y belleza de *Las Soledades*" [Clarity and beauty in *Las Soledades*]. According to Alonso, Góngora's clarity is not by any means semantic simplicity, but an effect of visual radiance that occurs from the metaphorical incorporation into the aesthetic object of some key ornamental or atmospheric elements associated with light or its reflection—dawn, gold, water, crystal, mirrors, bright color.[58] When Alonso calls this effect "hiperluminosidad" [hyperluminosity] in his essay, he seizes on an analogous corollary in Stephen's theory of beauty.

This insistence on preciosity and radiance as important *modern* aesthetic effects might explain why in Alonso's *Retrato* there is a calculated embellishment in the choice of words, a measured elision of the original's vulgarity, a tendency to make plain statements appear as figural language, of having metaphors predominate in the translation of idiomatic expressions.[59] The point is to make Stephen's aesthetic doctrine epitomize the postulations of the gongorist "poesía pura" [pure poetry] practiced by Alonso's generation. Thus it should not be a surprise that Alonso's translation invigorates the Paterian "purple" prose of the narrative in the last chapters of A Portrait with the atmospheric techniques of Góngora's poetry.[60] Indeed, in his letters to Joyce discussing and negotiating the translation, Alonso showed more interest in the linguistic preciosity of the prose than in the narrative or characterological aspects of the novel.[61] When transposed to Spanish, Joyce's English has the ring of the baroque idiom developed by Alonso and his generation.

As a consequence, the gongorist spirit of Alonso's translation instigated a significant loss in the ironic tone of the original. The translation's emphasis on A Portrait's symbolist aesthetic and style also brought about a weakening of its psychological subtlety, cutting down the distance between the narrator's perspective and the protagonist's voice and dissolving many ambiguities regarding Stephen's promise as an artist. The surprising result is that Stephen's fully documented attempt at poetry—the villanelle of chapter 5—does not sound *adolescent*—that is tentative, mannered, self-indulgent—in Alonso's stronger translation. Indeed, the word *adolescencia*—which Alonso used consistently in the text for "youth" or "boyhood"—seems to consistently suggest growing maturity rather than inmaturity, word and self-mastery rather than linguistic or moral turpitude. Alonso's Esteban thus became the "hero" the ironic Joyce never meant him to be. This might explain why A Portrait has been read among Latin American writers of Lezama's generation as a non-ironic book about the definitive emergence of artistic talent and sensibility in the young poet,[62] as a type of primer of a poet's formation, and why Lezama chooses to disregard some of its darker elements, dispelling its "Neronic" dimensions when rewriting A Portrait in Paradiso.

VII

The emergence of the poet's sensibility as a process of language acquisition gives A Portrait and Paradiso a modernist structural affinity that both extends and innovates the Bildungs- or Künstlerroman narrative tradition of the development of the artistic sensibility established by Goethe's Wilhelm Meister.[63] Critics have already noted how Joyce's modernist ironic distance in the design of A Portrait problematizes and subverts Goethe's model.[64] Paradiso's chapter 9 makes manifest Lezama's own position concerning the history and relevance of the genre through some metafictional comments on Goethe's novel and Foción's clever fabrication about "James Joyce's book on Goethe" commented above. In a way, what *Paradiso* says about *Wilhelm Meister* is a statement about how Lezama read Joyce's first novel. Following the important conversation with his mother after the riot at the university, the imsoniac Cemí reads by chance two passages from two very different books:

> De la primera lectura de esa noche, había saltado la palabra *neroniano*. Era lo que calificaría siempre el desinflamiento de una conducta sin misterio, lo coruscante, lo cruel, lo preconcebido actuando sobre lo indefenso, actor espectador, lo que espera en frío que la sombra de la gaviota pase por su espejo. Para el segundo desfiladero de esa noche, no acudió a Suetonio, sino al *Wilhelm Meister*. Fue buscando los párrafos que había subrayado y de pronto leyó: "A qué pocos varones les ha sido otorgado el poder de presentarse siempre, de modo regulado, lo mismo que los astros, y gobernar tanto el día como la noche, formar sus utensilios domésticos; sembrar y recolectar, conservar y gastar, y recorrer siempre el mismo círculo con calma, amor y acomodación al objeto." ¿Fue una arrogancia de adolescente lo que le llevó a poner al margen de esa frase: *Yo*? Puede ser que el sentirse enfermo, el reencuentro de la amistad y las palabras dichas por su madres, le otorgasen ese momentáneo orgullo, pero él sabía que era esa alusión a las costumbre de los astros, a su ritmo de eterna seducción creadora, a un Eros que conocía como las estaciones, lo que lo había llevado a esa frase, más con la aceptación de una amorosa confianza, que con la tentación de una luciferina vanidad omnisciente. (*P* 234/*R* 231)

> [Out of the reading he had done that night had come the word "Neronic." For him, this would always mean the detumescence of a conduct without mystery, the biting, cruel, premeditated working on the defenseless, the spectator-actor, waiting coldly for the shadow of the gull to pass over the mirror. For the second path out of that night he did not go to Suetonious but to *Wilhelm Meister's Apprenticeship*. He was looking for the paragraphs he had underlined and suddenly he read: "So few men have been awarded the power of always showing themselves in a regulated way. The same as the stars, and governing the day as well as the night, shaping their domestic utensils; sowing and reaping, saving and spending, and passing along the same circle, always with calmness, love and accommodation to the object." Was it the arrogance of an adolescent that made him write in the margin: "Me?" It might have been that his illness, the revival of friendship, and the words his mother spoke, all had given him a momentary pride, but he knew that the reference to the stars' habits, to their rhythm of eternal, creative seduction, to an Eros that he knew as he knew the Seasons,

had drawn him into that passage, more in the spirit of accepting an amorous confidence that of the temptation of an omniscient, Luciferine vanity.]

This passage reformulates the two principal themes in *A Portrait* analyzed in "Muerte de Joyce": one, the impact the emergence of Eros, which Lezama regards not merely as sexual yearning but as a sensual yet non-libidinous desire for knowledge, has on the adolescent and, two, the young artist's need to overcome Luciferine pride.[65] Cemí's realization of his own artistic vocation can be read as addressing the issue of the ironic ambivalence in Joyce's *A Portrait*. In their study of *A Portrait*, critics have argued heatedly whether the novel as a text incarnates or parodies the aesthetics it seems to espouse. Their arguments range from Stephen as an arrogant, proud, and immature aesthete doomed, as Satan, to failure and defeat, and derided by Joyce's detached portrayal, to Stephen as Joyce's model of an erratic but talented poet-to-be. Wayne Booth, Hugh Kenner, and Robert Scholes, among others, have participated in this debate.[66] The two passages Cemí reads represent the two divergent interpretations: Booth and Kenner see Stephen as "Neronic"; Scholes regards him in the light of *Wilhelm Meister*. With Cemí's personal justification of his poetic vocation, Lezama favors the positive reading of *A Portrait*. He sees Stephen-Cemí overcoming Luciferine pride and developing the required self-knowledge of poetry. Even when there is some irony in the high-flown language of this segment, Lezama presents a positive appraisal of Cemí as a future poet. As Scholes does in *A Portrait*, Lezama sees in the textual body of *A Portrait* the exemplification of its aesthetics: the novel is itself the *final* incarnation of the poetic "Eros" of adolescence. Thus Lezama makes *Paradiso* a parallel literary exercise. Following *A Portrait*, *Paradiso* establishes a *modern* difference with former bildungsroman as it incorporates into its own form the final linguistic and poetic development of its protagonist. The novel—be it *Paradiso* or *A Portrait*—is the concluding incarnation of poetry, the textual embodiment of the full adulthood of the artist, where language as substance replaces the body of the protagonist.

Nevertheless, though similar and symmetrical, the execution of this narrative design in *A Portrait* and *Paradiso* does not yield identical textual results. *A Portrait* and *Paradiso* employ different rhetorical strategies to evidence poetic growth. The "delicious" *A Portrait* becomes distorted as it is broken down and digested in *Paradiso*'s textual body. This distortion happens by means of a proliferating, refractive process in which the elliptical structure of *A Portrait*, built on the principle of exclusion, is inverted in *Paradiso*, where every gap in the narrative is filled by metaphor and description. Critics have thoroughly documented how the movement of writing in *A Portrait* is one of elimination—"the result of an extended process of refinement."[67] Turning from reproduction to a selective method of writing, Joyce engineered *A Portrait* as the result of the subtraction and revision of a longer original draft, *Stephen Hero*, and other versions. Many Joycean critics have commented and studied this process and illuminated the ultimate, distilled symbolist design of *A Portrait*.[68] *A Portrait*'s special process of refinement is reversed in the textual apparatus of *Paradiso*, which, while based on *A Portrait*'s synthetic schema, moves toward surplus and excess. The nodal motifs are the same in both narratives, but in *Paradiso* they undergo baroque elaborations, kaleidoscopic refractions, and anamorphic distortions in the concave mirror of Lezama's prose. It is as if Lezama were trying to rewrite *A Portrait* under the spell of the subsequent aesthetic of *Ulysses* and *Finnegans Wake*.

Lezama makes his new version of *A Portrait* an apotheosis of ornamentation. As a rewriting of *A Portrait*, *Paradiso* is—to use another Lezamian expression—a *hypertelic* revision in which the excess of the copy overflows the full cup of the original. Lezama writes in his diary: "La hipertelia, es un fenómeno que rebasa su finalidad, una decoración." [The hypertelos is a phenomenon that surpasses its end, a decoration.] (*Diario* 76) Lezama's rewriting moves in the opposite direction from Borges's radical condensations of Western modernist literature in *Ficciones*. Like the image in a concave mirror, Lezama's adaptation of *A Portrait* is not a faithful reflection; the mirror distorts the image, purposefully, and accidentally. The result is a splendorous, enriched refraction.

VIII

The Baroque revival was thus not limited to Madrid. Cuba's *Revista de Avance* participated in the celebration of Góngora's Tricentennary in 1927 and paved the way for Lezama's *Orígenes* generation's reappraisal of Baroque aesthetics during the 1930s, 1940s, and 1950s.[69] This reappraisal acts like a prism refracting Lezama's assimilation of Joyce, breaking the white light of *A Portrait*'s prose into the rainbowlike beams of *Paradiso*'s poetic discourse. Rather than devalorize, it revalorizes the Joycean aesthetic.

Lezama is the exemplar of this American valorization, setting himself opposite to Borges's rejection in a deliberate counter-position. The references to *A Portrait* in "Muerte de Joyce" constitute a systematic rebuttal to Borges's later assessment of Joyce's work. Likewise, *Paradiso* can be read as Lezama's triumphant *pièce de resistance* in his argument that the novel could be "resurrected" through *A Portrait*'s poetic mode despite Borges's vaticinations of the novel's doom.

3

Orphic Odysseus: Mythical Method and Narrative "Technology" in *Paradiso* and *Ulysses*

I

THE LEGENDS RELATING THE TROUBLED PUBLICATION PROCESS OF JAMES Joyce's *Ulysses* during the twenties are legion in literary history; the story of the reception of *Ulysses* in the Hispanic world could produce a similar wealth of anecdotes. If making Joyce's work known in the European literary world was something of an obstacle course, the dissemination of *Ulysses* in Latin America had to find its way through a transatlantic labyrinth of mutation and mediation. Dámaso Alonso's 1926 translation of *A Portrait of the Artist* made Joyce's early work fairly accessible by the end of the decade. But in order to reach Latin American shores (and Lezama's bookshelf), Joyce's second novel had first to traverse multiple and shifting textual spaces and to undergo complex refractions. Unlike other works of European modernism, Joyce's novel was neither immediately translated nor instantly imitated and assimilated, but underwent various stages of reception and adaptation.[1] Access in the New World to editions of Joyce's *Ulysses* was complicated by U.S. censorship laws. The confiscation by the U.S. Post Office of *The Little Review*, in which some chapters of *Ulysses* were first serialized, and the ensuing ban of the Shakespeare & Company edition hindered the availablity of Joyce's work in all countries in the Western hemisphere.[2] But, even when John W. Woolsey's district court decision exonerated *Ulysses* from the charge of obscenity on 6 December 1933 (more than eleven years after the first edition), twelve more years would pass before the novel was completely translated into Spanish and published in Buenos Aires.[3]

The late appearance of *Ulysses* in Spanish helps explain why Joyce's narrative techniques—the representation of inner con-

sciousness through interior monologue or "stream of consciousness"; the framing of plot according to an acknowledged
mythological story; the use of punning, wordplay, and parody over
linear narration as the motor of novelistic discourse— filtered fully
into the Latin American novel after Joyce's death in 1941. In the
late forties, a new generation of novelists paid homage to *Ulysses*
in novels that borrowed from Joyce's experimentation with narrative form and language to rebel against the stiff poetics of the "novela de la tierra" [regionalist novel].[4] These novels shifted the focus
of the Latin American novel from the countryside to the city and
from the telluric to the urban, seeking, as Joyce had done with
Dublin, to render in a new experimental fiction the proliferation of
voices and perspectives of the expanding Latin American metropolis. This new direction is seen in the novels of Miguel Angel Asturias (*El Señor Presidente* [The President], 1948), Leopoldo Marechal
(*Adán Buenosayres*, 1948) and Alejo Carpentier (*El acoso* [The
Chase], 1956). The use of Joycean technique would increase in
their later work.[5]

This belated interest in Joycean themes and narrative techniques
paralleled a brief "boom" of critical studies and commentary in
Spanish on Joyce during the forties. Borges's frequent references to
Joyce in the stories published in 1942 in *El jardín de los senderos
que se bifurcan* and in the essays appended to *Discusión* in 1954
should be counted as part of this trend. In Argentina and Uruguay,
journals such as *Alfar, Contrapunto*, and *Los anales de Buenos Aires*
featured translations of important European articles on Joyce and
reviews evaluating the Spanish version, which resurrected old debates about *Ulysses* and the possibility of its translation.[6] The *Revista de Occidente*'s translation of Jung's article on *Ulysses* and
Herbert Gorman's 1939 biography *James Joyce* were issued in book
format in Buenos Aires by Santiago Rueda in 1945 as companion
volumes to the Spanish edition of *Ulises*.[7] In 1946, Editorial Araujo
published Juan Jacobo Bajarlía's university lectures on the avant-
garde under the title *Literatura de vanguardia del Ulises de Joyce y
de las escuelas plásticas* [The Avant-Garde Literature of Joyce's
Ulysses and the Plastic Arts]. Conceived as the "continuation" of
Guillermo de Torre's 1927 book on the *vanguardias*, it featured five
chapters of exegesis on *Ulysses* that drew their quotations from
Subirat's translation.[8] This enthusiasm for Joyce's second novel
surfaced as well in Cuba. In 1940 José Lezama Lima commissioned
Oscar Rodríguez Feliú for a translation of the "Proteus" chapter
of *Ulysses* for the Havana journal *Espuela de plata*. Later, José
Rodríguez Feo translated, for Lezama's journal *Orígenes*, the last

chapter of Harry Levin's influential 1941 monograph on Joyce as well as Theodore Spenser's "Introduction" to the 1944 edition of *Stephen Hero*.[9]

Despite the twenty-three-year time lag, however, J. Salas Subirat's translation did not mark the first encounter of the Spanish-American intellectual with the monumental *chef d'oeuvre* of modernism. Subirat's contested version of *Ulysses* sparked a new wave of interest in the experimental novel; however, by 1945 *Ulysses* had already been widely read and commented upon in Latin America, not so much in the English original but in the 1929 French translation by Auguste Morel, Valery Larbaud, and Stuart Gilbert,[10] which cast a spell on the writings of many literary critics. Even though the Joycean seed fully germinated only after the forties, as Gerald Martin argues convincingly,[11] *Ulysses'* remarkable notability in Latin America had actually begun to develop during the previous two decades. The difficulty of reading *Ulysses*—not just for the impenetrability of its discourse, but for the scarce copies available to interested readers—led to an industry of exegesis and prolegomena that, to a degree, compensated for the public's scant access to the original work or its translation. Latin America's encounter with the "modernity" embodied by *Ulysses* thus gave interpretation primacy over the fiction itself, making the mediating activity of criticism as fundamental as—if not more so than—that of translation or creative imitation. Before being incorporated into the sphere of literary production, Joycean modernism demanded a process of critical conception—a type of textual imaging, an *a priori* picturing—that preceded the appropriation of technique in actual fictional writing. The scandal and the "newness" of books such as *Ulysses* prompted all manner of debate on literature (such as the polemic on the "death" of the novel), and inspired the invention of a new analytical vocabulary and a new critical idiom in discussions about aesthetics and genre theory. Arguably, *Ulysses'* modernity first stimulated the transformation of literary theory in Latin America before inspiring novelistic innovation.

Lezama's reading of *Ulysses* and *Paradiso*'s peculiar adaptation of *Ulysses'* narrative principles are shaped by the terms of the more influential interpretations of the novel that preceded its publication in Spanish translation. Before comparing Lezama's novel to Joyce's, we must examine the substance and origin of these terms. *Paradiso*'s "refractive mirroring" of *Ulysses'* textual aesthetic must be studied as part of a pattern of "critical dependence" that gave canonical status to previous exegeses of the novel. This is to say that Lezama's approach to *Ulysses* does not rely on an innocent reading of the English original, but also on a meticulous consultation of mediatory interpretations. Foremost among these are: Valery Larbaud's humanist commentary, Ezra Pound's technical valoration, T. S. Eliot's positive evaluation of "mythical method," Ernst Curtius's stylistic study, C. G. Jung's polemical interpretation, and Stuart Gilbert's analysis of the novel, among others.

Two other good examples of this dependence happen to be the first two reviews of *Ulysses* written for Hispanic journals: Jorge Luis Borges's 1925 essay in *Proa* "El *Ulises* de Joyce" [Joyce's *Ulysses*] and Antonio Marichalar's 1924 article in *Revista de Occidente*, "James Joyce en su laberinto" [James Joyce in his labyrinth].[12] Here both Borges and Marichalar relied extensively on Valery Larbaud's seminal 1922 article in the *Nouvelle Revue Française* (which is the text of the first conference ever given on *Ulysses*) to orient their interpretation. A close, panotic examination of these articles reveals that the Hispanic critics borrowed structures of argumentation, analytical vocabulary (like "interior monologue"), and aesthetics notions from Larbaud's *NFR* essay, thus bordering on plagiarism if not stark plunder.

This dependence is paradigmatic. All peninsular and Latin American approaches to *Ulysses* resort to "canonical" criticism, whether or not this operation is made explicit in the text. The dependence, however, does not overdetermine the Latin American's perspective; critical outlooks are refashioned, altered, refracted and anamorphosed. The Hispanic strategy in reading *Ulysses* thus evidences a process of research and consultation where guides and introductions are exhausted before any serious reading of the perplexing novel is done. Yet in the Hispanic reading a disfigurement, a recasting of the critical concepts, occurs: Borges and Marichalar's "promotional copying" of Larbaud's ideas does not produce an exact duplicate, but a baroque, distorted version that suits each critic's literary agenda at that time: *ultraísmo* in Borges's case, *occidentalismo* in the case of Marichalar.

This pattern of mirroring and distortion, reflection and refraction, occurs in Lezama's "Muerte de Joyce" [Death of Joyce], written for the Cuban journal *Grafos* on the ocassion of Joyce's death in 1941. Lezama adopts, in an analogous fashion, a posture of critical dependence in analyzing Joycean modernism. Lezama's essay on Joyce as well as those on other figures of European modernism repeat Borges and Marichalar's reliance on European criticism as the required first step before exercising a Hispanic interpretation. Borges and Marichalar's Joyce originates in Larbaud; Lezama's Mallarmé and Lezama's Valéry rely heavily on Albert Thibaudet's studies of the two symbolist poets.[13] Nevertheless, Lezama's Valéry and Lezama's Mallarmé are difficult to reconcile with Thibaudet's despite Lezama's "dependence." Likewise, Lezama's Joyce is not commensurate with the Joyce of his critical sources.

By the time Lezama wrote "Muerte de Joyce" there had been a displacement in the interpretations of *Ulysses* that reigned in the Hispanic world of letters. By 1941 Valery Larbaud was not the only authoritative source reflected in the Latin American critical approach to the novel. Stuart Gilbert's study *Ulysses* (1930)—with its description of the work's systemic structure and styles and the full disclosure of the "schema"—was quoted more frequently. Nevertheless, behind this critical effervescence of the forties lay the influence of two early advocates of Joyce whose poetry was widely discussed in the literary journals of Latin America during the thirties: Ezra Pound and T. S. Eliot.[14] With their work, the intricate role of Homeric parallels in the construction of *Ulysses* and the novel's rigorous application of realist techniques became popularized, and the understanding of *Ulysses* as an anarchical avant-garde work became a more complicated point of debate. What Joycean studies call the fact/symbol paradox of *Ulysses*—a duality synthesized in what has been called the Pound-Eliot debate[15]—began to "trickle down" to Joycean commentary by Latin Americans.

Pound's writings on Joyce determines a whole genealogy of Joyce appreciation. Pound was Joyce's first *de facto* literary agent who championed his early career. The novelty in Pound's essays on Joyce's work resides in the fact that these essays were produced as the Joycean works began to circulate, and the critical force of the essays can be explained by that chronological preeminence. Pound wrote while orchestrating the appearance of Joyce's short stories and the serialization of *A Portrait* in *The Egoist*; while coordinating the publication of chapters of *Ulysses* in Margaret Anderson's *The Little Review* in New York; while getting *Dubliners* published after harrowing persecution and censorship; and while having *A Portrait* widely reviewed by respected English critics as well as arranging its translation into French.[16] As part of his promotional labor, Pound's essays coined many of the terms by which Joyce's work would be considered in Europe and abroad.

Rather than a form of conventional book publicity, the energetic enthusiasm of Pound's commentary on Joyce stems from his emancipatory vision of literary culture. Pound interprets Joyce's writing as the extension and culmination in the English language of a revolutionary brand of realist prose initiated by continental narrators in the nineteenth century—Stendhal, Maupassant, the Gouncourt brothers, and Flaubert. Pound considers Joyce's style "the most clarifying," "most beneficial force in modern writing" (*PJ* 28). Pound's championing of Joyce is tied to a messianic concept of prose as a legislative civic force, a redemptive appliance for the revival of civilization. In discussing the importance of Joyce's early prose style, Pound's essays often make eccentric references to the current World War: "The hell of contemporary Europe is caused by the lack of representative government in Germany, *and* by the non-existence of decent prose in the German language" (*PJ* 90). In this context, the aesthetic achievement of the "clear, hard" realist style of *Dubliners* and *A Portrait* attains a redemptive, social importance: "The obstructionist and the provincial are everywhere, and in them alone is the permanent danger to civilization. Clear, hard prose is the safeguard and should be valued as such. The mind accustomed to it will not be cheated and stampeded by national phrases and public emotionalities" (*PJ* 91). Pound's essays on Joyce are rife with this obsessive sense of carefully calibrated "prose" as a requirement for the smooth functioning of culture and society: "A sense of style would have saved America or Europe. The *mot juste* is of public utility" (*PJ* 91).

Pound's vision of Joyce as a herald of this new "clear, hard prose" makes Joyce a modernist to the extent that, as a stylist, he is an innovator who can rid language of rhetorical superfluity and duplicity and restore the stark logic of its inner mechanisms. In Pound's eyes, the nature of this achievement is technical: the refinement attained by Joyce's prose—far from being elegant, romantic, or decadent—is the result of an efficient and industrious, almost scientific distillation. It is produced through "condensation," "rigourous selection," and "exclusion of all unnecessary detail," observing an "international standard of prose writing" (*PJ* 29). What Pound calls "prose" appears thus as an aesthetic form of engineering. Pound resorts to technological metaphors to illustrate the perfection of design in Joyce's writing: "he deals with subjective things, but he presents them with a clarity of outline that he might be dealing with locomotives or with builder's specifications" (*PJ* 27). Metallurgy is Pound's ultimate allegory: Pound promotes *Dubliners* and *A Portrait* as examples of a "metallic prose." In his essays, Pound plants the seed of the myth of Joyce as a *technician* of narrative language—the cold-blooded engineer who builds upon Flaubert's precise tinkerings with the prose machine.

Even when the "Sirens" chapter strains Pound's standards of prose realism to the point of exasperation,[17] Pound defends *Ulysses* as the culmination of Flaubert's technical project to forge a prose that can efficiently capture the fullness of reality without the burden of sentimentality or affectation. In both his essay on *Ulysses* and his lesser known article in the Paris *Mercure* "James Joyce et Pécuchet," Pound's main argument is still bound to the Flaubert-Joyce realist succession: *Ulysses* is the fulfilment of what Flaubert's *Bouvard et Pécuchet* left unfinished.[18] Pound sees Flaubert's unfinished novel as the last item in an ongoing project to reform narrative prose. The novel is, so to speak, the disposal site of old prose styles, the burial ground of bourgeois banalities. Just as *Dubliners* and *A Portrait* are the successors to *Madame Bovary* and *L'Education Sentimentale* respectively, *Ulysses* is the capping of Flaubert's last novelistic enterprise. In this estimation, Pound disregards the overflowing, baroque excesses of the narrative in *Ulysses* (especially because Pound writes about the leaner version serialized in *The Little Review*, which did not feature the proof accretions that doubled the length of the final Shakespeare & Company edition), and still sees in *Ulysses* a metallic tautness, a physical tension of design in its narrative force. Pound does not regard the alternation of styles in *Ulysses* as a literary conceit, but as part of the realist imperative to represent a plurality of characters with technical conciseness by filtering their representation and characterization through their own language. The innovations of *Ulysses*—the fragmentation of syntax, the use of abrupt phrases or single words in the cataloguing of perception in stream-of-consciousness—are justified because they are technical, determined by the naturalist imperative to devise the objective "clear, hard prose" that can portray with more accuracy how the mind registers the phenomenal world. To Pound, *Ulysses* is a purposeful assortment of discourses—a menu of "proses," so to speak—that heralds the new style while neutralizing archaic, irrelevant types through pastiche and parody, in the manner of Flaubert's *Dictionaire des idées reçues*. Pound minimizes the relevance of the "symbolic" dimension of the novel—the Homeric parallels, the esoteric cryptology that Stuart Gilbert analyzes in his study—regarding it as a minor aspect of prose "construction." To Pound, *Ulysses'* symbolic structure is merely a "scaffold," a way of organizing the narrative so that realist detail can stand out even more.

Eliot's interpretation privileges neither the representation of actuality nor the experimental innovations in prose technique, but concentrates on the use of myth as a way of giving order to the chaos of modern experience, thus producing a "continuous parallel be-

tween contemporaneity and antiquity" (201).[19] Rather than "realism," "prose," or "modernity," Eliot is concerned with the
harmonious, "timeless" elements in literature sheltered under the
rubric of Classicism. In "*Ulysses*, Order, and Myth," Eliot's evaluation of *Ulysses* as "the most important expression which the present age has found" (198) rests on the "significance" of the parallels
to the *Odyssey*, and not on any stylistic or technical justification, as
in Pound. Eliot's essay is written—at Joyce's and Pound's request—as a response to Richard Aldington's attacks against
Joyce's avant-gardism . According to Aldington's review, Joyce was
a "great undisciplined talent," a Dadaist "prophet of chaos" whose
sordid view of humanity reflected the empty nihilism of the avant-
garde movements.[20] Eliot's response is that the readers who only
recognize the avant-garde, contemporary "anarchy" in *Ulysses* disregard the more essential role of classical ingredients in the novel.
Although these readers "treat" the schema "as an amusing dodge,
or scaffolding erected by the author for the purpose of disposing
his realistic tale, of no interest in the completed structure" (198),
the opposite is true: *Ulysses* is revolutionary because it employs the
"sordid detail" of the present time and world to resurrect and reen-
ergize humanistic antiquity. The anecdotal presentation of the
present is, in fact, the scaffold that supports the revitalized appreciation of the universality and timelessness of Homeric myth. Thus
the parallel use of the *Odyssey*—"unprecedented" in the history of
the novel—has the "importance of a scientific discovery" (201).
The choice of words in Eliot's concise piece—especially the term
"scaffolding"—carries a riposte to Pound's emphasis on realist
technique in narrative and to his belittling of the role of "myth and
order" in the novel.

Although Eliot is ambiguous about the true importance of the
use of mythical correspondences, he is no less messianic about its
relevance to civilization than Pound is about the social importance
of "good prose." To Eliot the appearance of the mythical method
heralds the end of the novel, whose recent formlessness he sees as
an indication of its imminent "obsolescence" (201). Encoded in
this statement is a prediction of the end of prose narrative as such,
and thus of all the technical apparatus of realism. In a remarkable
reversal to Pound's approach, "*Ulysses*, Order, and Myth" neglects
the modern imperative to record actuality with "hard, clear prose"
and promotes a return to the faceless universals contained in myth,
where humanity can be made whole by being rendered anony-
mous. In a melancholic denial of the here-and-now—"the immense panorama of futility and anarchy which is contemporary

history" (201)—and an aggrandizement of "antiquity," Eliot appears to find in *Ulysses* an important juncture in the history of aesthetics since Joyce is "pursuing a method which others *must* pursue after him" [my emphasis]. Eliot's references in his essay to Einstein's studies of relativity are not meant to compare Joyce's prose to the new discoveries of physics, but to attest to the irreversibility of a monumental change in the writing of fiction. Just as the theory of relativity alters all former notions of linear time and of gravity as a constant force, *Ulysses* testifies to the resurgence of classical myth in culture inspired by the findings of research in folklore undertaken by the Cambridge School of Anthropology and in French classical studies.[21] The force of this revival of myth neutralizes the need to draw narrative from immediate reality. Thus, "psychology . . . , ethnology, and *The Golden Bough* have concurred to make possible what was impossible even a few years ago" (202). Joyce's discovery is not technical but paradigmatic; it is not related to realist prose, but to the devising of a *method* of "double writing" that organizes—through mythologization—the formless experience of modernity that straightforward narrative can no longer convey. Realist narrative, as a technique, is dead to Eliot: "we may now use the mythical method," he concludes (202).

In sum, Pound's hyperrealism breeds new technical concreteness in narrative prose. In Eliot, the use of classical parallels as structuring principles allows modern narrative to retain form and coherence, and guarantees the survival of classical tradition in modernity through the renewal of myth.

These antagonistic positions—pitting "narrative technology" against "mythical method"—are reflected in Latin American criticism on *Ulysses* during the forties. Juan Jacobo Bajarlía's tendentious rejection of the relevance of the Homeric correspondences in his study of *Ulysses*[22] is essentially the reapplication of the Pound technical/realist argument: "[No] hay claves ni simbolismos homéricos. . . . Sólo es verdad una cosa: la técnica. Cada capítulo tiene su lenguage propio que le distingue del empleado en los demás." (49) [There are no Homeric codes or symbolism. Only one thing is true: the technique. Each chapter has its own language that distinguishes it from the language used in the rest.] To Bajarlía, *Ulysses'* avant-garde achievement lies precisely in its camera-like registering of the minute phenomena of the modern urban chaos with an "objetividad casi morbosa" (51) [an almost morbose objectivity]. Bajarlía's invocation of Jung's reading in his conclusion can be seen as a way to explain Pound's idea of hyperrealism in *Ulysses* through Jung's point that the narrative style of the novel operates according to the lower functions of the psyche, discarding abstraction and thus detailing meticulously the objective world without reducing it.

On the other hand, Pound's *Mercure* piece on "*Ulysses* et Pécuchet" can be regarded as the inspiration for Borges's use of *Ulysses* and the Flaubert-Joyce equation in his essay on Flaubert's novel.[23] Nevertheless, Borges's position regarding mythical method and technical realism is a fusion of Eliot and Pound's arguments. Pound's assessment of the social importance of "good prose" implies that the novel—especially in its realist mode—is the true genre of the times, while Eliot mutedly announces in "*Ulysses,* Order, and Myth" that *Ulysses* marks the obsolescence of the genre. Although Borges adopts the Flaubert-Joyce relation elaborated by Pound, Eliot's pessimism regarding the future of the novel is magnified in the Ortega y Gasset-Borges debate. Borges incorporates and refracts Eliot's vision of the centrality of *Ulysses*'s "mythical method" and the relevance of Frazer's *Golden Bough* in this matter into his theory of magical structures in the novel developed in "El arte narrativo y la magia" [Narrative art and magic].

Lezama's "Muerte de Joyce" is a condensed revision of the many clashing critical outlooks concerning *Ulysses,* the novel. Despite the piece's brevity, a sophisticated familiarity with the novel and the critical debates is evident. Lezama explicitly mentions the analysis of the Homeric correspondences proposed in Stuart Gilbert's book—"Stuart Gilbert ha señalado en el *Ulysses* la parodia de las aventuras de Odiseo" (*OC* 2: 237) [Stuart Gilbert has pointed out in *Ulysses* the parody of Odysseus's adventures]. Lezama also demonstrates a close acquaintance with the novel in his estimations of its key chapters: "para aumentar sus peligros, los electores del cuantioso Ulysses [sic] reclamaban la escena del burdel, los monólogos, abandonando la polémica sobre el *Hamlet* en la Dublin Library, o la bellísima página sobre el color y lo vital" (*OC* 2: 236) [in order to exaggerate its dangers, readers of the bulky *Ulysses* praised the brothel scene and the monologues, and paid scant attention to the debate on *Hamlet* at the Dublin Library, or to the precious page on color and vitality (in the Ithaca chapter)]. When Lezama favors Stephen's discussion of *Hamlet* in "Scylla and Charybdis" and the stellar, poetic language of "Ithaca" over the brothel scene of "Circe" and the experimental stream-of-consciousness ("los monólogos") of "Penelope," he shows himself a discriminating reader of *Ulysses* as a whole.

Despite initially reading *Ulysses* in French and his acknowledged difficulties with English, Lezama seems to have engaged the original enough to quote, in "Muerte de Joyce," a line from "Ithaca" not mentioned in Gilbert's study.[24] It is clear that from the time Lezama first read *Ulysses* to when he wrote "Muerte de Joyce," he had become acquainted with more of the criticism and the debates surrounding the novel, particularly Stuart Gilbert's study and the specification of the tabular schema. Thus, the first responses to *Ulysses* in Hispanic letters—the stress on the force of imagery in the novel in Borges's ultraist interpretation; the emphasis on Stephen as exemplar of an elite, artistic intelligence in Marichalar's appreciation—were not the only influences in Lezama's estimation of Joyce.

That Lezama paid special attention to the Homeric parallels and the other symbolic elements in *Ulysses*' schema is evidenced in his postulation of a figural interpretation of the novel according to Jesuit demonology. In "Muerte de Joyce," Lezama proposes that the categories used by Jesuits for the exorcism of demons could constitute yet another column in the symbolic order of *Ulysses* chapters. Lezama's "secret" column shows each chapter to be constructed under the symbol of a particular vice or demon in need of exorcism, thus reaffirming the essential, if problematic, Catholicity of *Ulysses*: "igualmente podemos señalar la reminiscencia de la teología jesuítica en sus temas más utilizados. Asmodeo: ex querubín, dirigiendo el tema de la carne: burdel, parto, excrecencias; Mammon: los numerosos judíos que aparecen en su obra; Belzebuth: la magia, la cábala, la furia por penetrar y animar el mundo exterior, la parodia que hace la jerarquía infernal de la celestial" (*OC* 2: 237) [we can likewise point out the application of the most common themes of Jesuitical theology—Asmodeus, ex-cherub, orchestrating the motif of the flesh: brothel, excrescence, parturition; Mammon: the many Jews that show up in his work; Beelzebub: magic, the Kabbalah, the fierce desire to penetrate and animate the external world, the parody that the hierarchy of hell makes of the hierarchy of the Heavens]. Thus, Asmodeus can be thought of as a "ruling" symbol for prostitution in "Circe" chapter, for defecation in "Calypso" and ejaculation in "Nausikaa" (Bloom's), for menstruation in "Penelope," and for parturition in "Oxen of the Sun." Mammon dominates in "Calypso" and "Lotus Eaters," when Bloom, the ads canvaser, is introduced. Beelzebub determines the use of black magic in the transmogrifications in "Cyclops" and "Circe." The final vision of *Ulysses* that emerges from Lezama's piece is that of a Dantean *Inferno* where the soul undergoes a gnostic voyage through the underground of materiality, organized according to the severe yet sensuous imaginations of the Jesuits. Although his observations about the rhetorical relevance of Loyola's exercises seem more applicable to A Portrait, Lezama's observations about Joyce's quest for orthodoxy out of heterodoxy and his catalogue of human sins and demons produce an original, perceptive mapping of Ulysses.

Lezama also adopts terms from the Pound-Eliot debate. In the essay, Lezama explicitly rejects the overtly technical appreciation of the novel, affirming instead a poetic principle in Ulysses' use of symbolism and classical correspondences. When one penetrates the difficult discourse of "Muerte de Joyce," one finds that the essay makes a theoretical distinction between "technique" and "craft." Lezama recognizes the technical dexterity of narrative experimentation in Ulysses, but chooses to emphasize in it an "artesanía" [craftmanship] independent of sheer technical virtuosity. "Sí se le señala su artesanía, sus furias, pero separándole siempre la artesanía del modo, y la furia, que tiene que pegarse con sustancia, de la ironía filológica." (OC 2: 237–38) [We recognize his craftmanship and his fierceness, but always distinguishing craftmanship from mode, and fierceness—which needs to be joined with substance—from mere philological irony.] Lezama's description of "furia" [fierceness] in Joyce is probably drawn from Borges's observation in "El Ulises de Joyce" about his Irish "osadía" [daring]. "Modo" is Lezama's term for a technical device; thus, the elements listed as "technics" in the last column of Gilbert's schema—stream of consciousness, the catechistic format, the use of pastiche, and others—are not to be confused with Ulysses' "artesanía."

Beyond narrative technique, there is for Lezama a more important cohesiveness toward which prose has to strive. Lezama prefers to highlight the organic symbolism of Joyce's Ulysses rather than its fragmentary, technical virtuosity. In the Pound-Eliot debate on Ulysses, Lezama sides with Eliot against the technical realist tradition initiated by Pound. The objections voiced against narrative technology in "Muerte de Joyce"—Lezama's diatribe against those "obsessed" with creating a "special" avant-garde, technical Joyce—are echoed in Lezama's discussion of his own writing of fiction:

Yo soy renuente a usar en literatura expresiones como técnica o estructura, me parecen palabras comentadas. De las técnicas se derivan leyes. Por el contrario, un configurador de la expresión, un pintor, un

escritor, tienen experiencia de taller, la balanza secreta para la gravitación de cada palabra o de cada color. Si mi novela ha podido desen-
volverse ha sido por el desprecio de todas las técnicas, de los clichés
para construir novelas. Yo no tengo una técnica, yo no recomiendo
modos ni maneras, yo no tengo ningún *parti-pris* al enfrentarme con la
palabra. (P 728)

[Regarding literature, I am reluctant to use terms such as technique or
structure—these seem to me trite words. Laws are deduced from techniques. On the other hand, an expressive creator, a painter, a writer,
has a craftman's workshop upbringing that supplies the secret scale to
measure the weight of each word and color. If my novel has been able
to evolve, it is because I have rejected all techniques, the clichés used
to construct novels. I do not have a technique, I do not recommend
modes or manners, I have no *parti pris* when confronting language.][25]

In 1941 Lezama's Joyce is closer to Eliot's Joyce than to Pound's.
This may explain why *Paradiso*—which Lezama began conceptual-
izing in 1949—mirrors *Ulysses* in the use of the mythical method
rather than in "surface" narrative technique. Lezama's unique
adaption of *Ulysses'* mythical method in *Paradiso* can be con-
trasted with the more formulaic appropriation of Joycean narrative
technique and mythical method that occurs in Leopoldo Marechal's *Adán Buenosayres*.[26] The publication of *Adán Buenosayres* in
1948 might be considered the culminating moment on the 1940s
Joycean revival in Argentina. The formal and thematic proximity of
Marechal's metaphysical novel to the project of *Ulysses* became an
issue of debate in the early reviews of the novel. As with *Ulysses*,
the first responses to *Adán Buenosayres* were inspired by prudery.
The first issue of debate was the use of obscene language in the
novel; Eduardo González Lanuza's unfavorable review in *Sur* objected to the unelegant Joycean "desenfado" [informality] in the
novel's references to scathology and bodily functions. Noé Jitrik
adopted Pound's view of Joyce as a naturalist writer by highlighting
the novel's "objectivity of fact," while Adolfo Prieto and Graciela
de Sola contested the imputations of Joycean plagiarism.[27] Notwithstanding the imputations and the disclaimers (including Marechal's own), a systematic reading of *Adán Buenosayres* reveals a
derivative pattern not just of the technical and the mythical elements but of the very nature of anecdote in *Ulysses* and *A Portrait*.
    Setting apart its many merits and its moments of incontestable
originality, *Adán Buenosayres*'s immersion in Joyce is such that its
reflection of Joycean motifs could very well be labelled manneris-

tic. In terms of temporal framing and plot, it appropriates the one day paradigm as it follows its protagonist from dawn to a nocturnal, cathartic *walpurgisnacht* in a brothel. It repeats the opening scene of rental precariousness of the "Telemachus" chapter by turning the Martello tower into a student "pensión" (10–23). The novel's Stephen-like character protagonist has the equivalent biblical-mythical name of Adán Buenosayres and suffers from similar vacillating reveries, erotic frustrations, and phobia of water (39). He, too, is a schoolteacher who carries on a class in the spirit of *Ulysses'* "Nestor." His companion in the "pensión," the philosopher Samuel Tesler, is a Malachi Mulligan prototype who mocks Adán's account of dreams where his mother's death is morbidly visualized (24), thus recalling Mulligan's accusing Stephen of his mother's "beastly death." An old maid who accosts them for the rent symbolizes Argentina, the way the milkmaid represents Ireland in "Telemachus." At one point, a character proposes "the establishment of polygamy" in a "philogenetic festival," calquing Buck Mulligan's proposal of the "Omphalos" sperm farm in "Scylla and Charybdis." There is the obligatory wake, a rhymed poem to the inefable temptress in the manner of the villanelle in *A Portrait* (121), and a discussion of aesthetic theory that picks up where Stephen Dedalus left in his conversation with Lynch. After settling the problem of aesthetic apprehension, this symposium addresses the topic of artistic inspiration and production (266–73). The anecdotal mirroring is such that *Adán Buenosayres* unconsciously transposes snippets of dialogue from Joyce's fiction more in careless imitation than in respectful homage. The novel's cynical attitude toward Buenos Aires echoes conspicuously Stephen's vision of Dublin. "Buenos Aires es la perra que se come sus crías" [Buenos Aires is the bitch that devours its litter], says Tesler (47). In *Portrait*, Stephen tells Davin the nationalist, "Ireland is the old sow that eats her farrow" (*PA* 203). The major discrepancy regarding the overall shape of anecdote and plot in *Ulysses* and *Adán Buenosayres* is the absence of a Leopold Bloom figure in the latter, though Tesler's Jewishness appears to be modeled after Bloom's.

The most conspicuous Joycean appropriation in Marechal's novel is the use of multiple narrative techniques and the "scorched earth" alternation of styles. *Adán Buenosayres* utilizes the "dramatic" format of the Circe chapter (50, 262–74), the stellar-objective catechist question-answer technique of "Ithaca" (28–29, 236–37), the "labyrinth" orchestration of a street fight reminiscent of the design of "Wandering Rocks" (63–79), and the Protean metamorphosis of characters in the *Walpurgisnacht* at Saavedra

(in which the Gaucho Juan sin Ropa, like Zoe in "Circe," is meta-
morphosized into a giant and into the devil, 184–235). Marechal
concludes the "anecdotal" section of the novel with a extensive
stream-of-consciousness sequence in the manner of "Penelope."
Even though the latter is the discourse of a male mind
(Buenoayres's) and makes use of punctuation, the scope of the
flashback, which refers to Buenosayres's childhood, adolescence,
and his trips to Spain and Europe, covers the same intimate biographical space as Molly's. *Adán Buenosayres*'s greatest technical
debt to Joyce's *Ulysses* is the ability to shift modes of narrative discourse in the novelistic text without having to distill and maintain
one prose form. In other words, Marechal's novel dispenses with
the aesthetic ideal of a unified narrative style to become a show-
case of narrative techniques in the fashion of *Ulysses*.[28]

Marechal's dependence on Joyce is made even clearer in the essays and commentaries in which, while refuting the imputations of
Joycean influence, he reveals his full assimilation of the Joycean
system. In his essay "Las claves de *Adán Buenoayres*" [The keys to
Adán Buenosayres], Marechal explains how his novel also makes
use of Homeric parallels. Like *Ulysses*, *Adán Buenosayres* pretends
to be an allegorical national epic, an *argentinopeya* that draws insistently for its figuration on episodes and characters from the *Iliad*
and the *Odyssey* more explicitly than *Ulysses* itself. In *Adán Buenosayres* there is a "Polifemo," a "Circe," a "Proteo," and other
mythical characters whose outline proclaims—rather than hide—
their classical derivation. "Las claves de *Adán Buenosayres*" is written as a letter to the critic Adolfo Prieto in order to set the record
straight about the novel. Marechal goes full circle by replicating
Joyce's strategy with Stuart Gilbert and other exegetes of *Ulysses*.
In the face of the misunderstandings he perceives in the commentaries on his novel, Marechal writes his article with the purpose of revealing the "claves"—the code, the skeleton key, the
schema—to the critics. Marechal approaches Prieto to make him
his Gilbert; he thus discloses that *Adán Buenosayres* draws substantially from *Ulysses*' mythical method. His essay serves to show
that his novel is also an actualization of Greek epic. Marechal
takes care to note, however, that his novel has a metaphysical mes-
sage absent in Joyce's godless universe.[29] While it is true that the
classical correspondences have a distinctive farcical, light and
humorous effect in *Adán Buenosayres* missing in Joyce, *Adán
Buenosayres* tends to mirror *Ulysses* mechanically by drawing simultaneously from its techniques, its mythical method, and its
storyline.

Lezama does not mimic Joyce's menu of techniques as Marechal does. The prose of *Paradiso* has a unique, unified character that draws from parody, but is not suspended in pastiche. *Paradiso* adopts the mythical method, but does not do it in the often formulaic, caricature-like manner of *Adán Buenosayres*. *Paradiso*'s understanding and application of Joyce's mythical method is unique, since other generations of Latin American Joycean novels opt to appropriate Joycean technique without fully understanding the mythical principles to which this narrative "technology" is put to use. *Paradiso* does not reflect the surface of Joyce's novel the way *Adán Buenosayres* does, but probes the depth of its symbolic design.

This is not to say that *Paradiso* does not show sophistication in experimental technique. Lezama himself has revealed the extent of his technical appropriations by describing the switching of narrative point-of-view from the third to the first person in chapters 9 and 14 and other scattered instances in *Paradiso* as a device taken from Joyce, and not as a naive narrative lapse, as some critics have argued.[30] Furthermore, in *Paradiso* Lezama makes great use of what Joyce called the "technic of the labyrinth": the orchestration of stray, apparently disconnected stories in an interlacing, multiple narrative layering best demonstrated in the "Wandering Rocks" chapter but operating, as Joycean critics have shown, in the novel as a whole.[31]

This narrative technique is used overtly three times in *Paradiso*, to great effect. Critics have analyzed how, in *Ulysses*'s "Wandering Rocks," the labyrinth is treated not just as a symbol or a theme, but, in the correlation between theme and form, as a system in which the symbolic landscape determines narrative design.[32] In chapter 2 of *Paradiso*, the stories of Cemí, Juan, Petronila and Nila Cazar, Sofía and Adalberto Kuller, Martincillo, Vivo, Lupita, Tránquilo and Luva, are presented in an alternating rotation (the narrative design) that helps encapsulate, in an illusion of simultaneity, the quotidian life and customs of a *cuartería*, a working-class neighborhood behind Havana's Vedado (the symbolic landscape). In the enigmatic chapter 12, four disconnected narrations—the epic battles of the Roman Captain Atrio Flaminio, the games of an unnamed child under the care of his grandmother, the wanderings of an insomniac who prowls the Havana night heeding a mysterious call, and the fabulous story of the musicologist Juan Longo, whose life is preserved by a trance-like condition of "suspended animation" concocted by the spells of his Circe-like wife—slowly become intertwined, and finally merge at the center of the textual "labyrinth" in the conclusion. Chapter 13 is first divided into several storylines—José Cemí comes out of a *sesión espiritista* or spiritualist meeting; a collector of antiques (Oppiano Licario) leaves a shop after negotiating a purchase of Roman coins; Martincillo, a thief, tries to find money to buy a present for his girlfriend; and Vivo has just bought a magical accordion to neutralize a hex put on him by his lover (another temptress in the Homeric vein). All of these characters converge as they board an "infernal" bus recalling the carriage that rides through Dublin in *Ulysses'* "Hades" chapter. As in *Ulysses*, the labyrinth is the narrative principle that structures the totality of *Paradiso* as novel. It organizes the character's peripatetic wanderings in the streets and alleys of Havana. It represents the novel's search for a center, for a lost point of origin. It describes the efforts of two characters in the process of finding each other in the maze of the narrative: Theseus after the Minotaur; Telemachus after Odysseus; Stephen after Bloom; and Cemí after Licario.

Lezama does not, however, care to call attention to the dexterity of his use of modernist narrative techniques, nor does he presume to use technique for the mere sake of experimentation. Lezama does not pillage *Ulysses'* toolbox of styles to produce a "Joycean" novel, the way other Latin American and peninsular novelists would from the forties on: Leopoldo Marechal with *Adán Buenos-ayres*; Guillermo Cabrera Infante with *Tres Tristes Tigres* (1967); Fernando del Paso with *José Trigo* (1966) and *Palinuro de México* (1975); Carlos Fuentes with *Cristóbal Nonato* (1989); and Julián Ríos with *Larva* (1983).[33] Lezama rejects the exploitation of techniques and the "scorched earth" policy of a style-per-chapter. Lezama does not practice—at least with the same intensity—what he calls, in his essay on Julio Cortázar's *Rayuela*, "la ensalada verbal del Joyce filológico" [the word-salad of the philological Joyce]. Rather than the experimental Joyce of the avant-garde, Lezama prefers the mythopoetic Joyce who manipulates not syntaxes, points-of-view, and neologisms, but rather archetypes and legends. *Paradiso*'s use of the labyrinth technique is linked to the logic of a rigorous, consistent, yet expanded and refurbished mythical method. *Paradiso* adopts *Ulysses'* Homeric schema, but reinvents it in the process of assimilating it into a "baroque" interpretation of the origins of Greek mythology.[34]

Even though inspired by Joyce, Lezama's mythical method does not mechanically reproduce that of *Ulysses*. Lezama amplifies the method in the process of researching and writing *Paradiso*. Thus, we note, in Lezama's theoretical disengagement between mythical method and narrative technique, the assumption of Eliot's definition of "method" as a form of serious literary investigation into the classical past. Lezama's *Paradiso* documents classical myth and antiquity in an obsessive, informed fashion, in the way Eliot argues that *Ulysses* does. *Paradiso* does not limit itself to extracting motifs from a casual reading of the Homeric epics. It draws from a pool of information and contemporary scholarship about Greece and other ancient civilization: the Cretan, the Egyptian, and the Phoenician, just to mention a few. In the sheer multiplicity of allusions to ancient cultures, *Paradiso* is more akin to *Ulysses* than Marechal's novel is. The proximity of Lezama's range of sources to Joyce's confirms the crucial role of Stuart Gilbert's study in Lezama's understanding of the Joycean method, a "critical dependence" that is surpassed in Lezama's refiguration of Joyce's narrative fiction.

Lezama's *Paradiso* evidences a plan of construction and investigation resembling the creative process presented by Joyce to Gilbert. In adopting Homeric correspondences and esoteric symbologies, what Lezama adopts is Joyce's research strategy—the thorough and precise recreation of antiquity encoded or encrypted underneath an anecdotal surface which Gilbert's study excavates, as if the text were an archaeological site. To say that Gilbert's book is an "explicitation" of the Homeric parallels in *Ulysses* is only a partial statement; Gilbert's analysis is also the elaboration of Eliot's important observation about the role of new classicist, mythographical, and ethnological research in modernist literature. Gilbert does not rely exclusively on an isolated reading of the Odyssey to trace the "order of myth" in *Ulysses*; he also documents the presence of a number of recent archaeological, philological, and esoteric investigations about Homer's epoch in the fabric of *Ulysses*.

Joyce's "method" thus included consulting a body of contemporary scholarship concerning the sources of the Homeric poems and the migratory history that led to the colonization of the Aegean archipelago and the emergence of Greek culture. Joyce writes *Ulysses* after a turn-of-the-century resurgence in classical studies motivated by revolutionary archaeological discoveries, the development of new methods in philological and textual analysis, and the revision of the concept of "primitive" in anthropology. Joyce led Gilbert to realize that his vision of Greece was built on reading not just Homer and the other authors of antiquity, but also on the continuous consultation of the pionering works of the Cambridge

School of Anthropology—Gilbert Murray, Sir George Frazer, and Jane Harrison[35]—together with the controversial studies of the Homer specialist Victor Bérard, in particular, his *Les Phéniciens et l'Odysée*.[36]

In the chapter of his study titled *"Ulysses* and the *Odyssey,"* Gilbert makes sure to show that the novel's Homeric parallels represent more than the symbolic reproduction of an epic plot. According to Gilbert, the Babelic character of language in *Ulysses* is a modern transposition of the compounding of dialects that philology had discovered in the Homeric compositions. Quoting M. Breal's studies, Gilbert details Joyce's sophisticated knowledge of the linguistic hybridity of the *Odyssey*'s vernacular and of the scholarly theories addressing its production: "Homer's vocabulary presents some astonishing anomalies. . . . In the Homeric dialect we find Ionian, Aeolian, Cyprian, and even Attic elements; the philologist is bewildered by its phonetic variability and the diversity of grammatical forms employed" (*JJU* 77–78). The principal study in Joyce's understanding of the *Odyssey*'s discursive complexity, says Gilbert, is Bérard's *Les Phéniciens et L'Odyssée*. Victor Bérard's key contribution to the Homeric scholarship of this time was the determination of a historical Homer after Romantic scholarship had proclaimed the folk origin of the poem, regarding "Homer" as an imaginary author concocted by the Alexandrians of the second century. Bérard accomplished this by juxtaposing the stylistic consistency of the poems with excerpts from poems found in recently excavated Egyptian papyrii, thereby confirming the true antiquity of sections of the *Odyssey* which the German Romantic School had regarded as adulterated.

After fixing the composition of the Homeric poems to a time, a period, a culture, and an individual, Bérard discussed the inconsistencies between the regions through which Odysseus wanders in the poem and the Greek world-map of Homer's time. Some discrepancies in geographical names indicated to Bérard that the author of the poem was not truly familiar with the tales he rhapsodized, which led Bérard to conclude that the stories that inspired the creation of Homer's Odysseus—long taken to be Aechean, the culture of island-dwelling ancestors of the Greeks— were in fact of Semitic origin, probably taken from log books (*periplous*) describing Phoenician navigations in the westernmost part of the Mediterranean. The Phoenician source for Odysseus' adventures would then be the cause of the linguistic multiplicity of the Homeric dialect. Thus Odysseus and Homer were not contemporaries, but lived instead at very distant points in history and geography:

> I do not believe in Homer-Odysseus. I believe the *Odyssey* to be the work of a cultured poet who can write and read, and who borrows from a written source the material for his descriptions and legends. This source, direct or indirect, he owed to the Phoenicians; it was neither the work of one person's imagination, nor a collection of popular or old wives' tales. And the information which the Poet thus borrowed is a kind that points to some sailor's manual, a *periplous* prepared by a professional hand, as his original source.[37]

The novelty of Bérard's approach is that, instead of reaching this conclusion exclusively through the philological investigation of surviving manuscripts, he retraced the Odyssean voyage in the west Mediterranean region. Taking the *Odyssey*'s voyage to be a real one, Bérard combined his analysis of names in the poem with the information uncovered by recent archaeological discoveries (in this period archaeologists claimed to have found the palace of Menelaus in Crete), in order to pinpoint the different locales of the poem's shipwrecks and landings. Thus, Menelaus's kingdom is in Crete, Aeolos's island is really Stromboli, Circe's island is in fact a region on the coast of Egypt, and Calypso's island is Gibraltar. Bérard closed his book with a map of the Mediterranean tracing Odysseus's twenty-year wanderings. Extrapolating from the historical names of Homeric sites their linguistic transformation in the Greek language of Homer, Bérard analyzed the poem's mixed, hybrid idiosyncracy. According to Bérard's hypothesis, the original "Odysseus" was a Phoenician whom Homer made into an Aechean, hellenizing the names and terms attached to this legend or *periplous*.

Gilbert's exegesis of *Ulysses* is thus guided by the history of the *Odyssey* as chronicled in Bérard's elegant and influential book. Gilbert's approach follows the principles put forth by Eliot in his essay. With the term "myth" Eliot referred to the specificity of the body of Greek myth, not "the mythical" in general. In Eliot and Gilbert's reading of *Ulysses*, the Homeric parallels are not just a mask for the current time; by having the current time conform to the order of antiquity—an order best expressed in the complexity of its myths—a *total historical* picture of antiquity is preserved and conveyed. In meticulously recreating a Greek myth using a contemporary context, the modernist novel makes the anecdotal, plot-and-characters elements serve as the "scaffold" for a coherent, scholarly, fully coded representation of antiquity. Thus, according to Gilbert, Molly is born in Gibraltar because this is Calypso's island in Homeric lore, and Bloom is Jewish because of the Hebraic origins of Homer's language. Gilbert argues that this precision and attention to detail permeates every incorporation of Homeric motifs into *Ulysses*. More recent Joyce critics have dwelled on the high degree of accuracy in the application of Bérard's theories to the peripatetic symbolic design of *Ulysses*, drawing parallels between the maps featured in Bérard's illustrated version and the routes through Dublin that each chapter traces.[38]

In sum, *Ulysses'* use of the Homeric format is not mechanical, but defined by depth, by a compounded intertextuality cutting transversally through layers of scholarship to illustrate the ways and nature of antiquity. The result is *Ulysses'* erudite density, a condensation of rare, sometimes obscure information grafted into a deceivingly simple narrative fiction. This makes *Ulysses* a curious polyvalent text which highlights and reenacts the composite, hybrid, plural syncretism of the *Odyssey* by merging discrepant discourses and languages in its narrative.

II

Paradiso is interested in attaining the same depth of informed, studied syncretism as that achieved by *Ulysses'* mythical method. Lezama's use of classical scholarship exhibits the same profundity, the same condensation of knowledge as Joyce's. José Lezama Lima's investigation of the classics occurs in the context of a moment of Latin American enthusiasm for classical studies patterned after the turn-of-the-century European efflorescence of Homeric analysis. Pedro Henríquez Ureña has traced this "renaissance of the classical humanities" to the impact that the *generación* [generation] of the *Sociedad de Conferencias del Ateneo de la Juventud* [Atheneum of Youth Society of Conferences] had on the Mexican educational system.[39] As a reaction against the positivist orientation of scholarship in turn-of-the-century Mexico, the members of this *generación*—Alfonso Reyes, Antonio Caso, José Vasconcelos, Jesús Acevedo, Diego Rivera, and Pedro Henríquez Ureña— engaged in a methodical study of Hellenic civilization "leyendo y releyendo en coro lo central de las letras y estudios helénicos" [reading and rereading chorally the best of Hellenistic letters and studies][40] in order to rescue the humanist ideal they thought lost with the rise of the *científico* intellectuals of the Porfiriato. After the thirties and due to the powerful Mexican publishing industry, this system became the model for humanities programs in Havana and the rest of Latin America. In their late years, in a revisionist attempt to contain the expressionist promotion of the Baroque, Reyes and Henríquez Ureña would return to write on ancient Greece and update classical scholarship in Latin America. They regarded the "return to the rational Greeks" as the best humanistic remedy to the "existentialist cult" of irrationality that followed the Second World War.[41]

The renaissance in Greek studies in Mexico had its apex during the forties, when Alfonso Reyes returned to Mexico to occupy humanities chairs in the Colegio de México and the Universidad Autónoma. Despite having little formal training in the study of Greek, Reyes devoted the rest of his academic life to the scholarly promotion of the *afición a Grecia* [the devotion to Greece], thus earning the reputation of foremost *helenista* in Mexico and abroad.[42] Heralding a new interest in Greek civilization and armed with the pioneering scholarship of Victor Bérard, Gilbert Murray, Werner Jaeger, and other New Hellenists, Reyes published a great number of *textos de divulgación*: popular manuals of mythology and synopses based on the annotated research he conducted for his course lectures. The first texts that appeared during this period were *La crítica en la Edad Ateniense* [Criticism in the Age of Athens, 1941] and *La retórica antigua* [Ancient Rhetoric, 1942]. During the next decade he would produce a series of studies, under the title *Archivo de Alfonso Reyes,* devoted to the diffusion of the latest bibliography in classical studies: *Estudios helénicos* [Studies in Hellenism, 1957], *Libros y libreros en la antigüedad* [Book and Bookmakers in Antiquity, 1955], and *La filosofía helenista* [Greek Philosophy, 1959]. Reyes's most important work in this vein was his collection *Junta de sombras* [Assembly of Shadows, 1949], in which articles attempting a poetic and concise articulation of Reyes's vision of the Aechean civilization appear together with some ambitious and learned analyses of the work of Bérard and other scholars from whom Reyes drew his compendia. While his former works had dealt with theoretical issues of criticism which used classical examples as their illustration and his later *Archivo* studies functioned as compilations or book summaries, *Junta de sombras* was Reyes's foremost attempt to update Latin American scholars on the lastest trends in classical studies and recent discoveries in philology, anthropology, and archaeology.

Through Reyes's promotional work, his translations, and the *breviarios* [short introductions] on ancient civilizations published in

Spanish during the forties by the Fondo de Cultura Económica under Reyes's tutelage, José Lezama Lima read and became acquainted with classical scholarship, thus finding the background against which to recreate the "continuous analogy between antiquity and contemporaneity" in *Paradiso* that he had found in Joyce and Eliot. Reyes's work of making the classics known was to Lezama's generation what the work of Bérard, Frazer, Harrison, and Murray had been to Joyce, Lawrence, and Eliot. It was through Reyes that Lezama became acquainted with the work of Bérard, which had played, according to Gilbert, such a critical role in the design of *Ulysses*. In *Junta de sombras*, Reyes pays homage to Bérard's stature among classical scholars in an essay that later served as the basis for Reyes's introduction to the Spanish translation of Bérard's study, *La resurrection d'Homére* (written in 1930 and, like *Ulysses*, published in Spanish translation in 1945).[43] Reyes also highlighted in his book the work of Werner Jaeger, author of *Paideia: The Ideals of Greek Culture*. At the conclusion of *Junta de sombras*, there is a discussion of the first volume of *Paideia* with a consideration of Jaeger's importance as a scholar of the classics.[44]

The essays in *Junta de sombras* reflect the transformations and reorientation in classical studies expressed in the works of Bérard and Jaeger. Reyes's laudatory vision of Greek civilization is determined by Bérard's and Jaeger's positive appreciation. According to Reyes, the Greek world is a world of rationality and measure, the product of the "reasonable man" in early Ionian and Aechean civilizations that was expounded in Jaeger and Bérard's studies. Likewise, Reyes minimized the importance of the intellectual and political achievements of the Periclean period of the fifth century and the philosophical school of Athens, considering these late forms of Greek "reasonableness." Inspired by Bérard and Jaeger's belief in the centrality of Homer as the key to the Greek spirit, Reyes begins his book with essays exploring the nature of the Homeric pantheon. In "The Dawn of Civilization," "Mileto's Awakening," "The Island Philosophers," and "Aspects of Archaic Lyricism," Reyes developed the Bérard-Jaeger conception of the prehistory of Homeric "reasonableness" in Aechean and Ionian civilization. In this view, the development of Greek culture is measured according to its capacity to successfully resist Oriental influences. *Junta de sombras* ends with elegiac essays on the dissolution of the Athens school and the fall of Hellenic civilization—"The Last Seven Wise Men," "Elio Arístides, Executioner of Himself," "Demetrio Falereo's Ship," "Towards the Middle Ages"—as Greece is conquered by Macedonia and Rome and becomes orientalized with the rise of mystical Constantinople and the Ottoman Empire.

In organizing his essays with this ambitious scope, Reyes adopted two major tenets from Bérard and Jaeger's studies. First, despite the fragmentary geography and the influences from the East, Greek civilization was a unified phenomenon that began with the rise of an anthropocentric cosmology, originating in the culture of the Aechean islands, which is then adopted by the permanent city-states of the mainland. All of these cultures shared the same serenity, self-control, and curiosity about the spectacles of nature, values exemplified by the anthropomorphic ethos of the Homeric poems in which gods are neither uncontrollable nor awe-inspiring natural forces, but humanoids. Even if Bérard believed that the *Odyssey* had Phoenician or Semitic origins, Reyes concludes that it was nevertheless the product of a Greek mind that had hellenized the *periploi* information to the point of erasing its oriental component.

Second, even after this civilization spread from north to south or east to west, it remained unique and autonomous. It had a claim to many regions but was loyal to one mentality that stayed strong and integrated even when exposed to the East in trading and religious centers in the lower Mediterrenean. Initially an island culture stressing individualism, commerce, and survival, Hellenism grew unchanged as it was transferred to the mainland. Reyes, Jaeger, and Bérard assumed a contradiction between Hellenism and the Orient, with the oriental mindset regarded as backward, mystical, and inclined to superstition, religious awe, and quietude, while the Greek spirit, inquisitive and enterprising, was seen as the precursor of scientific knowledge and method. In Reyes, Jaeger, and Bérard, the Greek mind aimed toward the logical understanding of causation in the world.

José Lezama Lima's "classical temper" is thus inspired by the renewed interest in antiquity, the *afición a Grecia*, demonstrated by Reyes's generation. Many of the classical terms which Lezama frequently uses in *Paradiso* are drawn from Reyes's studies. For example, the Mexican Ateneo group regarded the Greek ideal of *sofrosyné* [moderation] as the binding spirit of their generation. Lezama incarnates this ideal in the character of Oppiano Licario and describes his temper—his "robusta ecuanimidad, la previa curación de las pasiones" [robust equanimity, prior expiation of passions]—with the language the members of the Ateneo used to define *sofrosyné*.

Bérard and Jaeger speculated that the resourcefulness of Ionian culture resulted from its being an island culture. This alleged self-sufficiency and the arrogance it inspired—which Reyes calls "la insolencia jonia" [the Ionic insolence][45]—may have fed Lezama's proud mystification of the richness of Cuba's insular heritage. The idea of Ionic insolence as an aspect of island culture—"insolencia" carries within it the poetic echo of "ínsula" [island] in Spanish—resembles Lezama's defense of "insularidad" [insularity] as a cultural mode and as a "teleology" in his "Conversación con Juan Ramón Jiménez" [Conversation with Juan Ramón Jiménez].[46] According to Gilbert, Joyce was equally attentive to the island motif in Bérard's navigational investigations concerning movements within the *Odyssey*, and was particularly sensitive to the possibility that Phoenician travel (and thus the original Odysseus) might have reached as far as Ireland.[47] It seems, however, that when Lezama resorted to Reyes's bibliographical sources for further research, he became more drawn to Jaeger's panoramic view of the *paideia* of Greek culture than to the obstinate minutiae in Bérard's geo-archaeological and philological corroborations. According to Cintio Vitier, Lezama repeatedly consulted Joaquín Xirau's and Wenceslao Roces' translations of the four books of Jaeger's *Paideia*, published by the Mexican Fondo de Cultura Económica from 1943 to 1945 with Reyes's encouragement.[48]

Jaeger's notion of *paideia*—the "biological" state of culture when it pursues a higher degree of permanence and perfection through the deliberate intellectual and ethical formation of its future citizens[49]—permeates the philosophy of *Paradiso*. In his article, Reyes defines it as "la modelación paulatina del ideal del Hombre, y aun de cada hombre en relación a ese ideal" [the progressive modeling of the ideal of humanity, and of each and every person under such ideal] (*Junta de sombras* 478). According to Jaeger, the term *paideia* embraces several concepts, including culture, intellect, education; yet, rather than a given cultural form, it is a potential perfection, a roster of ideals, that the collective culture sets for itself through natural and spontaneous strategies of instruction and training. These strategies operate in an organic fashion rather than through the coercion and the bureaucracy of institutions. *Paideia* is a cultural process that precedes the emergence of the state and happens "informally" in the master-pupil relationship set by craft apprenticeship or the tutelage of independent philosophers. Jaeger's book is an exploration of the spectrum of pedagogical ideals that Hellenism deemed worthy of teaching to future generations, and of the consistent distillation of those ideals through schools of philosophy and artistic and theatrical activity. These ideals—which have their origin in ancient systems of nobility—promote the celebration of measure, honor, and reason, the human capacity to understand natural cause and appreciate the harmony of the universe. Jaeger's work traced these ideals from the apex of their formulation in the Homeric poems through the work of the lyrical and dramatic poets, the pre-Socratic philosophers, and the teachings of Plato.

Paradiso derives from Jaeger a number of terms denoting paideic ideals. Lezama's concept of *eros* has its origin in Jaeger's discussion of the term, which Jaeger defines in his analysis of Plato's *Symposium* as "man's instinctive urge to develop his own higher self" (*Paideia* 2: 195). Terms like *areté* and *aristeia*—prominent throughout Jaeger's text—are central principles in *Paradiso*, as are the expressions of *sofrosyné* (moderation), *aidos* (sense of duty), *diké* (justice), *aristia* (divine protection in combat), *nemesis* (the stigma of blemished honor), and *ananké* (an inflexible and unchanging destiny), among others.[50] *Aristeia* (the sense of "individual intellectual achievement and sovereignty," of victory and disposition to sacrifice in battle, 1: 17) and *areté* (a "proud and courtly morality reinforced with warlike valour," 1: 5) recur with notable frequency through all of Lezama's writing. In his piece on Ché Guevara, for example, Lezama applies the concepts of *areteia* and *aristia*: "La *aristia*, la protección en el combate, la tuvo siempre a la hora de los gritos y la arreciada del cuello, pero también la *aresteia*, el sacrificio, el afán de holocausto"[51] [He was always in *aristia*, protected while in combat, in the hour of shouts and throat-seeking lunges, but also in *areteia*, in sacrifice, in the desire for holocaust].

According to Jaeger, what *paideia* seeks to inculcate in the young citizen is the nobility of soul and principle encapsulated in the term *areté;* other virtues are subsequent emanations of this primal moral force. The nobility of *areté* shapes a moral heroism, a self-possession and high-mindedness that feeds and is fed by a secure, confident, unpretentious love of self.[52] *Paradiso* is a chronicle of the growth of *areté* in the noble Cuban youth: the prime example is Fronesis, after whom Cemí shapes his own character in the communitarian context of friendship (the *sympathos)* and the ritual meeting (the *symposia*). The exemplary nature of Fronesis's character is constantly stressed in *Paradiso:*

> Cemí no había conocido a nadie como Fronesis que tuviese una más natural adecuación a la fuerza y a la seducción de la cultura viviente y a ese precio que las horas nos imponen por su deslizarse y por la oportunidad que nos brindan.
>   . . .

La raíz de Fronesis era la eticidad, entre el bien y el mal escogía,—sin que su voluntad o el dolor de su elección se hiciesen visibles,—el bien y la sabiduría. No había en él excesos verbales para apuntalar cualquiera de sus puntos de vista, se diría que no perseguía, sino que se le mostraban en su evidencia natural aquellas cosas por las cuales mostraba simpatía o una demora cariciosa. Su eticidad parecía un producto tan misteriorso como afianzado, brindado por la secularidad que había recibido por la calidad de su sangre, que le deba un impulso tenaz, pero llevado con serena confianza y tranquilo navegar dentro de sus fines. (P 322–23/R 326)

[Cemí had not known anyone like Fronesis, anyone with a more natural fitness to the strength and seduction of the living culture and to that price which the hours impose while slipping away and in the opportunity they offer us.
. . .
Fronesis's root was ethicism, he chose between good and evil, without his will or the pain of his choice being visible, goodness and wisdom. There were no verbal excesses in him to bolster up one or the other of his opinions, it could be said that he would not pursue, unless they manifested themselves with their natural proof, those things for which he showed sympathy or a caressing delay. His ethicism seemed a product both mysterious and tangible, a gift of the secularity he had received through the quality of his blood, which gave him a tenacious drive that he carried with serene confidence and tranquil navigation within its extremities.]

The "natural fitness to the strength and seduction of the living culture" that the text ascribes to Fronesis is a condensed definition of Jaeger's notion of *paideia*. This *paideia*—and Fronesis' *areté*—reaches its purest forms in Fronesis's gift of a poem to Cemí titled "Retrato de José Cemí" [Portrait of José Cemí]. The *fineza* [graciousness] of Fronesis's gift exemplifies a state of style and cultivation Cemí still needs to strive for:

No tenía el secreto afán de hacer visible un sentimiento que aunque podía ir más allá del rendimiento de la cortesanía, la expresaba en verdad, en una forma y con un ademán que la ingenuidad adolescente de Cemí hacía semejantes a las grandes épocas del estilo.

. . . Cemí era todavía muy joven para poder percibir un temperamento de la constitución espiritual de Fronesis, el esperado gesto de retirada después de una acción en que su afectividad se había entregado sin reservas.[53] (P 336/R 339–40)

[He did not have the secret urge to manifest a feeling which, though surpassing in courtliness, was expressed in truth, in a form and with a mien that Cemí's adolescent innocence likened to the great epochs of style.

. . . Cemí was still too young to be able to perceive a temperament like Fronesis's spiritual makeup, the expected gesture of withdrawal after an action in which his affection had been given without reserve.]

José Cemí's inmaturity distances him from Ricardo Fronesis. Fronesis has reached this ideal state; Cemí is still in the process of achieving it. The correct acquisition of *areté*, according to Jaeger, occurs not through a relationship between peers but through a transgenerational association between an adult teacher and a young pupil. Jaeger illustrates the subtlety of this ideal by describing the qualitative change that separates the values expressed in the *Iliad* from those in the *Odyssey*. According to Jaeger, the primitive, collective submission to military tribalism symbolized by Achilles's mechanical defense of his honor in the first Homeric poem is replaced by the proud individualism and refined resourcefulness of Odysseus's character in the second epic. To trace this difference in the poems' doctrines of exemplariness, Jaeger analyzes the significance of the first section of the *Odyssey*, the "Telemachia," in which Telemachus grows into the responsibility and the self-possession of *areté* as he sets out to sea determined to find his missing father.[54] The "Telemachia" narrative is the highest instance of the educational value and utility that Plato recognized in Homer's epic poetry because it gives a "step-by-step" method for bringing out the *areté* in the young man. This is accomplished through a mentor. Melenaus, Nestor, and, finally, Athena (disguised as Mentor) perform the task of honing Telemachus's capacities and virtues: poise, eloquence, respect, self-possession, and determination.[55] Among other things, James Joyce parodies this mentoring process in the "Proteus" chapter of *Ulysses*.

The Greek paideic function of mentorship to instill and sharpen the adolescent's *areté* structures the relationship between Oppiano Licario and José Cemí in *Paradiso*, and thus the novel's fundamental narrative design. As in *Ulysses*, *Paradiso* stages a *Telemachia*: the journey of a son seeking his missing father and acquiring wisdom and self-reliance on the way. Cemí is Telemachus in search of the legacy of the Absent Father and the transcendental power of poetry; Oppiano Licario is the Mentor and substitute father who will lead Cemí-Telemachus to assume Colonel Cemí's nobility of spirit through the dangerous exercise of poetry in the island of *Paradiso*. This mentorship is what the colonel asks from Licario in his deathbed: "Tengo un hijo, conózcalo, procure enseñarle algo de lo que usted ha aprendido viajando, sufriendo, leyendo" (*P* 154/*R* 154) [I have a son, acquaint yourself with him, try to teach him some of what you have learned traveling, suffering, reading].

While *Paradiso*'s plot might outwardly resemble a family saga in the style of Thomas Mann's *Buddenbrooks* or the project of recollection in Proust's *A la Recherche du temps perdu*,[56] the mythical method makes *Paradiso* a mythopoetic epic quest for transcendence symbolized in the Son's search for the figure of the Absent Father. Lezama takes into uncharted waters *Ulysses'* erudite and punctilious use of ancient arcana, replicating by a textual strategy of accretive allusions the encyclopedic dimensions of Joyce's novel. The mythical method also makes *Paradiso* a sourcebook of ancient mythology and cosmology, comprising the Greek universe and integrating in its far reaching raddii other sacred scriptural systems: the mystic Kabbalah, the Egyptian *Book of the Dead*, and the Confucian *Tao Te Ching*. One of the models for this expansiveness may be *Ulysses* itself. Joyce's novel does not just stage a parodic correspondence between Hellenic antiquity and modern life in Dublin, but integrates a vision of oriental culture and philosophy as well, as Gilbert pointed out in the introduction to his study.[57] Arguably, Lezama systematizes the mythical and symbolic method of *Ulysses* even further in order to produce the cosmology of the *era imaginaria* proposed in his essays of the late fifties and early sixties.[58]

In this light, "Muerte de Joyce" can be read as *Paradiso*'s prolegomena, an anticipatory description of its principal themes and design. Lezama's list of "preferences" in "Muerte de Joyce"—the motif of the quest, the debate on Hamlet, the stellar poetry of Ithaca, the exactness of Joyce's rhythm, the search for a new orthodoxy—marks the points of coincidence where *Paradiso* mirrors and refracts the content and composition of *Ulysses*. Both *Paradiso* and *Ulysses* feature scenes of philosophical debate that bring the Platonic Symposium into the present day, thus highlighting the relevance of Socratic dialogism in the constitution of the novel as genre. Both explore the possibilities of rhythm in the production of a poetic language fashioned to revitalize the contemporary novel. Both adapt Homer's epic to allegorize the search for a father figure that will harbor the fullness of knowledge. These parallelisms ramify into new pairings leading to multiple comparative configurations: The Cemí-Oppiano Licario dyad mirrors that of Stephen-

Bloom. The "Scylla and Charybdis" debate on the androgynous nature of creativity in Shakespeare's Hamlet at the Dublin Library echoes the discussion between Cemí, Fronesis, and Foción regarding the androgynous sexuality of the creatures of heaven in *Paradiso*'s chapter 8. Joyce's personification of Homer's Telemachus in the character of Stephen is reenacted in *Paradiso*'s Cemí. In *Paradiso*, Joyce's mythical method is kaleidoscopically enriched: The Homeric topoi are merged with still another schema—the myth of Orpheus—to form a polysemic configuration and allusive narrative system as dense as Joyce's.

The disposition of the chapters in *Paradiso* reflects the studied, deliberate patterning of the chapters in *Ulysses*. Under the proliferating arabesques of the prose, the skeletal joints of the novels' narratives are seen to be the same; the same pillars occupy the foundations of both prose labyrinths. *Ulysses* may occur in one day and *Paradiso* may span more than fifty years, but the encounters in the Dublin maze and in the Caribbean City happen at equivalent junctures in the text. Before "merging" in "Ithaca," Stephen and Bloom casually intersect at three points without recognizing each other: in the "Hades" trams, the "Scylla and Charybdis" library, and the "Oxen of the Sun" hospital. It is in the climactic "Circe" brothel and the stellar "Ithaca" chapter where their momentous encounter takes place. Licario and Cemí's lineage also casually intersect three times before the "merging" of Licario with Cemí. Oppiano Licario "rescues" Cemí's uncle, Alberto Olaya, from the snare of a demonic homosexual bar in chapter 3. In chapter 5 he meets the colonel at the Pensacola hospital and notices Cemí from afar, just as Bloom notices Stephen in "Hades." By a stroke of "luck," Licario has a brush with Cemí in the bus/tram of chapter 13, in which he arranges to have Cemí visit him at his apartment. Cemí and Licario finally "merge" in chapter 14, meeting at Licario's wake.

The best evidence of Lezama's careful awareness of the deliberate suspension of Bloom's and Stephen's encounter as a tactic to create a moment of revelation that can give meaning to what appears to be a senseless accumulation of trivial detail, is found in Lezama's annotations to his reading of *Ulysses* in 1939. In the short essay draft "Joyce y Proteo," found in Notebook 16 among his papers at the Fondo Lezama Lima in the José Martí National Library, Lezama comments on the aesthetic purpose of the postponement of the meeting between "Telemachus" and "Odysseus" in *Ulysses*. The document reads like a statement of purpose for the deferment of the encounter between Cemí and Oppiano Licario in *Paradiso*:

> El tercero de los diez y ocho episodios que componen el *Ulises* de James Joyce, termina la parte que corresponde a la Telemaquia de la Odisea. Bloom-Ulysse [sic], el hombre medio moderno, héroe poco heroico, no ha entrado todavía en escena y es el joven Stephen Dedalus (Telémaco), Hamlet irlandés, que ocupa el primer papel. Stephen es de pura cepa irlandesa, Bloom de origen judío, pero de esta misma oposición resulta que el uno encuentra su complemento en el otro y en toda la primera mitad del *Ulises* el lector presiente que pronto o tarde se establecerá una descarga que—uniendo estrechamente estos dos polos opuestos—aclarará hasta en sus menores detalles este vasto fresco de la vida moderna que es el *Ulises*, el cuadro más perfecto que se ha hecho hasta ahora de las sutilezas conscientes y subconscientes que constituyen la vida interior del hombre medio del siglo viente. Proteo contiene múltiples alusiones, ciertos pasajes oscuros que se aclaran solemente después de la entrada de Bloom, hacia el fin del *Ulises*. Tres veces durante el día 16 de junio de 1904, estos dos protagonistas pasan por el lado del otro sin establecer el menor contacto, y es tan sólo en la noche cuando de pronto la tempestad que se ha estado incubando durante todo el día encima de Dublín estalla, que Ulises y su hijo espiritual traban amistad.

> [The third of the eighteen episodes that comprise James Joyce's *Ulysses* concludes the section that corresponds to the "Telemachia" of the *Odyssey*. Bloom-Ulysse [sic], the modern everyman, hero of little heroism, has not yet come into the scene, and it is Stephen Dedalus (Telemachus), an Irish Hamlet, who occupies the premier role. Stephen comes from pure Irish lineage, Bloom is of Jewish origin, but it is out of this very opposition that one finds his complement in the other, and throughout the first half of *Ulysses* the reader foresees that sooner or later a flash will occur which, closely uniting these two opposite poles, will illuminate to the smallest details this vast fresco of modern life that is *Ulysses* . . . Proteus features multiple allusions, some obscure passages that are clarified only after Bloom's entrance, toward the end of *Ulysses*. Thrice during the day of June 16, 1904, these two protagonists come cross each other without establishing the slightest contact, and it is only at midnight when suddenly the tempest that has been brewing all day over Dublin explodes, that Ulysses and his spiritual son become friends.][59]

Likewise, the two protagonists of *Paradiso* encounter each other without meeting formally until the end, when the same flash of revelation that Lezama sees in *Ulysses'* climax illuminates "communion" between Cemí and Licario at the end of chapter 13 and in chapter 14. As *Ulysses, Paradiso* initially orchestrates a profusion of obscure episodes and allusions that only gain meaning ("que se aclaran") at the conclusion, when Licario and Cemí's meeting fulfills the young man's search for a mentor who can show him the way to a poetic interpretation of the world. Here Lezama visualizes in *Ulysses* the intricate interplay between enigma and decipherment, mystery and epiphany, opacity and transparency, darkness and light, *oscuro* and *claro*, that will determine the semantic and semiotic dynamics of *Paradiso*'s textuality. Like Bloom advising Stephen in the Ithaca chapter, like the obstinate Finnegan refusing to remain still in death, Licario will impart his knowledge to Cemí during his own wake at the conclusion of *Paradiso,* and will return from death itself to continue the mentoring in the sequel, *Oppiano Licario* (1977). The careful construction of *Paradiso* not only shows the same symbolic deliberation critics from Eliot to Kenner have found in *Ulysses*; it also shows the idiosyncratic adoption of *Ulysses'* Telemachia at the very core of Lezama Lima's conceptual inception of his novel.

III

In the *Ulysses-Paradiso* correspondence, Oppiano Licario takes Blooms's place as Odysseus. Lezama's exegesis of his character's name—Oppiano for a Roman senator who delved in esoteric mysticism; Licario for Daedalus's son's thirst for the altitude of perfection[60]—neatly corroborates a system of classical parallels as that found in Joyce. Nevertheless, Oppiano never performs as a statesman, and he does not show any of Icarus's hubris. Nor does Oppiano incarnate Odysseus the way Leopold Bloom does. When Oppiano finally meets Cemí in the novel, he is stationary, living on the first floor of an apartment building. Even though he has been an experienced traveler in his youth—he studied Ninivite art and numismatics in Paris and Harvard (an obscure homage to Werner Jaeger since Oppiano could have been potentially Jaeger's student)—Oppiano Licario is not made to undertake an elaborate voyage, a parodic Odyssean *epos* like Leopold Bloom's in the Dublin of *Ulysses* (although, as Odysseus, Licario is capable of returning from Hades to earth). A new schema appears that postulates new classical correspondences. Licario is not a simple prototype of the Homeric counselor. The esoteric nature of Oppiano's knowledge, the capacity of teaching "from death itself," his conveyance of serene rhythm as an antidote to the passions, and his dualistic and gnostic theological beliefs, associate Licario with the mystagogue heroes and philosophers of the hermetic "mystery" sects, specifically those of Orpheus and Pythagoras, that flourished in the sixth century B.C. just before the age of Pericles' Athens. Oppiano resembles Pythagoras in character and wisdom, and adopts Pythagoras's "musical education" as the main vehicle for purification, mentorship, and the attainment of resurrection. Through the Cemí-Licario relation, *Paradiso* conjures yet another mythical schema: the story of the reshaping of Orphism under the teachings of the Pythagoreans. By doing this, Lezama argues for an orientalized interpretation of Hellenism, thus partially challenging Reyes's rational vision of the Greek.

Reyes extolled the Ionian rationality of the Greeks. His celebratory profession of Greek reason is a *cri du coeur* against the irrationalism of the Second World War and the existentialism that flourished after the war. *La afición a Grecia*—Reyes's last collection of essays on classical Greece, published posthumously in 1960—is a synthesis of his Apollonian view of Greek culture. Reyes conveys this conviction best in his interpretation of the political unification at Delphos. The success of Apollo's priests in co-opting the shrines of the Dionysian cult and in integrating divergent sects into the worship of one god is the highest moment in the teleology of Greek rationality.[61] *Junta de sombras* is a deceiving title for Reyes's earlier book on the Greeks, since its essays portray classical Hellenism as an "age of enlightenment," and makes only marginal reference to the Orphic Hades to which the "sombras" [shadows] in the title allude.

Alfonso Reyes's vision is absorbed and debated in the works of the modern Latin American writers who use classical lore and mythology to investigate the role of unreason, excess, and violence—much in the fashion of Friedrich Nietzsche, E. R. Dobbs, and Georges Bataille—at the core of civilization: Borges, Carpentier, Cortázar, and, finally, Lezama.[62] Borges's revision of Homer in his story "El inmortal" [The Immortal] is a parable about the futility of reason, since Homer is literally made into both a savage and a man of modernity. In Borges's "La casa de Asterión" [The House of Asterion], the social function of Daedalus's labyrinth—to protect Cretans from anarchy and the threat of the monster—is called into question by the story's portrayal of the Minotaur as a type of romantic hero and its picture of Theseus as an indolent murderer. A similar inversion of the savage-civilized dyad occurs in Ariadne's secret motive for reaching the center of Daedalus's construction—

her bestialist, incestual passion—in Cortázar's recreation of the myth in *Los reyes* [The Kings]. As in Borges's story, in Cortázar's dramatic poem the Minotaur's humanity exceeds that of his captor. The bloodthirsty Maenads from the story in *Final del juego* can also be read as an Orphic reponse to Reyes's Apollonian vision. In his treatment of Greek and Roman mythology, Cortázar seeks to highlight the Dionysian element that survives beneath Apollonian repression; the timeless persistence, from antiquity to modernity, of this destructive instinct is the moral of "Todos los fuegos el fuego" [All the Fires the Fire].

Lezama participates in this revision of Reyes's promotion of Hellenic rationality. In *La cantidad hechizada* [The Measure of Enchantment], Lezama's essays on Orphism and the Egyptian and Chinese civilizations vindicate oriental religiosity and contest Reyes's depreciation of their "mystical irrationalism." Lezama remains faithful to the Ionian ideals of *paideia*, but incorporates Orphism as an integral part of such ideals. In fact, the picture of Ionian culture illustrated in *Paradiso* avoids the reverence for pure reason found in Reyes's work. Lezama appreciates the doctrine of paideia—of a culture in search of perfection and refinement and of the virtues of moderation and contemplation—that Reyes and Jaeger honor, while painting a critical canvas of the Hegelian optimism of Jaeger and Reyes's work by marking what both Reyes and Jaeger consider a marginal, ancillary movement—Orphism—as a prominent, essential Hellenic ingredient.[63] In his essay "Introducción a los vasos órficos" [Introduction to the Orphic vessels, 1961], Lezama discusses the importance of the period preceding the Periclean era. He writes: "En realidad, el período órfico trae una solución que no es ya la del período apolíneo. Trae un nuevo saber, una nuevo descenso al infierno." [In fact, the Orphic period brings a solution different from that of the Apollonian period. A new knowledge, a new descent into Hades.] (*OC* 2: 860) The myth of Orpheus displaces and merges with the Odyssean rectitude so admired by Bérard, Jaeger, and Reyes, and the elements of Orphic experience, cult, and myth serve as code and symbol of multiple moments and scenes in *Paradiso*'s narrative, much in the way various motifs of the *Odyssey* operate in Joyce's *Ulysses*. The narrative structure of *Paradiso* rests on its conveyance of an underworld, a topos more central to the Orphic myth than to the Homeric poem. Thus, the title *Paradiso* does not represent the narrator's Cuba; it points to a place outside of the narrative toward which Cemí's spirit—his *paideia*—moves. But the world of *Paradiso* is Orphic in the sense that, in the duality soul/body, sky/earth, heaven/hell, it belongs to the fallen dimension of existence. *Paradiso* stages a constant descent into an underworld from which Cemí only begins to emerge at the end, after the death of Oppiano Licario.

As a dualistic religion anticipating Gnosticism, Orphism believes in the divinity of the soul, and regards earthly existence as an accidental fall into sinful materiality, a descent figured by Orpheus's nocturnal trek into Hades to regain his "soul," symbolized by Eurydice. The way for the soul to climb back to heaven is through rituals of ecstasy and purification. Orphism is considered a variant of the Dyonisian cult: both the myths of Orpheus and Dionysus originated in Thrace.[64] The Orphics appeal more to Lezama because of the centrality of song and music—the *praxis* of poetry—in the myth. The doctrines of transmigration, resurrection, and afterlife propounded by this ritualistic faith are more adaptable to the Catholic dogmas of sin and fall, sacrament, expiation and redemption at stake in the theological arguments of Lezama's novel.

The essay that Lezama devotes to Orphism in *La cantidad hechizada* offers some clues as to how Lezama's poetic system amends Joyce's reliance on the Homeric poem. The reverence shown to Homer by both classical scholarship and the Joycean "modern" novel assumes an incompatibility between Homer and Orphism and "the mystery sects." The ecstatic rites of the Maenads "do not commend themselves to the unemotional nonsacramental Homeric tradition."[65] In his "Introducción a los vasos órficos," Lezama supersedes this discrepancy by positing the *Odyssey* as a derivation from the Orphic myth, as if Homer, instead of consulting the Phoenician *periploi*, had instead studied Apollonious' *Argonautica* or the Orphic hymns. Lezama thus reworks and rewrites the theories that situate the source of the myth of Orpheus in the Egyptian legend of the dismemberment of Osiris.[66] For Lezama, Odysseus is an outgrowth of Orpheus, and the Orphic dimensions of *The Odyssey* (the descents to earth by the gods and to hell by Odysseus) are the superior moments of the Homeric ethos and mythos. Orphism for Lezama is the Greek quintessence: the goal toward which *paideia* is mobilized.

> Aunque se le atribuye a Orfeo, a una regalía hecha a los pelasgos por iniciados egipcios, lo cierto es que el mito de Demeter lleva la dorada luz aprensible de lo homérico. Casi todos los vasos órficos responden a esa proyección del mundo homérico sobre el orfismo: Orfeo ha sido reemplazado por Ulises, y en lugar de relegar el período órfico prearcádico, se deja invadir por las visitas, reconocimientos, sombras paseadoras, madres que aconsejan el regreso a la luz, del descenso del Laertíada fecundo en recursos. (*OC* 2: 854)

[Even though the myth of Orpheus is thought of as an offering Egyptian initiates make to the Pelasgians, the truth is that the myth of Demeter holds within itself the tangible, golden Homeric light. Almost all the Orphic tales respond to this projection of the Homeric world upon the Orphic: Ulysses has replaced Orpheus, and instead of reflecting the pre-Arcadian Orphic period, he allows itself to be invaded by visitors, recognitions, passing shadows, mothers that counsel a return to the light from the descent of Laertes' son, rich in cunning.]

Lezama thus finds no contradiction in following the system of Homeric correspondence promoted by *Ulysses* and representing a documented Orphic vision in a contemporary novel. For Lezama, Orphic dualism is the best expression of the Homeric *epos* since it makes the hero's voyage a double movement of ascent and descent, sacralizing man and humanizing the gods. Lezama's erudite discussion of the crucial role of "canto" [song] and "sombra" [darkness] in Orphism at the beginning of his essay illustrates these counter-displacements. Rejecting the notion of Orphism as a purely ecstatic, carnal religion of no superior spiritual ideal, Lezama writes:

> El orfismo nunca se contentó con la hipóstasis en el reino de los sentidos, de una esencia o figura divinal derivada a la presencia de los dioses de la naturaleza, establecía como un círculo entre el dios que desciende y el hombre que asciende como dios. Impregna esas dos espirales, que se complementan en un círculo, en la plenitud de un *hierus logos*, es decir, en un mundo de total alcance religioso, mostrado en una teogonía donde el hombre surge como un dios, coralino gallo de las praderas bienaventuradas. (*OC* 2: 853)

> [Orphism was never satisfied with the hypostasis into a carnal kingdom; using a spirit or divine figure derived from the ever-present gods of nature, it established a kind of cycle between the god that descends and the man that ascends like a god. It impregnates these two spirals (the ascending and the descending), which together form a circle in the plenitude of a *hierus logos*; in other words, a world of absolute religious reach, exhibited in a theogony where man emerges like a god, a coral rooster of the blessed plains.]

Here Lezama is glossing Homer's Telemachia. In order for Telemachus to rise and achieve the godlike virtue of *areté*, a goddess (Athena) needs to descend from heaven to assist in his purification. She does the same to help Odysseus in his quest of regaining a higher post in the cosmic hierarchy. Lezama's essay rejects the assumption of absolute separation and impenetrability between the realm of heaven (reason) and hell (the irrational) adopted in

Reyes's vision of the Orphic. Lezama believes Orphism to be the most genuine Greek religion because it hypostatizes a porosity, a permeability between heaven and hell that song and poetry can traverse like a beam of light through darkness. Although in process of separation, these realms are still in communication in the Orphic segments of Homeric epic. Lezama's Orphism is a doctrine of necessary salvation; the proof of Homer's Orphism is the ritual role of the god who comes down to assist in the return of the soul to the source (Orpheus journeys to rescue Eurydice; Hermes goes down with Odysseus to Hades; Athena accompanies him dressed in the most humiliating costumes). In this economy of salvation, the transaction descent-ascent has its culmination in the "death" that the demi-god suffers as he strips himself of his divinity in his descent. To Lezama, Orphism is thus a theogony: in the sacrifice of Orpheus, man is rewarded with poetry (after his dismemberment, Orpheus's head is thrown into the sea with his lyre, floats from Thrace down to Lesbos, and, still singing, becomes an oracle)[67] to help him regain his original divine being. For Lezama, Orphism is Greece's point of intersection with Catholicism. Sacramental and salvational, it explains the crucifixion as a necessary deicide which facilitates man's ascent to his true angelic being. Lezama's Orphism regards earthly existence as infernal, and presumes a continuous two-way commute between the terrestrial Hades and the stellar realm. This ongoing contact is exemplified in the ubiquitous presence of the Orphic song, in its capacity to charm both the deities in heaven and the gnomes of hell.

In *Paradiso*, Cemí is the divine soul caught in Hades who requires release, and Oppiano is the Athenaic "god" who descends to assist him in his voyage back to the ether. Notions of Orphic ecstasy abound in *Paradiso*—the descent into the flesh is a necessary sacramental moment in the process of purification before returning to the One-before-the-Fall. But perhaps the most explicit identification of Cemí with the Orphic in the novel occurs in the poem Fronesis dedicates to Cemí. Fronesis acts as an anticipatory tutorial figure in *Paradiso*; like John the Baptist with Christ, Fronesis "announces" Oppiano's coming. Most of *Paradiso*'s meditations on Fronesis's diamantine virtue gloss the mysterious, selfless motivation that drives him to write "Retrato de José Cemí" [Portrait of José Cemí]. Fronesis's poem to Cemí crystallizes the highest expression of his *areté*; it is also the clearest statement of Cemí's Orphic orientation.

María Zambrano has recognized the Orphic symbolic movement of descent and ascent in Lezama's poetry. Zambrano writes: "[En

Lezama] la poesía atraviesa, sí, la zona de los sentidos, mas para llegar a sumergirse en el oscuro abismo que los sustenta. Antes que le sea permitido ascender al mundo de las formas idénticas en la luz, ha de descender a los infiernos, de donde Orfeo la rescató dejándola a medias prisionera. Y así la poesía habitará como verdadera intermediaria en el obscuro mundo infernal y en el de la luz, donde las formas aparecen" [In Lezama's work, poetry does traverse the realm of the senses, but it is to become submerged in the dark abyss that sustains that realm. Before poetry is permitted to ascend to the world of forms made identical in light, it is required to go down to Hades, from which Orpheus rescued her, leaving her half-prisoner. And thus poetry shall live as the true intermediary in both the dark, infernal world and in the world of light where forms are made].[68] Zambrano's observations—written eighteen years before the publication of *Paradiso*—apply to the trascendentalist dynamics of "Retrato de José Cemí." In Fronesis's lyrical "portrait" (the term is not fortuitous) of Cemí, Cemí is described as "paying reverence to friends and melody," "and loyal to Orpheus and Proserpine." Fronesis discovers Cemí's poetic strength in his capacity for dealing with the basest of material elements while continuing to extract, like Orpheus with Eurydice, the spark of the divine trapped within. Cemí's poetic will seeks "un cuerpo en la sombra" [a form in the shadows], even in the shadow of the tree standing "a la entrada del infierno" [in the gates of Hell]. Despite this journey into darkness, Cemí's Orphism is not ecstatic or orgiastic; rather than a violent, cathartic purification of the flesh through rituals of excess, what the poem describes in Cemí is the equilibrium of stoic serenity (Reyes's treasured *sofrosyné*) in the midst of the "fevers" of Orphic Nature: "la naturaleza le regaló su calma y su fiebre / Calmoso como la noche, / la fiebre le hizo agotar la sed / en ríos sumergidos . . . / Así todo lo que creyó en la fiebre, / lo comprendió después calmosamente." [Nature bestows her calm, her fever. / Calming as the night, / the fever made him quench his thirst / in sunken rivers . . . / So that everything he believed in fever / he later understood in calm.] (*P* 334–35/*R* 338–39).

The synthetic equilibrium between the Orphic feverish seizure and the poised, Homeric restraint is expressed in Fronesis's renaming of Cemí in the poem: "Su nombre es tambien Thelema Semí" [His name is also Thelema Semí]. Cintio Vitier has proposed a long list of possible interpretations for his appelation, ranging from Rabelais's use of the alchemic term "thelema" to the seer Telemus who predicts Cyclop's fate in the eighth rhapsody of the *Odyssey*.[69] Vitier misses the simpler and more elegant possibility of reading

Thelema as an abbreviation for Telemachus. Fronesis's poem represents Cemí as the son of an Orphic Odysseus by linking the Homeric onomastic (Telemachus) with the resonance of the Orphic theorem of *söma-sema* encoded in Cemí's last name. Scholars have indicated that Orphism "is characterized by its *söma-sema*, or body-tomb concept, which sees the body as a prison or tomb in which the soul—a divine element, akin to the gods—is incarcerated."[70] The name *Thelema Semí* illustrates the soul's journeys between heaven and the body-tomb.

Thus arises the possibility of picturing a Joycean schema for *Paradiso* where elements of the myth of Orpheus are grafted onto the narrative schema of the *Odyssey* so as to capitalize on what Lezama regards as "el perfeccionamiento de los símbolos en el momento en que Ulises desciende al sombrío Hades" (*OC* 2: 857) [the perfection of symbols at the point when Odysseus descends into the somber Hades]. The logical closure of the Orphic correspondences in *Paradiso*'s mythical method lies in the transfiguration of Oppiano Licario into Pythagoras. The prominence of Pythagorian doctrine and numerology is evident in many passages of *Paradiso*, most of which feature Licario: the text's lyrical pronouncements on the hermetic powers of the ten Pythagorean numbers in Cemí and Fronesis's "choral" symposium in chapter 11; the many references to the Pythagorean geometrical *portezuelas* [ritual doors] leading to the astral region in chapter 14. As a "mysteriosophical" movement that followed Orphism in Samos and Delphos, Pythagoreanism sought a consequential and methodical application of Orphic doctrine and ritual—it adopted the Orphic dualist vision of the divinity of the soul by incorporating the Orphic myths of metempsychosis and purification into its philosophical system, but attenuated the ecstatic bachanals with fasting and submission to the ordered and ordering "influences" of numerology and astrology.[71]

The focus on Oppiano Licario in the conclusion of *Paradiso* is conspicuous in a novel where he has been for the most part a hidden character. In chapter 14, Oppiano is seen in the context of a nurturing family life, preaching moderation and happy with his destiny, with no resentment toward his rivals, and satisfied with his anonymity, despite the danger of becoming insane because of his genius. Oppiano's hermetic and superhuman wisdom is conveyed in his exact answers to the grueling, even absurd questions of a baccalaureate oral examination. In chapter 13 he demonstrates his knowledge of the occult in the dietetic suggestions he makes to women in a bus. He is able to tell the specific time a poem is written according to the metrical rhythm of verses selected to designate an hour. He dies in peace, and the philosophical treatise he spent his life writing, the *Súmula nunca infusa de excepciones morfológicas* [Never Infused Summa of Morphological Exceptions], is mostly destroyed by a hurricane in the sequel to *Paradiso, Oppiano Licario*.

The life story of Oppiano Licario is modeled after the biographies of Pythagoras written by Porphyry, Iambichus, and Diogenes Laertes.[72] Pythagoras travels from the island of Samos to study with the Egyptians; Oppiano travels from Cuba to Europe and the United States for his studies. As a young man, Pythagoras was known to have dazzled his Egyptian examiners with precision and the range of his knowledge, like Oppiano in *Paradiso*'s examination scene in chapter 14. Like Pythagoras's, Oppiano's teachings continued to succeed after his death and in spite of his failure to leave behind a manuscript with his doctrines. In the biographies, Pythagoras's failure to transfer his doctrine through a written vehicle is a very contested point. Porphyry, Iambichus, and Diogenes Laërtes debate the existence of extant manuscripts by Pythagoras, and conclude that, even if Pythagoras did write, his teachings were "imparted by word of mouth," disseminated by followers or by the persistence of Pythagoras's ghostly, mystical presence after his death. Pythagoras possesses the knowledge of his former incarnations in the cycle of his soul's transmigrations, which explains his (and Licario's) immediate access to a core of wisdom unavailable to the mind of one human existence. Pythagoras leads Orphism toward an ordered view of the universe; Oppiano, in his mystical absence, will lead José Cemí to realize José Lezama Lima's "poetic system of the world."

The centrality of music in Pythagorean education is one of the aspects of Pythagorean culture that Jaeger best documents in *Paideia*.[73] Pythagoras's view of music as emanations of cosmic numerological patterns—the "harmony of the spheres"—and his conception of "musical education" as the highest form of instruction, determine the initiatory pedagogical gesture of Oppiano, who greets the student Cemí by beating the hesychastic style on a metal triangle. The Pythagorean belief in the soul's substance as an astral emanation of the constellations, and in the soul's eventual return to these luminous configurations, explains the stellar thrust in the imagery of *Paradiso*. This "constellatory" imagery can also be traced to *Ulysses'* "Ithaca," the "chapter of arrival," where the still, objective, sidereal poetry of the prose boosts Stephen and Bloom into the stars of the abstract heavens.

Oppiano's Pythagorean line of descent is not perfectly linear;

some ironic distortion occurs as a result of novelistic parody. Though Bloom has been said to embody many of Odysseus's qualities, he is a parodic and humane reversal of the grand heroism of the protagonist of the *Odyssey*. Lezama's own, ironic twist in his parodic adaptation of Pythagoras in Oppiano lies in the annulment of Pythagoras's stringent dietetic restrictions. Oppiano is represented as a discriminating *gourmet* who rhapsodizes about food with oracular expressions, in striking and humorous contrast to Pythagoras, who warned against feeding on flesh and overeating; yet, Oppiano's gastronomical enthusiasms show more Pythagorean mettle and sophistication than an outright Epicurean or sybaritic release into gluttony.

IV

The Orphic and Pythagorean bent of *Paradiso* does not displace or overwhelm the application of the Homeric epic model in the novel; one qualifies the other. The Joycean pastiche of the classical epic operates implicitly throughout *Paradiso*, and explicitly in a number of scenes. *Paradiso*'s clearest appropriation of the Homeric epic mode, consonant with *Ulysses*' mythical method, happens, however, in the story of Atrio Flaminio featured in chapter 12 (*P* 368, 373–74, 380–82, 390–93, 398). Flaminio's story is one of the several recurring nightmares José Cemí has after his father's death. In this tale, a Roman captain of a legion—a figure of Homeric measure and rationality who embodies the highest qualities of *areté*— confronts and is eventually defeated by the infernal creatures of an Orphic mythology. He is also a dream-simile for the colonel, Cemí's father.

Heading a Roman crusade against oriental superstition and unruliness during the *pax octaviana*, Atrio Flaminio successfully conducts three "battles." He suppresses a revolt of a Greek city-state in Mileto modeled after Sparta and addicted to athletic games. He defeats a plague of flying ghosts in Thessaly and Etruria. He prevents the infernal spirits of a Larisa cemetery from mutilating the corpses of Roman soldiers on their way to Hades. Flaminio is an example of the persistence of Greek virtue in the midst of Roman decadence; he defeats his enemies with the Odysseus-like cunning of the gifted strategist (his tricks are as clever as the ploy of the Trojan horse in the *Iliad*), yet shows the defeated the magnanimity and benevolence expected, according to Jaeger, from the most refined in *areté*. Flaminio protects his virtue by shielding himself from

the corruption of the East invading the Empire; he resists all oriental influences with the exception of the Chinese respiratory exercises which he adopts as part of his daily exercises. Flaminio's
Homeric spirit is expressed by the fact that he worships Athena,
not Minerva, and thus represents unaltered Hellenism within the
syncretism of Greek and Roman mythology and attitudes. Flaminio's battle tactics demonstrate the Greek roots of Roman military
culture. He celebrates the conclusion of one conflict with the staging of an Olympiad-like sports competition instead of calling for a
Roman circus. Imitating the practice of military leaders during the
Apollonian period of Greek civilization, he consults the Pythian oracle at Delphos to figure out his strategy against the airborn, ecto-
plasmic wizards of Thesally. Nevertheless, Flaminio's resolve—the
areté that makes him godlike—is broken by the implacable forces
of Hades and the Orient issuing from Capadocia, which infect him
with a mortal disease (a parallel to the flu that kills the colonel).
Flaminio is condemned to undergo the Orphic descent into Hell
and confront the mauled figures of the soldiers of his legion who
had fought the forces of Hades under his leadership. In a last Orphic twist to the epic story, Flaminio's soul transmigrates into the
body of the musicologist Juan Longo in a metempsychotic circle in
which the noble military hero (the first exhibitor of *areté* in Jaeger's
Greek teleology) is merged with the musician (the ultimate pur-
veyor of *areté* in the Orphic and Pythagorean *paideic* orientation).

The conflicts implicit in this miniature epic, grafted onto the textual dynamics of *Paradiso*, allegorize the debates that energized the
scholarship on classical Greece in Lezama's time: the dispute between superstition and reason, between Hellenism and oriental-
ism, between East and West, between the Apollonian and the
Dionysian, between Homer and Orpheus. Lezama's fiction
searches for a syncretic middle point in the dispute, taking the Orphic position that regards the clash between *areté* and *nemesis*, between the stellar and the infernal, as the irresolvable condition of
earthly existence. Armed with the tools of *areté*, Flaminio fights the
irrational chthonic entities, but death defeats him: he must compromise with Orphism in the underworld. He is resurrected, and
reappears as Juan Longo, the Orphic musician who defeats time.
In the symbolic order of Orphic metempsychosis in *Paradiso*, Juan
Longo also incarnates Cemí's father and Oppiano Licario. Partak-
ing of the Orphic and oniric elements in Joyce's *Finnegans Wake*,
Paradiso thus stages a merging juxtaposition of funerals, where the
corpse in the coffin undergoes dazzling, protean metamorphoses
before Cemí's gaze: the colonel becomes Oppiano who becomes

Flaminio who becomes Juan Longo who becomes the colonel. All of these figures are dreamlike projections of one single ur-wake, just as Bloom in *Ulysses* is the binding nexus of multiple deities and symbolic figures.

Lezama's Orphism is positioned between Cortázar and Carpentier's Dionysian view and Borges and Reyes's more Apollonian interpretation of Greek classicism. The staging of classical motifs in Lezama's syncretistic cosmology is meant to be the specular image of the polar confrontation between angels and demons in Catholic eschatology. Lezama applies Orphic dualism to his vision of a Christian universe, using Greek mythology to characterize the distinctions between benign divinities and evil spirits in Catholic dogma: Athena and St. Michael on one side, the Maenads and Lucifer on the other. In fact, Lezama uses the Greek and Roman pantheons to elaborate the intricate demonology of his novel—its catalog of "diosecillos" [minor gods] and "demonios" [demons]—and his view of hell, which is more pagan, more Orphic, than Christian.

Thus, in both *Paradiso* and *Ulysses* the use of the Greek motifs is not a mechanical support for narrative, but has a cosmological import. As in Joyce, there is in Lezama a reconfiguration of a Catholic cosmos through the strategic defamiliarization of dogma through references to pagan syncretism. Catholic orthodoxy in *Paradiso* and *Ulysses* is refashioned by means of the symbolic employment of heresy. Like Joyce, Lezama achieves a studied syncretism of pagan mythology and Christian angeology and hagiography, using classical allusions to create a more intricate scholastic vision.

In conclusion, Lezama does not adopt Joycean technique arbitrarily; he absorbs *Ulysses'* mythical method. Dedalus-Cemí is Telemachus in search of the spirit of his father under the mentorship of Bloom-Oppiano Licario. These pagan motifs are organized and hypostasized in the narrative by means of the principal images of Catholic dogma. Joyce manipulates the mystery of the Trinity in the relationship formed by Stephen, Bloom, and Molly; Lezama mirrors this gesture in the Cemí, Fronesis, and Foción triangle, and in the Oppiano Licario-Inaca Eco-Cemí configuration developed in the sequel to *Paradiso*, *Oppiano Licario*. Lezama expands the mythical method to include other schemas: Cemí is also Orpheus going down to Hades in search of his own Eurydice: his poetic vocation. In *Paradiso*, the Orphic myths thus play a role similar to that which the *Odyssey* plays in *Ulysses*. Finally, Joyce's novel can be taken as a model for *Paradiso*'s intertextual, mythological complexity since *Ulysses* does not restrict itself to the *Odyssey* for its form but relies on many other mythical schemas, as Richard Ellmann's *Ulysses on the Liffey* can testify.[74]

4

Oppianos Wake: Vico, Resurrection, and Neologisms in *Finnegans Wake* and *Oppiano Licario*

I

A TURNING POINT IN JORGE LUIS BORGES'S REEVALUATION OF JAMES Joyce's work—the point at which he shifts from enthusiastic approval of Joycean experimentation and erudition to a critique of what he calls Joyce's "baroque vanity"—occurs with his reading of the first installments of *Work in Progress* (the early version of *Finnegans Wake*) published in Eugene Jolas's journal *transition*.[1] In the 1939 article in *Sur* on *Work in Progress* entitled "Joyce y los neologismos" [Joyce and Neologisms], Borges's growing ambivalence toward Joyce is apparent in the metaphor he uses to describe the use of neologisms in *Finnegans Wake*.[2] Borges claims that Joyce's systematic fabrication of compound terms represents the core of the novel's technical inventiveness: "Es sabido que el rasgo más evidente de *Work in Progress* (que ahora se titula *Finnegans Wake*) es la metódica profusión de *port-manteau words*. . . . [En esto] reside la novedad de James Joyce" (160) [The most striking element of *Work in Progress* (which now is called *Finnegans Wake*) is the methodical profusion of portmanteau words. . . . Here lies James Joyce's novelty.] Although in his essay Borges uses several technical literary terms to describe neologism as a rhetorical device ("jitanjáfora," "portmanteau," "calembours," "retruécanos"), from the opening sentence he consistently refers to these puns as "monstruos verbales" [verbal monsters]. He reiterates this teratological metaphor—"these monsters," "another one of Joyce's monsters," "Ariachne's monstrous name"—up to the article's very conclusion. Borges had used this same concept of verbal monstrosity in *El idioma de los argentinos* (1928) to describe the "aberrations" of Góngora's poetry.[3]

132

To Borges, the "novelty" of *Finnegans Wake* is monstruous because its neologisms spring from a hybridization of language that shatters the classical harmony he had begun to privilege in his essays of the thirties and forties. Borges thus regards neologisms as linguistic corruptions or mutations, transgressions against the elementary structures of language. Nevertheless, in "Joyce y los neologismos" Borges still recognizes that despite this monstrous strain there is aesthetic value—although he qualifies it as "débil" [weak] (160)—to punning neologisms. Reviewing some of the "precursors" of the language manipulations in *Finnegans Wake*, he recalls Laforgue's calembours, which he describes as "hermosos y precisos monstruos verbales" [beautiful and precise verbal monsters]. Borges implies that *Finnegans Wake* continues the tradition of Laforgue's poetic triumph on a grander scale: "Laforgue . . . hizo del juego de palabras un instrumento lírico o elegíaco; en el vertiginoso *Finnegans Wake* este procedimiento es constante." (162) [Laforgue . . . made wordplay into a lyrical, elegiac instrument; in the vertiginous *Finegans Wake* this is a constant procedure.] Borges seems to accept with some reluctance that even though Joyce's neologisms are the product of semantic convolution and grammatical distortion, they *do* have literary merit. *Finnegans Wake*'s wordplay can be "terrible y majestuoso" (162) [awe inspiring and majestic] in some of its best segments.

The success of this strategy, however, depends on the tightness of diction and the flow and rhythm of a *sequence* of neologisms. Borges's example from the novel ("flick as flowflakes, litters from aloft, like a waast wizzard all of whirlworld. . . . Pride, O pride, they prize") demonstrates that he is more impressed by the "lyrical or elegiac" atmospheric sonority of the alliterative language of *Finnegans Wake* than by the semantic complexity of its neologisms. Viewed singly, Joyce's neologisms feel forced, unaccomplished, clumsy, or obvious. So says Borges after listing and explaining a random dozen and a half of these, dictionary-style: "Esos monstuos, así incomunicados y desarmados, resultan más bien melancólicos. Algunos . . . son meros *calembours* que no exceden las módicas posibilidades de Hollywood." (161) [These monsters, thus isolated and disarmed, become somewhat melancholy. Some of them . . . are mere *calembours* that fail to exceed the limited talents of Hollywood.][4]

Although Borges's article does not completely condemn the aesthetic project of *Finnegans Wake,* and in fact approaches the text with restrained enthusiasm, it bears the initial signs of the disappointment that is to become more pronounced in his later references to Joyce's work. The few, cautious words of praise in "Joyce y los neologismos" have misled some critics to think that Borges's assessment of *Finnegans Wake* is a positive one.[5] Borges's first piece on *Finnegans Wake* remains ambigious about the work's aesthetic achievement, though it succeeds in conveying the text's Babel-like, encyclopedic multiplicity. Despite its brevity (or because of it), "Joyce y los neologismos" is one of Borges's most densely erudite essays. In discussing the neologisms in *Finnegans Wake*, Borges refers to writers as diverse as Laforgue, Groussac, Swedenborg, Marcelino del Mazo, the Cuban Mariano Brull, and Edward Lear, and to works as disparate as Fischart's 1575 German translation of Rabelais's first book and the 1580 *Legend vom Ursprung*, a Latin translation of Lewis Caroll's *Jabberwocky* ballad, John Milton's *Samson Agonistes*, Shakespeare's *Troilus and Cressida*, Browne's "Urne Buriale," the ninth-century gospels, and Baltasar Gracián's *Criticón*. Interpreting the multilingual condensations in some of the neologisms in *Finnegans Wake* allows Borges to show off his versatility as a polyglot; he examines some very complex, hybrid word plays in Spanish, Latin, French, English, and German. Despite its erudite revelry, the article, however, neither clearly approves nor disapproves of *Finnegans Wake*.

Borges's vacillation becomes more evident when we compare "Joyce y los neologismos" with the exegetical sources that inspired the article. Following the pattern of "critical dependence" in Latin American commentary on European modernism that we have explained in earlier chapters, Borges's brief explications of neologisms in *Finnegans Wake* are based on "mediatory" essays by Stuart Gilbert. Borges's article (although published in 1939) borrows many ideas—including the term "neologism" itself—from Stuart Gilbert's 1928 *transition* article entitled "Thesaurus Minusculus: A Short Commentary on a Paragraph From *Work in Progress*." This piece, Gilbert's second on *Finnegans Wake*, was reprinted in 1929 under a different title in the notorious first collection of essays on Joyce's last work, *Our Exagmination Round his Factification For Incamination of Work in Progress*. Here Gilbert "spells out" a number of the "synthetic words" featured in a segment of Joyce's last novel published in *transition* in 1927.[6] Borges's list of annotated neologisms appropriates several from Gilbert's "Thesaurus" ("fairyaciodes," "voise," "ameising," "eithou"). But although Borges adopts the hermeneutic strategy and the "dictionary" format of Gilbert's introduction to the novel, he does not reflect Gilbert's conviction regarding the artistic quality of each single neologism. What Gilbert reverentially qualifies as original, lasting achievements—"a miniature treasury of new-minted words" that could "in course of time pass into general currency" (18)—Borges regards as mostly flawed artifacts of dubious permanence.

In his own early references to Joyce, José Lezama Lima demonstrates a muted awareness of the debate inspired by the neologisms in *Finnegans Wake*. In "Muerte de Joyce," Lezama, like Borges, devalues and satirizes the linguistic experiments of Joyce's later work—the "language physics incarnated in the Berlitz phonograph" (*OC 2:* 236)—and focuses on the poetic aesthetic of *A Portrait* and the mythographical and eschatological construction of *Ulysses*. When challenging the tendentious "special kind of reader" who insists on regarding Joyce as a member of the avant-garde, "Muerte de Joyce" specifically deprecates the efforts of the critics of the *Exagmination* to justify the Babel-like obscurity of *Work in Progress*, obstinate "in creating a special Joyce, regarding him as Surrealism's big brother, imbued with all Romance languages, Greek and Latin, impenetrable, Babilonic, Rabelaisian, the progeny of lesser symbolists" (*OC 2:* 237). Nevertheless, if the subject of *Finnegans Wake* is briefly—albeit obliquely— present in "Muerte de Joyce," it resurfaces more forcefully and explicitly in the essays that comprise Lezama Lima's book *La cantidad hechizada* [The Measure of Enchantment, 1970], where Lezama begins to articulate his hermetic theory of the "eras imaginarias" [imaginary eras].[7]

First published in the December 1959 issue of *Islas*, the third essay of this series, "La imagen histórica" [The Historical Image], illustrates the crucial concept of the *imagen* [image] in Lezama's poetic system. The *imagen* in Lezama is a transcendental theological, cosmological, and cosmogonical fiction; it is the point at which a higher realm of being penetrates into the human, a projection of the "lo incondicionado" [the "non-conditioned"] over "la causalidad" [causality], of the "invisible" over the "visible." It is a fantastic conceit transcending logic and realism which nevertheless defines the mentality of a cultural period. When Lezama calls the *imagen* historical, he is not referring to its historicity or to its national or social circumstance; he is characterizing the *imagen* as something that shapes any human history defined by a theological and teleological belief in an Afterlife, a resurrection.

According to Lezama, the cluster of mythemes, emblems, symbols, tropes, or motifs that make the *imagen* never coheres into a homogeneous icon. It is rather a network—a system—of mutually supportive, proliferating metaphors that never become synthesized into one stable, decodable allegory. Thus the *imagen* always remains a mystery. The dragon of the Chinese, the Buddhist turtle that supports the world, the dying blood-sun of the Aztecs, the Immaculate Conception, and Eucharistic transubstantion of Catholicism are examples of what Lezama considers historical *imágenes*. These *imágenes* determine the course of civilizations as they organize the social and political structures of these civilizations upon the certainty of an afterlife. Thus, when Lezama chooses the label "imaginary eras," he speaks not of fictional but rather fiction-making eras. The societies of these epochs exercise an anti-Kantian, anti-Cartesian imagination—based on "lo imposible creíble" [the "believable-impossible"]—and live and flourish under the suggestions of this culture-defining, fantastic *imagen* of resurrection.[8]

Lezama's project in his essays of *La cantidad hechizada* is to discuss the imaginary eras together with the *imagen* that structures them. Eight of these eras are identified in the second chapter, "A partir de la poesía" [Starting from poetry]. Lezama's method is a mode of reverse cultural hermeneutics. Since the *imagen*—like the Hegelian *Geist*—shapes the historical direction and cultural production of an *era imaginaria*, it can be, despite its final incomprehensibility as an ungraspable mystery, approximately intuited and deducted—in Lezama's terms, "reduced"—from any number of surviving artistic, paleographical, or archaeological sources: an Oriental painting, a tapestry, a Flemish landscape, a religious temple, a passage from scripture, or a literary text.[9] Lezama begins "La imagen histórica" with a speculation on the conditions that permit both the historical (culture-generating) and the hermeneutic (interpretive) recognition of the *imagen*. These recognitions can only be achieved by overcoming two main obstacles. The first is "la extensión" [the "expanse"] or "lo indiferenciado" [the "non-differentiated"]—a condition of physical and spiritual blankness and homogeneity where mythical imagination cannot "fix its gaze" to achieve any visual concretization, and thus fails to apprehend the *imagen* in some productive clousure. Lezama writes: "la ausencia de diversidad es el primer muro que la imagen encuentra en su camino" [the absence of diversity is the first obstacle that the *imagen* has in its way" (*OC* 2: 843)]. Second, the *imagen* can also perish in a context of hyperdiversity—"la diversidad más pintarreteada" [the most garish diversity]—where the central, defining *imagen* can be lost in a proliferation of detail. Thus, the *imagen* can only be produced out of a polarized context, between the fierceness of extreme change and the cold starkness of sameness:

La imagen nace de esa hirviente polarización, en que la problecita pre-imagen, enredado en lo diverso o fláccida frente a la extensión, lanza un reflejo, un rayo de penetración y disfrute. (*OC 2:* 844–45)

[The *imagen* is born out of this boiling polarization in which, enmeshed in diversity or flaccidly confronting the expanse, the frail pre-*imagen* is able to cast a shimmer, a beam of insight and pleasure.]

Lezama illustrates this polarization with a description of a Buddhist picture of the stages that lead to Nirvana, which consists of three sets of antagonistic realms. The strident juxtapositions of contrasting icons (a tiger's eye set next to a tree, a pagoda terrace next to a burning forest) creates a dynamic, oscillating movement between fierceness and serenity, diversity and sameness. This movement is the *imagen*: the *imagen* "rueda de la extensión vegetativa al furor, una antítesis de imagen placentera frente a otra colérica, un árbol frente a un ojo de tigre, una terraza frente a las lanzas infernales" (*OC 2:* 845) [rolls from the vegetating expanse to the furor, in the antithesis between a peaceful image and a choleric one, a tree in front of the tiger's eye, a terrace in front of the infernal spears]. Lezama's first explicit reference to *Finnegans Wake* appears here in relation to the *imagen*, which, "flowing like a river" between the two oppositional plains, facilitates their potential union:

Y entre las dos parejas antitéticas, el río que fluye, que arrastra, que llega a los contemporáneos en el río del *Finnegan's* [sic] *Wake*, lleno de nombres de príncipes indios y de pequeños ríos irlandeses. Vemos en esas dos suertes corridas por la imagen, la coincidencia entre la vida eterna y la eterna vida. (*OC 2:* 845)

[And between the two antithetical pairs, a river flows that rises and razes, that reaches contemporary man in the river of *Finnegans Wake*, filled with the names of Indian princes and of small Irish streams. We can recognize, between these two fates experienced by the *imagen*, the coincidence of life eternal with the eternal life.]

Finnegans Wake reappears as an important reference in Lezama's essay on Julio Cortázar's novel *Rayuela* "Cortázar o el comienzo de la nueva novela" [Cortázar or the beginning of the new novel], which, with the autobiographical piece titled "Confluencias" [Confluences], concludes *La cantidad hechizada*. Lezama discusses the labyrinth-structure in *Rayuela* as an *imagen* that mediates between the human and the divine through the phenomenon that Lezama calls "antropofanía" [anthrophany]. Lezama refers to "la ensalada filológica del último Joyce" [the philological salad of the last Joyce] to describe the textual mechanisms of the novel, especially Cortázar's invention of *glíglico*, a nonsense language of fabricated words that Lezama considers a Joycean, *Work-in-Progress* form of esperanto, an "idioma universal de claves y raíces" [universal language of codes and roots].[10] Lezama writes:

> Ese laberinto [en *Rayuela*] se deja recorrer por un idioma ancestral, donde están los balbuceos del jefe de la tribu, y un esperanto, un idioma universal del claves y raíces, que se reduce del primero por una decantación analítica. En el idioma ancestral hay una interposición, la acumulación de lo inmediato verbal, detrás de las palabras de comunicación, se esconden o se entreabren otras que pesan tanto como su otra manifestación externa. Secuestrados latidos, contracciones, crujimientos, que respiran secretamente detrás de una extendida y visible masa verbal. El otro idioma, un esperanto universal, aquella ensalada filológica del último Joyce, que coloca detrás de lo inmediato verbal una infinita escenografía, un dilatado concentrismo que procede por dilatadas irradiaciones. El idioma ancestral tiende a solemnizar la expresión, a entiesarla por escayolada o cartoné de abuelidad. El otro idioma, la ensaladilla, tiende a ironizar, a presentar irreconocibles y sucesivos derivados como los cañutos de un anteojo. Entre ambos idiomas se tiende un laberinto donde los énfasis y las carcajadas, los juramentos y los manotazos se entrelazan en núcleos y en la infinitud de pliegues arenosos. (*OC 2:* 1192–93)

> [(Rayuela's) labyrinth allows itself to be flooded by an ancestral tongue, which holds the first stutterings of the chieftain within itself, and an Esperanto, a universal language of codes and roots that is derived from the first by means of analytical distillment. In the ancestral tongue there is an obstruction, the accumulated force of verbal immediacy; behind the words used for communicating, other words hide or almost surface, which carry as much weigh as their external form. Hidden rhythms, contractions, grating sounds, that breathe secretly behind an extended and visible verbal mass. The other language, the Esperanto, the philological salad of the last Joyce places behind the verbal immediacy an infinite scenery, a dilated concentrism that operates in expanding irradiations. The ancestral tongue tends to solemnize expression, to stiffen it in a cast of ancientness. The other language, Joyce's salad, tends to ironize, to introduce crypticisms and successive kaleidoscopic [word] derivations. Between both languages a labyrinth spreads where emphatic statements and guffaws, lofty pledges and handslaps are interwined into nucleii that multiply into an infinite rippling of sand.]

The difficult, foliating, baroque discourse of Lezama's essays in *La cantidad* enunciates a discrepancy with Borges's estimation of *Finnegans Wake* as a work exclusively concerned with neologistic word play. As with *Ulysses*, Lezama performs an in-depth reading of *Finnegans Wake* rather than an analysis of the "surface discourse" on which Borges focuses his critique. In the two fragments quoted above, *Finnegans Wake* is represented as an organic text that operates with a broader, unified mythopoetic ambition; here Joyce's work is not the quilt of patchwork neologisms—well-stitched in some corners, unravelling at most points—that Borges's fragmentary reading purports it to be.

In the first fragment, *Finnegans Wake* is associated with the work of the *imagen* as it reconciles contrary realms in its flow. Lezama highlights here the unifying symbol of language as water (rather than as monster) in *Finnegans Wake*—the "along the river run" motif that unites all the strands and reattaches the end to the beginning—overlooked by Borges. In the second fragment, Lezama's interpretation of "dilated, irradiating concentrism" of the language in *Finnegans Wake* contradicts Borges's isolated concept of neologism. Rather than expanding or dilating in meaning, Joyce's "word-monsters" in Borges's estimation appear to be suspended in the static solitude of convoluted signification. The passage above presents *Finnegans Wake*—a model, according to Lezama, for *Rayuela*'s use of language—as a type of ultimate language; not an arbitrary collection of puns or witticisms, but an esperanto, an expanding synthesis of human tongues that stands as an apotheosis of language on the end opposite that of the semi-articulate tribal language of origin. To the Alpha of the tribal *Ursprache*, *Finnegans Wake* juxtaposes an Omega, the culmination of linguistic evolution which, in a circular way, becomes labyrinthically reconnected with the gestural urgency and the vitality of the *Ursprache*. To Lezama, *Finnegans Wake* and *Rayuela* represent the end of a cycle of civilization and language that is about to begin anew; it is the proof of resurrection, the *ricorsi* after the *corsi*.[11]

The disparity between Lezama's in-depth reading of the later Joyce and the emphasis on verbal surface in Borges's interpretation stems from Lezama Lima's recognition of a structural influence in *Finnegans Wake* not acknowledged by Borges: the strategic use of the principles of Giambattista Vico's *Scienza Nuova*. In his reading of *Ulysses*, Lezama follows an "upgraded" mythical method taken from a critical reading of Eliot and Gilbert's positions on the novel, but in his references to *Finnegans Wake* he follows the critical arguments concerning the applicability of Viconian concepts in the novel's construction. As in their analysis of Joyce's earlier novels, Borges and Lezama's understanding of *Finnegans Wake* is mediated by European criticism. Borges's reading of *Finnegans Wake* is partly determined by the thesaurus-like emphasis on the *portmanteau* and the neological decipherings of Stuart Gilbert's second article. Lezama's, on the other hand, is probably influenced by Gilbert's first piece on *Work in Progress*—"Prolegomena to *Work in Progress*"—which stresses the Viconian element, and by Samuel Beckett's essay "Dante . . . Bruno. Vico . . . Joyce," both published in *transition* and reprinted in the *Exagmination*.[12]

Vico's influence on Joyce's work was documented by the literary critics of Lezama's time, especially during the period of Joycean enthusiasm in the forties. According to several theories drawn from a literal reading of Joyce's letters to Harriet Shaw, the key to Joyce's confoundingly hermetic last work was to be found in the principles of Vico's *New Science*.[13] When *Finnegans Wake* confronted critical accusations of impenetrability, Joyce took specific steps to release some of the codes of his experimental fiction among his circle of affiliates. In the case of *Ulysses*, Joyce turned to Valery Larbaud and Stuart Gilbert to "leak" the Homeric schema; with *Finnegans Wake*, Joyce furnished Gilbert and Beckett with information to establish the Viconian structure of the novel.[14] According to their accounts, *Finnegans Wake* is to be read as a full-blown dramatization of many of the most controversial ideas of the *New Science*: the historical *corsi* and *ricorsi* of culture; the four ages (theocratic, heroic, vulgar, and decadent) of man; the poetic origin of language in both its oral and written mode; the role of barbarism and gigantism in the prehistory of the all great pagan civilizations; the historical, factual, nonallegorical character of classical myth; and the anti-archaic dimensions of philology. *Finnegans Wake* performs in its fiction the cycle of the four Viconian phases of mankind's development in a phantasmagoric, oneiric Ireland, much like *Ulysses* is a reenactment of the *Odyssey* in contemporary Dublin.[15]

"The subject of *Work in Progress* may be easiest grasped by a reference to Vico's *Scienza nuova*," writes Gilbert. "James Joyce's new Work, in fact, is, in one of its aspects, a realization of the Italian philosopher's conception of an ideal history [whose] eternal law all nations observe in their beginnings and developments" (53).[16] Vico's "theory of the origins of poetry and language, the significance of myth, and the nature of barbaric civilization," Beckett notes, are "aspects that have their reverberations, their reapplications . . . in *Work in Progress*" (4–5). Gilbert and Beckett argue that

Finnegans Wake adopts Vico's cyclical notion of human history as a fixed, constellatory "rotating progress," and explain the unstable, shifting constitution of the central "characters" HCE (H. C. Earwicker or Here Comes Everybody) and Ana Livia Plurabelle (both HCE's wife and the *anima* of the river Liffey) as the exemplification of Vico's understanding of the exclusively symbolic nature of the history-making, outstanding individual during the heroic age. According to Vico, the initial poverty of human language prompted young tribes to use the same name for all individuals who shared a common virtue (Achilles for bravery, Odysseus for shrewdness, Caesar for convenience). In time this practice was discontinued and became "corrupted" into the idea that these collective names had been actual historical agents when in fact the achievements attributed to each were dispersed across many generations. Joyce adopts this theory in his experimental fiction by telescoping multiple personalities and personifications into the "public," animistic-heroic-vulgar shifting personas of HCE and ALP, which nevertheless retain the archetypical, symbolic consistency of Vico's heroic names.

Gilbert also argues that *Finnegans Wake* replays the *Scienza nuova*'s eccentric yet scripture-faithful interpretation of pagan genesis. In Vico's bold metanarrative of origin, after the biblical deluge, pagan people survived as giants who roamed the earth like animals without any social organization, until they were "terrified into shame and justice" by the first thunderstorms, which formed when "the earth began to dry" two centuries after the Great Flood. The fear generated by the first thunder lighted the first spark of human consciousness in the form of an animistic and superstitious imagination that "understood" the rumbling sky to be the angry body of the first pagan god, Jove. This first event unleashed a process of cultural and historical development leading to the full-fledged evolution of every gentile civilization (*New Science* 110–20): the frightened giants hid and established the first cave dwellings; in settling down they limited their relations to one partner and thus created the first human institution, marriage; sedentary life induced the adoption of land as feudal property and the first form of writing in family seals or "coats of arms" as a way of marking an estate; class conflict arose as society was divided into heroes (patricians or nobles pretending to descend from the gods) and plebeians (former barbarians who settled as serfs in the estates of the more advanced families). *Finnegans Wake*'s plot is thus patterned after Vico's "providential" schema, beginning with its primal cause: a thunderclap. Gilbert: "It is significant that *Work in Progress* opens with a crash of thunder" (53). Beckett: "In the beginning was the thunder" (5).

Beckett's discussion of the Brunian element in both *La Scienza Nuova* and *Work in Progress* is reflected in Lezama's first qualification of the late Joyce in *La cantidad hechizada*. Beckett argues that Vico's cyclical vision results from his unacknowledged adoption of Giordano Bruno's principle of the identity of opposites. The last stage of Vico's historical schema, which marks a tendency toward societal "interdestruction," is followed by regeneration and the "replay" of the three former phases. "At this point," says Beckett, "Vico applies Bruno's . . . philosophical abstraction. There is no difference, says Bruno, between the smallest possible chord and the smallest possible arc, no difference between the infinite circle and the straight line. The maxima and minima of particular contraries are one and indifferent. . . . The maximum of corruption and the minimum of generation are identical; in principle, corruption is generation. . . . From these considerations Vico evolved a Science and Philosophy of History" (5–6). *Finnegans Wake* is a textual stage on which opposite phases of civilization meet to recommence riverlike cycles of gradualist differentiation. In the chapter and "character" structure of *Finnegans Wake*—moving from Finnegan to HCE to HCE's children Shem and Shaun—Joyce incarnates the evolution of human mentality from superstitious gigantism to religious heroism to humanistic philosophy and back to barbarism.

This Brunian-Viconian vision is also present in Lezama's essay, "La imagen histórica." The "el río lleno de nombres" [riverful of names] of *Finnegans Wake* flows to join antithetical couples, "arrastrando" [leveling] superficial contradictions. The sense of *ricorsi* is further communicated by the fact that, according to Lezama, *Finnegans'* textual river carries archaic symbols and emblems smoothly into the contemporary present, assuring a cyclical continuity and identity between modernity and antiquity. The river runs and drags in its wake the "nombres de príncipes indios y de pequeños ríos irlandeses" [names of ancient, primitive princes and sacred rivers] that reach contemporary man. In Lezama's text, *Finnegans Wake*'s effect is described as that of a Brunian coincidence of opposites, and its *ricorsi* represents the conjunction of regeneration and resurrection, the possible indistinction between "la vida eterna" (the spiritual afterlife) and "la eterna vida" (the everlasting, ever-renewing biological life).

Lezama's other reference to *Finnegans Wake* in *La cantidad hechizada,* on the other hand, reflect Gilbert and Beckett's observations concerning the compatibility between *Finnegans Wake*'s linguistic experimentation and the *Scienza nuova*'s vision of the origin of language. *Scienza nuova* corroborates Vico's ideal history by studying linguistic evolution in the contexts of etymological and lexical scarcity. In the theocratic age, language was not capable of abstract functions (such as allegory, symbolism, or logic); nevertheless, because of this inevitable concreteness, this first language was, by necessity, poetic. The scarcity of words during this age required that one word be used to identify several objects in nature. Metonymy and synecdoche were the first tropes of language, but they had a purely denotative, nonsymbolic function in the effort of imaginatively "stretching" out the few existing terms. These tropes then lead to an elaborate metaphoric economy that eventually drove human thinking into philosophical abstraction. In Beckett's example (taken from the 1732 edition of *La Scienza nuova*), the term "lex" begins depicting an immediate thing in nature (a crop of acorns). It is then transferred synecdochically to a compound object (a tree of acorns). Then it is associated metonymically to a human activity ("legere" as gathering), metaphorically to an analogous physical action ("lex" as people-gathering or assembly), and to a symbolic one ("legere" as to gather letters together in reading), and, finally, to an abstraction ("lex" as law).

Vico thus "denies the dualism of poetry and language," writes Beckett. For Vico, language is a late cultural product; it is less varied and diverse than what is assumed because words, in the course of human history, have had to serve "poetically" as signifiers for multiple, ramifying signifieds. Any single language is thus not an ideal nomenclature (Vico does not believe any single language has achieved absolute meaning), but the history of all idioms follows similar patterns of denomination. All languages evolve from muteness to expression, from emblems to symbols, from names to concepts, and thus are structurally equivalent. Most, in fact, share some elementary units. According to Vico, "pa" is in all languages an expression of fear and signifies god or the father; "jus" signifies law in Latin, Greek and German (*New Science* 148). Vico thus thought it conceivable to collapse all languages into one synthetic language since all had the same history and since philology told the same semantic story in every variant and dialect. Gilbert writes: "Vico's work . . . is preoccupied with the root-meaning of words (their associative rather than strictly etymological implications) and he contemplated the formation of a 'mental vocabulary' whose object would be to explain all the languages that exist by an ideal synthesis of their varied expressions. [A]fter two centuries, such a synthesis . . . is being realized by James Joyce in his latest work."

The Joycean neologism is thus the crystalization of the *New Science*'s philological project, for it clusters and fuses into single terms the equivalent "root-meanings" of several languages in its rigorous polyglossia. To Gilbert, *Finnegans Wake* is not written in English, but in a hybrid, multilingual dialect that draws foreign terms into its discourse, not to confound the reader but to illuminate the primordial commonality of all tongues. Lezama adopts this interpretation when he calls Cortázar's *glíglico* and the "word-salad" of *Finnegans Wake* a "universal root-idiom": "un idioma universal de claves y raíces." Furthermore, although to Gilbert the neologisms of *Finnegans Wake* are elements of aesthetic modernity, they are innovative precisely because they destabilize the contemporary abstract use of language through an antiquarian attention to the archaic, objective "root-meaning" of the lexical and phonetic units that compose them. Thus, to Gilbert, the neologisms of the *Wake* are Joyce's most accomplished instance of correspondence between content and form (a critical theme in Gilbert' study of *Ulysses*), since word structure itself is mutated in order to find a primitive, objective, magical, pseudo-onomatopoeic bond between the new term and the series of objects-concepts it describes. "The verbal difficulty and the literary device employed by Joyce is not . . . a mere caprice or tour de force, it has its justification in the origins of human speech . . . In carefully adapting his words to his subject-matter, Joyce is not performing a mere conjuring-trick with the immense vocabulary he has at his command but is going back to the original and natural methods of human speech." Beckett argues as well that the discourse of *Finnegans Wake* is an artistic, modern reconstruction of the original poetic language, in that it recovers the original's "direct expression." The Joycean neologism recaptures the gestural vitality, the metaphorical inventiveness, and the elemental concreteness of the first language: "Mr. Joyce has desophisticated [the English] language [which before had been] abstracted to death . . . [i.e.] Mr. Joyce recognizes how inadequate 'doubt' is to express a state of extreme uncertainty and replaces it by 'in twosome twinminds.' Here is the savage economy of hieroglyphics . . . with all the inevitable clarity of the old inarticulation" (15).

Lezama's account of the new language of *Finnegans Wake* (as reflected in *Rayuela*) incorporates Gilbert's "root-language" concept and Beckett's "direct expression." In Lezama's description, the Joycean neologism, which "mixes" word-stems in "salad-form," assumes the shape of a "dilating concentrism" where the "lo inmediato verbal" [the "immediate" synthetic term] irradiates an "infinite" series of meanings, like the ever-widening ripples of a stone cast on the pond of language. As the neologism simultaneouly incorporates into one expression the contemporary, archaic, and polyglossic meaning of several "roots" through punning, it conveys at once the layered meanings accrued through their history and produces, through the juxtapositions of this chain of meanings, new poetic configurations, multiplying like a kaleidoscope. Because of the limitless ripple effect of neologisms, Lezama does not pretend to gloss them in thesaurus form as Borges does. Lezama thus heeds Gilbert's warning in "Thesaurus minusculus" about the endless signifying potential—Lezama's "infinita escenografía"—of Joycean neologisms: "The commentary, however, does not claim to be exhaustive. . . . One of the fascinations of reading *Work in Progress* is that as a mine of suggestion and allusion it is practically inexhaustible" (67). Borges instead insists upon the limited, stagnant quality of most Joycean wordplay.

Like Beckett's, Lezama's characterization of *Finnegans Wake* argues for its recovery—not rejection—of the ancestral. Lezama speaks of Cortázar and Joyce's neologistical work as an intertwining, a "laberynthical interconnection," in Lezama's words, between primal and contemporary language. To Lezama, one is the "decantación analítica" [analytical distillment] of the other; the "abuelidad" [ancientness] of primal language and the "ironía" [ironic playfulness] of contemporary language do not make them irreconcilable. According to the passage, one feeds from the qualities of the other; the last language derives its emphatic force from the first. The rhetorical sophistication of the *omega* language is linked to the loud outbursts ("carcajada") of the *alpha*, the judicial formality of the modern ("juramentos") has its source in the clumsy and strident gestures of exclamation of the original ("manotazos"). In the Viconian progress, the first poetic language undergoes a not entirely successful process of annulment: the new abstract applications of **ur**-terms displace but do not absolutely cancel the original, poetic-objective meanings. The textual dynamic of *Finnegans Wake* recovers these displaced significations. Lezama agrees: "Behind the words used for communication, others hide that carry the same weight as their external form: *secuestrados latidos, contracciones, crujimientos.*" Joyce's "philological salad" pulls out the buried roots of the first language by knotting ("entrelazando") them into nuclei (what Gilbert calls *Finnegans Wake*'s nodal points) that "radiate" old and new meanings in what Lezama calls an "infinite rippling of sand."

Lezama's reading of the later Joyce demonstrates an active acquaintance with Viconian principles, and also may indicate a parallel textual adoption of Vico in Lezama's work. This Viconian presence in Lezama shows that there is a deep and subtle dialogue with the "sources" of Joyce's river-novel in Lezama's own late writings, especially in the essays about the *era imaginaria*, in *Paradiso*, and in the unfinished *Oppiano Licario*. Lezama's sophisticated interpretation of the function of neologisms in *Finnegans Wake* suggests a definite familiarity, if not with the English edition, possibly with Haroldo and Augusto de Campos's 1962 Portuguese translation of excerpts, *Panorama do Finnegans Wake*. In their introduction to the book, the de Campos brothers reviewed Gilbert and Beckett's interpretation of Joycean synthetic or telescoped neologisms as a form of Viconian "root-language" and played on the trope of Joycean language as kaleidoscope that Lezama elaborates in his essays.[17] Lezama might have known also the glosses in Campbell and Robinson's *A Skeleton Key to Finnegans Wake* (1944), whose introductory "plot" summary singles out the prominent role of Vico's *New Science* in the overall design and texture of the novel.[18] (The Campos's *Panorama* featured a Portuguese version of the first chapter of Campbell and Robinson's study in its conclusion.) Lezama probably came to know the chapter on *Finnegans Wake* in Harry Levin's study on Joyce through the encouragement of José Rodríguez Feo.

Arguably, Lezama's acquaintance with Vico's writings could have occurred in isolation from Lezama's reading of Joyce. The circulation of the first translations of Vico's work in Spanish took place around the time of the appearance of *Finnegans Wake* and the much discussed death of Joyce in 1941. Vico's *De antiquissima Italorum sapientia* appeared in 1939 as *Sabiduria primitiva de los italianos* in an edition from the University of Buenos Aires's Institute of Philosophy.[19] José Carner's translation of the *Scienza nuova* was published in 1941 in two volumes by the Colegio de México.[20] The analysis of Vico's work in Latin America occurred before his rediscovery in other countries—Thomas Goddard Bergin and Max Harold Fish published their English translation of the *Scienza nuova* in 1948—and was probably fueled by the influence of Benedetto Croce, whose essay on the "philosophy" of Viconian thought must have caught the attention of readers who were exposed to Croce's aesthetic ideas in Ortega's *Meditaciones del Qui-*

jote and the translation of Croce's essays published in the *Revista de Occidente*.[21] The vogue for Dilthean historicism established by Ortega's thinking encouraged a search for anti-Enlightenment, antipositivist visions of history, which Latin American scholars and writers found in figures like Vico and Herder. A symposium on Vico and Herder was organized in 1944 at the University of Buenos Aires to commemorate the bicentennial of Vico's death and Herder's birth. The papers were published in a important volume (*Vico y Herder: Homenaje en el Quinto Centenario*) in 1948, sixteen years before the publication of the essays by Isaiah Berlin that energized the study of these two figures in the English-speaking academia.[22]

What distinguishes Lezama's reading of Vico is that, as Joyce's, it is not a philosophical reading, but a literary appropriation. Like *Finnegans Wake*, the essays of *La cantidad hechizada* are a critical actualization of Vico's ideas. Like *Finnegans Wake*, *Oppiano Licario* can be read as Lezama's attempt to bring the Viconian metanarrative of origin into an "espacio novelable americano" [Latin American fictional space] much in the way *Finnegans Wake* "dublinized" *The New Science*.

II

Despite some recent breakthroughs, critics have barely begun to sort out the complexities of Lezama Lima's reading of the work of Giambattista Vico.[23] The concerted assimilation of Vico in the work of the late Joyce constitutes a model with which to explain an analogous appropriation of Viconian principles in the later part of Lezama's creative and essayistic work. The heuristic application of notions taken from *La Scienza nuova* increased in Lezama's writing after the 1957 publication of his lectures on *La expresión americana*. Alhough Viconian principles can be seen to operate in some of his early work, Lezama's work did not make any overt references to Vico's ideas before 1957. The 1948 essay "Las imágenes posibles" [Possible images] contained the first sketches of the morphological ponderings on ancient civilizations that *La cantidad hechizada* was to elaborate, including the discussion of a "mythical age" and the analysis of the Egyptian afterlife and Greek Orphism. The fact that terms used in Carner's translation of *La Scienza Nuova* are echoed in "Las imágenes posibles" encourages dating Lezama's first reading of Vico in the forties. It is, however, in *La cantidad hechizada* that Lezama openly debated, dissected, and appropriated Vico's method.[24] Like Joyce's, Lezama's late work demonstrates an *explicitation* of Viconian principles analogous to the way *Finnegans Wake* openly refers to Vico, starting from the "commodius vicus of recirculation" phrase in the novel's first sentence.[25]

Lezama's intent interest in Vico at the end of his writing career is a sign of a new strategy of fabulation that links the last Lezama with the last Joyce. In Lezama's earlier book of essays, *La expresión americana*, he explored the cultural specificity of the New World, and postulated a theory of a syncretic or hybrid American aesthetic.[26] In each chapter, Lezama dealt with different aspects of this mixed cultural etiology: the emergence of New World myths that replace the "exhausted" fables of antiquity; the appearance of the American baroque as a period of plenitude in which a dynamic, transcultural equilibrium of ethnic creative forces is achieved; the progress of a New World *imagen* which Lezama traced through the analysis of the chronicles of the Conquest, of sacred pre-Columbian texts like the Popol Vuh, and the baroque elements in the works of Sor Juana Inés de la Cruz, Carlos Sigüenza y Góngora, Kondori, and the Aleijadinho; and the development of an irreversible, Romantic nationalism shown in the persistent idealism of patriots (Fray Servando Teresa de Mier, Francisco Miranda, Simón Rodríguez, and José Martí) who were imprisoned during the Latin American Wars of Independence. Lezama's exclusively Americanist focus in *La expresión americana* contrasts with his fascination for extinct, non-Western, esoteric civilizations as expressed in the essays of *La cantidad hechizada*.

Like the fictions of *Finnegans Wake* and *Oppiano Licario*, the essays of *La cantidad hechizada* demonstrate a centrifugal impulse, a counter-insularity, a movement away rather than toward the "islands" of the New World. The representation of Dublin in *Finnegans Wake* is subverted by the "invasion" of foreign names into its textual topography: the references to the Dublin cityscape and the Irish landscape are confused by the Joycean wordplay with towns and regions taken from all over history and the world.[27] The persistent foreignization in Joyce's last novel is heightened by the systematic grafting on to the text of the arcana of ancient hermetic scriptural traditions far removed from the Irish context: the Egyptian *Book of the Dead*, Nordic mythology, and the Kabbala. (With one exception: *Finnegans Wake* draws plentifully on the lore and the baroque ornamentality of the native ancient manuscript *Book of Kells*).[28] The essays of *La cantidad hechizada* detour from the exploration of Americanness and *cubanía* that occupied Lezama's early essays, and traverse an uncharted, absolute Otherness. Like

Finnegans Wake, these essays exercise, through pastiche and commentary, an examination of the surviving sacred texts of non-Western, esoteric, extinct philosophies: the Chinese *Tao Te Ching* and *I Ching*, the *Book of the Dead*, the Orphic hymns. After *La expresión americana*, there is a universalizing expansion in Lezama's novelistic and essayistic work that mirrors *La Scienza nuova*'s range of speculation regarding antiquity, the same range that determines the Joycean mythographical apparatus in *Finnegans Wake*. The visionary breadth that leads Vico to pursue—for many years, according to his own testimony[29]—the foundation of a "new science" that would reveal the main operating principles of all human history, shapes Lezama's ambition to generate a "poetic system of the world" that would reach beyond the regional cultural boundaries of Latin America and the New World.

This ambition is born from the need—philosophical and religious in Vico and Lezama; blasphemous and atheistic in Joyce—to harmonize the orthodox doctrine of Catholicism with the principles of a compelling pagan heterodoxy. In its most basic form, Lezama's *La cantidad hechizada* is, like *La Scienza nuova*, a meditation on the place of gentile religions in Judeo-Christian eschatology. Lezama's examination of the diverging journeys of the *imagen* in Christian and pagan civilizations reflects Vico's evaluation of Judeo-Christian exceptionalism in the context of universal history. Starting from the assumption that Judeo-Christian teleology is the standard measure of human destiny and that biblical tradition is "Truth," Vico and Lezama seek to understand the transcendental justification of religious and cultural diversity. *La Scienza nuova* deals exclusively with the "ideal history" of Gentile tribes; Lezama's catalogue of *eras imaginarias* encompasses mostly non-Christian civilizations.

Both Vico and Lezama dwell on the study of pagan cosmologies to argue the polemical, theologically-suspect notion that all variants of human civilization are under divine guidance, and that all arrive at a final, analogous interpretation of God and the world.[30] This guidance is of a complex, multiple nature, but its many manifestations take two main forms: active Providence (or Revelation) and immanent Providence. Revelation involves the explicit presence of the Godhead "personally" guiding and shaping Jewish and Christian history. It is the active participation of the Trinity in the events of the Judeo-Christian people: God the Father in the time of the Old Testament; God the Son in the figural culmination of the New; the Holy Spirit in the time after, as Revelation becomes the Truth of Christian society before Judgment. According to *La Scienza nuova,* the Hebrew tribes do not go through stages of barbarism, idolatry, and mythology because active Providence—through Revelation—has them preclude these periods.[31] All other cultures go through a circuitous route of superstition and fabulation to develop a "rational," non-idolatrous religious sense that finally mirrors the "truth" of Revelation. The "other" Providence concerns those histories that do not feature any apparition of God in his true "form"; it organizes the teleological dialectic of the non-Christian culture in a different fashion, leading it through cycles of barbarism, heroism, and rationality that eventually shape it into a monotheistic society believing in a Christian-like higher realm of resurrection.

In Lezama's essays, Vico's immanent Providence adopts the form of the *imagen,* the projection of the *incondicionado* over the *condicionado*—what in "A partir de la poesía" Lezama describes as the "poetic causality" encapsulated by the progress of the *imagen.* Lezama's notion of poetic causality—the other causality (*otra causalidad*) incarnated by poetry—is derived from Vico's "other" Providence. According to Lezama, in poetry the creative imagination projects the impossible upon the possible. Poetry, as absolute fiction, is based on the unreal—Lezama speaks of the ethereal, phantasmagoric "nothingness" of poetry—but the fact that it is insubstantial does not make it arbitrary or irrational. Poetry reveals a new, unknown order which Lezama compares to an alternative form of logic: "Es para mí el primer asombro de la poesía, que sumergida en el mundo prelógico, no sea nunca ilógica. Como buscando la poesía una nueva causalidad, se aferra enloquecedoramente a esa causalidad" (*OC 2:* 821). [To me the first, amazing aspect of poetry is that, even though it is submerged in the prelogical world, it is never illogical. As if searching for a new causality, poetry becomes maddeningly faithful to this causality.] When a metaphor produces a fantastic juncture of images, the apparent absurdity opens "a gateway" into a patterned field of fantastic possibilities that are somehow preordained, since new tropes "flow logically" from the associations posited by the primary image. Poetry is thus not an expression of fancy, but the recognition of an "other" realm of relations and declensions invisible to, but parallel, with what Lezama calls Aristotle's "causality of the visible."[32] An unpredictable yet inexorable narrative is generated by the progress of the "magical," metaphoric relations inaugurated by the shimmering, initial verse. This narrative overcomes causal shock—the awe and incredulity inspired by the verse's challenge to "visible" causality—and normalizes the logical rupture through its promise of establishing a new set of cause-and-effect connections which,

because of its "natural, breath-like rhythm," can be as coherent
and sensible as those of the natural world:

> ya una vez en esa región, la de la otra causalidad, se gana después una
> prolongada duración que va creando sus nudos o metáforas causales.
> Si decimos, por ejemplo, el cangrejo usa lazo azul y lo guarda en la
> maleta, lo primero, lo más difícil es, pudiéramos decir, subir a esa frase,
> trepar al momentáneo y candoroso asombro que nos produce. . . . Des-
> pués, mantenernos en esa región donde vamos ya de asombro en
> asombro, pero como de natural respiración, a una causalidad que es
> un continuo de incorporar y devolver. . . .
>   Tenemos, pues, que el cangrejo de lazo azul nos hizo ganar otra re-
> gión. Si después lo guardó en una maleta, nos hizo ganar una morada,
> es decir, una causalidad metafórica. (OC 2: 822–23)

> [once in this region, the region of the other causality, one gains a pro-
> longed temporality which gradually creates its own nodes or causal
> metaphors. If we say, for example, that the crab wears a blue bow tie,
> and he keeps it in his briefcase, the first, most difficult thing is, so to
> speak, to climb on that [first] phrase, mount on the sudden and candid
> astonishment it produces in us. . . . [If] we can remain in that region,
> where we go from one amazement to another, although no less natu-
> rally than breathing, [we move] toward a causality that absorbs and
> returns [things] continuously. . . .
>   Thus, the crab with the blue bow tie helped us conquer another re-
> gion. When he put it in his briefcase, he helped us conquer another
> realm, a metaphoric causality.]

Poetry opens a new causality since it does not operate as a single
image but as a chain of linked metaphors that follow, one after another, according to a mysterious yet consistent and unending succession. This chain is "providential" because the compelling
logical power produced by the sequence and the rhythmic (in other
words, systematic) emergence of its units, corroborates the existence of a higher, invisible realm of determination. This other region ("morada") is won ("ganada") with the subsequent metaphor
(the crab puts the tie in his briefcase), the trope derived from the
first or former (the crab likes wearing a blue tie), which normalizes
the irrational elements of the first image and activates the network
of poetic correspondences that acts as the *figura*—the prophetic
announcement—of "another" causality.

According to Lezama, this "other" metaphoric causality organizes the religious visions of the transcendentalist societies he
studies under the rubric of *era imaginaria*. In Lezama's aesthetic,
poetry and ancient culture cannot be separated. "En los milenios,

exigidos por una cultura, donde la imagen actúa sobre determina-
das circunstancias excepcionales, al convertirse el hecho en una
viviente causalidad metafórica, es donde se sitúan esas eras imaginarias. La historia de la poesía no puede ser otra cosa que el es-
tudio y expresión de las eras imaginarias" (*OC 2*: 833). [In those
millenia that a culture needs for its development, in which the *imagen* acts upon specific, exceptional circumstances, when fact and
event become a living metaphoric causality, is where the *eras imaginarias* are situated. The history of poetry is nothing more than
the study and the expression of these imaginary eras.]

The "imaginary" in Lezama's *era imaginaria* is drawn from
Vico's characterization of *fantasia* as the exclusive "thought-
format" of the mindset of the ancient gentile civilizations.[33] Lezama
appropriates Vico's anatomy of *fantasia* or "poetic wisdom" in the
second book of *La Scienza nuova*, and organizes his representation
of the imaginary according to the epistemological categories presented there by Vico. The ideas that the first barbaric tribes could
only express themselves through poetic thought and language, and
that fables and fantastic cosmologies were the creations of the
theological poets of these first societies, is well incorporated into
the Lezamian discourse. Lezama's system adopts and deploys
Vico's notions that the first language was gestural and emblem-
atic—"en el signo queda siempre el conjuro del gesto" (*OC 2*: 811)
[in every sign there is the residue of a gesture's conjuration]—, that
writing is immemorial and appears simultaneously with speech—
"el afán primero . . . rodea el nacimiento de la escritura" (*OC 2*:
812) [the first impulse . . . accompanies the birth of writing]—, and
that augury is the first semiotic system available to man.

Lezama's "feast-like" incorporation of Vico is not without refractive distortions. In *La Scienza nuova*, Vico paints "poetic wisdom"
as a primitive, limited, hyperbolic expression of sense experience
with no capacity for abstraction or reason, thus excluding the possibility of philosophical nuance, of deduction or induction.[34] Lezama interprets what Vico considers a weak and rustic stage of
language as a sublime imaginative *and* conceptual strength; in Lezama *lo poético* is an extremely complex and sophisticated force.
Like Heidegger, Lezama believes that poetry represents both the
primordial springing-forth of human consciousness and the final
synthesis and crystallization of the ultimate possibilities of higher
thought.[35] Alpha and Omega, poetry to Lezama is the praxis of "lo
difícil" [the difficult] at every point of human evolution: it represents the most demanding mental task required of humankind in a
given historical circumstance.[36] Poetry in Lezama thus carries with

it an ethical burden, for poetic practice demands (morally and imaginatively) ascetic dedication and sacrifice. The thirst for absoluteness and exhaustiveness in Lezama's *conocimiento poético* goes far beyond the elementary, mostly cognitive functions exercised by "poetic wisdom" in Vico.

The redemptive, atemporal manifestations of poetry in Lezama also destabilize the immanent logic of Vico's providential schema. In the *era imaginaria*, the structuring influence of the metaphoric causality of the *imagen* sets off a process of religious imagination which—even if resulting in visions that orthodoxy would consider idolatrous or fetishistic—always prefigures the Judeo-Christian conception of divinity and resurrection. The work of the *imagen* makes all *eras imaginarias* reconcilable with Christian eschatology, and all tales of tribal origin and consolidation can be subsumed as scriptural equivalents of biblical Genesis. All pagan mythologies can be read as variants of the Old Testament that prefigure—in Auerbach's definition of *figura*[37]—the good news of the Messiah's coming in the New Testament. Thus, in "A partir de la poesía," the philogenetic myth of sexless procreation among the *idumeos* is comparable to the generation of Eve from Adam's rib. Such reasoning leads Lezama to heretical readings of scripture: he claims that the *idumeos* are "levemente aludidos" (*OC 2:* 835) [latently alluded to] in the book of Genesis. Orpheus' "human" death, his descent into Hell, and his sacred-profane nature—"de origen divino, su canto es para los humanos" (*OC 2:* 836) [despite his divine origin, his song is meant for humanity]—prefigures the coming of Christ. The Egyptian underworld and the reconstitution of the body of Osiris is a pre-Christian intuition of the dogma of Hell and the certainty of resurrection. The Buddhist conception of The One is the manifestation of the one Christian God. The Confucian *imagen* of dragon-as-library signals the primacy of sacred scripture as insisted upon in the biblical tradition.

Lezama considers the transcendentalist, quasi-orthodox inclinations of pagan cosmologies as the consequence of "poetic wisdom" since the poetic imagination—Lezama's *sujeto metafórico* [metaphorizing subject]—guarantees the vision to the "other" causality of Providence. Lezama thus quotes as one of the principal elements of his definition of the *era imaginaria* Vico's dictum on *lo imposible creíble*, the believable-impossible, since both study "poetic" civilizations where the "impossible" generated by the poetic imagination defines what is believed.[38] But while Vico considers such belief a temporary period of delusion, Lezama sees it as a glimpse into sacred truth.

Thus we see that Lezama did not adopt Vico's schemas and concepts mechanically. In fact, Lezama misreads Vico's historicism even more radically. In addition to refashioning Vico's poetic theory, Lezama reads the sequence of Viconian ages in an eccentric, ahistorical way. *La cantidad hechizada* debates and redefines the terms of Vico's poetic wisdom, challenges and modifies Vico's Providence, and categorically refutes Vico's historicism. While appropriating and refracting the principles predicating the theocratic "poetic system" of gentility, Lezama rejects the crux of the social and historical argument that organizes Vico's project. Lezama's first explicit reference to Vico in "A partir de la poesía" voices an objection to Vico's view of the way religion participates in the origination of class struggle:

> Vico cree que las palabras sagradas, las sacerdotales, eran las que se transmitían entre los etruscos. Pero para nosotros el pueblo etrusco era esencialmente teocrático. Fue el más evidente caso de un pueblo surgido en el misterio de las primeras inauguraciones del dios, el monarca, el sacerdote y el pueblo unidos en forma indiferenciada. El convencimiento que tenía el pueblo de que el dios, el monarca y el sacerdote, eran la misma persona, le prestaba a cada una de sus experiencias o de sus gestos, la participación en un mundo sagrado. . . . Vico podía creer en la transmisión sacerdotal, pero se le hacía muy difícil la concepción del pueblo de sacerdotes. (*OC* 2: 831)

> [Vico believes that it was the sacred, priestly words that were transmitted among the Etruscans. But to us the Etruscans were essentially theocratic. They were the most evident case of a people emerging from the mystery of the first inaugurations, of a god, a monarch and a priest which were not differentiated from the people. The people's conviction that god, monarch and priest were the same person allowed each of their experiences or gestures to participate in a world made sacred. . . . Vico believed in sacerdotal transmission, but had a hard time acccepting the idea of an entire people made up of priests.]

Here, Lezama attacks Vico's understanding of the process through which, with the foundation of the first cities, a noble priest-caste rose to power by manipulating and monopolizing ritual and superstitious beliefs through the creation of a secret or exclusive language that was "transmitted sacerdotally" [among priests]. At first, barbaric superstition created a sparse handful of gods and associated them with basic natural forces (Vico lists twelve essential gods present at every early stage of barbarism); as society matured, there occurred a process of class division that influenced the con-

tent and function of the theocratic fables. After the recognition of
Jove as the "being-in-the-sky," the heavenly elements (climactic
phenomena such as thunder and lightning, the flight of birds, and
the movement of the stars) were understood as either emanations
of Jove's body or the articulations of Jove's language. The practice
of augury emerged thus as the first human art that "read" the signs
in heaven as Jove's divine instructions or announcements of the
future.[39] Eventually, augury as a science became an exclusivist
knowledge-domain of the founders of the city, who used it to dominate the lower castes. The arcane sciences of sidereal interpretation (augury and astrology) were developed as the first conflicts
over landed property arose, exacerbating the tensions and class
differences between patricians (landowners) and plebeians (serfs).
The practice of augury and astrology thus degenerated into an opportunistic use of the dieties in gentility absent from Judeo-Christian orthodoxy. During the heroic period, Jove becomes an
ideological instrument for the patrician class' domination of its feudal serfs.

Lezama contests Vico's picture of the corruptibility of poetic wisdom. He does not see poetic wisdom as facilitating an arcane form
of knowledge that manipulates auguries in order to coerce and
dominate. For Lezama, the "believable-impossible" is not a revelation for the privileged, but the entitlement of the whole social body.
In the *era imaginaria*, the entire society is capable of sharing in this
belief, because of the "democratic" permeability of poetic vision
among the people. Lezama uses the example of the Etruscans, a
civilization never mentioned outright in *La Scienza nuova*, to contradict Vico's generalization concerning the inherent opposition
between the priest-caste and the plebians. With the Etruscans,
augurial science was public knowledge, "the most evident case of
a people emerging from the mystery of the first inaugurations."
There are no social tensions as "the monarch, the priest and the
people [are] united undifferentiatedly," making the Etruscan a
classless system, or rather a one-class society: a society of priests.
Lezama presents here his medieval notion of the conflict-free *unidad coral*—the choral unity of religious societies enlightened by the
imagen.[40]

Lezama's disagreement is starker yet in his objection to Vico's
presentation of the euhemeristic meaning of the dragon in the Hercules myth cycle. Freely paraphrasing Viconian discourse, Lezama
complains about Vico's decision to include a confrontation with a
dragon, after Hercules' victory over the lion and the hydra, as part
of the hero's labors: "Pero el surgimiento del dragón en la tradición

occidental, nos parece difícil y paradojal. . . . ¿Cómo pudieron
llegar esas fábulas griegas a los japoneses, se pregunta Vico, o a la
China donde existe una Orden de Caballeros del Hábito del
Dragón?" (OC 2: 832) [But the appearance of the dragon in the
Western tradition seems difficult and paradoxical to us. . . . How
could these Greek fables reach the Japanese, asks Vico, or China,
where a Dragon Order of knights exists?] Lezama refers here to the
section of the 1732 edition of La Scienza nuova in which Vico interprets the labors of Hercules as a encoded summary of the morphological events of the heroic period. In book 5, chapter 10, whose
title Carner translates as "Uniformidad de la Edad de los Héroes
en la Naciones antiguas, demostrada en el carácter de Hércules"
[Unity of the Gentile Heroic Age, shown in the character of Her-
cules], Vico explains that the Hercules myth cycle belongs to a second period of fabulation, in which the emphasis on a mystical,
supernatural universe governed by the gods of the theocratic period shifts to the predominance of a domestic orbis terrarum that
serves as theater for the feats of extraordinary figures born from the
marriage of gods and humans. These creatures—heroes or titans—
are wholly identified with the human region. In his offbeat, euhe-
merist approach, Vico regards the prominence of the epic,
semidivine hero (Hercules, Achilles) or the hero that can confer
with the gods on an egalitarian basis (Odysseus), as standing for
the entire social class of the patricians rather than for one mythi-
cized individual in history. Considering the extreme geographical
displacement and multiplicity of the Hercules adventures, Vico
does not think of the hero as one figure, but the telescoping or fusion of the travails of many Herculeses—the Greek, the Egyptian,
the Celtic, the Scythian, the Libyan, the Ethiopian, the Phoenician,
the Thirian, and the Theban (New Science 185)—under one name.
The fire associated with the chimeras that Hercules battles—the
dragon, the serpent, the hydra, and the lion—represents the practice of land clearing through fire for agriculture which the noble
class began after leaving the caves they first dwelled in. The dragon
is thus a totemic term for patrician land ownership, and the labors
of Hercules represent the efforts of the patrician class to establish,
cultivate, and defend their estate. The dragon in the Hercules fable
articulates in narrative form what the sign of the dragon represents
as a hieroglyph in heraldry. In the archaic coats of arms discussed
by Vico, the dragon-emblem designates domesticated land as
property. I translate from Carner's translation since its language
imprinted Lezama's interpretation of the passage:

[Hércules mató] en Hesperia el dragón: y el dragón de Hesperia vomit-
aba llamas, y la hidra fue matada con fuego, así como el león Nemeo
con sus llamas prendiera fuego en la selva, fábulas todas que deberán
de significar una especie de fatiga de varios Hércules griegos, eso es, la
selva de la tierra por el fuego reducida al cultivo. . . . Con este anti-
quísimo lenguaje de las armas se explican las Empresas públicas que
se cargan o encuadran con dragones, pintados espinosos y escuálidos,
como era la gran selva de la tierra. (*Ciencia nueva I* 85–86)

[(Hercules killed) the dragon in the Hesperides. This dragon vomited
flames, and the hydra was killed with fire, just as the Nemean lion
sparked a fire in the forest. All of these fables should be seen as representations of a specific form of labor of several Greek Herculeses—that
is, the jungle covering the earth is cleared for cultivation with fire. . . .
This ancient language of emblems explains the coats of arms in which
dragons abound, thorny and frail as was the great jungle that covered
the Earth.]

The hybrid, chimerical nature of the creatures that Hercules battles after the hydra, the lion and the dragon (symbols of the patricians' relationship with the land) reflects, according to Vico, the
mongrel, monstrous race of the plebeians, the primitives who first
invade and steal from the properties of the first patricians and are
later allowed to settle on the patrician's property in exchange for
their labor and tribute. When Hercules fights the monsters and the
tyrants, he fights and kills "impíos vagabundos nacidos de concú-
bitos nefastos . . . y . . . los ladrones de mieses, hombres sin tierra,
deseosos de ocupar la ajena" (*Ciencia nueva II* 188) [faithless vag-
abonds born out of nefarious wedlock . . . and . . . harvest thieves,
men without land, eager to occupy any property]. Hercules's battle
with Anteus is similarly framed as a heroic battle for land, when
the heroes refused to grant the plebeians control over the fields
(*Ciencia nueva II* 189). Through Vico's method, the Hercules fables
in toto can be decoded to signify the defeat and subjection of the
plebeian races under the superior force of the patricians. The
dragon is a sign—in fact, the universal denomination—for feudal
property defended from a lower, threatening caste. Due to the distortion and corruption of the Hercules fables in the vulgar period—
which recasts fables as abstract allegories and regards the trials
and feats of gods and heroes as anthropomorphic symbols for
human virtues and vices—the dragon loses this concrete social
and historical designation.

    In chapter 11 of the 1732 edition of *La Scienza nuova*, Vico refers
to the ancestral appearance of the dragon among the Japanese and

the Chinese as an example of an equivalent situational emblem of social conflict in these other civilizations. In "A partir de la poesía," Lezama objects to this association, alluding to the *extensión crono-lógica*, the distance in space and time that separates Hercules from the Chinese dynasties—the same distance, argues Lezama, that separates "la tortuga agrietada para la adivinación, en la China arcaica, y la lira de concha de tortuga, pulsada por Orfeo" (*OC 2*: 832) [the cracked turtle used for divination in archaic China from Orpheus's turtleshell lyre]. Lezama interprets Vico's rhetorical question regarding the antiquity of the dragon as a symbol in China and Japan as implying that the oriental notion of the dragon has its source in the Greek version of the Hercules myth. Lezama disagrees: "[T]enemos que llegar a la conclusión que era en extremo difícil esa influencia de la Grecia mitológica sobre una lejanía casi irreconciliable" (*OC 2*: 843) [We have to reach the conclusion that it was extremely difficult for that Greek mythological influence to survive an almost irreconcilable distance]. Vico is not concerned, however, with making a statement about the geographical reach of the myth's diffusion. On the contrary, Vico mentions the presence of the dragon in remote civilizations to illustrate the emergence of identical elements at equivalent periods of evolution in absolutely unrelated civilizations. The negative rather than affirmative answer to the question is clear from the full quote:

> Y si alguien siguiera diciendo que esta Empresa hubiere sido tomada por algún duque de Borgoña de la fábula Griega de Jasón, responderemos preguntando: ¿de dónde llegaron las fábulas griegas a los Japoneses, que guarnecen de dragones todo el solio de su Emperador? ¿de dónde a los Chinos, que hasta hace dos siglos mantuvieron impermiables sus confines para los extranjeros, y cuyos Emperadores instituyeron una Orden de caballeros del hábito del Dragón? (*Ciencia nueva* I 88)

> [If someone told us that the (use of the Dragon coat of arms) by some Burgundy duke is taken from the Greek myth of Jason (i.e., has one historical source), we would answer: How was it possible for the Greek fables to reach the Japanese, who use dragons to adorn the Emperor's throne? How could they reach the Chinese, who, until very recently, kept their boundaries sealed to foreigners and whose Emperor instituted a Dragon Knight Order?]

What Vico maintains here is that, despite the mutual isolation of the cultural contexts, the same heroic emblems recur in many pagan civilizations and represent equivalent periods of social

conflict. Vico thus makes the emblem of the dragon a unit of signification—akin perhaps to Jung's archetype or Levi-Strauss's my-
theme—of a universal mythical language operating in both East
and West. It is in this respect that Lezama formulates his sharpest
objection: the dragon does not bear the meaning Vico pretends in
these contrasting cultural contexts. To attempt such parallelism is,
to Lezama, misguided—"difícil y paradojal" [difficult and paradox-
ical]—for, in the Japanese and the Chinese examples, the dragon
does not act as a symbol for a land war and a class conflict. On the
contrary, it represents a unifying dynastic rule (the Fou Hi, Chin
Noum, and Houan Ti kingdoms) that brings enlightment to the
masses by promulgating the sciences that augury and astrology ad-
umbrate—ideogrammatical writing and mathematics, "la letra y el
número" [the letter and the number] (43). In other words, the
dragon is not a heroic symbol, but a regal one. It represents, as in
the case of the Etruscans, a choral monarchy where populace and
Mandarin share and exchange privileges. In Lezama, the Oriental
dynasty crowns a monarch who is both sacred and popular, who
prefigures the harmonious system of governance that Vico deemed
characteristic of the "vulgar" or human period that begins when
the appearance of the figure of the king achieves the reconciliation
of patricians and plebeians.

Lezama's interpretation of Vico's Hercules myth exemplifies his
elliptical style of erudite gloss and his selective appropriation of Viconian principles. "A partir de la poesía" never challenges Vico's
qualification of the "flaccidez vencida" [defeated frailty, *OC 2*: 832]
of the dragon in the Hercules myth (the expression is Lezama's recasting of the "espinoso y escuálido" [thorny and frail] description
quoted above that Carner uses to translate Vico's characterization
of the heraldic dragons). Nevertheless, Lezama neglects to explain
the euhemeristic signification of this "flaccidez." A full knowledge
of Vico's text is required to unknot the enigma of Lezama's meticulous, almost pointillistic allusion. Lezama abides by Vico's social-
euhemeristic definition of the Herculean dragon, but by devising a
less heroic meaning for the oriental use of the emblem, Lezama
casts a shadow of doubt over the Viconian method of historical discernment that takes care not to evolve into a full negation of Vico's
system. Vico himself propounds the principle of kingship as an ecumenical institution of social harmony in his detailing of the vulgar
period, and Lezama echoes this favorable interpretation at many
points in his writing, making the *rey-como-metáfora* [king-as-meta-
phor] his fifth *era imaginaria*.[41] In Lezama, however, this societal
structure happens before its due time in Viconian metahistory (in

the barbaric times of the early Chinese dynasties). In the example of the Etruscans, Lezama fuses the theocratic, heroic, and vulgar periods into one epoch. In other words, Lezama's *era imaginaria* is a synthesis of the three Viconian periods that eliminates the diachronic dialectic of conflict that, according to Vico, energizes historical progress. In Lezama's discussion, the king, the heroic-priest class, and the peasant class participate in the religious literacy Vico considers arcane.[42] Lezama regards Vico's assumption of the exclusivity of sacred knowledge in the heroic age the great flaw in his postulations in *La Scienza nuova*. Vico neglects "the choral possibility": "Vico no podía comprender el hechizo entero de la ciudad, de la marcha del campesinado penetrando en lo irreal, en lo imposible. . . . Vico no pudo conocer esa otra naturaleza del pueblo como penetración de un coro en los designios" (*OC 2*: 832) [Vico could not understand the betwitched state of a city when the peasantry invades, as if it were entering the unreal, the impossible. . . . Vico never knew that other nature of the people as a choir interpreting auguries].[43] Lezama thus collapses the temporality inscribed in Vico's periodizations into a joyous, kaledoscopic simultaneity. He prefers to regard the specifics of Vico's epochs as nonevolving potentialities that accumulate and coexist in virtual instantaneity.

The one historical and literal judgment on fables Lezama acknowledges in Vico's science is the assumption of an inexorable mutation of *fantasia* into new, abstract modes of thought, and the opinion that this philosophical transformation of fables entails a loss of poetic power: "En nuestra época la poesía no muestra ninguna de esas decisivas ocupaciones . . . la poesía había perdido los esplandores inaugurales, el gran sillón calendario para el jefe de la tribu" (*OC 2*: 815). [In our time poetry does not evidence any of the decisive occupations. . . . Poetry has lost the splendors of augury, the great calendar stone on which the chieftain was seated.] Here Lezama takes pains to summarize Vico's refutation of Descartes's claims concerning the timeless universality of the rational as the defining category of the human mind.[44] Lezama interprets Vico's great achievement to be the discovery of the existence of a sublime, "fabulous" reason which is lost as its obscurity is refigured and abstracted first as mythology and later as philosophy:

> Vico intuye que hay en el hombre un sentido, llamésmole el nacimiento de otra razón mitológica, que no es la razón helénica ni la de Cartesio, para penetrar en esa conversión de lo fabuloso en mitológico. Frente al mundo de la *physis*, ofrece Descartes el resguardo de sus

ideas claras y distintas. Frente a los detalles "oscuros y turbios" de los orígenes, Vico ofrece previamente a las platónicas ideas universales, la concepción de sus universales fantásticos o imaginarios. . . . Esos universales imaginarios, los mitos, nacen de la apetencia, según la frase de Vico, de "homerizar a Platón y de platonizar a Homero." (*OC 2: 847*)

[Vico intuits that there is in Man a [special] sense—let us call this the emergence of mythological reason—which is neither Hellenic nor Cartesian reason—in order to pierce through the conversion of the fabulous into the mythological. In the face of the world of *physis*, Descartes provides the safeguard of his "clear and distinct ideas." In the face of the "obscure and turbid" details [that remain] from the origin [of Man], Vico conjures up the idea of fantastic or imaginary universals that precede Platonic idealism. . . . These imaginary universals—myths—are born, according to Vico, from the desire to "homerize Plato and platonize Homer."]

What Lezama glosses here is Vico's critique of classical mythology from Plato on, and its systematization of fables into an allegorical genre that represents the gods as the anthropomorphization of human virtues and vices. Mythology as a system implies a domestication of fabulous reason: according to Plato and the commentators that followed him, myth expresses rational universals. Vico, however, is interested in the time when myths were "obscure and turbid" fables according to the modern mind, but comprehensible and exacting as concrete language: the *vera narratio* of the barbaric mind.[45] The whole *Scienza nuova* is a challenge to "mythology" as an abstract, transparent figuration. Like Vico, Lezama is interested in the stage where the imagination is still obscure and has not achieved the "esclarecimiento de las imágenes en el mito" [clarification or stylization of images in myth]. This is a period prior to that of symbols as they exist now in our imagination. Like Vico in his effort to dispense with abstract thought in order to understand the primitive mentality of fables, Lezama wishes to access a similar form of reminiscence in which he can retrieve "en el símbolo como un recuerdo de la cifra que lo atesoraba" (*OC 2: 847*) [in a symbol the reminiscence of the cipher from which it issued]. To Vico this cipher, this first image, is the idea of Jove not as an anthropomorphic god, but as an animistic figure of heaven on which only some aspects of human behavior are projected. The same applies to Apollo (the sky), Diana (water), and the other dieties of Vico's elementary pantheon.

Lezama wants to restore the enigmatic, animistic power of fables since the *imagen* operates within this irrational force: "La imagen extrae del enigma un vislumbre, con cuyo rayo podemos penetrar, o al menos vivir, en la espera de la resurrección" (*OC 2:* 848) [The *imagen* extracts from the enigma (of fables) a source of light, an insight, and with this ray we can enter in, or at least live waiting for, resurrection]. Here is the essence of Lezama's dispute with Vico. Vico believes that "fabulous reason" is a primitive state of mind, and that the animistic interpretation of the universe is a form of superstitious pre-thought that is transcended through the abstract conception of a single deity present from the beginning in the Hebraic-Christian tradition or dominating the Homeric-cum-Platonic mythology. Revelation spares the Judeo-Christian religious mind the needless profusion of gods, chimeras, and monsters of the pagan religions. Lezama, however, invests these fantastic forms with a real sacred value; they are not simply the products of a perverse or retrograde fancy. In fact, these primal animistic images have little to do with a rustic imagination, according to Lezama. Lezama's assumption is that Jove's apparition is in fact a divine manifestation and that the barbaric sacred fear is not just before a nature-that-reflects-God's-designs, but before the real God. By recognizing Jove in the sky, the primitive poetic imagination allows mankind to access the other causality and thus participate in the godly realm. Thus, to dwell in the *otra causalidad* of these fables brings about a transfiguration of the atavistic believer that situates him or her in a state akin to Catholic grace (the eighth *era imaginaria*).

This is Lezama's eccentric interpretation of Vico's *believable-impossible*. It is not a condition of stammering brutishness (as Vico so vividly characterizes it), but a metaphysical and supernatural transfiguration: "Es decir, el que cree vive ya en un mundo sobrenatural, cualquier participación en lo imposible convierte al hombre en un ser imposible, pero táctil en esa dimensión. Acepta un movimiento sobrenatural, una propagación sobrenatural, un sobre natural estar en todas las cosas" (*OC 2:* 848). [In other words, whoever believes lives already in a supernatural world, any relationship with the impossible turns man into an impossible being that [remains] 'tactile' in that dimension. He accepts a supernatural movement, a supernatural expansion, a supernatural being in all things.] Lezama agrees with Vico's observation concerning the displacement of poetic wisdom by reason, but he deplores this development. Thus, Lezama's portrayal of atavistic antiquity does not prove how immanent Providence leads from superstition to a pre-Christian monotheism, but shows that the *imagen*'s progress is multiform and ecumenical: it is the Holy Spirit of the gentiles. The *imagen* is a polyglossic, revelatory Providence that offers a parallel vision of inmortality to multiple cultural contexts in antiquity.

The points of agreement and disagreement between Lezama and Vico's systems become more obvious in the two authors' discussion of gigantism. Both the Viconian and the Lezamian system reconceptualize primitivism through the figure of the giant, but this revaluation leads to contrasting results. To Vico, gigantism is an actual period in biblical history. After the flood, the rugged terrain and natural chaos transformed the physique and the customs of the pagan men that survived. Again Vico gives an euhemeristic explanation of myth: the giants mentioned in Homer and in the Bible are not fantastic beings but historical creatures belonging to gentility's barbaric, anarchic, semi-imbecilic and superstitious first state. It is during this period of gigantism that humankind witnesses the first thunderstorm and mythical consciousness begins. The theocratic period follows this age of men as troglodytes.

For Lezama, gigantism is a period just as important and as real as for Vico. Its presence in mythology is not a mere fabulation, but indicative of a stage in man's sacred transfiguration. Contrary to Vico, gigantism is not the farthest state from godliness possible to humankind; it is rather a sign of communal proximity. *La Scienza nuova* argues that the assumption that the giants were born from the union of gods and men was a fabrication used by the nobles to disguise their origins and subject the lower classes. This interpretation is not adopted by Lezama. For Lezama, gigantism is an angel-like hypostasis of the divine on the human, a prefiguration of the incarnation of God in Christ, where the divine and the earthly are joined. Ironically, to support this interpretation, Lezama uses terms and notions from the *Scienza nuova*'s analysis of gigantism, including Vico's observation that the myth of the giants—like Homer's misunderstood representation of Cyclops—precipitates the conversion of fable into mythology. Lezama writes: "La lucha de los gigantes contra Júpiter . . . prevalec[ió] en el vencimiento de las fábulas por los mitos" (*OC 2:* 850–51) [The giants' war against Jupiter . . . prevailed in myth's victory over fable]. "La imagen histórica" rehashes Vico's own catalogue of giants: Jupiter's rebel sons that climbed the sky; Licaon's murder attempt against Jove; Hesiod's reference to the Titans; Ovid's mention of "hulking giants"; the dolmens of the Karnak giants; and, most importantly, Saint Agustine's reference to giants in *The City of God* (*OC 2:* 851). Like Vico, Lezama speaks of the Egyptian pyramids as a curious remnant of the existence of giants in that civilization. Lezama uses

Vico's material to arrive at a very different conclusion. The giant's primitivism in Lezama is not barbaric, but an angelic condition akin to sacred innocence:

> La existencia de los gigantes en la mitología, en las cronologías y en la reminiscencia, forman la imagen del hombre transfigurado, alcanzando otra especie, rompiendo las murallas del ser, adquiriendo la lanza de Baal, que es el mito del fuego en el cielo, del hombre llevando el fuego a las moradas celestes. . . . Todavía San Agustín, en *La ciudad de Dios*, cree en ese encuentro de los hijos de Dios, los ángeles, con las hijas de los hombres, que engendraron los gigantes, nacidos de la confusión de las semillas, que vienen a ser arrastrados por el diluvio. Acaso los espíritus puros pudieron conocer en la carne. Una nueva cultura surgiría si los ángeles llegaran a hipostasiarse, si toda la materia adquiriese la transparencia y la transparencia el espíritu puro. (*OC* 2: 851)

> [The existence of giants in mythologies, in chronologies and in reminiscence, forms the *imagen* of man transfigured, mutated into another species, breaking the barriers of being, stealing Ball's spear: (it is the) the myth of the fire in the sky, of man taking fire (from) the celestial realm. . . . In *The City of God*, St. Augustine himself believed in the marriage of the children of God, the angels, with the daughters of men, from whose confused seeds were born the giants that the flood killed. Perhaps the caste spirits [the angels] were once able to know man's flesh. A new culture would arise if the angels could become hypostasized, if all matter could take on the transparence of pure spirit.]

The conclusion of "La imagen histórica" deals with myths that envision a merging of the divine and the earthly (Peleus's education under Chiron, Julius Caesar's claim that his aunt descended from the gods) (*OC 2*: 851–52). The essay ends discussing the *imagen,* founded by Catholic dogma, that exemplifies this impossible possibility: the Immaculate Conception of the Virgin Mary.[46] Lezama pictures gigantism as a prefiguration of what he calls in his essay on Cortázar *antropofanía*: the participation of the human in the divine. Arguably, this is Vico's eventual argument (gigantism is the first stage of an immanent providential order that takes the pagan from barbarism to revelation), but Lezama ascribes to it an immediacy that adds to Vico's immanent providence a tangible, precocious element of revelation through the *imagen.*

To summarize: In his appropriation of Vico, Lezama both sacralizes and aestheticizes the principles of *La Scienza nuova* by rejecting Vico's historicist argument and implementing a gnoseology of the fabulous as a virtual state belonging to all the *eras imaginarias.*

Unlike Vico, Lezama does not ridicule primitivism, nor does he consider it a state to be transcended. He regards it as a condition of innocence necessary for the sacred, revelatory force of poetry to manifest itself. Unlike Vico, Lezama minimizes the relevance of human progress toward reason and deplores the disappearance of "poetic wisdom" in modern society. Both Vico and Lezama contest Cartesian rationality, but in the end Vico favors the formation of philosophical thought, while Lezama wants to restore the fantastic mindset of the *era imaginaria*. While both Vico and the rationalists would categorize poetic wisdom as a form of magical superstition, Lezama regards it as an intuition into the sacred nature of the world.

In this Lezama makes the mistake—common among readers of Vico—of reading *La Scienza nuova* as an aesthetic system rather than a historicist epistemology.[47] To Vico, the poetry of the primitive tribes was a purely cognitive form of knowledge; its sublimeness—a deceiving term in the Viconian text—is generated by the excesses of an underdeveloped, aphasic mind. In *La Scienza nuova*, the poetic is an almost inarticulate mode of fancy that cannot evoke Lezama's systematic realm of symbolist correspondences; it offers only a diminished vision of reality as a system of mysterious forces on which man can only impose his own nascent emotions and thoughts. In Lezama Lima's system, poetry is not an archaic remnant in the archaeology of the mind, but an eternal visionary presence that obviates the distinction between past and present and re-interprets the experience of modernity with the recast fabulations of antiquity.

III

Despite the obvious differences in linguistic strategy, the narrative-anecdotal dimension of both *Finnegans Wake* and *Paradiso-Oppiano Licario* features similar "plot developments" that illustrate Vico's stages in an ideal history of man. Not the least of these is the wake scene as a nodular figure in the text.[48] *Finnegans Wake* is, among many things, the staging of multiple wakes amalgamated with an overwhelming array of religious and ethnographical information concerning burial ceremonies. All of these wakes issue from and flow into one: Finnegan's epic funeral.[49] Following Vico's postulation that the three institutions that evidence the radical commonality of all human societies are religion, marriage, and burial, *Finnegans Wake* builds elaborate scenes illustrating each institution, but concentrates on the paraphernalia of funerals.⁵⁰ The instrumentalia of wakes—the "inhumationary bric a brac" (*Finnegans Wake* 77)—resurfaces constantly; the framing narrative of Finnegan's wake is mirrored and multipled in subordinate scenes of interment, such as HCE's.

A similar, magnified recurrence of the corpse-in-coffin motif occurs throughout *Paradiso*: the mortuary rituals of *velorio de cuerpo presente* or *capilla ardiente*; the showcasing of dead "saints" in Catholic cathedrals; the unearthing of tombs. Oppiano Licario's wake is prefigured by a number of mortuary visions glimpsed in Cemí's childhood: the face of the deceased father whitewashed before Cemí's gaze by the waters of oblivion; the church urn with the prostate saint's "corpse" that terrorizes and fascinates Cemí; the tale of the disentombment of his grandfather, whose corpse magically dissolves as soon as it is struck by air. The wake as a nodular topos that ties together the many narrative strands in the total textual network of *Paradiso* is repeated in the metamorphosis of the musician's body in the crystal urn at the conclusion of chapter 12. This wake scene amalgamates all former funereal images in the novel, from the colonel's death on, into a synthetic kaleidoscope of transformations with a powerful cumulative effect. This kinetic, cinematic convergence of burial scenes climaxes with Licario's wake. Cemí experiences these repeating visions as he approaches Licario's coffin: "Recordó el relato de doña Augusta, su bisabuelo muerto, con uniforme de gala, intacto, y de pronto, como un remolino invisible, se deshacía en un polvo coloreado. La cera de la cara y las manos, en su runa de cristal, de Santa Flora, ofreciendo una muerte resistente, dura. . . . De nuevo la voz de su padre, escondido detrás de una columna" (*P* 457/*R* 464) [He remembered Doña Augusta's tale, his dead great-grandfather in a dress uniform, intact, who had suddenly, like an invisible whirlwind, breaking up into colored dust. The wax of St. Flora's face and hands, inside the glass casket, offering a resistant death. . . . Suddenly his father hidden behind a column].

The wake in both Joyce and Lezama's text represents a Viconian ritual process of transition and succession. The anticipated encounter between José Cemí and Oppiano Licario—constantly suspended and deferred, like Stephen Dedalus and Leopold Bloom's in *Ulysses*, in the halting architecture of the novel—occurs in the concluding chapters. Chapter 14 shows Cemí undertaking a complex, hermetic, Orphic journey though a nocturnal underworld to stumble by chance upon the house where Oppianio Licario, like Finnegan in the first part of Joyce's novel, is mourned in his coffin.

Although the parodic representation of Finnegan's wake belies the solemnity of *Paradiso*'s conclusion, Joyce's *walpurgisnacht* of transformations stages, like *Paradiso*'s last chapter, a similar ritual descent into Hades. Faithful to the Homeric and Dantean versions of hell, messages that mark a ceremony of succession are exchanged between the living and the dead in *Paradiso* and *Finnegans Wake*. When dead Finnegan springs up at the mention of whisky, the twelve mourners have him lie down, announcing that he has already been succeeded by HCE.[51] Thus the first section of *Finnegans Wake* obeys the Viconian tenet concerning the replacement of the barbaric age of the giants by the age of heroes.[52] Cemí's appearance at the wake represents a similar displacement of one stage by another by means of an inheritor: a substitute son, as Stephen is for Bloom. In Lezamian jargon, this is the replacement of the *eros del conocimiento absoluto* [Eros of absolute knowledge], Licario's pleasurable search for total knowledge, by the *creación en la imagen* [creation in the *imagen*], Cemí's poetic pragmatics.[53] This succession is "sealed" by Ynaca Eco's ritual delivery of the poem and the hermetic manuscript that contains the teachings of Licario, and, as we shall see, by the establishment of erotic cosanguineity through the body of Licario's sister.

Resurrection as a trope for regeneration—Viconian *ricorsi*—appears conspicuously in both texts. Book two of *Finnegans Wake* tells of the rise and fall of HCE, Finnegan's successor. This story, which deals with HCE's disgrace and public trial due to an alleged misdemeanor, ends (if such a verb can be used for the impossible textual closure of *Finnegans Wake*) with HCE's funeral and burial in a Dublin lake.[54] Soon after, HCE rises from the dead and is reported to be seen in very bizarre circumstances by several people.[55] Thus, after his "death" HCE obsessively reappears in the text, even after the story of his children Shaun and Shem (and all their subidentities) takes over the narrative.

In Lezama's second novel, Oppiano Licario is also resurrected in conditions as cryptic and mysterious as those of HCE's revival in *Finnegans Wake*. Cemí feels his ghostly presence and holds conversations with Licario's *corporización* (apparition) well into the evening. Like HCE, who is seen in the shape of a merchant and fish-monger, Licario wanders the earth assuming multiple, eccentric, ghostly guises. Purgatory in Licario's case assumes a circuslike appearance. Licario, in the colorful apparel of a trapeze artist, "corporizes" as a diner in several restaurants or a stroller in the park after midnight. Sometimes, imbued with the power of his mythological namesake, Licario is capable of flight. Like HCE's confrontation with his witnesses, Licario's encounter with the red-haired youth—Foción's promiscuous friend in *Paradiso*—is full of cryptic developments: a demonic cat attacks and viciously bites the arm of the youth, a mad doctor performs some dubious treatment on the wound. The eerie circumstances that accompany Licario's corporization in Havana resemble the strange consequences of HCE's wanderings after rising from the dead.[56]

Both novels also deal with the reconstitutions of lost or destroyed manuscripts. According to drafts and annotations left by Lezama detailing the projected evolution of the unfinished novel, *Oppiano Licario* was to conclude with the restoration of Licario's manuscript, *Súmula nunca infusa de excepciones morfológicas*.[57] According to these notes, the central plot of the missing chapters of *Oppiano Licario* concerns the process in which Cemí and Fronesis collaborate to piece together Licario's manuscript after Cemí's copy is ruined in a hurricane. Cemí labors to reconstruct the surviving pages (of which only one, containing a poem, is left intact), and Fronesis consults the writings that Licario leaves to the architect Abatón. *Finnegans Wake* features a parallel—though satirical—paleographical examination of an ancient manuscript buried and found damaged after several years: great attention is paid to this confusing piece of writing that seems to be different documents at once (Ana Livia Plurabelle's letter, a laundry list, an early Celtic attempt at writing).[58] Like Licario's *Súmula*, Ana Livia's letter is a metaphor—albeit a parodical one—for scripture, the sacred text of cultural and religious foundation.

Nevertheless, the principal Viconian motif developed in both narratives is the event which, according to Vico, initiates conscious human history: the thunderstorm that gives rise to religious dread. This notorious element of Viconian metahistory is adopted by the two twentieth-century authors in very idiosyncratic fashion; each novel gives this motif its own peculiar twist. In *Finnegans Wake*, the rumble of the thunderclap indicates a discursive shift or a change of focus.[59] This rumbling is a form of Godspeak, and is represented by long, compound, nonsense words.[60] Echoing Vico, the thunder-words in *Finnegans Wake* are considered the undecipherable voicings of God. On several occasions in Joyce's novel, the thunder surprises lovers "in the act," and compels them to marry. Thus, the various appearances of thunder in *Finnegans Wake* parody the Viconian giant's primitive understanding of the thunder as a Jovean admonishment to settle down with the woman he is with at the moment of the storm. Vico's "thunder-complex" thus provokes the founding of the institutions of marriage and religion.

Finnegans Wake satirizes the thunder-complex in the passage that "verbalizes" Kate's testimony at the wake when she recalls what compelled her to marry Finnegan. Through puns and neologisms, Joyce conflates references to Oriental and Western deities, nuptial augurial symbols, and details concerning the Deluge myth in order to relate Vico's "primal scene." Kate's sardonic delivery, sexual word-play and *double entendres* desacralize the experience by diluting and trivializing sacred fear, and inscribe the supernatural Jove into the ordinary by making his call a simple paternal admonishment. But despite its domestic tone, the passage communicates a folkloric sense of atavistic origin. (The bracketed comments represent my exegesis):

> For hear Allhighest sprack [speak, brack] for kwishnians [Christians, Khrishna] as for propagana [propaganda for pagan gentility] fidies and his nuptial eagles sharped their beaks of prey [Jove's "language" includes the flight of birds, according to Vico]: and every morphyl [mortal, morphological, gigantic] man of us, pome by pome, falls back into this terrine [terrain, Earth]: as it was let it be, says he! And it is as though where Agni araflammed and Mithra monished [admonished] and Shiva slew as mayamutras the obluvial waters [oblivion, diluvial: reference to the biblical deluge] of our noarchi [Noah's ark, archaic] memory withdrew, windingly goharksome [augurial sign], to some hastyswasty timberman torchpirest, flamenfan, the wads of the wind that lightened the fire that lay in to wood that Jove bolt, at his rude word [Jove's words are accompanied with lightning, which starts a fire in the forest, a conflagration]. Posidonius O'Flucturary [Poseidon, poisonous, fleuve, tributary: all these water names and symbols refer to Finnegan]! Lave [leave, wash] that bloody stone [reference to both Finnegan and Kate's sexual organs] as it is! What are you doint your dirty minx [Kate] and his beg treeblock was up your path [sexual word play]? Slip around, you, by the rare of ministers [admonishment to marry]! And, you, take that barrel back where you got it, Mac Shane's and go the way your old one went, Harchettsbury Road [admonishment to settle down]! And gish! (*Finnegans Wake* 80)

In *Oppiano Licario*, the Viconian thunderstorm is also associated with sex, superstition, and foundation, but it also acquires a special baroque, Caribbean flourish: Lezama translates Vico's primal scene into the "ab-original" experience of the tropical hurricane. The hurricane in chapter 6 has the peculiar effects that Vico associated with the "first" thunder. It advances the human state of consciousness and society as it orchestrates and authorizes a foundational act of coupling; it is thought of as the personification of an angry god; it inspires a sacred, atavistic fear and anticipation;

it "fixes" things in their place. Vico spoke of how thunder inhibits the giants from traveling and "fixes" them in their caves. *Oppiano Licario*'s chapter 6 opens with the sound of the "claveteo" [hammering] of boards and objects being fixed into place.

Lezama's peculiar adaptation of the Viconian thunderstorm is filtered through the prism of Fernando Ortiz's study of the mythology of the tropical hurricane, in his 1947 book *El huracán*. Many of the climatological terms and anthropological observations in Lezama's chapter are taken from Ortiz' book—the explication of the effects of the *ras de mar* [flooding], the discussion of the calm in the eye of the storm, the account of the superstitious practices that engulf the island as the hurricane approaches.[61] Ortiz's account of the hurricane's mythology—which ranges from pre-Columbian times to the present—has a Viconian metastructure. Ortiz studies the hurricane as a type of Jove, a primal deity that serves as the cornerstone of the mythological system of the region. Like Vico's Jove, this god drives the primitives into the caves and there inspires the writing of the first hieroglyphs. Reviewing the current archaeological data of this time, Ortiz minutely studies the iconology of the most antique inscriptions left on stone by the Cuban aborigines, and identifies the "figure of the spinning arms," known among experts as the "most typical of Cuba," as an emblem for the hurricane. Ortiz recognizes in the arching arms figured as a helix the gyrations of the hurricane's wind, and traces the diffusion and formalization of this symbol from the stylized and abstract spiral or spiroid emblems that abound in Antillean pre-Columbian archaeological deposits.

The encyclopedic fact-crunching of Ortiz's book—together with its references to the work of Sir James Frazer, whom Lezama also quotes in *La cantidad hechizada*—suggests that, in the investigation of the mythical ramifications of the hurricane phenomenon, Ortiz was attempting to produce the Cuban counterpart to *The Golden Bough*.[62] Moving beyond the Caribbean, Ortiz studies all type of coiled forms in archaeological remains from all over Latin America, concentrating on the Orinoco river system and the Yucatán and Veracruz regions in Mexico. In his ambition, Ortiz does not restrict his studies to Latin America, but studies isomorphic spiral symbols in Egyptian, Greek, Roman, Polynesian, and North American archaeology, following Vico's universalist imperative. By focusing on the hurricane as the initial, Jovian godform in the Old and New World, Ortiz aims to reconfigure a bold new system—a Viconian "new science"—of archaeological and mythographical interpretation. *El huracán* probably served as the American inspiration for Lezama's attempt to produce a mythopoetical system of the world through the examination of a consistent *imagen* in antiquity.

In Ortiz's account, the hurricane is a composite god, but, like Vico's Jove, it is first identified with the sky as one homogeneous "element":

> Para el indio de las Antillas, en el fenómeno del huracán intervenían los cuatro elementos: el aire, el agua, el fuego y la tierra. Sin duda pensaron los indoantillanos que en esos cataclismos intervenía así mismo un 'quinto elemento.' es decir, el de los cielos. . . . En el cielo, es decir, por encima de los vientos, los rayos, los truenos, las lluvias, los astros y las estrellas, es donde está el ente que los gobernaba a todos y los lanzaba sobre la tierra y sus habitantes. (54)

> [The Antillean aborigine believed that all four main elements intervened in the occurrence of a hurricane: air, water, fire, and earth. Surely the first Antilleans also thought that in these cataclysms a 'fifth' element intervened—that of the sky. . . . It was in the sky above the winds, the lightning, the thunder, the rains, and the stars, that the being that ruled them and wherefrom he unleashed those elements onto the earth and its dwellers.]

Ortiz considers "Juracán" to be among the first words created by the pre-Columbians, and, following the Viconian etymological method, assumes and traces its existence in all the regions where some form of the name has been used: among the Venezuelan and Guyana Arawaks, the isthmus Nahuas, the Maya-Quiché in Yucatan. The *pièce de resistance* in Ortiz's argument concerning the primacy of Hurricane as American god is the identification of the most ancient Mexican deity, Quetzalcoatl (whose Quiché name *kukulcán* is a variant, according to Ortiz, of the term *huracán*), with the god of the hurricane. Ortiz reads the account of the genesis in the *Popol Vuh* (whose cosmogonical principles are also studied by Lezama in *La expresión americana*, pages 65–70) as proceeding from the deluge-like experience of the hurricane, and pores over the colonial chronicles for descriptions of the climatic phenomenon and its representation in theological discussion and evangelization.

Although Ortiz demonstrates how many pre-Columbian societies considered the hurricane a demon or evil spirit, he takes pains to show that despite its destructive capacity the hurricane was generally regarded as a deity capable of regenerative effects on the productivity of the soil, bringing in its wake—when the storm's eye did not devastate the land— sorely needed water. Ortiz uses Fernández Oviedo's description of the Indian veneration of the hurricane

as evidence that the fear inspired by the hurricane was not hysterical but reverential, and that rituals were used to placate the wrath
of the god and reorient his energy in beneficial ways. The climatological indications preceeding the hurricane—the still, foamless
sea; the symmetrically curving cirrus clouds—are read as "expressions" of the god, just as the priests in Vico's theological era read
Jove's auspices, and ceremonies are celebrated to encourage a dialogue with the deity. Quoting Fernández Oviedo, Ortiz characterizes the hurricane as a demon the aborigines wished to placate and
petition in exchange for water for their planted fields. Evil, benign,
or both, the hurricane appears in Ortiz's pre-Columbian mythography as the foremost incarnation of divine omnipotence in the Antil-
les, the first and highest among the gods: "Antes y después de las
aguas del bautismo . . . entre los indios precolombinos de América
y sus sucesores el huracán fue la expresión de la omnipotencia div-
ina" (105) [Before and after the waters of baptism . . . the hurricane
was thought of as the expression of divine omnipotence among the
American pre-Columbian Indians and their successors].

By combining historical and modern testimonies of the phenomena associated with the hurricane, Ortiz seems to argue that the
actual witnessing of a hurricane inspires a regression to a forgotten,
primitive state. The experience triggers a mitigated remembrance of
the original fear. Although Vico argues that the fears of superstition
had disappeared by the vulgar era, his cyclical argument holds that
such regression is possible.[63] In Ortiz's uneven, sometimes tedious
study, there are frequent lyrical passages that contemplate the hurricane from a contemporary perspective. In the conclusion to the
first chapter, Ortiz refers to modern scientific sources and journals
to describe the meteorological and atmospheric particularities of a
hurricane's arrival—the distortion in cloud formation, the erratic
behavior of waves and tide—but he restores some of the underlying superstitious "primitivism" of the experience by inserting
verses from José María Heredia's romantic poetry and passages
from the autobiographical reminiscences of Lino Novás Calvo into
his "objective" account. By quoting from literature, Ortiz attempts
to convey some of the atavistic awe inspired by the voice of Jove
and thus circumvents the sanitized and dispassionate scientific de-
piction, though the conveyance of sacred fear is attenuated by the
stylizations of verse and literary prose. The lyricism of Heredia and
Novás Calvo's account contaminates Ortiz's style—known for its
aesthetization of the discourse of the social sciences[64]—in those
passages where the atavistic feelings revived by the hurricane are
considered. One example follows:

El sofoco de la estación aumenta hasta hacerse angustioso, en la calma serena del ambiente resuena el creciente rugir de la lejana marejada que se acerca a gran velocidad bajo el azote del vendaval, las mareas crecen, se van sintiendo de cuando en cuando algunas ráfagas precursoras, la electricidad sensibiliza la atmósfera, caen chubascos muy copioso y racheados, la humedad lo impregna todo de cierta viscosidad, el cuerpo se siente intranquilo . . . algo está pasando que "no es natural" . . . es el huracán. En esto estriba su mayor misterio, en que no parece "natural." Hay algo de "sobrenatural" en sus orígenes y causas, como en sus expresiones. "Se va a acabar el mundo," os dirá el campesino cubano. Todos los antillanos se llenan de pavor. Se encierran en sus casas, atrancan sus puertas y ventanas, clavándolas o amarrándolas por dentro con cabuyas, y el miedo al peligro inminente e irresistible hace poner en práctica todos los medios deprecatorios de las religiones. Es un momento de pavor en que el ser humano se encuentra impotente ante la inmensidad de la naturaleza encolerizada. Heredia lo expresó en un maravilloso verso:
     ¡El huracán y yo solos estamos! (48)

[The climate becomes increasingly suffocating and anguishing. Into the serene, atmospheric calm rushes the increasing roar of the still-far ocean surge that rapidly approaches, lashed by the windstorm. Tides rise; once in a while some precocious gusts are felt. Electricity animates the atmosphere. It rains copiously and forcefully; the humidity covers all things with a strange viscosity, our bodies become uneasy . . . something "unnatural" is taking place . . . the hurricane approaches. There is something "supernatural" about its origin and cause, in its expressions. "The world is going to end," a Cuban peasant will tell you. All the Antilleans are terrorized. They seal themselves shut in their homes, and secure doors and windows, nailing or tying them down with useless string. The fear of the imminent danger makes all the possible, preventive rituals of every religion resurface. In this moment of dread man finds himself impotent while confronting the immensity of an irate Nature. Heredia expressed this feeling in a marvelous verse:
     The hurricane and myself, stark alone!]

Against the representations of science, Ortiz adamantly juxtaposes a Jovian deification of the hurricane. In Ortiz's prose, the atmospheric "behavior" mirrors Vico's characterization of the first thunderstorm; like the thunderstorm, the hurricane arrives suddenly and unexpectedly after a period of great precipitation. The arbitrariness of the trajectory of such "meteors" inspires the belief in a willful, unpredictable deity that keeps man constantly under vigilance and in check. Ortiz so visualizes the apparent capacity for self-determination in the hurricane. Its erratic, spontaneous direction—like the stray explosions of lightning and thunder—seems to have "a mind of its own." This sense is reinforced with the *torna-són*, the inversion of the wind's direction with the crossing of the eye. The primitive mind conceives the *tornasón* as if the hurricane first lashed out with one of its arms and then with the other, ascribing human vengefulness and gratuitousness to the deity, and inspiring the hieroglyphic representation of the gyrating hurricane wind as swinging arms (50–51).

Lezama produces a picture of the hurricane influenced by Ortiz's study, incorporating the strategies of lyrical atavism fashioned by Ortiz's prose. In Lezama, as in Ortiz, the hurricane is the manifestation of a willful, capricious, destructive god that "sacralizes" the time and space of its apparation. Lezama traces the atmosphere of magic and exceptionality generated by the hurricane's approach. The hurricane's Jovian capacity to intimidate is reflected in the hysterical, and regressive, behavior of Cemí's sisters as they give him their dog to protect. The sisters' nervous stiffness as they attempt to board up the house is a symptom of the "neurosis of fixation" induced by Jove: the text highlights the injuries to the sister's fingers left by the mis-hammering of nails. Despite their will for flight, they appear hypnotically petrified, "absortas por el exceso de trabajo que les imponía el ciclón, como una divinidad que viene a cobrar sus ofrendas" (*OP* 183) [hypnotized by the excessive work that the hurricane imposed upon them, like a divinity that arrives to collect its offerings], "suavemente enajenadas"(*OP* 184) [softly alienated], so unable to move that "el miedo las orinaba a gotas" (*OP* 184) [fear peed from them drop by drop]. They finally manage to escape to Jaguey Grande, a place whose Arawak name suggests a primitive protective dwelling like that of Vico's cave.

In Lezama's account, however, the primitive dread inspired by the climatic auguries of the approaching hurricane is mixed with a peculiar sense of carnavalesque mirth and hieratic celebration—the nervous side-effects of sacred anxiety and the surface manifestation of the atavistic sexual energy that the "exceptionality" of the hurricane-god's visit unleashes. This sexual dimension of the Jovian "meteor"—unacknowledged by Ortiz, implicit in Vico's association of Jove's appearance with the institutionalization of marriage, explicit in the salacious thunder-scenes of *Finnegans Wake*—is well illustrated in Lezama's description of the naked youngsters who plunge into the Havana *malecón* [seaboard] before the gaze of schoolgirls and old women.[65] The arrival of the hurricane officiates over a semi-orgiastic carnival, where sacred dread and holy terror feed festive exaltation and sexual license:

Pero el grave del martillo . . . era constrastado por un aleluya, por un ambiente verbenero que como una comparsa avanzaba de cantina a barrio, de barrio a serpiente que iba jadeando y suspirando por toda la ciudad. (*OP* 174)

[But the grave baritone of the hammer . . . was antagonized by screams of hallelujah, by a carousel atmosphere that moved from bar to barrio like a conga line, like a serpent panting and sighing all around the city.]

Un dios irritado, cautelosamente traslaticio y engañador, cuya cólera, al alcanzar su plenitud se hacía dueña de toda la llanura, era recibida con chumba, con risotadas, con hollijos volantes, con paga doble en las cantinas. Con risitas y orinadas en todas las esquinas. El comienzo del ciclón venía a sustituir entre nosotros a las antiguas faloroscopias sicilianas. Antes de la llegada del dios irritado se preparaba un gigantesco espejo en semi-luna en cuyo centro oscilaba una llama fálica . . . Pero lo más curioso es que ese primer umbral abierto frente al ciclón, grostesco y de una sensualidad helénica, era acatado, transcurrido y paseado en silencio, como si todos estuviese acordes en aceptar sin aspavientos esa entreabierta franja del paraíso. Lo concupiscible latía en secreto enloquecido, pero ofrecía una forma inalterable en toda su extensión; nunca podremos saber si esa incólume contemplación del esplendor de los cuerpos era ese fingido paraíso que se entreabre antes o después del terror o en los avisos de la visita de un dios desconocido. (*OP* 174–75)

[An ill-humored god, shrewdly mobile and misleading, whose ire ruled the plain when it reached its zenith, was greeted with mirth, with guffaws, with flying fruit, with double rounds in the canteens. With hissing and pissing at every corner. Among us the arrival of the cyclone played the role of the old Sicilian festivals of the Phallus in which, shortly before the arrival of the ill-humored god, a gigantic mirror in the shape of a half-moon was built with a phallic flame dancing in its center. The most curious thing was that this first, grotesque gateway of Hellenic sensuality that opened in front of the cyclone was heeded, experienced and traversed in silence, as if everybody had agreed—harmoniously, without outbursts—to enjoy this half-open strip of Paradise. Concupiscence pounded madly but in secret, showing an inalterable form all throughout . . . We will never know for sure if this healthy contemplation of bodily splendors was the fake Paradise that stood ajar before or after the terror of the doorknocks of an unknown god who had come to visit.]

Lezama performs here a Joycean refashioning—what Harold Bloom would term a strong misreading[66]—of Vico's and Ortiz's texts. The hurricane Jove is also the equivalent of the god of the

Sicilian Festival of the Phallus and of the Greek Bacchus; even as the hurricane admonishes, its presence unleashes sexual desire. The hurricane-god instills both shame and shamelessness. This arousal is not, however, anarchistic or wholly orgiastic; like the original Jove, the hurricane liberates but also regulates sexual behavior. The strict, ritualized, ceremonial gestures that prefigure the sexual encounter of Ynaca and Cemí at the end of chapter 6 are reminiscent of Finnegan and Kate's in *Finnegans Wake* during the storm, and of Vico's assertion that the thunder's "first spark" of superstition fixed men in their cave and prompted them to remain faithful to one partner, inaugurating shame and channeling desire through the institution of marriage. The hurricane becomes the deity officiating over the sacrament of Cemí and Ynaca's union: like Vico's thunderclap, it "marries" Ynaca to Cemí. It sacralizes their sex by subjecting it to the rigor of the "inalterable forms" of ritual, which require a hieratic language of gestures and signs—hieroglyphics like the half moon with the standing lighted candle, symbols for the female and the male organs—which is the language expressed by the *sacerdotisa* [priestess] Ynaca Eco as she draws signs on the wall and the floor, cleanses Cemí following Orphic rites of purification, and inscribes on their bodies yoga junctures and energies. In *Oppiano Licario*, the hurricane thus becomes the second incarnation of Vico's atavistic imagination: Juno, the goddess of fertility.[67] Cemí's sister, *las solteronas* [the "old maids"], only recognize the inhibiting commands of Jove; Cemí and Ynaca Eco heed Juno's call to be fruitful and multiply within the strict ritual rules required by Viconian-Joycean mythography.

IV

So far we have shown the mythographic parallels between Joyce and Lezama's appropriations of Vico. The overlapping of Viconian elements in Joyce and Lezama's texts occurs not only in the configuration of the mythical, but on the linguistic, discursive level as well. Gilbert and Beckett interpreted the heuristic profusion of neologisms in *Finnegans Wake* as the crystalization of Vico's wish to create a universal root-language that would reveal the common declensive history of all tongues. This ambitious project is also apparent in the neologistic inclination of Lezama's texts, which, flouting Borges's prejudices, coin many synthetic terms whose purpose appears to be the deliberate mutation of the fabric of Spanish. Lezama's own peculiar use of "monstrous," fabricated terms (like "ingurgite," "cerveceo," "entreacabó," to mention a few) helps explain his positive appreciation of the similar practice in *Finnegans Wake*.⁶⁸

Although Lezama's neologisms have been evaluated by Cintio Vitier and others, analysis of these coinages requires more attentive work.⁶⁹ Although infrequent when compared to the ubiquity of Joyce's, they are just as conspicuous and reflect some of Joyce's heuristic force, even when they never approach the latter's creative extremes. In *Finnegans Wake* a neologism is never repeated; terms mutate constantly and indiscriminately. Lezama is more faithful to the production of a consistent new language not based on the principle of permanent self-sabotage, as is the case in *Finnegans Wake*. Fabricated words in Lezama participate in the reiterative and incantatory dimensions of language; they develop a restrained fixity in the conditioned entropy of Lezama's discourse, while that relative stability is absent in the perpetual kaleidoscopic shifting of Joyce's "echoland."

There is a theoretical basis for neologisms within Lezama's poetic system: the concept of the *súbito* [the "sudden"]. Although this term appears with the frequency of other key eccentric notions—like *vivencia oblicua* [oblique experience] or *potens*—in Lezama's essays, it is one of the least defined, and requires critical elaboration. Lezama's cryptic and fanciful definition of the term in his essay "Preludio a las eras imaginarias" [Prelude to the Imaginary Eras] goes as follows:

> La contracifra de lo anterior, lo incondicionado actuando sobre la causalidad, se muestra a través del súbito, por el que en una fulguración todos los torreones de la causalidad son puestos al descubierto en un instante de luz. En los idiomas donde el ordenamiento latino no gravitó con exceso, en el tránsito de la nominación, que fija al verbo, que ondula sobre la extensión, cobraban de repente la distancia que hay entre el nombre y el verbo. *Vogelon* (en alemán, el acto sexual), aislada tiene la oscuridad de lo germinativo. Esa oscuridad se rinde cuando vamos precisando dos sustantivos previos, *vogel* (pájaro) y *vogelbauer* (jaula para pájaros), no obstante, al llegar a la palabra *vogelon*, penetramos por un súbito la riqueza de sus símbolos, súbito que penetra en la acumulación de sus causalidades con la suficiente energía para hacer y apoderarse de su totalidad en una fulguración. (*OC* 2: 816)

> [The counterpoint to what I have explained above, the case of the inconditioned acting on causality, can be seen in the *súbito*, which produces an instantaneous flash that brings to light all of the towers of

causality. In those languages on which Latin syntax did not exert a great influence, the transit from an action to the naming of the action ... stretches further the distance between the name and the verb. "Vogelon"—German for fornication—by itself conveys only an idea of germinative darkness. This obscurity disappears when we begin to recognize two nouns within it, "vogel" (bird) and "vogelbauer" (birdcage). Thus when we return to the world "vogelon," in a *súbito* ("sudden" or "surprise") we penetrate the richness of its symbols and its accumulated causal meanings with enough energy to grasp its semantic totality in one flash.]

Lezama's philosophy of language is based on the postulation of the three functions of words which he adapts from Pythagoras via Vico.[70] According to Lezama, these are the simple word, the hieroglyph, and the symbol: "el verbo que expresa, el verbo que oculta y el verbo que significa" (*OC 2:* 810) [the verb that expresses, the verb that hides, and the verb that signifies]. The *súbito* is that instant in language at which this three-way distinction collapses, forming what Lezama calls the "triple verbo" [triple verb]. In the *súbito* the functions of expression, occultation, and signification converge simultaneously. A *súbito* might blow open the hidden significations of a word while retaining the word's hermetic, "hieroglyphic" articulation; it can show how a purely emphatic or rustic emotional utterance can also have sophisticated, symbolic meaning. The *súbito* cannot be the understanding of one term in synchronic language (Saussure's *langue*); it is rather the sudden visualization of a diachronic layering of meaning and rhetorical usage of the term that has been suppressed or eroded but is still latent. The *súbito* is an instantaneous glimpse into the archaeology of a word, revealing an unknown causality. As we saw in Lezama's reading of *Vogelon*, the *súbito* reveals a connection or affinity of a verb to an unrelated, "distant" noun(s)—a connection between "copulating" and "bird" and "birdcage." The *súbito* creates thus an unexpected kinship between disparate semantic terms by highlighting their homonymous elements—exactly in the way a pun merges conflicting significations into one term by manipulating phonic similarities. This new "kinship" between the terms unearths a "blinding causality," a potential system of etymological associations previously unknown. Thus the *súbito* can only occur as a compact, synthetic term whose newness triggers a surprising revelation that forces one to reconfigure established knowledge, as in the baroque, Jesuit concept of wit or *ingenio* in Baltasar Gracián.[71] The term *Vogelon* as *súbito* might indicate the unsuspected metaphoric origin of all action terms in the language, or suggest an ancestral ritual or totemic conceptualization of the sexual act.

Lezama's *súbito* as the instant understanding of how the history of naming ("tránsito de la nominación") develops a "distance" between the original, nominative "hieroglyph" and the verb that is derived from it, is an application of Vico's eccentric account of how etymology not only reveals the evolution of language but also demonstrates the transition of mankind from one age to another. Vico believes that Pythagoras's categorization of the three functions of language—expressive, occultatory, and symbolic—also describes the linguistic functions prevailing in each of the three ages of man (theocratic, heroic, and vulgar). In his analysis of the term *legere*— quoted in Beckett's essay—Vico performs *avant la lettre* Lezama's hermeneutic of the *súbito*. By assuming that the meaning of "lex" (acorn) is connected to the meaning of "legere" (to read) through a chain of lexical transformations, Vico prefigures Lezama's similar analysis of the term *Vogelon*. Though represented as a diachronic transformation, the determination of this connection is made on fictional etymological grounds that are grasped synchronically: on the assumption that the modern word contains and preserves within itself the archaic word. One term is simultaneously many terms, as puns are.

Thus, in the *súbito* and in Vico's fanciful etymologies, the flash of revelation occurs through the simultaneity of meanings; like Borges's Aleph, the word triggers many associations that cannot be hierarchized in a sequence, and thus may overwhelm its audience. In this way, despite the difference in neologistic practice between Lezama's discourse and Joyce's, Lezama's notion of the *súbito* as a punning word-play that triggers endless revelations becomes an accommodating definition for the Joycean neologism that Borges was not capable of appreciating. Lezama's *súbito* fitfully describes Joyce's synthetic terms. The *súbito* is the Joycean-joyous-jocular enlightenment that occurs with the "centering" or concatenation in one "invented" word of the several meanings accrued in one or several roots. This is what Lezama means when he speaks of the concentric emanations of the Joycean neologisms in his essay on Cortázar.

The discussion of the *súbito* together with the two references in *La cantidad hechizada* might be interpreted as the only instances where the achievement of *Finnegans Wake* is explictly considered in the work of Lezama Lima. Thus an argument could emerge that though Lezama did contemplate the creative implications of the poetics of Joyce's last novel, he did not attempt to implement such experimentation in his own novelistic work. Both Lezama's and Joyce's styles deploy a hermetic concept of literary language, but the difficulty in *Paradiso* and *Oppiano Licario* achieves a level comparable only to that in *A Portrait* and *Ulysses*, not *Finnegans Wake*. This assumption is contradicted by one segment in *Paradiso* that can be read as a pastiche of *Finnegans Wake*'s textual experimentation. In Tío Alberto's letter (P 170–73/R 168–71), full of close-to-impenetrable double entendres in which words referring to ocean zoology are to be interpreted as sexual signs that communicate an obscure warning against venereal disease, Lezama recreates the principles of the "ensaladilla verbal" [verbal salad] he recognizes in the late Joyce. This text is a dynamic fabric of punning *súbitos* that demonstrates Lezama's positive appropriation of the aesthetic project of *Finnegans Wake*.

Tío Alberto's letter marks a break with the textual mechanisms that predominate in *Paradiso*. It is not absolutely hermetic—the way the discursive constructions in *Finnegans Wake* are not, either—but the difficulty of the passage is especially strenuous. The effect is one of wonderment; Lezama's poetic manipulation of language here reaches the apex of its fabulous obscurity. Lezama's literary system, however, is less concerned with "primordial" obscurity than with the *esclarecimiento* [clarification] that follows. While illustrating the linguistic dynamics of *Finnegans Wake*, the language in Tío Alberto's letter functions as check and as boundary. Though dangerously close to *Finnegans Wake*'s "illegibility," Lezama's novelistic discourse will be produced on this side of the legible, with Tío Alberto's letter marking the limits of its hermetic density.

Like the sacred river of the *imagen*, Lezama's novelistic discourse rides the middle way between the opposites of the early Joyce's diaphanous concreteness and the later Joyce's experimental obscurity. Lezama's fiction is thus situated at the center of the equilateral triangle formed by the aesthetics of *A Portrait*, *Ulysses*, and *Finnegans Wake*. We could thus read Lezama's novels as some type of Cuban hypostatis of Joyce's literary trinity.

5

Joyce Wars, Lezama Wars: The Scandals of *Ulysses* and *Paradiso* as "Corrected" Texts

Ojalá que mi tentativa concite intereses, despierte polémicas,
ojalá arda Troya si es necesario.

[I hope my project inspires interest, provokes polemics, I hope
Troy burns if necessary.]
     —Julio Cortázar in a letter to José Lezama Lima, 28 July 1966

I

WHAT CAN THE HISTORY OF WHAT IS KNOWN TODAY AMONG LITERATURE scholars as the "Joyce Wars"—the notorious polemic led by John Kidd against Hans Walter Gabler's attempt to establish a definitive, "corrected" edition of Joyce's *Ulysses* in 1984—tell us about similar disputes concerning the editing of *Paradiso*? The 1966 Cuban novel has not only attained a canonic stature and reputation for difficult interpretation in Latin American fiction that rival those of Joyce's novel in the English language; its hazardous textual and editorial history bears uncanny parallels to that of *Ulysses*. At first glance, however, differences between the ideological and institutional configurations of the academic fields in which these two controversies are held would belie the possibility of a comparative analysis.

First, there is a significant contrast in the amount of professional investment and interest in these polemics and the measure of their exposure in the international media. A complete, well-structured establishment of scholars numbering in the hundreds worldwide—what is often known as the international "Joyce industry"[1]—was attentive to the seven-year process in which Gabler established his unprecedented methods for editing *Ulysses*. This industry documented, commented, commended, and/or criticized Gabler's enterprise in a wealth of conference papers, journal articles, books, and internet discussions that is still going strong in 1998. Because of

181

the novel's reputation as the major work of English literary Modernism and its prominent place in English academic curricula, popular journalism from the *Washington Post* to *Newsweek* and influential literary magazines like *The Times Literary Supplement* and *The New York Review of Books* have monitored or featured—often in rather sensational fashion—the subsequent, heated five-year reaction following Kidd's "first salvo" in 1985 against Gabler's 1984 "critical and synoptic" edition and the 1986 "corrected" trade paperback based on Gabler's work. These "wars" eventually led Random House to reinstate the 1961 trade version of the novel, thus deauthorizing Gabler's to a significant degree.[2] In the case of Cintio Vitier's 1988 "corrected" edition of *Paradiso* for the prestigious Archivo series, the interpretative and critical "wars" have only taken place in a few academic articles, the most outstanding being Brett Levinson's critique of Vitier's philological and logocentric approach to the novel, Enrico Mario Santí's dissension in a 1992 article for the Mexican journal "Vuelta," and Bernardo Teuber's analysis on how the contradictions of autobiographical discourse in *Paradiso* disqualify any attempts to "fix" the text.[3] The objections of these Lezama Lima scholars, however, have not led yet to consequences as drastic as those that have befallen Gabler's edition in the "Joyce wars."

Moreover, the technological and institutional resources available to these editorial enterprises have markedly different magnitudes. For Gabler's project, the German government donated a $300,000 grant to be used, among other things, for fact-checking throughout the many libraries and collections accross the Atlantic where the manuscripts, typecripts, notes, and correspondence related to the writing of *Ulysses* are kept. A sophisticated computer programing and processing system was used to collate manuscript and printing information, and there was continous encouragement from the Joyce estate to arrive at a substantially different document in order to secure a copyright extension.[4] To evaluate the "critical and synoptic" edition and the objections from Kidd and other scholars, international conferences were held in Monaco (1986) and Miami (1989).[5] In the case of *Paradiso*, resources were predictably more limited. Cintio Vitier's four years of what he calls "exclusively artisan work" was done without any major technological support.[6] Vitier's only monetary remuneration was a $1,000 payment from the Archivos publishers (an amount which can only be understood in the context of the schismatic distance between the current Cuban economy and the global market). Nevertheless, with the support of Cuba's Ministry of Culture, Vitier put together a team of critics and researchers that assisted him in establishing the text, which is supplemented by copious critical notes, interpretative essays, and explanatory addendas that make the Archivos edition recall simultaneously various staples in *Ulysses*' bibliography—Gifford's *Notes on Ulysses*, Thornton's *Allusions in Ulysses*, and Hart and Hayman's *James Joyce's Ulysses: Critical Essays*—as much as Gabler's 1984 edition.[7] Ironically, the Archivos *Paradiso*—printed in Spain and Mexico with UNESCO funds—is too expensive to be made available in Cuban bookstores, while the English language press has been generally indifferent to this new version of the text. The option of publishing a critical edition of Gregory Rabassa's 1970 English translation, "updated" according to Vitier's 1988 amendments and notes, was turned down by the Pittsburgh University Press due to lack of cooperation by the owners of the English translation copyright.[8] It would appear that, on the arena of international literary publishing, the "wars" regarding Vitier's edition of *Paradiso* are less consequential than the Joyce wars; that the problematics of editing Lezama's novel scarcely have textual or institutional implications equivalent to those associated with Joyce's novels.

I want to argue here that the opposite is true. If the controversies surrounding the editing of Lezama's novel do not appear to yield the same "casualty costs" as the Joyce wars, this only happens if we consider a quantitative evaluation of these phenomena. When we shift to theoretical, hermeneutical, ideological, even geopolitical dimensions, it is clear that what is at stake in the "Lezama wars" is something perhaps more urgent and pertinent than what is debated in the frays about *Ulysses*. In fact, institutionally speaking, the repercussions of the 1988 critical and revised edition of *Paradiso* on the current literary scene in Cuba and on Cuban cultural officialdom are quite proximate to those of Gabler's *Ulysses* in the Joyce industry. Just as Viking Press replaced all previous printings of *Ulysses* in 1986 with a massive trade paperback that adopted the text established by Gabler, the state-owned press Letras Cubanas released in 1991 a 13,000 copy printing of a new edition of *Paradiso*—the first done in Cuba since the 4000-copy first edition of 1966—that incorporates the 1988 revisions and an introduction by Vitier. This gesture is significant, since it has been generally acknowledged that, during the period of the 1970s known as the "quinquenio gris" (the "grey" five years), Lezama Lima was effectively "silenced" as a writer until his death in 1976.[9] Despite his persistent (if somewhat heterodox) Catholic beliefs, the modernist-prone aesthetic and demanding hermeticism of his work, and occasional attacks in some revolutionary journals against the "elitist" nature of his writing, during the sixties Lezama was employed by some of the Revolution's principal cultural agencies and was able to publish consistently throughout the decade.[10] After the notorious 1971 Padilla affair—in which Lezama was denounced as a writer ingrateful to the Revolution by Heberto Padilla himself in a staged ceremony that many compare to a forced "Stalinist" confession[11]—he was ostracized and his work was not published again in Cuba until after his death.[12] Some argue that this backlash was due in no small measure to petty resentment regarding the international success of *Paradiso* and the fact that much of this success was due to praises made in journals that were noxious to the regime—like Emir Rodríguez Monegal's *Mundo Nuevo*—and by exiled intellectuals who, at the time, had been openly denounced and abhorred within Cuba, like Severo Sarduy. The institutional support for Vitier's work—culminating with the second Cuban edition and printing of *Paradiso* after twenty-five years—could be thus interpreted as an act of critical reparation against injustices committed against Lezama's person and *oeuvre*.

Paradiso is thus "corrected" within the wider frame of the regime's "correction" of its own mistakes. In other words, Vitier's work occurs in tandem with (although not necessary subordinate to) institutional mechanisms of revolutionary *auto-crítica* [self-criticism] or *rectificación* [rectification], where correcting policy "error" often works as a co-opting strategy to confirm the Revolution's historical telos. Vitier underlines this need for "rectification" when declaring that republishing *Paradiso* and the rest of Lezama's work should be the duty of the Revolution after such missteps: "no lo publicamos porque queramos responder a las pretensiones de la contrarrevolución de hacerlo suyo, sino porque es un deber nuestro" [we are not republishing him in order to respond to the pressures of the counter-revolution, but because it is our duty].[13]

If the polemics around the Gabler critical and synoptic edition stimulated the organization of two international conferences and dynamized Joycean scholarship in new, unexpected ways, the Archivos edition of *Paradiso* directly contributed to the organization of two major academic events in Havana. First, the colossal international *Orígenes* colloquium of 1994 that celebrated Lezama Lima's work of cultural promotion as editor of the journal that first serialized *Paradiso* was buoyed by the appearance of *Paradiso*'s "definitive" version in Cuba and abroad and the added prestige that Vitier—the most outstanding (and outspoken) living member of Lezama's *Orígenes* group and the conference's chairman—had

acquired as its "establisher." Second, Vitier's work directly motivated the organization of the 1996 international conference cele-
brating the thirty years since the appearence of the novel, which he
introduced.[14] This event was sponsored by the "Casa Museo Lezama Lima," a museum set in Lezama's house recently (and luxu-
riously) renovated by the Ministry of Culture.

Nevertheless, after years during which the novel was disre-
garded—sometimes demonized—by the cultural bureaucracy, the
process of officializing *Paradiso* that began in the eighties with Vitier's rectifications reached its apex not with the celebration of
these conferences, but with the Cuban cinematographical industry's decision to produce *Fresa y chocolate* (*Strawberry and Chocolate*). This 1993 film was based on Senel Paz's prize winning short
story, in which *Paradiso* has a pronounced iconic importance. Perhaps the most important representation of a reformist cultural ideology in the Cuba of the nineties, the film openly encourages its
viewers to read *Paradiso* as it subliminally orients its interpretation,
underlining passages and scenes in the novel (such as Abuela Augusta's "almuerzo" or banquet in chapter 7) that promote a celebratory, inclusive concept of Cuban charm, generosity and
refinement: *la cubanía* [cubanness]. Diego's gift of Lezama's
novel—referred to in the film as "la más gloriosa novela que se es-
cribiera jamás en esta isla" [the most glorious novel ever written
on this island]—to David after the *almuerzo lezamiano* [Lezamian
banquet] happens at the climatic moment of the film. Nevertheless, Diego's line—"después de esto podrás decir que eres parte de
la cofradía de adoradores del maestro, faltándote sólo el conocimiento de su obra" [after this you can say that you have been initiated in the society of admirers of the Master, and you will only
need to get to know his work][15]—also implies that the book is a
transparent reflection of the cultural openness and ethics David
has learned from Diego, thus deemphasizing the novel's notorious
moments of demonic opacity, cloacal obsession, and subversive
irony. *Fresa y chocolate* minimizes the scandalous, hermetic, and
erratic elements in *Paradiso*, thus demonstrating the same facilitating and popularizing purpose in Vitier's "correction" of the novel
as stated in his introduction to the Letras Cubanas edition: "de lo
que se trata ahora es de apartar sencillamente los dos obstáculos
apuntados (escándalo, hermetismo) para abrir las puertas de *Paradiso* a un público no necesariamente de 'iniciados', público que en
Cuba le pertenece por derecho propio ya que la versión lezamiana
de lo cubano . . . tiene raíces profundas en las mejores tradiciones
de nuestra cultura" (iii–vi) [what matters now is to simply do away

with the two obstacles noted above—scandal, hermeticism—to open the doors of *Paradiso* to a public that is not made up by 'initiates,' a public to whom the novel rightly belongs since Lezama's vision of Cubanness . . . . has deep roots in the best traditions of our culture]. Both Vitier and the film project an accessible, transparent, scandal-free, "error-free" version of *Paradiso* that supports the vision of a tolerant, inclusive, festive, transcendental (Diego is, like Lezama, a *creyente* or believer), luminous, yet light-hearted ontology of Cuban culture.

Thus, the current official vogue of *Paradiso* in Cuba could be seen as part of a complex, oddly coordinated process that includes the island's film industry, literary criticism, cultural tourism, and academic exchange.[16] Within Cuba and within the intellectual circles defined by Cuban affairs, the consequences of Vitier's edition are thus enormous: Vitier's work frames the official recognition of the novel as *the* major work of Cuban literature in this century, assuming the status previously held in the Revolution by Carpentier's *El siglo de las luces* [*Explosion in a Cathedral*]. The publication of such a painstakingly prepared edition in such a generous printing in the stringent *período especial* underlines this final legitimation of the novel under the Revolution while it vindicates at the same time a Revolution now "corrected" of its former homophobia and intellectual intolerances. Clearly, Vitier's revision of *Paradiso* has institutional and ideological implications parallel to the magnitude of what the "corrected" edition of *Ulysses* had in First World academic studies.

Given that what is at stake is so considerable in both cases, it should not come as a surprise that the "corrections" of canonized texts such as *Ulysses* and *Paradiso* have motivated very strong reactions and similar patterns of polarization. In both cases two contending, empassioned camps of scholars can be clearly outlined. In the case of *Ulysses*, there are those who support the principles of Gabler's editorial work (i.e., Michael Groden, Vicky Mahaffey) and see the 1984 edition as an important contribution to Joyce studies; against this position are those spearheaded by John Kidd who consider Gabler's work seriously flawed and have called for its removal from print. In the case of *Paradiso*, the polarization is surprisingly more theoretically complex but not any less piercing. On one side there are the prominent Cuban nationals, Catholic or philological scholars who read in Lezama an ontology of affirmation, transcendentalism, or recuperable textual meaning and thus support the edition (i.e., Vitier, Prats Sariol, Samuel Gordon); on the other are exiled or foreign critics who, intepreting *Paradiso* from a post-structuralist, anti-ontological perspective, object to it (Santí, Levinson, Teuber). Inversely, some of the responses to Vitier's work operate within a theater of operations not that distant from Kidd's reliance on media other than just specialized bibliographical journals to launch his attacks. Santí's position commands an equivalent public exposure since his strongest denouncements have appeared in Octavio Paz's highly visible politico-cultural magazine *Vuelta*, which has been characteristically critical of the Cuban Revolution. Levinson's critique appeared not in a literary journal but in the *Cuban Studies Annual*, whose topics extend beyond aesthetic, bibliographical, or philological scholarship to address ideological and geopolitical issues about the consequences and developments of the Castro Revolution in Cuba and the Americas. Like the Joyce Wars, Vitier's promotion of a "sanitized," error-free *Paradiso* and Santí and Levinson's critique occur in an institutional framework that goes beyond exclusively literary or aesthetic concerns.

Thus, when scholars and editors address the peculiar role of "error" and indeterminacy in Joyce and Lezama's textualities, they bring up extraliterary issues of institutional power, of the mechanisms that set out to fix canonical authority. We could call the procedures that determine such a fixing foundational, since these critical, editorial, bibliographical, and archival strategies function to adjudicate foundational and ideological power to a text: they establish "scripture," as does biblical exegesis, constitutional documents, or Fidelista pronouncements. What motivates such strikingly similar debates is the way in which Joyce and Lezama's writings consistently question the possibility of setting up "scripture"—how they challenge the ontological foundations of any error-less, canonical, transparent, or divine authority. This is not to say that Joyce and Lezama are anti- or counter-foundational (as an extreme reading of Levinson and Santí's position might assume), but that they deliberately ironize solemn conventions by delving boldly into the prohibited, the demonic, the counter-scriptural, the gnostic, the heretical, the apochryphal, the scandalous. That Lezama and Joyce explore that "error" which erodes pious, patriarchal, or national foundations right at their core of legitimation becomes particularly clear in the way their works unswervingly address topics of "deviant" or "erratic" sexuality, breaking taboos in the midst of modernist prudery or revolutionary *machismos*, and in how they mangle stylistic correction in the process of heightening literary expression. As Catholics, both Joyce and Lezama are concerned with how orthodoxies are constructed *and* deconstructed. Their interest in heretics—the consistent allusions to Giordano Bruno, Pico della Mirandola, Jacob Bohme, and other heterodox thinkers in their work—transmutes into an obsession with impropriety—linguistic, sexual, moral, and political. While in Joyce this purpose might be anticlerical and iconoclastic and in Lezama a spiritual exercise—"un ejercicio de soga de la fe" [faith's jumprope workout]—in order to arrive at a more inclusive and syncretic ecumenism where even the demonic is not banished, both Lezama and Joyce investigate how sexual, religious, or ideological orthodoxies proceed from scriptural and foundational notions of "good" writing. This is why scandal—the breaking of taboos, of societal interdictions—and "bad" writing are so prominently joined in Lezama and Joyce, and why they instigate attempts at "correction" that are bound to fail. In order to probe these similarities, we will offer a comparative account of the publishing histories of *Ulysses* and *Paradiso* to distinguish two phases: an early phase when the text is corrected as a response or while responding to censorship and/or imputations of scandal, and a later phase (the period of the "wars" of our title) when the text is "corrected" after it has been canonized.

II

FROM SEXUAL CORRUPTION TO TEXTUAL CORRECTION:
RESPONDING TO SCANDAL

Like the case of *Ulysses*, the repeated appeals for a "corrected" version of *Paradiso* are motivated by the historical problem of a highly "corrupted" first edition. What is fascinating is how in both cases textual corruption transcends the typographical or linguistic realm to involve moral and ideological issues. The inherent complexity, formal novelty, compositional irregularities, and verbal obscurity of these novels undoubtedly created situations of transmission that were conducive to the proliferation of printing errors. Nevertheless, the imperative to correct these texts—to rid them of their "faults"—cannot be disengaged from the scandals provoked by the equally graphic and sexually "perverse" content of their most notorious chapters (the "Nausicaa" and "Circe" episodes in *Ulysses*, chapters 8 and 9 of *Paradiso*). The energy first invested in expunging errata from *Ulysses* and *Paradiso* seems to accrue in relation to the need to legitimate, explain, or hide their sexual excesses.

Joyce's biographers have thoroughly documented the circumstances that made *Ulysses* so prone to typographical mistakes. After the serialization of the novel as "work-in-progress" in the *Little Review* was interrupted by a U.S. court's obscenity ruling against the "Nausicaa" chapter (in which Leopold Bloom masturbates while watching Gerty MacDowell expose herself), the reluctance of publishers to print a book bound to be censored by government authorities in all English-speaking countries led Joyce to pursue unorthodox venues for publication. In association with Sylvia Beach's Shakespeare and Company, Joyce contracted a French press in Dijon to set the pages of his novel. The complications of French typesetters working on a very unconventional and unruly English text—with the typemaster Maurice Darantiere often "correcting" Joyce's English against the latter's wishes—was compounded by Joyce's terrible sight problems and the famous fact that Joyce treated the proofs like drafts, adding almost one third of the total volume of the novel in the process of revising it.[17] Thus, the ignominy of the "sexual" errors lead, in a way, to the novel's typographical corruptions. Joyce would later complain about all these errors, revise proofs for the 1924, 1926, and 1931 printing, or have associates like Stuart Gilbert work on such revisions in later editions. This work never achieved a final, "definitive" version of the novel since new corruptions were introduced with each resetting.[18] As it were, there was a intense, continued attempt on Joyce's part to correct the novel throughout the period when it was censored in Britain and America and only circulated clandestinely. Joyce's interest in the typographical "cleanliness" of his text waned after the ban was lifted.[19] Joyce's concern for typographical decorum only appears when there is a need to counter charges alluding to a different type of corruption, as if the professional or literary "cleanliness" of the text were the best evidence to counteract imputations of pornography or degeneration.[20]

In the case of *Paradiso*, the 1966 edition was judged as profoundly "corrupt" as the 1922 edition of *Ulysses* and, at first, not solely on typographical grounds. It shocked many in Cuba who saw it as a text that catered to prurient reading. The chapters that had appeared in serial form more than a decade before in *Orígenes* had raised expectations about a great masterpiece. Just as the episodes of *Ulysses* in the *Little Review* impressed Hemingway, Yeats, and Wells enough to sign up for subscriptions, writers like Vicente Aleixandre, Julio Cortázar, and Octavio Paz congratulated Lezama on his "work-in-progress" and expressed the wish to read the finished opus.[21] Unlike *Ulysses*, *Paradiso* did not broach during serialization the more explosive topics of androgyny or polymorphous homo- and heterosexuality that would become so central to its final version. Even when suggestions of sexual debasement occur in the episode in chapter 5 that tells of Alberto Olaya's first "nocturnal" adventure, very little of what appeared in *Orígenes* foreshadows the extremities of the three Farraluque orgies, the Leregas-Albornoz scene, and Foción's account of his incestuous Manhattan adventures, or the centrality of the colloquium on homosexuality in chapter 9.[22]

At the time of *Paradiso*'s publication, Lezama worked as a researcher in the Instituto de Literatura y Lingüística de la Academia de Ciencias de Cuba, preparing for the Consejo Nacional de Cultura what would become one of the most significant historical anthologies of Cuban poetry published during the Revolution. In 1966, an article in *Bohemia*, an influential popular journal, would announce with praise the appearance of the anthology and proclaim Lezama as an important poet and scholar.[23] At this point, the accusations that had been leveled in 1959 against Lezama and *Orígenes* by *Lunes de Revolución* intellectuals had lost their force.[24] It seems that, after having secured enough prestige to guarantee support for the novel's publication without intervention, Lezama decided at this point to continue, finish, and publish *Paradiso* while risking a higher dose of erotic boldness, as evidenced by Lezama's outline for the second part of *Paradiso*, a document significantly missing from the dossier in Vitier's critical edition. In envelope 410 of the José Lezama Lima Manuscript Collection at the Biblioteca Nacional José Martí in Havana,[25] there is a rough outline in Lezama's handwriting for chapters 7 through 16, probably sketched when Lezama decided to return to the novel after a long hiatus in the early sixties. Although many elements noted were rendered without change in the novel (Alberto's confrontation with his mother in chapter 7, the yaquis episode with Rialta and her children, the student revolts), the characters of Fronesis and Foción were still vaguely drawn under the names of Jacobo Damaster and Percón Pergroida. More surprisingly, Oppiano Licario appears earlier in this outline. In this prospected version, the character was to conduct in chapter 9 the talk about sexuality that Cemí, Foción, and Fronesis eventually carry on. In chapter 11, the outline indicates that in a "visita crepuscular" [twilight visit] to Jacobo Damester's firm, Licario would talk "de la driada indefinida, de la sexualidad que no se encuentra en el sexo" [the undefined driad, the sexuality not found in sex] and his other personal "anti-sexual" proclivities. Added to the fact that in the outline the theme of sex-

ual excess is highly visible ("Farraluque," the *Kamasutra*, "lo fá-
lico" [phallicness], "Rabelaisian allusions to the phallus," and
Godofredo el Diablo are also mentioned), clearly issues of sexual
taboo and deviance came more into the foreground when Lezama
returned to the novel. Thus, the completed novel came as an absolute surprise (and was meant to be) not only because, compared
to what was being published in Cuba that year, the frankness of
Paradiso's sexual scenes was a striking anomaly, but also since
Lezama's scholarship under the Revolution had followed so far
such a conformist, unintrusive tenor. (The critical and biographical
notes in Lezama's anthology of Cuban poetry are unusually unad-
venturous.)

Despite all the debates, there are not many written accounts detailing how *Paradiso* was received by its first readers and the revolutionary establishment. Nevertheless, the defensive nature of the
first essays praising Lezama's novel testifies indirectly to the vehe-
mence of some early denunciation. Salvador Bueno's review in *Bohemia*—the first on the novel—begins by referring to the constant
gossip and buzz that the novel's "episodios atrevidos" [audacious
scenes] had spawned—"no se hablaba en los corillos literarios de
otra cosa" [this was the only talk at all literary circles]. He then
suggests that the initial readings of *Paradiso* situated it capriciously
in a tradition of deliberate pornography, albeit sophisticated and
exquisitely rendered:

> En seguida que se puso a la venta en la librería de la UNEAC la
> novela "Paradiso" de José Lezama Lima empezaron los comentarios y
> los rumores. Unos opinaban que la nota obscena era demasiado fuerte.
> Otros consideraban que la calidad literaria de la obra estaba por en-
> cima de cualquiera de sus elementos constitutivos. Algunos hablaban
> de ciertos escritores picarescos del siglo XVIII. Otros, no tan modestos,
> citaban a Henry Miller.[26]

> [As soon as José Lezama Lima's novel was on sale at the UNEAC
> library the rumors and comments began. Some thought that the ob-
> scene note was too strong. Others that the literary quality of the work
> was above any single one of its constitutive elements. Some mentioned
> some picaresque writers of the eighteenth century. Others, not so prud-
> ish, quoted Henry Miller.]

Bueno writes his essay to warn against exaggerating the lewd-
ness of the sexual episodes in the novel, arguing that Cuban prudishness and conservatism had not allowed readers to appreciate
other, more important aspects. "Nuestro público lector es bastante

pudibundo y pacato: se asombra de cualquier nota atrevida, hacen gestos de consternación ante cualquier rasgo que se aparte de la rutina consabida." [Our reading public is quite prudish and conservative: any bold note offends them, they show consternation before anything that breaks the trod-on routine.] Bueno defends Lezama's sensational use of eroticism by considering the "picaresque" episodes part of the allegorical richness of José Cemí's progress toward poetic wisdom. They are tactically introduced in the phase of Cemí's adolescence to represent the "intenso sacudimiento" [intense awakening] of sexual awareness that is part of human growth; the strategic function in the total narrative and superb literary quality save these scenes from being "pornografía barata" [cheap pornography]. Yet, the conclusion of the review suggests that Bueno was not really concerned with the reactions of a titillated public that needs enlightenment, but with those of scandalized *comisarios* that would proscribe the text for its "indecency" and the potentially corruptive influence of such fiction on the public: "Algunos han estimado que el desarrollo de estos temas en una novela puede causar un efecto deplorable en cierto lectores" [Some have claimed that the development of these topics in a novel could cause deplorable effects in a number of readers]. Bueno responds that only those already afflicted with "morbid inclinations" could read those episodes in a prurient fashion; that, in the end, the novel is harmless since, given its difficult reading and hermeticism, "no está destinada a la mayoría de los lectores" [is not destined to the general public] and, therefore, out of the para-epidemiological official concern for public morality. In this way, Bueno's review recalls arguments wielded by Ezra Pound, T. S. Eliot, and even Morris L. Ernst defending *Ulysses* against charges of obscenity.[27]

The profile of the revolutionary prude offended by Lezama's *osadía* [daring]—obliquely sketched in the first text written on *Paradiso*—becomes frighteningly stark with the appearance of a polemic published in a subsequent issue of *Bohemia*, clearly the first salvo in the interpretation "wars" around Lezama's novel.[28] The article in favor of the novel was written by Lezama's friend, Loló de la Torriente. A formidable appreciation of the novel, it is lucidly and thoroughly conversant with Lezama's poetic philosophy. The essay appears to have been written in consultation with the author since it gives away codes not yet available to readers, such as the revelation that the enigmatic chapter 12 recreates Cemí's dreams and nightmares after his father's demise, and the clearheaded glossing of the esoteric symbolism of the novel's confusing and fantastic concluding scene at Licario's funeral. The "con" article, written under the pseudonymn Juliosvaldo, is, on the other hand, a rabid, homophobic condemnation of *Paradiso* read as an open, unapologetic promotion of "Greek love." In a caricature-like diatribe teeming with spleen and disgust, Juliosvaldo calls the novel the pretentious work of an "orfebre satánico" [satanic artisan] who is out to humiliate the readers with "una exhibición circense de su innegable erudición" [a circus-like exhibition of his undeniable erudition] or assault them with "a fárrago implacable de un vocabulario capcioso" [implacable torrent of his obtuse vocabulary]. According to Juliosvaldo, Lezama "quiso crear un cosmos y no pudo obtener sino el caos" [wanted to create a cosmos and only could come up with chaos]. Juliosvaldo argues that the novel is a colossal failure not just because its use of a impenetrable hermetic, amphibolous language will not survive the Revolutionary "prueba de fuego" [test of fire] of communicating and holding "una conversación con el pueblo" [a conversation with the people], but especially because its "Machiavellian defense" of homosexuality as articulated in the dialogues of chapter 9 will not redeem a "long lost cause" given that evolution and biology had "marginalized" homosexual customs to the verge of extinction.

The article is written as a systematic refusal of Bueno's (not Torriente's) appreciation. To Bueno's reference to Lezama's reputation as one of the country's best poets as proof of the literary seriousness of *Paradiso*, Juliosvaldo counters that the novel must "stand on its own"; to Bueno's point that the central theme of the novel is Cemí's poetic progress and not homosexuality, Juliosvaldo responds that Cemí could not have been unaffected or uncontaminated by the "apetitos malsanos" [degenerate appetites] that surrounded him. Juliosvaldo is especially insidious in his evaluation of *Paradiso*'s "degenerate" characters—"los personajes más revulsivos de toda la literatura contemporánea" [the most revulsive characters of contemporary literature]—and in his imputation of base, prurient purpose to Lezama's erotic prose: "Con la descripción detallada de sus desviaciones y vicios comete *Paradiso* una de sus faltas más graves, pues el regodeo deliberado y descarnado de los hechos . . . hiere a fondo al más impávido y . . . no aportan nada a la cristalización de la novela como obra de arte." [By describing in detail all sorts of deviations and vices *Paradiso* makes one of its most serious faults, since the deliberate and explicit delight in description offends even the most blassé and does not contribute to the novel's crystalization as a work of art.] According to Juliosvaldo, the novel's assault on the reader's decency is rein-

forced significantly by the lack of care in its revision and printing—
"la gran cantidad de errores ortográficos que la novela . . .
demuestran poca consideración para el público lector" [the great
amount of orthographic mistakes . . . shows little consideration to
the reading public]—thus establishing a link between textual errancy and the author's moral corruption. Juliosvaldo's outrage recalls that of the typist's husband who put into the furnace fire those
pages from Joyce's manuscript for "Circe" in which a fantastic, sexually transformed Leopold Bloom is engaged in masochistic relations with the "virilized" madam of a brothel. Clearly, Juliosvaldo
would have supported such a fate for the full printing of Lezama's
Paradiso.

The vibrations from Juliosvaldo's seismic diatribe are felt in the
subsequent essays written to defend Lezama's novel as a masterpiece. Many of the early commendatory reviews carried the hidden
agenda of protecting both Lezama and his novel from the possibility that attitudes like Juliosvaldo's could lead from cheap scandal
to real censorship (or worse) in a Revolution that had a heavy
machista imprint and had for some time attempted to "rectify" homosexuals in special military camps.[29] This agenda is evident in
the next polemic to appear in print. Mario Vargas Llosa and Emir
Rodríguez Monegal's exchange in *Mundo Nuevo* concerning the
novel's treatment of homosexuality was triggered by a note in
which Monegal expressed surprise at Vargas Llosa's failure to acknowledge this topic in an essay on *Paradiso* published in *Amaru*.[30]
Rejecting the suggestion that this silence might be a measure of his
own "puritan" prudishness, Vargas Llosa responds in a letter that
recapitulates Bueno's argument. Out of "irritation" with the fixation Cuban readers had on the sensational sexual episodes, which
in his view only occupy "un lugar relativamente modesto en la
novela" [only a relatively modest place in the novel] (89), Vargas
Llosas chooses not to address sexual issues in his piece. He opts
to focus on other themes he considers central in order not to add
fodder to an interpretation that "denaturalizes" the novel by reducing it to a militant "treatise, manual, or apology of homosexuality,"
an "encubierto manifiesto sodomita" [a veiled, sodomitical mani-
festo] (90). That Vargas Llosa is responding not to Monegal but to
Juliosvaldo's evaluation of the novel as "pura pornografía" [pure
pornography] is clear in the concluding passage:

> lo peor es que se consolidara y propagara en torno a él en nuestras
> tierras, tan ávidas de pintoresquismo sexual y de escándalo barato, el
> rumor disparatado de que *Paradiso* tiene algo que ver con la porno-

grafía, es un panfleto sexual, o puede servir de alimento y estímulo a voraces onanistas. (89)

[the worst would happen if, in our (Hispanic) countries so avid for colorful sexual exploits and cheap scandals, a ridiculous rumor spreads and establishes that *Paradiso* has something to do with pornography, is a sexual pamphlet, or could feed and stimulate hungry onanists.]

In a brilliant answer, Monegal shows overwhelming evidence about the omnipresence of homoeroticism as it intermingles with and overwhelms heterosexuality across the novel. Monegal clarifies that he is not just concerned with the novel's few graphic depictions of intercourse, but with the many indirect references to alternative sexualities throughout the book; among the latter he lists the obscene grafitti that appears on Marticillo's door, Fibo's pen, sexual insinuations young Olalla receives in a movie theater, and Foción's exposure of his penis to Cemí after Fronesis' departure. However, Monegal does not acknowledge Vargas Llosa's hidden purpose of preventing the inflation of Juliosvaldo's charges of degeneracy against Lezama. Monegal's subtle and perceptive, almost clinical catalogue of *Paradiso*'s numerous instances of sexual "deviancy"—which are not limited to homosexuality but include castration anxiety and fetishism, thus bringing up a wider array of sexual issues—should have appeared particularly galling to Juliosvaldo and his ilk. Monegal probes into that prohibited arena that Vargas Llosa fears might further stigmatize the book and play into the censor's hand.

Both Emir Rodríguez Monegal and Mario Vargas Llosa refer in their exchange to the then recently published article by Julio Cortázar, today generally recognized as the piece that mitigated the first scandal of *Paradiso* and the "wars" it unleashed.[31] Vargas argues that, by only making two passing allusions to the problem, in his important essay Cortázar adopts a position fraternal to Vargas's deemphasis on homosexuality. Monegal counters brilliantly by reading Cortázar's introductory section on the intertextual use of Verne in *Paradiso* as a discrete way of foregrounding Verne's closet homosexuality. What Vargas and Monegal fail to note is that Cortázar skirts altogether the polemic about the novel's sexual "deviances"—Cortázar makes no mention of the critics who regarded *Paradiso* as gay pornography in disguise—and instead circumscribes the problem of corruption only to the realm of the textual. Dealing obliquely rather that overtly with the novel's problematic sexuality, Cortázar redefines the notion of the novel's scandalous-ness and thus reorganizes the warring camps. None of the other reasons he offers for the "silence" around Lezama's novel deal with questions of obscenity; only with its "instrumental difficulty" and the "circumstances of underdevelopment" in which the U.S. embargo hampers the circulation of the novel in Latin America. In relation to the textual errors, Cortázar writes:

> Queda, quizá, una tercera y más agazapada razón del torvo silencio que envuelve la obra de Lezama; voy a hablar de ella *sin pudor* alguno precisamente porque las escasas críticas cubanas que conozco de esa obra no han querido mencionarla, y en cambio *conozco su fuerza negativa en manos de tantos fariseos de nuestras letras*. Me refiero a *las incorrecciones formales* que abundan en su prosa y que, por contraste con la sutileza y la hondura del contenido, suscitan en el lector superficialmente refinado *un movimiento de escándalo e impaciencia* que casi nunca es capaz de superar. (49–50, my emphasis)

> [There is also, perhaps, a third, and more hidden, reason for the oppressive silence that surrounds Lezama's work: I am going to speak of it *without mincing words* ("sin pudor," without shame) precisely because the few Cuban critics familiar with his work have chosen not to mention it, but *I know its negative effect in the hands of many Pharisees of Latin American letters*. I am referring to the numerous *formal errors* in Lezama Lima's prose, which, in contrast to the subtlety and profundity of its content, produce a *scandalized impatience* that the superficially refined reader can rarely get beyond.] (87–89, my emphasis)

Rather than obscenity, Cortázar brings up instead the topic of Lezama's *formal* naiveté as a writer, manifested in errors in grammar, spelling (specially of foreign names), phrase quoting, composition, novelistic form, and other issues of stylistic decorum that had only been emphasized before by Juliosvaldo. (Torriente, in contrast, speaks of the novel's "great polish," *Bohemia* 38.)

By expounding the idea of Lezama as the great American innocent, Cortázar erases the picture of the corrupting, demonic, artless degenerate implied by Juliosvaldo; by reducing the issue of "corruption" in the novel to Lezama's textual incorrections, he banishes the rumors about sexual errancy. Cortázar argues that the magnification of, and condescending response to, "formal" errors by Latin American intellectuals when reading Lezama's works is a "defense mechanism" to avoid following Lezama "en su implacable sumersión en aguas profundas" (50) [implacable dive into the deepest waters]. What Cortázar means here is the refusal to tackle Lezama's poetic system in its own terms for fear of being over-

whelmed or humiliated by Lezama's erudition and originality. Cortázar avoids referring to strategies of self-repression and censoring
that arise in the reader when confronting the novel's illustrations of
sexuality. Contrary to what Rodríguez Monegal claims, the "aguas
profundas" in Cortázar's phrase suggests only in a tangential, elliptical way the centrality of the erotic in *Paradiso*. Cortázar redemar-
cates pruddishness and scandal by narrowing these down to
responses to textual corruption. Censorship or banning by comi-
sars (the "fariseos de nuestras letras") would only be contingent to
typographical or stylistic improprieties. Cortázar's solution to this
danger is to exert his energy (which is not at all exempt from erotic
investment) revising the text, making it formally "correct," errata-
less, with the right quotations, as the best remedy against the vision of the novel as a degenerate, corrupt one.

Thus, Cortázar's intense work with Carlos Monsiváis in preparing the Mexican 1968 Era edition can be thought to be motivated
secretly by the wish to rid *Paradiso* not only from textual scandal
but from the misreadings of its sexual content: in sum, from ill re-
pute. A similar drive also energizes many of Joyce's exegetes like
Stuart Gilbert, who wrote highly elaborate interpretations that drew
from classical philology and "proper" academic methods of analysis to deflect fixating on the more heterodox and scandalous elements in the text.[32] Sarduy's famous objection to Cortázar's textual
prudery ("hablar de los errores de Lezama es ya no haberlo leído"
[to speak of Lezama's mistakes is not to have read him yet]) might
be read here as a declaration that "cleaning up" Lezama's writing
is to disregard as well the deeper exploration of sexuality in his
work.[33]

III
FROM THE ORIGIN OF ERRORS TO THE ERROR OF ORIGINS:
HOARDING CANONIZATION

Gabler and Vitier's corrections of the texts of *Ulysses* and *Paradiso* occurred in a moment when obscenity and censorship were
not at issue; by this time the canonicity of both novels had been
generally established. The polemics that they have inspired thus
bring up other hermeneutical and philosophical matters, although
there is still an attempt to domesticate the demonic side of Lezama
in Vitier's punctilious expiation of mistakes. Therefore, the anxie-
ties in confronting sexual errancy still motivate the obsession to

"cleanse" the text, but new issues of "origin," meaning, and dissemination in textual theory are foregrounded.

Both Gabler and Vitier make unusual innovations in the methods they use to clean up *Ulysses* and *Paradiso* in order to avoid the compounded corruption that has plagued previous attempts to correct the texts. In the case of *Ulysses*, the wish for a revised edition—after a long history of printings in which Joyce and his associates attempted to produce an accurate version—was restated by John Dalton's denunciation of 4,000 errors in the 1961 reset edition of the Random House *Ulysses*, arguing that, like Joyce, the edition was unable to eradicate all incorrections while adding new ones.[34] Following Dalton's prerogative, the backcover notes to Gabler's trade edition claim to "fix" around 5,000 errors (although Gabler himself did not view his work as a correction, as we shall see).

Vitier's description of the insufficiency and inadequacy of Cortázar and Monsiváis's Era edition recalls Dalton's complaint. Even when done without consulting the manuscript, Lezama subscribed Cortázar and Monsiváis' edition as "impecable," "sin el sobresalto de las erratas, esos piojos de las palabras, como decía Flaubert" [without the interference of typos, words' headlice, as Flaubert used to say].[35] In his philological note to the Archivos edition, Vitier writes that, despite having achieved the fame of "haber salvado las numerosísimas erratas de la edición cubana" [having corrected the great numbers of errors of the Cuban editions], the Era edition is shown to be as corrupt as the Union edition after collation with the manuscript and the chapters published in *Orígenes*. In fact, while Vitier counts 798 errors in the Cuban edition, he finds 892 in Era—489 remaining from the Union and 403 which have been added to the text, among these some 70 "amendments" to Lezama's style that Vitier annuls (xxxv–xxxvii). Vitier does not include in these numbers emended errors in punctuation, capitalization, italics, or spelling—only those plausible but erroneous interpretations of Lezama's handwriting that appeared in the printed text. Thus a total sum of items changed throughout all the "corrected" editions of *Paradiso* could easily approach Dalton's estimate for mistakes in *Ulysses*.

Confronting the intricate and labyrinthine history of corruption in both *Ulysses* and *Paradiso*, Gabler and Vitier choose similar— but not identical—procedures to set down and revise a copytext or "texto-base." Vitier's rejection of the Era edition as copytext in order to give authorial primacy to Lezama's extant manuscript of *Paradiso* (even over copies of the Cuban Unión or Mexican Era editions corrected in Lezama's own hand) echoes Gabler's decision to establish a copytext not according to any extant edition but to a "continuous manuscript copy."[36] Both Gabler and Vitier's purpose is to circumvent error in the stage of transmission by drawing on documents related to the compositional phase of the novel. Both Vitier and Gabler privilege the idea of *Ulysses* and *Paradiso* as "inscriptional" rather than published works: as manuscripts and not as books, pointing to an "origin" before printing, book production, and public consumption—before reading and interpretation, before dissemination—that precedes any corruption. Like Gabler with *Ulysses*, Vitier wishes to present *Paradiso* as "Lezama wrote it," trying to recover the most pristine emanations of creativity before it becomes smudged by clumsy reading eyes.

This, however, does not mean that Vitier regularizes or eliminates the extravagances and peculiarities of Lezama's prose style. As Gabler, by making a distinction between documents of composition (the manuscript) and documents of transmission (the typescripts, proofs, and editions), Vitier differentiates between Lezama's idiosyncrasies and the gaffes of *Paradiso*'s printers. Vitier thus adopts a more permissive attitude toward Lezama's extravagances than Cortázar. Vitier in fact objects to Cortázar's attempt to regulate Lezama's prose, especially verbal constructions, in the Era edition:

> Por otra parte, la edición *Era* plantea problemas de diversa índole, que tienen que ver con la sintaxis, el uso de los tiempos verbales y la puntuación. En estos tres aspectos se nota un bien intensionado deseo de "regularizar" la prosa lezamiana, propósito que, salvo cuando se trata de *lapsus* obvios, no compartimos. Nuestro criterio, en esta edición, ha sido el de la máxima fidelidad posible a las características personales de la escritura de Lezama. (xxxviii–xxxix)

> [On the other hand, the Era edition presents several sorts of problems, which have to do with syntax, verbal tenses, and punctuation. In these three aspects we detect a well-intentioned wish to "regulate" Lezama's prose, a purpose which, except in case of obvious *lapsus*, we do not share. Our criterion in this edition has been to uphold maximum fidelity to the personal idiosyncrasies of Lezama's writing.]

Levinson is thus wrong in saying in his critique that Vitier's enterprise is exclusively corrective, that Vitier doesn't acknowledge any participation of error in Lezama's writing. ("Vitier cannot admit that Lezama himself might be responsible for the damages found in *Paradiso*, that those errors existed from the beginning . . ." "Strange Notes": 199.) As a rule, Vitier restores many of the commas omitted by Cortázar and many of the eccentric phrase constructions Cortázar found so "primitive." He also glosses with lucidity the peculiarites of Lezama's often Finneganesque transmogrifications of grammar, clearly investing a premium on the artistry of Lezama's "improper" use of language. Thus, Vitier's edition is not exactly "error-free." As Vitier, Gabler also restores "mistakes" in *Ulysses* as long as these are authorized by the manuscripts and make sense in the narrative context.[37]

Since by now canonization is a fact, Vitier does not suffer from Cortázar's anxiety about making the text look perfectly "clean" and uncorrupted. Nevertheless, Vitier's edition uses other means to placate possible scandalized reactions before Lezama's boldness. As Levinson has pointed out, the edition overdetermines the novel's readings with a series of interpretive essays that, for the most part, stress an ontological, Cuban, historical, and logocentric reading of the novel, while militantly discouraging (in Prats and Vitier's interventions) deconstructionist, Freudian, or Lacanian approaches that argue for the endless deferral of meaning or irrecuperable origin in Lezama's system.[38] Sarduy and Ortega's collaborations are the only exceptions to this rule.

What Vitier still subscribes to in Cortazar's "new and improved" *Paradiso*—which Levinson accurately criticizes—is not the myth of Lezama the American innocent but that of Lezama the tropical indolent, who, according to Vitier, cared less than most writers about revising transcriptive or transmissional mistakes.[39] This recalls Gabler's distinction between Joyce the brilliant, disciplined, and workaholic writer and Joyce the careless scribe so given to "eyeskipping" when transcribing or proofreading his work.[40] However, by applying this distinction, both Vitier and Gabler dismiss the possibility of a deliberate poetics or theory of error and chance in Lezama and Joyce's creative writing. Clive Hart has objected to Gabler's scriptural imperative since it paints the image of an infallible writer who does not treasure lapsus or error when these are in fact volitional "portals of discovery" in the Joycean world, according to Stephen Dedalus's famous quote.[41] Gabler's method eradicates those lapsi or errors in transmission that frequently inspired Joyce to produce new portmanteau words or invent out of the associations triggered by the typographical mistakes. Hart's objections apply as well to Vitier's treatment of Lezama. What Vitier considers to be Lezama's far-from-hearfelt (in fact, indolent) passive authorization of corruptions and their proliferation in the transmitted texts is, according to Santí and Levinson, a different creative and poetic position altogether.

One final word about Gabler and Vitier's affinities: the critical presentation and apparatus of their "revised" texts differ markedly. Gabler's synoptic text on the recto page uses complex diacritical signs to show in a synchronic, spatial layout the genetic, diachronic history of the text; Vitier uses the more conventional method of footnoting variants in former editions to his established version. Vitier's notes are, in fact, more limited than what one would expect, since there is no clear indication of how the historical collation with all the former editions was done: the reader often does not know when a mistake should be attributed to the Unión or the Era edition. On the other hand, there is, as in Gabler, a presentation of the compositional progress of *Paradiso* since Vitier consistently highlights the differences between the printed texts and the manuscript, thus offering the reader scriptive options and the opportunity to compare variants. Vitier allows some valuable synoptic and genetic vision into the text, although, as Levinson has pointed out, much is missing.

Gabler and Vitier's works have inspired powerful responses, but there are important differences in these responses. The main battle cry in Kidd's objection to Gabler is that of carelessness. Kidd is not preoccupied with defining a phenomenology of error or in trying to theorize what is correct in a Joycean text; his critique is mostly procedural, and, despite protestations about Gabler's methods and principles, he seems to be vying for a state of perfection and correctness more stringent than that proposed by Gabler. Kidd's whole work can be characterized as a longer "listing" of mistakes. Kidd's lists do not really address matters of Joyce's creative approach to error, which critics like Hart have brought up; they simply put Gabler under a higher demand for precision. This explains the title of Kidd's first piece: "Errors of execution in Gabler's *Ulysses.*" Kidd's article "The Scandal of Ulysses" is mostly an elaboration of this critical strategy.[42] Despite the theoretical nature of the first thirty pages of his book-length analysis "An Inquiry into *Ulysses: The Corrected Text,*" Kidd still pursues incorrections, sloppiness, and missteps in Gabler's practice. According to Kidd, Gabler's impropriety was not attempting to expunge error from the book, but going about his effort in an inappropriate, unrigorous fashion. Thus, Kidd argues for errors in Gabler but implies an absolute infallibility to Joyce the creator, seeing him as an unerring officializer of his word in print. For Kidd (as for Gabler and Vitier) there is a recoverable, *original* text; Kidd believes, however, that Gabler has recuperated the wrong one.

Santí and Levinson's critiques of Vitier are *profoundly* different. I stress the word "profound" here to argue that they show a more sophisticated vision than Kidd's by postulating a phenomenology of error in Lezamian textuality which also operates in Joyce, yet remains unrecognized by Kidd. In this sense, while Vitier and Gabler's projects have many points in common, Santí and Levinson in no way share Kidd's prerogatives. Santí and Levinson's critiques have, however, some limitations as well, as we shall see. Since Levinson is in great part influenced by Santí, I will conclude by discussing the fascinating, complex debate waged between Santí and Vitier over Lezama's work.

Santí's comments on the Archivos *Paradiso* in *Vuelta* cannot be deemed as constituting a review of Vitier's work, even though they did appear in the journal's books section and were presented in review format (with the title of the "reviewed" book and its bibliographical information preceding the essay). Even when the semiotic presentation of these comments encourages reading them as part of a book review, they happen to be an essentially testimonial account of Santí's relationship with the novel (and with the Archivos 1988 edition in particular), a paper whose first version Santí read in a panel on Lezama at the Kentucky Foreign Language Conference in April 1992. Santí does not consider this "testimony" a review or even a piece of scholarship, and makes this clear from the start: the opening paragraph warns that "no es el típico *paper* académico. Más cercano a un extracto de mis memorias, está a medio camino entre la reminiscencia y la respuesta, entre el desahogo y la confesión" (45) [this is not a typical academic paper. It is closer to an extract from my memoirs, in the middle ground between recollection and response, release and confession]. The paper is a personal, even evocative retelling of his experience reading fifteen years ago (at the same Kentucky Foreign Language Conference of April 1977) his paper "Parridiso" (a neologism roughly translatable as "parricide in Paradise" or "Parridice") in front of his peers and his mentor, Emir Rodríguez Monegal. In this brilliant paper (later published in *MLN* but which Santí does not fully summarize in his comments), Santí interpreted errors in Lezama's writing from a Derridean, Freudian perspective, arguing that they reflect (or allegorize) an intrinsic stance against the authority of the Father, Society, and Convention. Santí deftly narrates the history of this very important and disseminated essay, describing the positive and negative responses it provoked, and remarking both on its persisting influence in the States on young Lezama scholars like Brett Levinson and on the fact that it has not been yet officially printed and distributed in Cuba. The second half of Santí's "testimony" concentrates on the very negative and condescending fashion in which "Parridiso" is discussed—more than ten times, according to Santí—in the annotations and essays of Vitier's Archivos edition.

Even though Santí asserts that a full discussion of the problems in the textual assumptions and editorial principles of Vitier's work "would require a small book," Santí's brief "testimony" is a complex rhetorical piece that suggests a very peculiar view of Vitier's edition: that it was done in part to negate Santí's claim in "Parridiso" (as well as that made by other writers and scholars like Severo Sarduy and Irlemar Chiampi) that *"Paradiso es un libro irrevisable"* [*Paradiso* is an incorrigible book].[43] Santí appears to interpret Vitier's edition as a deliberate philological panacea—an antidote, a pharmakos—to the terrible errancy that Sarduy, Santí, Chiampi's, and other deconstructive readings of the novel let loose. Santí writes:

> *Paradiso* es un texto que lleva las capacidades de la escritura hasta sus límites más radicales, cuestiona la capacidad de la filología para crear una lectura totalizante, y reta a sus más diligentes editores. Por eso, dentro de la economía de esta edición, que aspira a una fijación textual prácticamente teológica, 'Parridiso' y Santí tienen que figurar como chivos expiatorios de un ceremonia en la que no sólo se sacrifica una lectura heterodoxa, sino se intenta con ella una nueva y perfeccionada domesticación del texto (47).

> [*Paradiso* is a text that takes the capacities of writing to their most radical extremes, questions philology's claim to produce totalizing readings, and challenges the most diligent editors. This is why, within the economy of this edition, which aspires to a practically theological textual fixity, 'Parridiso' and Santí appear as expiatory victims in a ceremony that not only sacrifices any heterodox interpretation of the novel, but seeks, through this sacrifice, a new and perfected domestication of the text.]

This argument creates a breach in the comparative narrative which would regard the Vitier-Santí conflict as a symmetric reflection of the Gabler-Kidd debate, since, in *Paradiso*'s case, the chronology is much more complex and phantasmagorical. Santí's critique of the philological and methodological principles of Vitier's attempt to edit and "sanitize" *Paradiso* was written eleven years before the publication of the Archivos edition. This is why Santí is not compelled to write a "typical academic paper" or review, but instead refers the reader to the primacy of "Parridiso" as one paradoxical and uncanny "source" for Vitier's work. Only with the sacrifice of the sacrifice—the "killing" of the revealed parricidal complex—can the fixing of the highly erratic Lezamian text occur. This makes Vitier's editorial work posterior to Santí's insight, while Kidd's critique follows Gabler's work chronologically and conceptually in an absolute fashion—and, thus, in the end, remains derivative, especially when it protests its differences and objections more loudly.

Clearly, part of Vitier's work responds to Santí's erratic (or "erotic") reading of *Paradiso*, but only to some extent. Santí emphasizes the number of times his work is criticized in Vitier's notes in an undoubtedly dismissive and condescending fashion that nevertheless, because of its profusion, calls attention to and strengthens Santí's position. There are, on the other hand, thousands of other comments and notes in the text that do not allude to Santí's interpretations. Vitier's persistence in defending a logocentric or antieccentric reading of Lezama might not be just a reaction to Santí's and other deconstructive readings but to something greater which Santí indeed begins to point out in his "testimonial review": Lezama's fascinating and highly ambivalent relation to Freud and to psychoanalytical theory. Santí writes: "deberá quedar claro que la polémica de estos dos señores no es ni con 'Parridiso' ni con Santí sino con Sigmund Freud, el psicoanálisis, y, tal vez, el siglo veinte" (47) [it should be clear that these gentlemen's polemic is not with 'Parridiso' or Santí but with Sigmund Freud, psychoanalysis, and, perhaps, the twentieth century]. Vitier has a profound dislike for a theory of a deep subconscious operating in Lezama since it would oppose the ethical ideal of luminous, willful Cubanness (which, in essence, is a theory of willful nationalism) so central in Vitier's reading. Although such a *paideia* informs *Paradiso*, it is clear that Lezama in *Paradiso* also enters in a dialogue with Freudianism that is not a mere shouting match or a persistent negation.

If there are episodes in the novel that read like an overt dismissal of psychoanalytical principles—like the Colonel's joke about those who follow "Edipos de bolsillo" [paperback Oedipus] or Oppiano's negation of the Oedipus complex on his deathbed (which Santí interprets in "Parridiso" as another case of bad quoting and thus, in the end, parricidal[44])—other segments from the novel seem as if they had been extracted from Freud's *The Psychopathology of Everyday Life*. The list of this sort of episode is truly considerable: Foción's affair with the "redheaded boy" (where homosexuality is explained as an unresolved attraction to the mother: thus Foción's revelation to Cemí that it was the boy's mother who wants her child's seduction); the mad priest who commits self-mutilating masturbation; the punished voyeurism of Godofredo el Diablo. Although arguing for a type of innocence that is fundamentally disauthorized by psychoanalysis, the representation of desire and sexuality in *Paradiso* does not dismiss Freud outright. Even the dialogue about homosexuality in chapter 9, with all its scholastic and cosmological framings—its heterodox "Aquinas"—does not fail to refer to him. Levinson has been particularly perceptive in developing this line of analysis by studying Lezama's errors and theory of the *"eras imaginarias"* in relation to *Jokes and Their Relation to the Unconscious, Moses and Monotheism,* and other works by Freud.[45]

Nevertheless, banishing philology (which could be defined here as the principle of the "recuperable" text) altogether might be an extreme solution when approaching *Paradiso*'s problematic textualities. Other people have followed Santí in his interpretation of the novel as a disseminating text, but without surrendering some philological principles of textual corroboration, postulating a deliberate, calculated, constrained indeterminacy. Such is the work of Irlemar Chiampi that focuses on the "lectura interrupta" or the *stokeino* in Lezama's text—those moments where the text short-circuits itself through complicated yet coordinated strategies of misquotings and strategical error that "stops reading from achieving a final gestalt."[46] Chiampi's reading is not an allegorical reading of errata as an emblem of the flight of meaning in Lezama, but an operative, pragmatic one; it recalls the work of critics who argue for studying the paradox of intentional error in Joyce's work.

I want to conclude by proposing another way of approaching "error" in Lezama's work, one that can be helpful in distinguishing "meaningful errors" from "accidentals," fruitful accidents from unfruitful ones, and thus help establish coherent editorial procedures when approaching Lezama's writing. Lezama does have a theoretical postulation for a case of language fracture that does not always occur out of a psychosexual struggle or repression (although Lezama's illustration of such a linguistic situation contradicts this). This is the notion of the *súbito* (which I would translate once again as the "abrupta" or the "sudden"), something not too distant from but not identical to Freud's concept of the pun. Influenced by Vico (and, as I have noted earlier elsewhere, in a way very much like Joyce was influenced by Vico), Lezama sees the *súbito* as a moment not of endless linguistic dissemination or deferral of meaning, but as an epistemological moment in which a telescopic condensation of signifieds create a rupture in the signifier, allowing a glimpse through the archaeology of language. Thus errors in *Paradiso* would be like *súbitos* that trigger epiphanies which "open" the text. This is what happens when Joyce uses errors or accidentals heuristically to engineer multiplying meanings derived from exceptions in the graphic forms of language. This would explain Lezama's approval of even the most notorious mistakes in *Paradiso*, at least of the one most often pointed out as an example of Lezama's carelessness: the repetition by the typesetter of a line in chapter 6 which Lezama, in a letter to his English translator, explains with a straight face.[47] It would also explain the title of Oppiano Licario's hermetic manuscript: "Summa nunca infusa de *excepciones* morfológicas."

Chance or the accidental allows for a *súbito*, for a new interpretation as language reorders itself into new patterns of meaning. This is what Severo Sarduy means with his reference to Burrough's experiments in aleatory incongruity to explain Lezama's aesthetic of brutally approximating opposites, cutting great distances between terms.[48] These *súbitos*—so kin to the notion of pun or to Gracián's *ingenio*—are not necessarily arguments about errancy or indeterminateness, but refer to a particular, breakable fixity (*fijeza*) in language from which proliferation ensues. It is in the *súbito* where Joyce and Lezama's poetics of difficulty merge more successfully, where the mirrors join to form one image.

Notes

Throughout this book, certain works are cited repeatedly and their reference given simply as title abbreviations with page numbers in parentheses.

- The Spanish version of *Paradiso* used is *Paradiso*, ed. Cintio Vitier (Paris: ALLCA/UNESCO, 1988); the title abbreviation is *P*. The English translation is from *Paradiso*, trans. Gregory Rabassa (New York: Farrar, Strauss & Giroux, 1974); the title abbreviation is *R*.
- Quotations from Lezama's essays (except for *La expresión americana*) are taken from *Obras completas* (Mexico: Aguilar, 1975–77), vol. 2; the title abbreviation is *OC 2*. All translations of the essays are my own.
- Quotations from Lezama's posthumous novel are from *Oppiano Licario* (Madrid: Alianza Editorial, 1983). All translations of this text are my own.
- Quotations from Lezama's poetry are taken from his *Poesía completa* (Havana: Editorial Letras Cubanas, 1985); the title abbreviation is *Poesía*. All translations of Lezama's poetry are my own.
- Quotations from James Joyce's first novel are taken from *A Portrait of the Artist as a Young Man* (Middlesex: Penguin Books, 1964). The title abbreviation is *PA*.
- The edition of *Ulysses* referred to throughout this book is *Ulysses. The Corrected Text*, ed. Hans Walter Gabler with Wolfhard Steppe and Claus Melchior (New York: Vintage Books, 1986). The title abbreviation is *U*. The page numbers appear first, then the line numbers.
- The edition of *Finnegans Wake* referred to throughout this book is *Finnegans Wake* (New York: The Viking Press, 1959). The full title is used to identify the text.
- Quotations from Ezra Pound's essays on James Joyce are take from *Pound/Joyce. The Letters of Ezra Pound to James Joyce*, ed. Forrest Read (New York: New Directions, 1970). The title abbreviation is *PJ*.

LEZAMA'S JOYCE: AN INTRODUCTION

1. Julio Cortázar, "Para llegar a Lezama Lima," *La vuelta al día en ochenta mundos* (Mexico: Siglo XXI Editores, 1967), 41–81. A English translation by Thomas Christensen of this essay, "To Reach Lezama Lima," is available in Julio Cortázar, *Around the Day in Eightly Worlds* (San Francisco: North Point Press, 1986), 82–108.

2. In an evaluation of Cuban literary studies from 1959 to 1989, Roberto González Echevarría reviews recent critical scholarship on Lezama, and concludes: "The study of Lezama is not a passing fashion, but a subdiscipline in itself that will continue unabated in the future; it may well be the Craved Text." "The Hu-

manities and Cuban Studies, 1959–1989," in Damián J. Fernández, ed., *Cuban Studies Since the Revolution* (Gainesville: University Press of Florida, 1990), 212. Eight years hence, the number of critical books on Lezama has almost doubled. The most comprehensive critical bibliography published on Lezama's work is Justo Ulloa, *Sobre José Lezama Lima y sus lectores: Guía y compendio bibliográfico* (Boulder, CO: Society of Spanish and Spanish-American Studies, 1987). The famed Cuban librarian Araceli García-Carranza—author of important bibliographical studies on Alejo Carpentier, Fernando Ortiz, and other Cuban authors—is currently at work on an updated, comprehensive bibliography of the growing field of Lezama studies.

3. The letter, dated 3 April l967 and written in Delhi while Paz was Mexico's ambassador to India, is reprinted in Pedro Simón, ed. *Recopilación de textos sobre José Lezama Lima* (Havana: Casa de las Américas, 1970), 316.

4. Severo Sarduy, "A Cuban Proust," *Review* 12 (Fall 1974): 43–45; Jaime Valdivieso, *Bajo el signo de Orfeo: Lezama Lima y Proust* (Madrid: Orígenes, 1980).

5. Raymond D. Souza, *Major Cuban Novelists* (Columbia: University of Missouri Press, 1976), 53.

6. Leonard Orr, "Joyce and the Cuban Novel," *Neohelicon* 19 (1992): 217–25.

7. See the chapter titled "Textual Epiphany: A Return to Bibliomancy," in Gustavo Pellón, *José Lezama Lima's Joyful Vision: A Study of Paradiso and Other Prose Works* (Austin: University of Texas Press, 1989), 69–84.

8. Robert Martin Adams, *Afterjoyce: Studies in Fiction After Ulysses* (New York: Oxford University Press, 1977), 169–84, esp. 179–84. The expression "polyphlusboious richness" appears on p. 183.

9. José Lezama Lima, *La expresión americana*, ed. Irlemar Chiampi (Mexico: Fondo de Cultura Económica, 1993).

10. I quote from pages 246–47 Mark Schafer's stupendous translation of the last chapter of *La expresión americana*, "Summa Critica of American Culture," included in Ilan Stavans, ed., *The Oxford Book of Latin American Essays* (Oxford: Oxford University Press, 1997), 244–59.

11. Lezama made many illuminating, carefully conceived remarks on Joyce in a 1964 Havana round table on Julio Cortázar's 1963 novel *Rayuela*. Roberto Fernández Retamar and Ana María Simo also participated. Their discussions were transcribed in Ana María Simo et al., *Cinco miradas sobre Cortázar* (Buenos Aires: Tiempo Contemporáneo, 1968), 7–82.

12. Frank Boas, "Evolution or Diffusion?" In *Race, Language and Culture* (New York: Free Press, 1940), 290–94.

13. Translated by James E. Irby. In Jorge Luis Borges, *Labyrinths. Selected Stories and Other Writings*, ed. Donald A. Yates and James E. Irby (New York: New Directions, 1964), 126.

1: JOYCE AND THE ESCHATOLOGY OF THE NOVEL: JORGE LUIS BORGES'S AND JOSÉ LEZAMA LIMA'S ANTAGONISTIC READINGS

1. Among Borges's pieces dedicated exclusively to Joyce published in Argentine journals are: an early essay on *Ulysses*, "El Ulises de Joyce" [Joyce's *Ulysses*], *Proa* 2.6 (1925), 3–6; his translation of the last segment of "Penelope," with the title "La última hoja del Ulises" [The last page of *Ulysses*] which appeared in that same issue, 8–9; two brief notes on *Finnegans Wake*: "Joyce y los neologismos"

[Joyce and Neologisms], *Sur* 9 (November 1939), and "El último libro de Joyce" [Joyce's Last Book], *El Hogar* (16 June 1939); a short, panoramic evaluation of Joyce's work written on the occasion of Joyce's death, "Fragmento sobre Joyce" [Fragment on Joyce], *Sur* 10 (February 1941); his negative review of J. Salas Subirat's 1945 Spanish translation of *Ulysses*, "Nota sobre el Ulises en español" [Note on the Spanish *Ulysses*], *Los anales de Buenos Aires* 1, no. 1 (1946): 49.

2. Although Lezama Lima's commentary on Joyce is not as extensive as Borges's, it is still very significant. In his career as a literary critic in Havana, Lezama published only one article strictly devoted to Joyce—"Muerte de Joyce" [Death of Joyce], *Grafos* 9 (Feb.–Mar. 1941): 16. Nevertheless, as I pointed out in the introduction, reflections about the significance of Joyce's work comprise pivotal sections in some of Lezama's most important critical writing. Like Borges, Lezama made countless references to Joyce in his fiction and poetry. Interestingly, Joyce's name appears insistently in notebooks, diaries, and other personal forms of writing that went unpublished during his lifetime. Lezama annotated his reading of the 1945 Spanish translation of *Ulysses* in his diary of 1939 to 1949, published as "Diario" [Diary] in *Revista de la Biblioteca Nacional José Martí* 29 (May–August 1988), 154; reprinted in José Lezama Lima, *Diarios [1939–49/1956–58]*, Ciro Bianchi Ross, ed. (Mexico: Ediciones Era, 1994), 15–94. In the notebook known as the *Carpeta II* that is part of the "Fondo Lezama" [Lezama Lima manuscript collection] in the José Martí National Library, there is an unpublished draft of an essay with the title "Proteo y Joyce" [Proteus and Joyce], which I consulted during a visit in July 1993.

3. José Ortega y Gasset, "Ideas sobre la novela" (1925), reprinted in Ortega y Gasset, *Ideas sobre el teatro y la novela* (Madrid: Alianza Editorial, 1975), 15–56. An English translation, "Notes on the Novel," is reprinted in José Ortega y Gasset, *The Dehumanization of Art and Other Writings on Art and Culture* (Princeton University Press, 1948; rptd. Doubleday Anchor). The debate on the "death of the novel" had a trajectory in Hispanic letters distinct from that which it took in the Anglo-European context. For a different approach to the topic of literary exhaustion in the work of Borges that does not address genre issues, see John Barth's influential 1967 essay "The Literature of Exhaustion," reprinted in *The Friday Book* (New York: G. P. Putnam's Sons, 1984), 62–76 (originally published in *The Atlantic*, 1967), and John O. Stark, *The Literature of Exhaustion: Borges, Nabokov and Barth* (Durham: Duke University Press, 1974).

4. Ortega writes: "In short, I believe that the genre of the novel, if it is not yet irretrievably exhausted, has certainly entered its last phase, the scarcity of possible subjects being such that writers must make up for its deficiency by the exquisite quality of other elements that compose the body of a novel," *Dehumanization*, 56. I take the English terms for these "exquisite elements" from the Princeton University Press translation of the essay. My edition does not identify the translator.

5. Although best summarized by Ortega's essay, the debate on the crisis of the novel had its full articulation in the pages of Ortega's influential journal *Revista de Occidente*, published from 1923 to 1936, in the period between the World Wars. The *Revista*'s reviewers of foreign literature, Benjamín Jarnés and Antonio Marichalar, authored the most relevant articles on the genre's decline that appeared in "Notas" and "Asteriscos," the sections the journal dedicated to literature. See Jarnés, "Frente a la novela nueva," 16 (1927): 398–400, and "Libros sin género," 30 (1930): 205–9; Marichalar, "Síntomas," 5 (1924): 394–98, "Mutaciones," 7 (1925): 366–72, "Nueva dimensión," 24 (1929): 380–83, "Ultimo grito," 31 (1931): 100–107, and "Musarañas," 44 (1934): 305–17.

6. An open expression of Borges's dislike for Ortega's writing can be found in a piece Borges wrote on the occasion of Ortega's death for José Rodríguez Feo's Cuban literary journal *Ciclón* 1, no. 2 (1956): 28. For further discussion of Borges's antagonism toward Ortega, see Roberto González Echevarría, "Borges, Carpentier y Ortega: dos textos olvidados," *Revista Iberoamericana*, 100–101 (1977): 697–704.

7. Although he acknowledges Borges's allusions to the crisis of the novel, Dario Puccini believes that Borges held the novel in high regard and "never hesitated in giving literary primacy to the novel, since he believed the genre showed enduring quality more frequently [than any other genre]": "Borges como crítico literario y el problema de la novela," *El ensayo y la crítica literaria en Iberoamérica*, ed. Kurt L. Levy and Keith Ellis (Toronto: University of Toronto Press, 1970), 145–54.

8. Jorge Luis Borges, "Vindicación de *Bouvard et Pécuchet*," in *Discusión* (1932; with additions, 1957; reprint, Madrid: Alianza Editorial, 1983), 21 (my translation). "Vindicación" was added in 1957 to the third edition of *Discusión* (1932). It is thus written after the publication of *Finnegans Wake* and the death of Joyce.

9. Borges makes a similar, slighting reference to *Ulysses* in another important essay in *Discusión*: "But the most perfect example of an autonomous orb of confirmations, omens, and monuments is Joyce's preordained *Ulysses*. One need only look into Gilbert's study or, in its absence, into the dizzying novel itself." Jorge Luis Borges, "Narrative Art and Magic," trans. N. T. di Giovanni, in *Borges: A Reader*, ed. E. Rodríguez Monegal and Alistair Reed (New York: Dutton, 1981), 38. Or see Jorge Luis Borges, "El arte narrativo y la magia" in *Discusión* (Buenos Aires: M. Gleizer, 1932), 121, for the original Spanish.

10. Andrés Sánchez Robayna, "Borges y Joyce." *Insula* 38, no. 437 (1983): 1, 12.

11. For an account of Borges's participation in the ultraist movement, see Guillermo de Torre, *Historia de las literaturas de vanguardia* (Madrid: 1967), and Thorpe Running, *Borges's Ultraist Movement* (Michigan: International Book Publishers, 1981). For an analysis of the ensuing transformation in Borges's mature style and literary philosophy, see Nicolas Shumway and Thomas Sant, "The Hedonist Reader: Literary Theory in Borges," *Latin American Literary Review* 9, no. 17 (1980): 37–54.

12. Jorge Schwartz, "Borges y la primera hoja de *Ulysses*," *Revista Iberoamericana* 100–101 (1977): 722. "Borges's diverse opinions on *Ulysses* throughout the years, although not unilateral, demonstrate . . . his profound admiration and recognition of its cathedral-like grandeur."

13. I translate from "El Ulises de Joyce," reprinted in Jorge Luis Borges, *Inquisiciones* (Buenos Aires: Editorial Proa, 1925), 20.

14. For information about the Góngora Tricentenary, consult Gerardo Diego, *Antología poética en honor de Góngora* (Madrid: Revista de Occidente, 1927), and Dámaso Alonso, "Góngora y la literatura contemporánea," *Obras completas*, vol. 5, *Góngora y el gongorismo* (Madrid: Gredos, 1978), 725–54.

15. I translate from Jorge Luis Borges, "Para el centenario de Góngora," *El idioma de los argentinos* (Buenos Aires: M. Gleizer, 1928), 123. For other similar sardonic attacks against gongorism, see the following essays in this collection: "Otra vez la metáfora," "El culteranismo," and "La simulación de la imagen."

16. Walt Whitman, *Hojas de hierba* (Buenos Aires: Lozada, 1979), 29. In "Borges y Joyce," Sánchez Robayna also refers to other instances where Borges

associates *Finnegans Wake* with Góngora's *Soledades,* Quevedo's wordgames, and the work of another notoriously difficult baroque writer of the Golden Age, Gracián.

17. "Joyce y los neologismos," reprinted in *Páginas de Jorge Luis Borges seleccionadas por el autor* (Buenos Aires: Editorial Celtia, 1982), 160–62. I quote, with one modification indicated in brackets, from Mark Larsen's translation in Rodríguez Monegal and Reed, ed., *Borges: A Reader*, 103–4.

18. Jorge Schwartz writes: "Borges's attraction toward Joycean verbosity would turn into a greater fascination after the publication of *Finnegans Wake*." "Borges y la primera hoja de *Ulysses*," 721. My translation.

19. Stuart Gilbert, "Thesaurus Minusculus: A Short Commentary on a Paragraph of Work in Progress," *transition* 16–17 (1928): 15–24. Borges identifies Gilbert as a source in his article.

20. I translate from "El último libro de Joyce," reprinted in Jorge Luis Borges, *Textos cautivos: Ensayos y reseñas en 'El Hogar'*, ed. Enrique Sacerio-Garí and Emir Rodríguez Monegal (Barcelona: Tusquets, 1986), 328.

21. Although in the poem "Invocación a Joyce" [Invocation to Joyce] Borges nonchalantly describes Joyce's work as "arduos laberintos, / infinitesimales e infinitos / admirablemente mezquinos, / más populosos que la historia" [laborious labyrinths, / infinite and infinitesimal, / admirably vulgar, denser than history], at the end he voices an uncharacteristic appreciation of Joyce's total artistic achievement. He praises Joyce's "obstinado rigor" [obstinate rigor] and his use of exile as the "arma de tu arte" [weapon of your art] for making even the shoddiest avant-garde experimentation significant, and speaks of "los oros de tu sombra" [the gold in your shadow], as if Joyce's obscurity were a source of something glowing and precious. I quote and translate from Jorge Luis Borges, *Obra poética* (Madrid: Alianza Editorial, 1972), 350–51.

22. "Fragmento sobre Joyce," reprinted in Borges, *Páginas de Jorge Luis Borges*, 167–69. From here on I quote, with some modifications indicated in brackets, from Mark Larsen's translation in Monegal and Reed, eds., *Borges: A Reader*, 134–36.

23. See Stuart Gilbert, *James Joyce's Ulysses* (New York: Vintage Book, 1955), esp. the preface and part 4.1 and 4.2 of the introduction, "Dubliners-Vikings-Achaeans" and "*Ulysses* and the Odyssey."

24. *Introducción a la literatura inglesa* (Buenos Aires: Columba, 1965), 60–62. I quote from Jorge Luis Borges, *An Introduction to English Literature*, trans. L. Clark Keating and Robert O. Evans (Lexington: The University of Kentucky Press, 1974), 68–69. In what is surely his last published comment on Joyce, Borges restates this position by declaring Joyce a creator of a "musical idiom" in a conference on "Blindness" transcribed posthumously in *Siete noches* (Mexico: Fondo de Cultura Económica, 1980): "[From Joyce] we have these vast and—why not say it—unreadable novels, *Ulysses* and *Finnegans Wake*. [. . . Joyce] wrote in a language invented by himself, difficult to understand but marked by a strange music. Joyce brought a new music to English." I quote from Jorge Luis Borges, *Seven Nights*, trans. Eliot Weinberger (New York: New Directions, 1984), 118–19.

25. For an analysis of how Borges's critical vision of Joyce as a novelist is reflected in his fiction, see my article "*Barroco* Joyce: Jorge Luis Borges's and José Lezama Lima's Antagonistic Readings," in Karen Lawrence, ed. *Transcultural Joyce* (Cambridge: Cambridge University Press, 1997), 63–92.

26. I translate from "Muerte de Joyce," reprinted in José Lezama Lima, *Obras completas* vol. 2 (Madrid: Aguilar, 1972), 236–38. Further references to this text will be indicated in parentheses with OC 2: followed by page numbers.

27. See note 1.542 in Don Gifford, *Ulysses Annotated* (Berkeley: University of California Press, 1988), 23.

28. That Lezama was quite familiar with most of these critics' positions on Joyce can be ascertained from a comment about the uses of literary criticism in an interview with Salvador Bueno printed in Cintio Vitier's critical edition of *Paradiso* for the UNESCO Archivos series (Paris: ALLCA/UNESCO, 1988). "La mejor crítica de Joyce, la hicieron Eliot y Pound, no Curtius aunque éste fuera una gran maestro de la sabiduría literaria, pero Eliot y Pound tenían una unidad más profunda con las experiencias de la ensalada filológica que está en la raíz de Joyce, por eso vieron más, pudieron profundizar más en sus sones creativos." (730) [Eliot and Pound, not Curtius, wrote the best criticism on Joyce, even though Curtius was a great master of literary wisdom, but Eliot and Pound had a deeper unity with the experiences behind the philological mixture at the core of Joyce's work. This is why they could see more, and probe more deeply into Joyce's creative rhythms.]

29. "The demand that I make of my reader is that he should devote his whole life to reading my works." Quoted in Richard Ellman, *James Joyce* (Oxford: Oxford University Press, rev. ed., 1983), 703.

30. For an excellent analysis of the Egyptian Book of the Dead as subtext to *Finnegans Wake*, see John Bishop, *Finnegans Wake: Joyce's Book of the Dark* (Madison: University of Wisconsin Press, 1986), esp. chap. 4. The Book of the Dead plays a similar hypertextual role in Lezama's last novel, *Oppiano Licario*. Bishop writes: "Archeologists have inferred that every individual who could afford it consulted with his priest and scribes in the course of his lifetime and more or less ordered . . . the writing of a guidebook that would answer his own particular needs and desires in the next world," 89–90.

31. I quote from James E. Irby's translation, "Funes the Memorious," in Jorge Luis Borges, *Labyrinths* (New York: New Directions, 1964), 66.

32. Lezama's dazzling "poetic world system" and his theories concerning the *eras imaginarias* [imaginary eras] and the role of metaphor and poetic "imagen" [image] in the construction of cosmologies, are impossible to summarize here. I discuss these topics thoroughly in chapter 4. For the best accounts of how Lezama's poetic system explores the possibility of resurrection, see Cintio Vitier's "Introducción" to Lezama's *Obras completas*, vol. 1; Rubén Ríos Avila, "A Theology of Absence: The Poetic System of José Lezama Lima," Ph.D. thesis, Cornell University (1983); Alina L. Camacho-Gingerich, *La cosmovisión poética de José Lezama Lima en Paradiso y Oppiano Licario* (Miami: Ediciones Universal, 1990); Enrique Márquez, *José Lezama Lima: Bases y génesis de un sistema poético* (New York: Peter Lang, 1991); Emilio Bejel, *José Lezama Lima, Poet of the Image* (Gainesville: University of Florida Press, 1990); and Ben Heller, *Assimiliation/ Generation/Resurrection. Contrapuntual Readings in the Poetry of José Lezama Lima* (Lewisburg: Bucknell University Press, 1997). Bejel writes: "We see [in Lezama's poetics] not only an insight into the relation of subject and space, but also the distinction between Heidegger's concept of the human subject as a being-for-death, who exists in order to die, and Lezama's metaphorical subject as a being-for-resurrection, who exists in preparation for a timeless life," 27.

34. "Que las posibilidades de la novela van siendo pocas, pues enseguida me pongo a hace una novela." From a letter to José Rodríguez Feo dated June 1953. José Rodríguez Feo, *Mi correspondencia con Lezama Lima* (Havana: Ediciones Unión, 1989), 130.

2: INCARNATING THE WORD: POETRY, ADOLESCENCE, AND
AESTHETIC THEORY IN *A PORTRAIT OF THE ARTIST AS A
YOUNG MAN* AND *PARADISO*

1. "Muerte de Joyce" was first published in the Cuban magazine *Grafos* (9
[89–90]: [16] February–March 1941). It was reprinted in Lezama's first collection
of essays, *Analecta del reloj* (La Habana: Orígenes, 1953). My page numbers refer
to the text as it appears in vol. 2 of José Lezama Lima, *Obras completas* (Mexico:
Aguilar, 1975–77).
2. Harry Levin discusses James Joyce's and Stephen Dedalus' admiration for
heresiarchs like Giordano Bruno in *James Joyce: A Critical Introduction* (Norfolk:
New Directions, 1941): "in [the] very first sentence [of "The Day of the Rabble-
ment] Joyce proclaims the isolation of the artist by authority of the Italian arch-
heretic of Nola, Giordano Bruno. . . . Bruno played the same role in Joyce's development that he did in the history of philosophy. . . . At the moment, this anti-
Aristotelian heresies were beckoning Joyce away from Thomistic orthodoxy" (23).
Stephen's conversation with Cranly takes place in chapter 5 of *A Portrait of the
Artist as a Young Man* (Middlesex: Penguin Books, 1964). All quotations come
from this edition.
3. Giordano Bruno is mentioned in page 324 of Cintio Vitier's critical edition
of *Paradiso* (Paris: ALLCA/UNESCO, 1988): "La *res universalis*, desde la unidad
de Parménides hasta el Uno de Giordano Bruno, ayudaban [a Fronesis] a estar
siempre en el centro de todas las *quaestio* que se presentaban" (*P* 324/*R* 328) [The
res universalis, from the unity of Parmenides to the One of Giordano Bruno,
helped him always to be in the center of every *quaestio* posited]. He is also mentioned in chapter 6 of *Oppiano Licario* (Madrid: Alianza Editorial, 1983), 188.
4. For a classical analysis of messianic figuration in *A Portrait*, see C. G. Anderson, "The Sacrificial Butter," *Accent* 12, no. 1 (1952): 3–13. "Chapter V of *Portrait* is controlled by three principal symbols: the Daedalus myth; the poet as
God—creator, redeemer, and priest; and the betrayal-crucifixion . . . '[O]ld father,
old artificer' Daedalus corresponds to God the Father and Creator. God the Father
is united with Christ the Son, who as the Word joins in creation and as the first
priest becomes a creator in Joyce's special sense. Christ, the Creator as a young
man, is betrayed and crucified in a way which corresponds to the betrayal of the
artist as a young man by his family, his national society, and his church" (4).
Cintio Vitier is the critic responsible for the most transcendentalist and commit-
tedly Catholic reading of Lezama. See his "Introducción a la obra de José Lezama
Lima," *Obras completas*: xi–lxiv. In "Lo tradicional cubano en el mundo novelístico de José Lezama Lima," José Juan Arrom writes: "[A] muchas personas les he
oído que las iniciales de José Cemí aluden . . . a Jesus Cristo" [I have heard many
people say that José Cemí's initials refer . . . to Jesus Christ], *Revista Iberoamericana* 92–93 (1975): 194. On the same page he adds: "José Cemí es para Lezama
lo que Stephen Dedalus fue para Joyce" [José Cemí is for Lezama what Stephen
Dedalus was for Joyce].
5. Despite its respect for Lezama's creative achievement and its instrumental
importance in helping the reader overcome his or her resistance to the difficulty
in Lezama's prose, Julio Cortázar's important article on *Paradiso* ("Para llegar a
Lezama Lima," *La vuelta al día en ochenta mundos*, Mexico: Siglo XXI, 1970, 2:
47–81) makes an argument about Lezama's "naive" or amateurish treatment of
the techniques of the novel: "Más importante es observar que faltan en *Paradiso*

lo que yo llamaría el reverso continuo, la urdimbre que 'hace' una novela por más fragmentarios que puedan parecer sus episodios" (58–59) [More importantly, *Paradiso* lacks what I would call the unifiying reverse-field, the fabric that makes a novel, however fragmentary its episodes]. I quote from Thomas Christensen's translation of this essay, "To Reach Lezama Lima," included in *Around the Day in Eighty Worlds* (San Francisco: North Point Press, 1986), 92. Gustavo Pellón discusses critically this line of reasoning in Cortázar's analysis in "Conclusion: The Henri Rousseau of the Latin American Boom," the last chapter of *José Lezama Lima's Joyful Vision* (Austin: University of Texas Press, 1990), 85–118.

6. "Entrevista con Salvador Bueno," published as an appendix to Cintio Vitier's critical edition of *Paradiso*, 727.

7. In some notes for a conference on writing *Paradiso* reproduced as an appendix in Cintio Vitier's critical Archivos edition (710–14), Lezama describes in very lucid terms the symbiosis between poetry and the novel that he seeks to establish:

> Sin perder su pureza la poesía [empezó a] inclinarse a la fabulación. . . . Una tendencia al relato, al asunto, que vino a unirse a las terribles y decisivas excursiones de la metáfora por el subconciente, que iba poblando mundos, desprendiendo ciudades misteriosas. / El proceso de la novela se hacía inverso: del sujet, del asunto, del entrecruzamiento trágico de la anécdota, se iba a la experiencia del lenguaje, a la meditación del tiempo, al hundimiento de la cultura. / Paralelo al sistema poético comenzaron a surgir los capítulos del Paradiso. Era como su ilustración, su iluminación. Los personajes comenzaban a relacionarse como metáforas y las situaciones se comportaban como imágenes. / La poesía y la novela tenían para mí las misma raíz. El mundo se relacionaba y resistía como un inmenso poema. (711)

> [Without losing its purity, poetry [started to] lean towards the fable. . . . An inclination towards telling, towards plot, became enmeshed with the decisive and terrible outpours of metaphor throughout the unconscious, thus populating worlds, letting mysterious cities emerge freely. / The novel's progress became reversed: from the sujet, from plot, from the tragic crossroad of anecdote, it moved to language as experience, to the philosophy of time, to a deepening in culture. / The chapters of *Paradiso* began to surface in tandem with my poetic system. The novel was the exemplification, the illumination of the system. Characters began to manifest themselves like metaphors and the dramatic situations behaved like images. / Poetry and the novel thus shared the same root. The world (of the novel) developed and resisted like a tremendous poem.]

Thus Lezama argues for overcoming the dualism that separates poetry from the novel.

8. Enrique Márquez includes some penetrating pages on the relationship between *fijeza* and *ecphrasis* in Lezama's poetic system in his *JLL: Bases y génesis*, 101–5.

9. In the sequel to *Paradiso*, the unfinished and posthumous novel *Oppiano Licario*, José Cemí will discuss with Ynaca Eco the way in which the *imago* of poetic language ends up generating a "cantidad novelable" [measure for the novel]: "En esa dimensión la imago viene para completar esa *media visión*, pues si no existiese lo posible de la visibilidad de lo increado, no podría existir la cantidad novelable" (*OP* 167) [In this dimension the *imago* enters to complete that *half vision*, for if the possibility of making the uncreated visible (through the *imago*) did not exist, the measure of the novel could not exist either].

10. On the *imago* (or *imagen*) and its "overabundance," Emilio Bejel writes: "For Lezama, the Image is the creative force stemming from a fundamental lack

of a natural order. He bases his poetry on the Image of the *supranatural*, which is basically a vacuum that demands a constant exploration of the unknown. This process [of exploration] is achieved through the metaphor, which, by means of similarities, associates terms that previously had no relation to each other. Furthermore, this metaphoric process always leads to an 'exceptional' and 'excessive' poetry that breaks with the classical concept of harmony in an idealized Nature." *Poet of the Image*, 44. The "excesses" of Lezama's poetry make it novelistic, in Ortega y Gasset's sense of the word.

11. This complex scene in *Paradiso* also illustrates the reputation Joyce's work had at the time—even in Havana—as being as lewd and obscene as it was difficulty, of interest only to dilletantes and eccentrics. At a bookstore in Havana Foción makes up an apocryphal book, James Joyce's *Goethe*, and asks the bookseller for it to trick and cruelly ridicule an eavesdropping naive and pedantic young man who instantly orders the book. Foción knows that his young man "was having a sexual crisis which showed itself in a false and hasty cultural greed that became pathological when faced with the novelties in books and the publication of strange works"; he chooses Joyce precisely because of the rarity of the editions of his books, the foregrounding of sexual and obscene themes in his later work, and so on. Foción might also be referring obliquely to *A Portrait of the Artist as a Young Man*, whose exquisite Spanish edition came out in 1926 and should have been a coveted novelty in Havana during the time this episode takes place. Gustavo Pellón argues in favor of the latter thesis in *José Lezama Lima's Joyful Vision* (Austin: University of Texas Press, 1989), 76.

12. Lezama's concept of *paideuma* is inspired by ethnologist Leo Frobenius's use of the Greek term to describe not only the effervescent creative imagination of children but of "primitive" cultures in Africa. See Leo Frobenius, *La cultura como ser viviente: contorno de una doctrina cultural y psicológica*, trans. Máximo Jose Kahn (Madrid: Espasa-Calpe, 1934), a work often mentioned by Lezama in his essays and part of his extant library kept at the Biblioteca Nacional José Martí. Arnaldo Cruz-Malavé has brilliantly discussed how, in *Paradiso*, the *paideuma*'s state of intense creativity is consistently attributed to children, "primitives," poets, and homosexuals. However, Cruz-Malavé makes the mistake of considering *paideuma* synonymous with *paideia*, a different cultural concept in Hellenic studies related not to an innocent and spontaneous condition of expressiveness but to a coordinated process of civic and philosophical education. See Arnaldo Cruz-Malavé, *El primitivo implorante. El "sistema poético del mundo" de José Lezama Lima* (Amsterdam-Atlanta, GA: Rodopi, 1994), 94–99. Also see chapter 3 of this book for a full discussion of the use of *paideia* in Lezama's work.

13. For a discussion of the constructivist model of language acquisition, see Jean Piaget, *The Language and Thought of The Child*, trans. Margaret Gabain (New York: Meridian Books, 1955).

14. For an account of the nativist model, see Noam Chomsky, *Reflections on Language* (New York: Pantheon, 1975), and Ferdinand de Saussure, *Cours de linguistique general* (Paris: Payot, 1949). For a debate between Chomsky's position and Piaget's, see *Language and Learning: The Debate between Jean Piaget and Noam Chomsky*, ed. Massimo Pietlli-Palmari (Cambridge: Harvard University Press, 1980).

15. For the terms and characteristics of the stages of language acquisition, I have consulted Herbert C. Clark, *Psychology and Language: An Introduction to Psycholinguistics* (New York: Harcourt, Brace, 1977), and Helen Cairns, *Psycholinguistics: A Cognitive View of Language* (New York : Holt, Rinehart & Winston, 1976).

16. I quote from Joyce's 1904 essay "A Portrait of the Artist," reproduced in Robert Scholes and Richard M. Kain, eds., *The Workshop of Daedalus: James Joyce and the Raw Materials for A Portrait of the Artist as a Young Man* (Evanston: Northwestern University Press, 1965), 60. The essay begins with this intriguing sentence: "The features of infancy are not commonly reproduced in the adolescent portrait for so capricious are we, that we cannot or will not conceive the past in any other than its iron memorial aspect" (60). Joyce's and Lezama's *bildungsromane* seek to narrate precisely the opposite.

17. For a discussion of aesthetic epiphany in Lezama Lima that bears in mind Joyce as literary precedent, see Gustavo Pellón, "Textual Epiphany: A Return to Bibliomancy," *José Lezama Lima's Joyful Vision*, 70–84.

18. The Virgin Mary is another frequent *topos* in Lezama and Joyce's Catholic discourse. Lezama's "Sonetos a la Virgen" appear in *Enemigo rumor* (1945), included in *Poesía completa* (Havana: Editorial Letras cubanas, 1985), 46–48. For an early commentary of Joyce's treatment of the topic, see C. G. Anderson, 12–13.

19. H. G. Wells and Ezra Pound read *A Portrait* as an essentially nonsymbolic work of stark psychological realism. Wells wrote in his review: "[The novel] is a mosaic of jagged fragments that does altogether render with extreme completeness the growth of a rather secretive, imaginative boy in Dublin. The technique is startling, but on the whole it succeeds." "James Joyce," *Nation* 20 (24 February 1917), reprinted in Robert H. Deming, ed. *James Joyce: The Critical Heritage*, vol. 1 (London: Routledge & Kegan Paul, 1970), 87.

20. Not just Cortázar judges this to be so. Noé Jitrik adopts a similar position, admitting the difficulty of classifying *Paradiso* as a novel but recognizing the coherent articulation of a consistent semiotic system behind its disjointed narrative. See "*Paradiso* entre desborde y ruptura," *Texto Crítico* 5, no. 13 (1979): 71–89. Raymond D. Souza also believes that Lezama's novelistic discourse distorts the rules of the genre; *The Poetic Fiction of José Lezama Lima* (Columbia: University of Missouri Press, 1983).

21. For a succinct articulation of how naturalism and symbolism "come to terms" in *A Portrait* and the rest of Joyce's work, see the chapter titled "The Uncreated Conscience" in Harry Levin, *James Joyce*, 3–20 ("Reality"), 41–62 ("The Artist").

22. For another approach to *A Portrait*'s symbolism, see David Hayman, "Daedalian Imagery in *A Portrait of the Artist as A Young Man*," *Hereditas: Seven Essays on the Modern Expression of the Classical*, ed. Frederick Will (Austin: University of Texas Press, 1969), 31–54. In "The Portrait in Perspective," Hugh Kenner argues that the allusive and symbolic construction of *A Portrait* is related to the intricacy and "concentration" in *Ulysses* and *Finnegans Wake*: "For the *Portrait*, as the painstaking revision it received at the *Stephen Hero* stage would suggest, must be read with unrelaxing attention. Indeed, such attention goes a long way toward revealing what *Ulysses* is about. . . . The reader who returns to the *Portrait* with the remainder of Joyce's output will be able to see how much symbolic material is controlled by images [in *Portrait*]," *James Joyce: Two Decades of Criticism* (New York: Vanguard Press, 1948), 132–74.

23. Kenneth Burke, "Fact, Inference, and Proof in the Analysis of Literary Symbolism," *Terms for Order*, ed. Stanley Edgar Hyman (Bloomington: Indiana University Press, 1964), 145–72.

24. On the rhythmical appreciation of poetry in *A Portrait*, see Thomas E. Connolly, "Kinesis and Stasis: Structural Rhythm in Joyces's *Portrait*," *University Review (Dublin)* 3 (1966): 21–30.

25. Lorenzo García Vega uses this expression to describe the condition of Cemí's [and Lezama's] social class in his vitriolic testimony about his years as a member of Lezama's "Grupo Orígenes" [Orígenes circle], *Los años de Orígenes* (Caracas: Monte Avila, 1978).

26. For an account of the sources and the consequences of this colonial displacement, see Louis A. Pérez, *Cuba Under the Platt Ammendment: 1902–1934* (Pittsburgh: University of Pittsburgh Press, 1986).

27. I refer to J. C. Austin, *How To Do Things With Words* (Cambridge: Harvard University Press, 1975). See also John Searle, *Speech Acts: An Essay in the Philosophy of Language* (London: Cambridge University Press, 1969).

28. Kenneth Burke considers literary statements "symbolic acts" which, like magic utterances, have efficacious consequences beyond their linguistic function of denotation, ostentation, or signification. One extralinguistic result of a "symbolic poetic act" is a kind of homeopathic mending or protection of the psyche. On poetic language as both medicine and poison, he writes: "[P]oetry is produced for purposes of comfort . . . as a ritualistic way of arming us to confront perplexities and risks. [Thus] poetry is 'medicine,' therapeutic or prophylatic [for] discomfort (actual or threatened). . . . The poet is, indeed, a 'medicine man. . . .' As 'medicine man,' he deals with 'poisons'. . . . The poet, in his pious or tragic role, would immunize us by stylistically infecting us with the disease. As we move towards the impious response, on the other hand, we get an 'allopathic' strategy of cure. We get the recourse to 'antidote.' " *The Philosophy of Literary Form* (Berkeley: University of California Press, 1973), 61, 63–64.

Derrida writes: "This *pharmakon*, the 'medicine,' this philter, which acts as both remedy and poison, already introduces itself into the body of the discourse with all its ambivalence" (70). In his reading of Plato's *Pharmacy*, Derrida examines the polysemic and contradictory semantic applications of the term to show that language suffers a disease of meaning: "In this way we hope to display in the most striking manner the regular, ordered polysemy that has, through skewing, indetermination, or overdetermination, but without mistranslation, permitted the rendering of the same word by 'remedy,' 'poison,' 'drug,' 'philter,' etc." (71). See "Plato's Pharmacy," *Dissemination*, trans. Barbara Johnson (Chicago: University of Chicago Press, 1981), 65–156.

In "Words and Wounds," Geoffrey Hartman also considers the pathogenic and homeopathic power of language, and studies how names in some contexts represent a "balm" that may "redress the wounds that words inflict," *Saving the Text* (Baltimore: Johns Hopkins, 1981), 118–55. The quotation is from p. 122.

29. On the opening pages of *Portrait* see Kenner, "The Portrait in Perspective," 139–48.

30. For an intriguing study of water imagery in Joyce, see Randolph Splitter, "Watery Words: Language, Sexuality, and Motherhood in Joyce's Fiction," *ELH* 49, no. 1 (1982): 190–213.

31. Gustavo Pellón, "The Aesthetics of Excess: The Novel as Fibroma," *Joyful Vision*: 13–27.

32. On Dedalus's aversion to water, see Splitter, 194–97. A study of the meanings of water in *Paradiso* has yet to be written.

33. After a gigantic wave overtakes Cemí in his dream, "llegaba después un pez anchuroso, con su rosado ingenuote y navideño, moviendo la iridiscencia de sus aletas como si se peinase. El pez contemplaba el dedo desamparado y se reía. Circulizaba alrededor del dedo, como si le diese alegría. Después se llevaba el dedo a la boca y comenzaba a impartirle su protección. Tirándolo por el dedo lo

había llevado a unas flotaciones muscíneas, donde comenzaba la música acompasada, de fino cálculo, de su nueva respiración. Luego, ya no veía la salvación por el pez, pero veía el rostro de su madre" (P 133/R 132–33) [A broad fish swam up in ingenious Christman pinkness, moving its iridescent fins as if combing itself. The fish eyed the forsaken finger and laughed. Then it took the finger into its mouth and began to afford it protection. Towing him by the finger, it brought him to a patch of floating moss where the carefully calculated rhythm of his new breathing began. Then he no longer saw salvation in the fish, but instead his mother's face]. The dream becomes more elaborate and surreal (a team of dwarfs disembark and invite Cemí to dinner); still, in the dream, Cemí's mother is consistently associated with fish and with the restitution of a regular, serene rhythm for breathing.

34. On Derrida and Lezama's critique of logocentrism, see Bejel, 47–48.

35. As in A Portrait, graffitti inscriptions in Paradiso tend to have an obscene nature, and carry violent sexual and demonaical significations. Consider, for examples, the drawing of male genitals on Martincillo's door (P 26/R 25) and the misoginistic, bestial scene scribbled in the urinals where Cemí sees Foción (now gone mad due to a venereal disease and to Fronesis's absence) for the last time (P 348–49/R 354–55).

36. The essay "Confluencias" concludes La cantidad hechizada (Havana: UNEAC, 1970). I quote from Obras completas vol. 2, where the essay is reprinted (1208–28).

37. Maurice Merleau-Ponty, Consciousness and the Acquisition of Language (Evanston: Northwestern University Press, 1973). Lezama was an avid reader of Merleau-Ponty; he read and annotated the Spanish translation to Merleau-Ponty's In Praise of Philosophy and Indirect Language and the Voices of Language. These were translated as Elogio de la filosofía and El lenguage indirecto y las voces del silencio (Galatea Nueva Visión, no date). A paper is yet to be written about Merleau Ponty's presence in Lezama.

38. See Irlemar Chiampi's analysis, "Sobre la lectura interrupta de Paradiso," Revista Iberoamericana 54, no. 154 (1991): 65–76.

39. Regarding the arguments as to Stephen's homosexuality, see William T. Noon, S. J., "A Portrait: After Fifty Years," in James Joyce Today (Bloomington: Indiana University Press, 1966): 54–82. "I surmise that Joyce himself was conscious of the submerged homosexual material of Portrait." (76)

40. The debate on the authorial ironic distance in A Portrait has inspired a smaller polemic concerning the literary merits of chapter 5's villanelle. See Charles Rossman, "Stephen Dedalus' Villanelle," James Joyce Quarterly (1976): 292–93, and Bernard Benstock's response, "The Temptation of St. Stephen: A View of the Villanelle," James Joyce Quarterly (1976): 31–38.

41. For an epiphanic interpretation of the aesthetic theory of A Portrait's chapter 5, see Connoly, Scholes, Link, and Rossman.

42. The notebooks of epiphanies and aphorisms of Joyce's annotating his early aesthetic theory can be found in The Workshop of Daedalus: James Joyce and the Raw Materials for "A Portrait of the Artist as a Young Man," collected and edited by Robert Scholes and Richard M. Kain (Evanston: Northwestern University Press, 1965).

43. See the section on "La fijeza" in Severo Sarduy, "Dispersión/falsa notas: Homenaje a Lezama," Mundo nuevo 24 (June 1968): 5–17. Sarduy elaborates more on this topic in La simulación (Caracas: Monte Avila, 1982): 59–60,115–19. In "La mascára y la transparencia," an essay on the prose of Carlos Fuentes, Oc-

tavio Paz writes: "[Su] enorme, dolorosa, delirante materia verbal podría hacer pensar en el barroquismo de *Paradiso* de José Lezama Lima. . . . Pero el vértigo que nos producen las construcciones del gran poeta cubano es el de la fijeza: su mundo verbal es el de la estalactita." [His enormous, hurtful, and delirious verbal matter makes one think of the baroqueness of José Lezama Lima's *Paradiso*. . . . But the vertigo that the great poet's constructs induce is that of fixedness: his verbal world is that of the stalactite.] Octavio Paz, *Corriente alterna* (Mexico: Siglo Veintiuno, 1967), 47.

44. For an analysis of how Aquinas's "integritas, consonantia, claritas" influence yet are not truly reflected in Joyce, see William T. Noon, *Joyce and Aquinas* (New Haven: Yale University Press, 1971). More needs to be done about Lezama's eccentric appropriation and refiguration of Aquinas's doctrine. Arnaldo Cruz Malavé does a penetrating reading of how, in chapter 9's symposium on homosexuality held by Cemí, Fronesis, and Foción, Lezama manipulates and distorts St. Thomas of Aquinas's teachings on beatific vision and sexual sin in the *Summa Teologica* by having Cemí misquote Aquinas's dictums on the "vicio contra natura" in order to represent homosexuality not as a fallen condition caused by lust but as an equivalent of the "innocent" and sinless sexual drive of beasts and animals (*P* 268/*R* 267–68). Cruz-Malavé argues that Lezama reinvents Aquinas in *Paradiso* by inscribing an ideological and theological "rupture" between his teachings and those of St. Augustine, thus corroding the lines of patristic succession and tradition. This heretical ploy is what Foción calls, at the end of the chapter, Cemí's "Santo Tomás de Aquino heterodoxo" [heterodox St. Thomas Aquinas] (*P* 269/*R* 269). See the section titled "Cemí. La ruptura como sucesión" in Cruz-Malavé, *El primitivo implorante*, 101–16.

45. This specularity is not one of perfect likeness ("semejanza"), but analogical. "[T]hings generated by the power of the sun have a certain likeness to the sun, although it is the likeness of genus, not of specific form. Now if there be an agent which does not belong to any genus, its effect will reflect its likeness all the more remotely. It will not reflect the form of the agent by possessing the same specific nature, not by having the same genus, but by some kind of analogy, since its existence is common to all things. The things which God has made are like him in this way. In so far as they are things, they are like the first and universal principle of all being," "The Perfection of God," *Nature and Grace: Selections From the Summa Theologica of Thomas Aquinas*, trans. and ed. A. M. Fairweather (Philadelphia: Westminster Press, 1954), 74–75. Lezama's "sujeto metafórico" [metaphorical subject] seeks to understand the mechanism of this analogy; i.e., how man is, in a way, a metaphor of God.

46. Dámaso Alonso published the translation under a pseudonym. James Joyce, *El artista adolescente. Retrato*. "Traducido del inglés por Alfonso Donado" [Translated from English by Alfonso Donado] (Madrid: Biblioteca Nueva, 1926). On the choice of the term "adolescente," Joyce writes to Dámaso Alonso on 31 October 1925: "As regards the Spanish title of my novel, from what you say it seems better to use the word Adolescente. As you say the Spanish Joven is impossible. Nevertheless, I believe that the classical meaning of adolescence is a person between the ages of seventeen and thirty-one and this would cover only the fifth chapter of the book and represents about one fifth of the entire period of adolescence, whereas in English at least, while the word adolescent is quite inapplicable to the person represented in chapters 1, 2 and even 3, the term young man can be applied even to the infant on page one, of course in joke." *Letters of James Joyce*, vol. 3, edited by Richard Ellmann (New York: The Viking Press, 1966), 128–29.

47. About this search for precursors, see Dámaso Alonso's 1927 essay "Góngora y la literatura contemporánea," reprinted in vol. 5 of his *Obras Completas*: *Góngora y el gongorismo* (Madrid: Editorial Gredos, 1978), 725–54.

48. For Walter Benjamin's analysis of allegory in baroque theater, see *The Origin of German Tragic Drama*, trans. John Osborne (London: NLB, 1977). On the German expressionist revival of the Baroque, see René Wellek's comments in "The Concept of the Baroque," *Concepts of Criticism* (New Haven: Yale University Press, 1963), 95.

49. José Ortega y Gasset, "La voluntad del barroco," *España* (12–VII–1915). Reprinted in *Meditaciones sobre la literatura y el arte*, ed. E. Inman Fox (Madrid: Castalia, 1987), 237–52.

50. For information on the Góngora Tricentenary, consult Gerardo Diego's *Antología poética en honor de Góngora* (Madrid: Revista de Occidente, 1927, reprinted recently in Madrid: Alianza Editorial, 2d ed. 1979).

51. See the following essays in volume 5 of Dámaso Alonso, *Obras completas* (Madrid: Gredos, 1979–85): "Claridad y belleza de *Las Soledades*," 11–32; "Góngora y el modernismo," 558–70; Góngora y América," 416–29.

52. On Lezama speaking about "escribir claro" [clear/luminous writing] and "escribir oscuro" [obscure/hermetic writing], see "Entrevista con Armando Alvárez Bravo," *Orbita de Lezama Lima* (Havana: Unión, 1966).

53. See Albert Thibaudet, *La poésie de Stéphane Mallarmé* (Paris: Editions de la *NRF*, 1912). "Cette préciosité émaillé (de Mallarmé) rappelle plus que le XVIIIe siècle, l'*Adone* ou le poètes de l'âge d'Élisabeth et plus encore que ceux-ci Góngora," 74.

54. For an interpretration of the revival of the Baroque as a condition of modernity and postmodernity, see Severo Sarduy's essays on the subject, collected in *Ensayos generales sobre el barroco* (Mexico: Fondo de Cultura Económica, 1987), and his "El barroco y el neobarroco," in César Fernández Moreno, ed. *América Latina en su literatura* (Paris: UNESCO, 1972), 167–85.

55. See Alfonso Reyes, *Cuestiones gongorinas* (Madrid: Espasa Calpe, 1927), esp. "De Góngora a Mallarmé." Dámaso Alonso says of Reyes: "Es el primero que se ha acercado a Góngora con ciencia y ecuánime compresión," *Obras completas*, 7: 533.

56. "Un minuto para Mallarmé." In Alfonso Reyes, *Mallarmé entre nosotros* (Mexico: Ediciones Tezontle, 1955).

57. On Joyce and Mallarmé, see David Hayman, *Joyce and Mallarmé* (Paris: Lettres Modernes, 1956). On Lezama and Mallarmé, consult Rubén Ríos Avila, "The Origin and the Island: Lezama and Mallarmé," *Latin American Literary Review* 8, no. 16 (1980): 242–55.

58. "Hay que añadir, en seguida, a la claridad de expresión, la claridad del objeto representado, la luminosidad del mundo poético gongorino. Claridad esta de íntima, profunda iluminación" [We have to add immediately to the clarity of expression the clarity of the represented object, the luminosity of Góngoras' poetic world. A clarity born out from an intimate, profound ilumination]. "Claridad y belleza de *Las Soledades*." In Luis de Góngora, *Las Soledades* (Madrid: Sociedad de Estudios y Publicaciones, 1956 [3d ed.]), 32.

59. Alonso tends to make metaphors of what in *A Portrait* are idiomatic or colloquial expressions. Alonso also tends to emphasize the brilliant presence of light in atmospheric descriptions. Here are some examples of "restrained embellishment" in Dámaso Alonso's translation of *A Portrait*:

A Portrait: "He felt his belly craved for food." *Retrato*: "La voz del vientre le rogaba" [His belly's voice begged him for food].

A Portrait: "The theater looked like a festive ark, anchored among the hulk of houses, her frail cables of lanterns looping her to her moorings." *Retrato*: "El teatro tenía la apariencia de un arca iluminada entre casas como barcos arrumbados y sujeta a sus amarras por los finos cables de sus hileras de farolillos."

60. The patina of baroque embellishments that Alonso's translation adds to the prose of *A Portrait* can be summarily illustrated by analyzing an apparently innocuous sentence in the Spanish version. Lying on his bed early in the morning after what many critics consider a "wet dream," Stephen writes his "temptress" villanelle. After jotting down, self-absorbed, two stanzas, Stephen hesitates, loses his inspiration, recovers it, finishes his poem, and remarks on his surroundings, noting that it is now late morning. The text says:
"The full morning light had come." (*PA* 221)
Alonso translated this as:
"La mañana estaba inundada de luz plena." [The morning was flooded with full light.] (*Retrato* 229)
Alonso's supplementary embellishment of the "full morning light" as a flood transposes Gongora's image of poetic luminosity as "light/water" from the *Soledades* into Joyce's text. By placing the "luz plena" at the end of the sentence, he suggest that it represents not a weather effect or a temporal change but the effusions from Stephen's state of accomplished poetic inspiration.

61. Joyce's letter to Dámaso Alonso answers Alonso's questions concerning mostly Irish colloquialisms, expressions, and idiomatic phrases—"Toasted boss," "Slim Jim," "Sums and cuts," and others—in *A Portrait*. See Joyce, *Letters of James Joyce*, vol. 3, ed. Richard Ellmann (New York: The Viking Press, 1966), 129–30.

62. Eliseo Diego, a member of Lezama's *Orígenes* group, has recently spoken about the great impact the quality of Alonso's translation of *A Portrait* had on his generation. According to Diego, the *Retrato* was read reverentially, as if it were a guide to poetic achievement. Some Cuban poets considered Alonso's translation of the villanelle so exquisite that they memorized it, Diego among them. Interview with César Salgado, Havana, 9 July 1993, unpublished.

63. On the history of the Bildungsroman, see Jerome Hamilton Buckley, *Season of Youth: The Bildungsroman from Dickens to Golding* (Cambridge: Harvard University Press, 1974).

64. Buckley, "Portrait of James Joyce as Young Aesthete," *Season of Youth*, 225–47. Buckley writes: "[Joyce] was fascinated from the beginning by the image of the aloof dispassionate craftsman and until the end was alert . . . to the problems of involvement and the possibility of betrayal [typical of the genre]. He therefore approached his Bildungsroman with deliberate caution and eventually in the final drafts succeeded in reducing the emotional content of the form and at the same time enlarging its capacities for self-protective ironic statement. . . . Joyce sums up, even as he transforms, the traditions of the nineteenth-century Bildungsroman" (225–26).

65. For important analyses of the allusive complexity of this passage and its relations to the Bildungsroman tradition initiated by Goethe's *Wilhelm Meister*, see the chapter "Textual Epiphany: A Return to Bibliomancy" in Gustavo Pellón, *José Lezama Lima's Joyful Vision*, esp. 70–76, and the section titled "El destino del Padre" in Arnaldo Cruz-Malavé, *El primitivo implorante*, 79–88.

66. The debate on the condemnatory or affirmative nature of Joyce's ironic treatment of Stephen Dedalus's character and poetic musings is best presented in Hugh Kenner, "The Portrait in Perspective"; Wayne Booth, "The Problem of Distance in *A Portrait of the Artist*," *The Rhetoric of Fiction* (Chicago: Chicago Univer-

sity Press, 1960), 323–36; and Robert Scholes, "Stephen Dedalus, Poet or Esthete?," *PMLA*, 84 (1964): 484–89. Kenner argues for Joyce's negative assessment of Stephen by taking *Ulysses'* unrealized and frustrated Stephen Dedalus as evidence of an unflattering vision of Stephen's pride and dilettantism in *A Portrait*. Writes Kenner: "The insufferable Stephen of the final chapter is explicable on the assumption that Joyce is preparing his bridge into *Ulysses*; but the moral difficulty of accepting the *Portrait* as satisfactorily finished off in its own right imposes an intolerable strain on the reader. . . . We are compelled to take Stephen seriously so that *Ulysses* may have its desired tragic effect . . . , but to take him seriously is very hard indeed" (172–73). Booth leans toward the ironic reading and masterfully summarizes how *A Portrait*'s aporia has puzzled the critics—"[Is] Stephen always to be viewed with the same deadly seriousness with which he views himself? Is it to artistic maturity that he grows?" (327) Scholes believes affirmatively in the promise of Stephen's aesthetic inclinations by arguing for the poetic soundness of Stephen's villanelle: "Joyce has deliberately set out in his description of Stephen's inspiration to fulfill the theoretical requirements he had himself set up for such inspiration. The inspiration and the poem are both intended to be genuine." (489)

67. On the extended process of revision and refinement of Joyce's episodic *Stephen Hero* manuscript into *A Portrait of the Artist*, consult Richard Ellman's biography *James Joyce* (Oxford: Oxford University Press, rev. ed. 1982), 295–99. See also Hans Walter Gabler's excellent essay on the textual history of *A Portrait*, "The Seven Lost Years . . ." in *Approaches to Joyce's Portrait: Ten Essays*, ed. Thomas Staley and Bernard Benstock (Pittsburgh: University of Pittsburgh Press, 1976), 25–60.

68. For a comparative study of the many condensations, alterations, and subtractions Joyce made in *Stephen Hero* as he rewrote it into *A Portrait*, see Theodore Spencer, "Introduction," in *Stephen Hero: A Part of the First Draft of A Portrait of the Artist as a Young Man* (Binghamton: New Directions, 1944), 7–19. According to Spencer, among the elements Joyce excises from *Stephen Hero* in *A Portrait* is the explicit discussion of aesthetic epiphany developed in Joyce's early notebooks. Harry Levin writes: "As Joyce rewrote his book he seems to have transferred the scene of action from the social to the psychological sphere. As he recollected his 'conflicts with orthodoxy' in the comparative tranquility of exile, he came to the conclusion that the actual struggles had taken place within the mind of Stephen. Discussions gave way to meditations, and scenes were replaced by *tableaux*. Evasion and indirection were ingrained in Joyce's narrative technique. The final effect is that which Shakespearean actors achieve by cutting out all the scenes in *Hamlet* where the hero does not appear," *James Joyce*, 48. Jerome Buckley writes: "[T]he *Portrait* as a whole evinces a remarkable economy. It has evolved from the earlier manuscript by a process of ruthless exclusion and steady narrowing of focus," *Season of Youth*, 238.

69. 1927: *Revista de Avance* 1, no. 4 (30 April 1927): 69. The editorial note "Directrices" goes as follows:

GONGORA: 1627–1927. Vivimos años de centenarios. El 23 de Mayo próximo cúmplese el tercero de la muerte de Góngora. . . . Tiene este acontecimiento exceptional significado para la gente nueva. Tal vez no se haya visto nunca en la historia de la evolución literaria de un pueblo caso tan patente de filiación como el de las actuales letras hispánicas respecto del "gongorismo." Puestos los poetas de hoy a la búsqueda de una alcurnia noble, en ese afán inevitable de querer hallar en el pasado algo así como la justificación ilustre, autorizada del presente, han dado con el arte raro, aristocrático, personalísimo, único en las letras castellanas, de Don Luis de Góngora y Argote: tronco de mantenido verdor, que dio sus primero brotes en el siglo XVI y que tres centurias después se orna todavía con floraciones maravillosas.

[Gongora: 1627–1927. We live in centenary years. Next May 23 will be the third since Góngora's death. . . . This event has exceptional meaning for the new generations. Perhaps there has never been in the history of literary evolution a more evident case of filiality than that contemporary Hispanic letters have with Góngora's poetics. Searching for a noble pedigree in that inevitable wish to find in the past an illustrious justification that could authorize the present, the poets of our day have found the rare, aristocratic, individualist spirit of Don Luis de Góngora y Argote, unique in Castellean letters: a tree of persistent greenness that began flourishing in the sixteenth century and that, three centuries later, is still producing marvelous blooms.]

The note ends with an announcement for a commemorative activity by the journal.

3: Orphic Odysseus: Mythical Method and Narrative "Technology" in *Paradiso* and *Ulysses*

1. Borges's translation of Virginia Woolf's *A Room of One's Own* and *Orlando* appeared in Buenos Aires in 1936. His version of Franz Kafka's *The Metamorfósis* was published (together with other Kafka stories) in Buenos Aires in 1938. His translation of William Faulkner's *The Wild Palms* came out in Editorial Sudamericana in Buenos Aires in 1940. Many modernist novels came to be known in Spanish before *Ulysses*. See Emir Rodríguez Monegal, *Jorge Luis Borges: A Literary Biography* (New York: E. P. Dutton, 1978), 293, 311–12, 372–73.

2. For an account of the *Ulysses* scandal—the United States Post Office confiscation of the *Little Review*, the censorship of the novel, and the trial of *Ulysses* for obscenity in the United States District Court—see Richard Ellman's biography, *James Joyce*: 497, 502–4; 666–67. For a personal account of the story of Shakespeare & Company's publication of *Ulysses*, see Sylvia Beach, *Shakespeare & Company* (Lincoln: University of Nebraska Press, 1991 [1st ed. 1951]); for an academic account, see Noel Riley Fitch, *Sylvia Beach and the Lost Generation: A History of Literary Paris in the Twenties and Thirties* (New York: Norton, 1983).

3. Ulises, translated by J. Salas Subirat (Buenos Aires: Editorial Rueda, 1945). For a profile of the translator of *Ulysses*, see César Tiempo, "El traductor de U-lises," *El Radical* (Chile, 17 October 1945). Salas Subirat published an article on his experience of translating *Ulysses*, "La experiencia de traducir el Ulises," in the Argentine journal *Contrapunto* 1, no. 4 (1945): 12.

4. "The *novela de la tierra* [which in 1933 was enjoying its heyday] continued the tradition of the nineteenth-century novel; it was essentially a bourgeois novel written within realistic conventions. Thematically it protested against social injustice and made a plea for progress in positivistic and liberal terms. Time is seen as a continuum, character and setting blend according to the established rhetorical norms of the nineteenth-century novel, and the narrative is given from the perspective of an omniscient narrator whose academic, standard Spanish gives the novel an even texture in which all differences are subsumed," Roberto González Echevarría, *Alejo Carpentier: The Pilgrim at Home* (Ithaca: Cornell University Press, 1977), 64–66. In *The Spanish-American Regional Novel* (Cambridge: Cam-

bridge University Press, 1989), Carlos J. Alonso presents a bold interpretation of the problematic modernity of the *novela de la tierra* that refutes some of the ideas espoused by González-Echevarría above. For another account of how the Latin American experimental *nueva novela* [new novel] broke with the poetics of the *novela de la tierra,* see Carlos Fuentes, *La nueva novela latinoamericana* (Mexico: Joaquín Mortiz, 1970).

5. On the occasion of Joyce's death, both Marechal and Carpentier published articles praising Joyce's technical innovations in the genre while, at the same time, trying to distance their own creative project from his influence. (A complete anthology could be made of these critical epitaphs on Joyce written in Latin America.) Discussing *Ulysses* in his note on Joyce's death, Marechal takes a cue from T. S. Eliot and writes: "Yo me atrevo a sostener que dicha obra es la primera y la mayor tentativa que se haya hecho últimamente para devolverle a la novela su lineamiento clásico y su raíz tradicional. El 'Ulises' es algo menos que una epopeya y algo más que una novela. . . . Con todo, su 'efecto literario' es bastante parecido al de la epopeya tradicional" (32, 34) [I'd wager that Joyce's work is the first and greatest attempt in recent years to restore to the novel its classical structure and its roots in tradition. *Ulysses* is something less than a epic and something more than a novel. . . . With all its literary 'effects', it still resembles the traditional epic]. With this, Marechal conceded that his own novelistics of the *argentinopeya* [epic of Argentina] had been inspired by Joyce. Then he adds: "Pero no dejo de reconocer que a Joyce, algunas veces, se le ha ido la mano en la pintura, y que su obra nada gana con ese alarde blasfematorio." (35) [But I have to recognize that Joyce lays it on too thick and his work does not gain anything from his shows of blasphemy.] "James Joyce en su gran aventura novelística," *Macedonio* 1, no. 3 (1969): 31–37. As Marechal, Lezama exposed the principles of his own novelistic writing when he wrote his 1941 note on Joyce; Carpentier rehearsed the same self-projection when he wrote about Joyce. Carpentier published five articles on Joyce in the column "Letra y Solfa" of *Revista Carteles,* including "¡Ha muerto James Joyce!" [James Joyce has died]. First published on 18 January 1941, the latter piece is reprinted in *Crónicas del regreso,* ed. Salvador Arias (Havana: Ediciones Unión, 1991), 52–56.

6. Many "canonical" essays on Joyce were translated and published in literary journals during the forties: Valéry Larbaud, "*Ulises,*" trans. J. M. Guarnido, *Alfar* 23, no. 85 (1945); Edmund Wilson, "James Joyce y el '*Ulises*' " trans. J. Salas Subirat, *Davar* 1, no. 2 (1945); Jacques Mercanton, "James Joyce," trans. J. M. Guarnido, *Contrapunto* 4, no. 5 (1945). Borges published a mostly negative review of Salas Subirat's translation, "Nota sobre el Ulises en español" [Note on the Spanish *Ulysses*"], *Los anales de Buenos Aires* 1, no. 1 (1946): 9. On the problems of translating Joyce, Borges wrote:

> Salas Subirat juzga que la empresa [de verter el *Ulises* al español] no presenta serias dificultades; yo la juzgo muy ardua. El inglés (como el alemán) es un idioma casi monosilábico, apto para la formación de voces compuestas. Joyce fue notoriamente feliz en tales conjunciones. El español (como el italiano, como el francés) consta de inmanejables polisílabos que es difícil unir. En esta primera versión hispánica del *Ulises,* Salas Subirat suele fracasar cuando se limita a traducir el sentido. Muy superiores son aquellos pasajes en que el texto español es no menos neológico que el original. *A priori,* una versión cabal del *Ulises* me parece imposible. (9)

> [Salas Subirat believes that the task of translating *Ulysses* does not present serious difficulties: I regard it as extremely arduous. English (like German) is practically a monosyl-

labic language, apt for forming compound voices. Joyce was notoriously fortunate in such conjunctions. Spanish (as Italian, as French) consists of unmanagable polysyllables difficult to connect. In this first Spanish version of *Ulysses*, Salas Subirat tends to fail when he restricts himself to the translation of meaning. Those passages in which the Spanish text is not any less "neologistic" than the original are much superior. *A priori*, it seems to me that a faultless version of *Ulysses* is impossible.]

7. C. L. Jung, *¿Quién es Ulises?* (Buenos Aires: Santiago Rueda, 1945); Herbert Gorman, *James Joyce: El hombre que escribió Ulises*, trans. Máximo Siminovich (Buenos Aires: Santiago Rueda, 1945). The latter book was part of Lezama's library at the time of his death.

8. Juan Jacobo Bajarlía, *Literatura de vanguardia de Ulises de Joyce y las escuelas poéticas* (Buenos Aires: Editorial Araujo, 1946). In the conclusion of the section on Joyce, Bajarlía refutes Borges's critique of Salas Subirat's translation by describing Subirat's great effort rather than by defending the merits of the translation: "Yo creo que el *Ulises* es traducible. Salas se ha enfrentado con una labor titánica, ciclópea. Buscad un espíritu que renuncie a todo para pasarse los años sobre el texto, y no le hallaréis. Y tal es la gloria de S. S., cuya versión le llevó cinco años (1940–45) acosado por toda clase de problemas" (54) [I believe that *Ulysses* is translatable. Salas has confronted a titanic, cyclopean project. Try finding someone with the disposition of giving up everything to spend years on this text, and you will not find him. Such is S. S.'s glory, whose work took him five years (1940–45) while plagued by all sorts of problems].

9. Oscar Rodríguez Feliú's translation of *Ulysses*' "Proteus" chapter, "Proteo" appeared in two issues of *Espuela de Plata*, no. E–F (1940), 22–27; no. G (1941), 3–7. José Rodríguez Feo translated the following: Theodore Spencer, "*Stephen Hero*: El manuscrito inédito de 'El Retrato de un Artista Adolescente,' " *Orígenes* 1, no. 3 (1944): 11–21; Harry Levin, "James Joyce: un epitafio," *Orígenes* 3, no. 10 (1946): 7–16.

10. James Joyce, *Ulysse*, "traduit de l'angiais par M. Auguste Morel, assisté par M. Stuart Gilbert; traduction entièrement revue par M. Valery Larbaud, avec la collaboration de l'auteur" (Paris: Achienne Monnier, 1929).

11. In the chapter titled "Into the Labyrinth: Ulysses in America" of his panoramic literary history, *Journeys Through the Labyrinth: Latin American Fiction in the Twentieth Century* (London: Routledge, 1988), Gerald Martin makes a convincing argument of why Joyce's writings become belatedly so influential in the Latin American novel, especially in that of the "boom" period (when *Paradiso* is published). Martin proposes that, after the twenties, there is a transition from the dominance of the "novela de la tierra" or telluric novel—tied to national and rural or authoctonous themes—to the "Ulyssean" novel—dealing with a cosmopolitan urban experience and a journey in search of modernity to Europe and back. Martin writes: "the 'Ulyssean novel' [is] an abbreviation for a certain kind of literary text existing before and after 1922, but for which *Ulysses* constituted the watershed, and, up to now, the archetype" (130). Mediating this transition, argues Martin, are the influences of Joycean writers William Faulkner and John Dos Passos, "more accessible influences in the Latin America of the 1930s, 1940s and 1950s whilst Joyce . . . would finally exercise his full impact only in the 1960s and 1970s" (130). Martin then synthesizes seven modernist principles and four conditioning factors that the Latin American novel of the "boom" and their precursors assimilated from *Ulysses*' legacy; all of these are present, in some way or another, in *Paradiso* and *Oppiano Licario*. The principles are: 1. the structural incorporation of myth; 2. the exploration of language through and in fiction; 3. the phenom-

enological exploration of consciousness in narrative fiction; 4. search for totality; 5. journeys to or through cities; 6. "petty-bourgeois" search for Otherness; 7. perfectionist approach to aesthetic technique. The conditioning factors are: 1. cosmopolitanism; 2. exile; 3. Catholicism; 4. a politically charged approach to language. Martin concludes asking a series of questions that are very pertinent to our analysis of Lezama vis-á-vis Joyce: "Is the new (post-Joycean) novel truly a sign of the independence and liberation of contemporary Latin American fiction . . . ; or is this final catching-up merely a deepening of its dependent neocolonial phase as detractors often suggest?" (140). However, Martin makes the mistake of considering *Paradiso* (1966) a novel of the late 1960s boom period, posterior to *El Señor Presidente* (1946), *Hombres de maíz* (1949), *Rayuela* (1963), *Tres tristes tigres* (1963), and so on, when in fact Lezama began writing *Paradiso* and publishing it serially (as *Ulysses* was at first) in 1949. Martin calls Leopoldo Marechal's *Adan Buenosayres* (1948) "the most comprehensively Joycean" of all the Latin American novels published before the 1960s boom; later in this chapter we will show that Marechal's novel is *mimetically* Joycean while Lezama's *Paradiso* is *genetically* Joycean instead.

12. Jorge Luis Borges, "El Ulises de Joyce," *Proa* 2, no. 6 (1925): 3–6; Antonio Marichalar, "James Joyce en su laberinto," *Revista de Occidente* 6 (1924): 177–202.

13. In a letter to José Rodríguez Feo Lezama speaks of his admiration for Albert Thibaudet's essays while invoking a line by Joyce: "Qué necesario, qué buena sangre encontrarse con lo que es una petición violenta, una reclamación casi y no esa inútil erudición de cetrería de que habla Joyce. Por un Thibaudet o un Du Bois, cuánto profesorucho que extrae de los libros lo que después devuelve en papilla de calabaza. Recuerdo que Thibaudet, al hablar de Mallarmé, evocaba la médula del saúco. Al principio, parece una delirancia, pero después distingue al que lo apresó del retardado." José Rodríguez Feo, *Mi correspondencia con Lezama Lima* (Havana: Ediciones Unión, 1989), 105. [How necessary, what good luck finding what could be considered a forceful critical demand, almost a reclamation, and not that 'useless erudition of falconry' that Joyce speaks about. For each Thibaudet and each Du Bois, how many lousy professors that extract (ideas) from books to then regurgitate like pumpkin mash. I remember that when Thibaudet wrote about Mallarmé, he used the expression 'sambucus marrow.' At first it sounds delirious, but soon it distinguishes he who inmediately understands it from the retarded reader.] Lezama thus takes his famous expression *médula de saúco* from Thibaudet, but deploys it with a higher cryptic power in his writing.

14. Borges's essays "Reinvindicación de Bouvard y Pécuchet" [Reinvindication of Bouvard et Pécuchet] and "El escritor argentino y la tradición" [The Argentine Writer and Tradition]—in very special ways, calques of Pound's "James Joyce et Pécuchet" and Eliot's "Tradition and the Individual Talent"—are proof of Pound and Eliot's great influence in Latin America.

15. See A. Walton Litz, "Pound and Eliot on *Ulysses*: The Critical Tradition," in *Ulysses: Fifty Years* (Bloomington: Indiana University Press, 1974): 5–17. Litz argues that "*Ulysses* criticism can be seen as a continuing dialogue between the spiritual descendants of Pound and Eliot." This judgment can be extended to Latin American criticism of *Ulysses* as well.

16. On Pound's work of promoting modernism, see Hugh Kenner, *The Pound Era* (Berkeley: Berkeley University Press, 1971), and *Pound/Joyce. The Letters of Ezra Pound to James Joyce*, Forrest Read, ed. (New York: New Directions, 1970).

17. Ellmann documents Pound's ambivalence toward *Ulysses* in *James Joyce*:

"Joyce was elated when he finished [Sirens], but on June 18 he received a letter from Pound, disapproving of the *Sirens*, then modifying his disapproval and protesting against 'obsession' and wanting to know whether Bloom . . . could not be relegated to the background and Stephen Telemachus brought forward." *James Joyce*, 459.

18. "James Joyce et Pécuchet" appeared in *Mercure de France* 575 (1 June 1922): 307–20. "Ulysses" appeared as the 'Paris Letter' in *The Dial*, New York 72, no. 6 (June 1922).

19. From here on, quotations come from T. S. Eliot, "*Ulysses*, Order, and Myth," in Seon Givens, ed., *James Joyce: Two Decades of Criticism* (New York: Vanguard Press, Inc., 1948), 198–202.

20. Richard Aldington, "The Influence of Mr. James Joyce," *English Review* 23 (April 1921), reprinted in *Critical Heritage*, 186–89. "From the manner of Mr. Joyce to Dadisme [sic] is but a step, and from Dadisme to imbecility is hardly that" (186–87). "*Ulysses* is a tremendous libel on humanity. *Ulysses* is dangerous reading for anyone whose style is unformed" (188).

21. On this topic, see John Vickery, *The Literary Impact of The Golden Bough* (Princeton: Princeton University Press, 1973), particularly the chapters on *Ulysses*, and Geoffrey Hartman, "Virginia's Web," in *Beyond Formalism* (New Haven: Yale University Press, 1970).

22. Juan Jacobo Bajarlía, *Literatura de vanguardia del Ulises de Joyce y las escuelas poéticas* (Buenos Aires: Editorial Araujo, 1946).

23. See my analysis of Borges's essay in chapter 1.

24. The page is from "Ithaca" and it refers to the constellations that Stephen and Bloom contemplate together, "the heaventree of stars hung with humid night-blue fruit": "Which various features of the constellations were in turn considered? /The various colours significant of various degrees of vitality (white, yellow, crimson, vermillion, cinnabar): their degrees of brilliancy; their magnitudes revealed up and including the 7th: their position: the wagoner's stars," etc. (*U* 574–75)

25. "Entrevista con Salvador Bueno" (*P* 728).

26. I quote from Leopoldo Marechal, *Adán Buenosayres* (Buenos Aires: Editorial Sudamericana, 1976). For other views of *Adán Buenosayres* as a novel inspired by Joyce, see Gerald Martin, *Journeys Through the Labyrinth*, chap. 8; Ambrose Gordon, "Dublin and Buenos Aires, Joyce and Marechal," *Comparative Literature Studies*, 19, no. 2 (1982), 208–19.

27. Eduardo González Lanuza, "*Adán Buenosayres*," *Sur* 16, no. 169 (1948): 87–93; Noe Jitrik, "*Adán Buenosayres*: La novela de Marechal," *Contorno* (1955); Adolfo Prieto, "Los dos mundo de Adán Buenosayres," *Las claves de Adán Buenosayres* (Mendoza: Azar, 1966), 31–50; Graciela de Sola, "La novela de Leopoldo Marechal: *Adán Buenosayres*," *Idem*, 51–77.

28. Julio Cortázar's lapidary observation on the content-form correspondence of the episodes in *Adán Buenosayres* can be transferred to *Ulysses*, and in fact rehashes the early critical impressions inspired by Joyce's novel. Cortázar's essay on Marechal's novel reformulates Joyce's own explanation for *Ulysses*' "scorched earth" stylistic strategy:

> Marechal . . . no se esfuerza en resolver sus antinomias y sus contrarios en un estilo de compromiso . . . sino que vuelca rapsódicamente las maneras que van correspondiendo a las situaciones sucesivas, la expresión que se adecúa su contenido. Si el "Cuaderno de Tapas Azules" dice con lenguaje petrarquista y giros del siglo de oro un laberinto de amor en el que sólo faltan unicornios para completar la alegoría y la simbólica, el velorio del

pisador de barro de Saavedra está contado con un idioma de velorio nuestro, de velorio en Saavedra allá en los veintitantos. . . . En ningún momento . . . cabe advertir la inadeuación fondo-forma que, tan señaladamente, malogra casi toda la novelística nacional. Marechal ha comprendido que la plural dispersión en que lucharon él y sus amigos de "Martín Fierro" no podía subsimirse en un estilo.

[Marechal (in *Adán Buenosayres*) . . . does not exert himself to resolve his antinomies and his contradictios in a style of compromise . . . instead, he rhapsodically delivers the modes that correspond to the sucessive situations. Expression is adjusted to content. If the "Notebook of Blue Covers" narrates with Petrarchian language and Golden Age embellishments a love labyrinth in which only unicorns are needed to complete the allegory and the emblematics, the wake of the peasant of the Saavedra hamlet is told in the autochthonous idiom of an Argentine wake. . . . At no point can we discover the maladjustment of form and content that plagues so saliently almost every Argentine novel. Marechal has understood that the plural dispersion with which by him and his colleagues of "Martin Fierro" (an important avantgarde journal of the twenties and thirties) struggled could not be subsumed under a common denominator, under a style.]

Julio Cortázar, "Leopoldo Marechal: *Adán Buenosayres*," first published in *Realidad* 14 (March–April 1949), reprinted in *Las claves de Adán Buenosayres*, 23–30. I quote from pp. 25–26 of the latter.

29. Leopoldo Marechal, "Las claves de *Adán Buenosayres*," *Las claves de Adán Buenosayres*: 7–21.

30. "Otros rastacueros con desviaciones medulares fingen asombro de clarisas porque comienzo las oraciones en tercera persona y las termino en primera, olvidando que esas mutaciones verbales son, desde Joyce, un hallazgo de la novela contempóranea" ("Entrevista con Salvador Bueno," *P* 727) [Some perverse show-offs fake gasps of maiden surprise because I begin sentences in the third person and finish them in the first, forgetting that these verbal mutations have, since Joyce, been a discovery of the contemporary novel].

31. On Joyce's "technic of the labyrinth," see Wendy Farris, *Labyrinths of Language: Symbolic Landscape and Narrative Design in Modern Fiction* (Baltimore: Johns Hopkins University Press, 1988).

32. See Wendy Farris, "Introduction," 15–17.

33. On Joyce's many influences on Latin American literature consult the special issue, "James Joyce and His Contemporaries," of *Comparative Literature* 19, no. 2 (1982), featuring Ambrose Gordon, "Dublin and Buenos Aires, Joyce and Marechal" (208–19); Robin Fiddian, "A Case of Literary Infection: *Palinuro de México* and *Ulysses*," 220–35; Wendy B. Faris, "*Ulysses* in Mexico: Carlos Fuentes," 236–53; and Morton P. Levitt, "Joyce and Fuentes: Not Influence But Aura," 254–71. On Joyce's impact in Spain, see Carlos G. Santa Cecilia, *La recepción de James Joyce en la prensa española (1921–1976)* (Sevilla: Universidad de Sevilla, 1997).

34. Curiously, Lezama criticizes the "criticismo crepuscular" [crepuscular criticism] of what Lezama thinks is T. S. Eliot's reductive reading of Joyce's "mythical method" while he celebrates Joyce's mythopoetic creativity. See my article "*Ulysses* en Paradiso: Lezama, Joyce, Eliot y el método mítico," *Inti. Revista de Literatura Hispánica* (Spring 1997) 45: 223–33.

35. On the revival in classical studies, see Geoffrey Hartman, *On Formalism*, note 21 in this chapter. See also John Vickery, *The Literary Impact of the Golden Bough*.

36. Victor Bérard, *Les Pheniciens et l'Odyssée* (Paris: Armand Colin, 1902–1903), 3 vol.

37. Victor Bérard, *Did Homer Live?* trans. Brian Thys (New York: E. P. Dutton, 1931), 136.

38. See Michael Seidel, *Epic Geography: James Joyce's Ulysses* (Princeton: Princeton University Press, 1976).

39. See the section on "El Ateneo de la Juventud" in Pedro Henríquez Ureña, *Estudios mexicanos* (Mexico: Fondo de Cultura Económica, 1984), 225–68, esp. the essays "El positivismo independiente," "La cultura de las humanidades," and "Alfonso Reyes."

40. See Ernesto Mejía Sánchez's preliminary study to the volumes on classical studies of Alfonso Reyes, *Obras completas* (Mexico: Fondo de Cultural Económica, 1958–1985). The quotation is from page 12, vol. 20.

41. For Reyes's low opinion of existentialism, see his introduction to *La afición a Grecia* (Mexico: Editorial del Colegio Nacional, 1960).

42. See Ingemar During, ed., *Alfonso Reyes, helenista. Homenaje del Instituto Ibero-americano de Gotemburgo a Alfonso Reyes* (Madrid: Insula, 1955). As part of his work as *helenista*, Reyes translated the first ten rhapsodies of the *Iliad* and studies by Gilbert Murray, Bérard, and others.

43. Víctor Bérard, *Resurrección de Homero*, trans. Alfonso Alemán (Mexico: Editorial Jus, 1945).

44. "De cómo Grecia construyó al hombre" [Of How Greece Built Man], 477–519 in vol. 7 of *Obras completas*. Reyes met Jaeger at Harvard in 1932. We have consulted the English translation: Werner Wilhelm Jaeger, *Paideia: The Ideals of Greek Culture* (New York: Oxford University Press, 1945), 3 vols. Lezama read Alejandro Xirau's three volume translation, *Paideia, los ideales de la cultura griega* (México: Fondo de Cultura Económica, 1942, 1945). His copies are still kept at the José Martí National Library.

45. "La insolencia jonia," *La afición a Grecia*, 35–55.

46. Many critics have pondered the "insular sensibility" that Lezama postulates in his conversation with Juan Ramón Jiménez: "La tesis de la sensibilidad insular, aparentemente orgullosa, tiene tanto de juego como de mito. No desearía ser el reverso en la búsqueda de una expresión mestiza, pues lo que intenta articular es menos que un mito. Se limita, humilde, a una justificación, una vida legitimista." [My thesis of an insular sensibility, even if seemingly insolent, has as much of play as it has of myth. It is not meant to be the other side of a *mestizo* poetics of expression, since what it attempts to articulate is something less than a myth. It humbly seeks a justification, a legitimacy of living.] "Conversación con Juan Ramón Jiménez" was first published in Lezama's journal, *Verbum* 1, no. 1 (1937). I quote from Lezama's *Obras completas II*, 57. On Lezama's discussion of a "sensibilidad insular" or "insularismo," see the chapter "Los orígenes, la 'sensibilidad negra' y el insularismo" in Arnaldo Cruz-Malavé, *El primitivo implorante: El 'sistema poético del mundo' de José Lezama Lima* (Amsterdam-Atlanta, GA: 1994), 31–39.

47. On the complexities of island navigation and its figuration in both antiquity and in Joyce's *Ulysses*, see chapter 4, "1. Dubliners-Vikings-Achaeans, 2. *Ulysses* and the Odyssey," in Gilbert's study, 65–84.

48. "Las ideas de Pitágoras, Platón y Aristóteles sobre el papel de la música, y especialmente del ritmo, en la formación espiritual del joven, es tema largamente tratado por Werner Jaeger en uno de los libros más releídos por Lezama: *Paideia: los ideales de la cultura griega*" [Notions expounded by Pythagoras, Plato, and Aristotle about the role of music, rhythm in particular, were dealt with in detail by Werner Jaeger in one of the books that Lezama reread more often]. Vitier's observation appears in an annotation to chapter 13 of his edition of *Paradiso*, 523.

49. *Paideia*, 1: xxv–xxvii.

50. The chapters "Nobility and Areté" and "The Culture and Education of Homeric Nobility" list the set of virtues promulgated by *paideia*. *Paideia* 1: 3–34.

51. José Lezama Lima, "Ernesto Guevara. Comandante nuestro." Included in *Imagen y posibilidad*, ed. Ciro Bianchi Ross (Havana: Editorial Letras Cubanas, 1981), 231.

52. See "Nobility and Areté": "There is no complete equivalent for the word Areté in modern English: its oldest meaning is a combination of proud and courtly morality with warlike valor. But the idea of Areté is the quintessence of early Greek aristocratic education," *Paideia* 1: 5.

53. For an analysis of Fronesis's poem-gift, of Lezama's notion of "fineza," and generally of gift-making in *Paradiso*, see my "Finezas de Sor Juana y Lezama Lima," *Actual: Revista de la Universidad de los Andes*. (September–December 1997) 37: 75–102

54. See *Paideia* vol. 1, book 2: "The Culture and Education of the Homeric Nobility." Jaeger writes about the special merits of the Telemachia rhapsodies in the *Odyssey*: "Was the Telemachia at one time an independent poem, or was it written for the epic as we have it at present? Apart from the bare facts of Telemachus' birth and home, tradition offered no nucleus of concrete fact for creative imagination, but the poet developed the tale of Telemachus' youth on its own logical basis, and introduced it into the *Odyssey* by a fine device—bringing gradually together two separate figures: Odysseus and his son. Both at once start to move toward each other . . . ," 30. Note the similarity with Lezama's description of *Ulysses'* design in "Joyce and Proteus," quoted in this chapter.

55. "[The] educational motif which runs through the whole Telemachia deserves closer examination. It is clear that the poet's purpose was not merely to set down a few scenes from high life. The core of his charming narrative is the problem of converting the young son of Odysseus into a thoughtful man whose high purpose shall be crowned with noble achievement." *Paideia* 1: 29. On Athena, Jaeger writes: "It is Athena . . . who trains Telemachus to be a man of strong decision and ready daring. In book 1, Athena herself expressly describes her advice as education. Her speech serves to bring Telemachus' resolution to maturity. This resolution and this journey are the *Telemachou paideia*, the schooling of Telemachus." *Paideia* 1: 30–32.

56. Rubén Ríos-Avila compares some aspects of Thomas Mann's novels with those of Lezama: "There is also a Mannian presence in *Paradiso*. Not only is the novel, like *Buddenbrooks*, also the chronicle of the decadence of a Cuban bourgeois family, but it is also, like *The Magic Mountain*, a philosophical novel." "A Theology of Absence," 168–69.

57. Gilbert points out themes of theosophy and Oriental philosophy in *Ulysses* in the third part of his introduction to *Ulysses: A Study*, 33–41.

58. Lezama's *eras imaginarias* are discussed in detail in chapter 4.

59. Lezama probably wrote this essay as a draft for an introduction article to Oscar Rodríguez Feliú's translations of *Ulysses'* "Proteus" chapter that appeared in "Espuela de Plata." See note 9 in this chapter. No part of this draft has ever been published before.

60. "Fijemos ahora el inocente terrorismo nominalista. Oppiano, de Oppianus Claudius, senador estoico; Licario, el Icaro, en el esplendor cognoscente de su orgullo, sin comenzar, goteante, a fundirse" (P 433/R 439) [Let us now define innocent nominalist terrorism. Oppiano, from Oppianus Claudius, Stoic senator; Licario, Icarus, in the cognitive splendor of his pride, not yet starting to deliquesce and come to ruin].

61. "Apolo—necesidad de orden, la ley, la paz—domesticó a Dionisio en Delfos, dándole un templo en su vencidad, lo convirtió en dios del teatro" (*La afición a Grecia*, 51–52) [Apollo—the need of order, law, peace—domesticated Dionysus at Delfos, assigning him a neighboring temple, he made Dionysus god of theater]. Reyes thus defines Ionian insolence as the "denuedo con que los primeros helenos se enfrentaron a las supersticiones y solemnidades de Oriente . . . se burlaron de las tiránicas mentiras que obstruían como esfinges" [self-assurance with which the first Greeks confronted Oriental superstitions and solemnities . . . they made light of those tyrannical lies that act like Sphinx-like obstructions]. From the essay "El asombro de Delfos" [Delphi's Awe], *La afición a Grecia*, 54.

62. See Jorge Luis Borges, "The Inmortal" and "The House of Asterion" in *Labyrinths*; Julio Cortázar, *Los reyes* (Buenos Aires: Gulab y Aldabahor, 1949), "Las ménades" in *Final del juego* (Buenos Aires: Sudamericana, 1964), and "Todos los fuegos el fuego" in the book of the same name (Buenos Aires: Sudamericana, 1966); Alejo Carpentier, "Semejante a la noche," in *Guerra del Tiempo* (Mexico: Compañía General de Ediciones, 1958).

63. That Lezama did not agree with Reyes's Apollonian vision of the Greeks is clear from a letter he wrote Rodríguez Feo in May 1950: "Leo en estos días *Junta de sombras*, de Alfonsito. Erudición americana todavía un poco ingenua. Al lado de la presunción de grandes tesis: negación de la influencia egipcia y oriental en Grecia; una descripción de la batalla de Maratón, candorosa y banal" [These days I am reading little Alfonso's *Junta de sombras*. An American erudition that is still naive next to the presumption of a grand thesis: the negation of Egyptian and Oriental influence in Greece; a candid and banal description of the battle of Marathon]. Rodríguez Feo, *Mi correspondencia con Lezama Lima*, 129.

64. On the Dionysian background of Orphic religions, I have consulted "Orphism," in *The Encyclopedia of Religion*, Mircea Eliade, gen. ed. (New York: MacMillan), vol. 11; and the *Larousse World Mythology*, 320–24. Also useful is *Orpheus: The Metamorphosis of a Myth*, Jon Warden ed. (Toronto: University of Toronto Press, 1982).

65. On the incompatibility of the Orphic and the Homeric see the section on "Mystery Religions" of the *Encyclopedia of Religion*, 835.

66. For theories relating the myth of Orpheus to that of Osiris, see "Orphism," in *Encyclopedia of Religion*.

67. In *A Portrait of the Artist: The Legends of Orpheus and Their Use in Medieval and Renaissance Aesthetics* (New York: Garland Publishing Inc, 1987), Elizabeth A. Newby studies how in the medieval and Renaissance periods Orphic song and harmony were consistently regarded as divine instruments for achieving transcendence beyond the human.

68. María Zambrano, "La Cuba secreta," *Orígenes* 20 (1948): 3–9.

69. *Paradiso*, Archivos edition, 514–15.

70. *Encyclopedia of Religion*, 703. Also: "The Orphics, Plato suggests in one of his curious etymologizings, calls the body *soma* because it keeps the soul as a prison keeps its inmate until that inmate has served his sentence or paid his penalty. . . . In this same passage (Crat 400B) Plato tells us that 'some [Orphics] say that the body is the tomb *[sema]* of the soul.' " In James A. Philip, *Pythagoras and Early Pythagoreanism* (Toronto: University of Toronto Press, 1966).

71. Because of scant evidence, scholars are still debating whether in the 6th century B.C. any contact existed between the Orphic sects in Thrace and the Pythagorean brotherhoods that formed in Southern Italy and all over the Mediterrenean. What is not contested is the great number of shared beliefs and rituals.

Through Cemí and Licario, Lezama posits a necessary, symbiotic relationship between these two religious movements. For an account of the debate concerning Orphic influence in Pythagorean philosophy, see *Pythagoras and Early Pythagoreanism*, 137–39. For a speculation on how Orphic musical concepts structure the Pythagorean concept of harmony, see Newby, 12–27.

72. See Iamblich of Syria Chalcis, *The Life of Pythagoras* (Alpine, N.J.: Platonist Press, 1919). This edition also includes the biography by Porphyry, 129–49; the biography by Photius, 150–55; the biography by Diogenes Laërtius, 156–77. See also José Vasconcelos, *Pitágoras, una teoría del ritmo* (n.p. Tip. Murgia, 1921). Lezama most certainly read the latter volume.

73. Jaeger's account of Pythagorean and Orphic education can be found in pages 161–69 of *Paideia*, vol. 1. His analysis of Plato's critique of Pythagoras's musical education is on pages 211–30 of vol. 3.

74. Richard Ellmann, *Ulysses on the Liffey* (London: Faber & Faber, 1972). Ellmann concentrates on detailing the "oversystematized," "harsh geometry" (57) of the many symbolic and mythical references in *Ulysses*, and not only reproduces and analyzes the Linati schema and Gorman-Gilbert schema specifying the different symbolic categories of the novel (color, person, science, organ, and so on). Ellmann produces a third, new, and richer diagram that identifies symbolic orders not included in Joyce's original schemas.

4. Oppianos Wake: Vico, Resurrection, and Neologisms in *Finnegans Wake* and *Oppiano Licario*

1. Nineteen installments of *Work-in-Progress* appeared in *transition* from 1927 to 1932. Sections from *Work-in-Progress* were also published in the *transatlantic review, Criterion, Navire d'Argent*, and *This Quarter* from 1924 to 1925.

2. Jorge Luis Borges, "Joyce y los neologismos," *Sur* 9, no. 62 (1939). I quote from *Páginas de Jorge Luis Borges* (Buenos Aires: Celtia, 1982), 160–62, where the essay is reprinted.

3. "Góngora—ojalá injustamente—es símbolo de la cuidadosa tecniquería, de la simulación del misterio, de las meras aventuras de la sintaxis. Es decir, del academismo que se porta mal y es escandaloso. Es decir, de esa melodiosa y perfecta no literatura que he repudiado siempre" [Góngora—maybe unjustly—has become a symbol for meticulous but superfluous games of technique, for the simulation of mystery, for mere aventures in syntax—in other words, for that melodic and perfect non-literature that I have always repudiated]. Jorge Luis Borges, *El idioma de los argentinos* (Buenos Aires: M. Glizer, Editor, 1928), 123.

4. I quote here, with one modification, from Eric Larsen's English translation, "Joyce and Neologisms," included in *Borges: A Reader*, Emir Rodriguez Monegal and Alistair Reed, ed. (New York: Dutton, 1981), 38.

5. "Esta atracción temporaria por la verbalidad joyceana," writes Jorge Schwartz, "habría de despertar en Borges una fascinación mayor, con la publicación de *Finnegans Wake* en 1939" [This temporary attraction to Joycean verbality would awaken in Borges a greater fascination with the publication of *Finnegans Wake* in 1939]. "Borges y la Primera Hoja de *Ulysses*," *Revista Iberoamericana* 100–101 (1977): 721.

6. Stuart Gilbert, "Thesaurus Minusculus: A Short Commentary on a Paragraph of *Work-in-Progress*," *transition* 16–17 (June 1928): 15–24.

7. *Las eras imaginarias* (Madrid: Editorial Fundamentos, 1971) is an abridged edition of the collection of essays Lezama published in Havana under the title *La cantidad hechizada* (Havana: UNEAC, 1970). The selection is the same, only that the former does not include the pieces in *La cantidad*'s third section on Cuban topics. The Madrid edition has the advantage of featuring all the essays that develop the concept of the *era imaginaria*—the essays on Cuban culture are written in a different spirit. This makes the Madrid edition a more cohesive work about interpreting great civilizations in the mode of Toynbee or Spengler.

8. Much has been written about the hermetic, transcendental concept of the *imagen* in Lezama. Consult the pages in Ríos-Avila, Bejel, Molinero, Camacho-Gingerich, Heller, and Márquez mentioned in previous chapters for the best approximations.

9. Lezama's last adumbration on the *era imaginaria* is the essay "Imagen de América Latina," which Lezama wrote at the request of César Fernández Moreno. It is the closing essay of the Fernández Moreno's important anthology *América Latina en su literatura* (Mexico: Siglo Veintiuno Editores, 1972), 462–68. Lezama writes there about the capacity for permanence—and for resurrection—of an extinguished culture's defining image in the culture's surviving art objects: "En los últimos años, de Spengler a Toynbee, el tema de las culturas ha sido en extremo seductor, pero las culturas pueden desaparecer sin destruir las imágenes que ellas evaporaron. Si contemplamos una jarra minoana, con motivos marinos o algunos de sus murales, podemos, por la imagen, sentir su vivencia actual, como si aquella cultura estuviese intacta en la actualidad, sin hacernos sentir los 1.500 años a. de c. en que se extinguió. Las culturas van hacia su ruina, pero después de la ruina vuelven a vivir por la imagen. La imagen . . . favorece su iniciación y su resurrección" (462) [During these last years, from Spengler to Toynbee, the theme of the great cultures has become very seductive, but the fact that cultures disappear doesn't mean that the *imágenes* they gave forth were also destroyed. If we look at a Minoan jar with their marine motifs, or any of their murals, we can, through the *imagen*, feel their actual livingness, as if that culture would remain intact even today, without feeling the weight of the 1500 years B.C. when it became extinct. Cultures move towards ruin, but after their ruin they live again through the *imagen*. The *imagen* . . . favors their initiation and their resurrection]. A critical edition of *Las eras imaginarias* should include this essay as a chapter or appendix, given its exposition of *eras imaginarias* that Lezama did not elaborate in *La cantidad hechizada*.

10. Only a careful reader of Cortázar's *Rayuela*—who has studied the "capítulos prescindibles" [dispensable chapters]—can understand Lezama's reference to a Joycean language of "claves y raíces" [roots and codes]. *Glíglico* is the term used in *Rayuela* to describe the babbling, "nonsense" language that intrudes often in the text, especially in the dispensable chapters of the second part. Rather than nonsense, *glíglico* is a proto-Joycean refiguration of words where prefixes, roots, and suffixes are randomly recombined into neologisms that acquire shades of meaning in the normative syntax of grammatically correct sentences.

11. A remarkable change in Lezama's critical appreciation of Cortázar's novel *Rayuela* can be noted when comparing Lezama's comments in the 1964 roundtable on the novel (in which Lezama debated Ana María Simo and Roberto Fernández Retamar) and Lezama's 1968 essay, "Cortázar y el comienzo de la otra novela," first published in *Casa de las Américas* 9, no. 49: 51–62 and later used as the prologue of the Casa de las Américas edition of the novel. In the roundtable transcribed in Ana María Simo et al., *Cinco miradas sobre Cortázar* (Buenos Aires:

Editorial Tiempo Contemporáneo, 1968), although Lezama celebrates the craft behind Cortázar's fluid prose and the profound dramatic effect of the novel's best scenes (Bertha Trepat's concert, Rocamadour's death, Horacio's lovemaking with the *clochards*), Lezama considers Cortázar as a novelist "que forma parte de un grupo que inicia una reacción a ese tipo de novela wagneriana" (10) [part of a group that reacts against the Wagnerian novel] represented by Joyce, Proust, Mann, and Hesse. To Fernández Retamar's claim that *Rayuela* is the equivalent of *Ulysses* in the history of the Latin American novel, Lezama responds that Cortázar's creative achievement in *Rayuela* is inferior to Joyce's ' "Wagnerian" capacity to completely reinvent the novel as a genre through the use of myth and parody since, according to Lezama, Cortázar's "dones críticos . . . son superiores a sus dones de creador" (48) [critical talents . . . are greater that his creative prowess]. Lezama implies that, due to an excessive and inhibited awareness of the burdens of tradition, Cortázar is not as able tapping the deep, "secret" reserves that constitute the source of Joyce's explosive creativity. Thus, even if, like *Ulysses, Rayuela* "tiene suficiente nitroglicerina para reventar la literatura antigua . . . no creo que llegue a habitar una nueva isla, una nueva región" (47) [has enough nitroglicerine to destroy the old literature. . . . I don't think it will inhabit a new island, a new region].

Nevertheless, in "Cortázar y el comienzo de la otra novela" (one of the most hermetic and challenging pieces in all of Lezama's critical prose), Lezama's evaluation is much more enthusiastic. He acknowledges in *Rayuela* an element of *paideuma*, the child-like or primitive state of spontaneous creativity that Lezama thought was the key to overcome the constraints of critical or conventional modes of thought and art, and proposes that, as a novel, *Rayuela* reinvents, reenergizes, and make contemporary the device of the labyrinth, making the novel a sacred site for the issuance of "antropofanía" [anthropophany]: the revelation of man as fundamentally a divine being that the experience of the labyrinth is supposed to engineer. In saying that, with *Rayuela*, Cortázar inaugurates a new, "other" novel and by using Joyce's as the only running analogy to Cortázar's achievement in the modern age (Lezama dismisses André Breton's *Najda* as a comparable text), Lezama concedes Fernández Retamar's claim that *Rayuela* is as important and innovative as *Ulysses*.

12. Both Beckett's "Dante . . . Bruno. Vico . . . Joyce" and Gilbert's "A Prolegomenon to *Work-in-Progress*" first appeared in *transition* 13 (Summer 1928): 242–53, 65–70. Both were reprinted in 1929 in *Our Exagmination Round his Factification for Incamination of Work in Progress* (London: Faber & Faber, 1929). Gilbert's two essays are merged into one with the latter's title. I believe Borges consulted Gilbert's "Thesaurus Minusculus" in its first *transition* format, not in *Exagmination. Exagmination* was not among the books in Lezama's library at the time of his death.

13. On 25 March 1925, Joyce wrote to his benefactor Harriet Shaw Weaver (editor of *The Egoist*): "I should like to hear Vico read to me again in the hope that some day I may be able to write again." James Joyce, *Letters Vol. III* (New York: Viking Press, 1966), 117–18. Later, writes Richard Ellman, "[t]he first faint signs of disaffection with his new work had begun to reach Joyce, and in February he wrote McAlmon of his concern over Miss Weaver's reaction . . . [Joyce] urged her to read Vico's *Scienza nuova*, as with *Ulysses* he had urged her to read the *Odyssey*." Richard Ellman, *James Joyce*, rev. ed. (Oxford: Oxford University Press, 1983), 563–64. Harry Levin's study—published two years after the appearance of *Finnegans Wake*—takes Vico to be the methodological key to the novel: "To inte-

grate [all the myths that emanate from *FW*], we need not a classical epic but a universal history. We desert Homer for the Neapolitan polymath of the eighteenth century who raised the so-called Homeric question. 'The producer (Mr. John Baptister Vickar)' is better known as the philosopher, Giambattista Vico." Harry Levin, *James Joyce: A Critical Introduction* (Norfolk: New Directions, 1941), 142.

14. "Joyce admitted to Larbaud he had stood behind 'those twelve Marshalls [the writers in *Exagmination*] more or less directing them what lines of research to follow' " (Ellmann, *James Joyce*, 613).

15. I have consulted Giuseppe Ferrari's 1859 edition of Giambattista Vico's *Principi di una Scienza nuova d'intorno alla comune natura delle nazioni* (Napoli: Stamperia de Classici Latini), which includes the texts of both the 1725 and the 1744 editions. Vico published three editions of the *Scienza nuova* in his lifetime. The third edition rebuilds and expands generously upon the first two; many scholars thus consider it the definitive edition. Other scholars—Ferrari, for example—have preferred to study the 1725 edition for both its concision and expressive boldness (see Ferrari's introduction). In his essay, Beckett refers to the edition of 1725, which was the edition that José Carner translated into Spanish and published in Mexico in 1941. Since this is the version Lezama consulted, most of the analysis and discussion of the *Scienza nuova* in the chapter refers to the 1725 edition. Significantly, this edition does not develop the idea of the *ricorsi*—the last phase of gentile history in which the "barbarism of reflection" would make a civilization regress to its first stage—in the decisive way the 1744 edition does. Nor does it include the sections in which Vico questions the existence of a Homer and analyzes the Homeric poems "not as the product of a single poetic personality, but the continous autobiography of the Greek people" (Levin 142). This may explain the differences between Borges and Lezama's approach to Vico. Borges's story "The Immortal" is a super-condensed parody of the 1744 edition of *La Scienza nouva* (not of the 1725) since the *ricorsi* and the dissolution of Homer's character into a continuous biography of humanity happen to be the crucial themes in the story. A copy of Carner's translation (annotated by Lezama) is catalogued in the *Fondo Lezama* at the National Library in Havana.

16. This and all subsequent quotations by Gilbert and Beckett come from *Our Exagmination Round his Factification for Incamination of Work in Progress* (London: Faber & Faber, 1928).

17. Augusto and Haroldo de Campos, *Panorama do Finnegans Wake* (Sao Paulo: Conselho Estadual de Cultura, 1962). The Mexican writer Salvador Elizondo has also worked on the Spanish translation of passages of *Finnegans Wake*. See "La primera página de *Finnegans Wake*," included in *Teoría del Infierno y otros ensayos* (Mexico: El Colegio Nacional/Ediciones del Equilibrista, 1992), 155–62. Elizondo follows faithfully the annotations in Campbell and Robinson's *Skeleton Key*. Elizondo's translation of *Finnegans Wake*'s first page is meant to mirror Borges's translation of *Ulysses' last* page in 1922.

18. Joseph Campbell and Henry Morton Robinson, *A Skeleton Key to Finnegans Wake* (New York: The Viking Press, 1961).

19. Giambattista Vico, *Sabiduría primitiva de los italianos* (Buenos Aires: Instituto de Filosofía, 1939). Vico's *Autobiography* was also translated in the forties as *Autobiografía* (Buenos Aires: Espasa-Calpe Argentina, 1948). Both books are part of Lezama's library in the Lezama Manuscript Collection.

20. Giambattista Vico, *Principios de una Ciencia Nueva en Torno a la Naturaleza Común de las Naciones*, 2 vols., trans. José Carner (Mexico: El Colegio de Mexico, 1941).

21. See Benedetto Croce, *The Philosophy of Giambattista Vico*, trans. R. G. Collingwood (New York: Russell and Russell, 1964).

22. Instituto de Filosofía, *Vico y Herder. Ensayos conmemorativos del segundo centenario de la muerte de Vico y el nacimiento de Herder* (Buenos Aires: Universidad Nacional, 1948). Like the "Joycean enthusiasm" of the forties, the boom in Viconian studies was a Latin American—not peninsular—phenomenon. It had two centers: Buenos Aires and Mexico City.

23. Bejel dedicates some pages to the topic of Lezama's relation to Vico, but fails to document the Viconian references in Lezama's writings. See Emilio Bejel, *José Lezama Lima, Poet of the Image* (Gainesville: University of Florida Press, 1990), 22–23, 48–49. The mostly lucid analysis regarding the proximity of Lezama's poetic system to Vico's *New Science* is Enrique Márquez's study. The virtue of Márquez's approach is his understanding of most of Vico's writings (Márquez does not limit himself to a reading of *La Scienza nuova*), given that Lezama himself was interested in the totality of Vico's life and *oeuvre*, as his library demonstrates. See *Bases y génesis de una sistema poético* (New York: Peter Lang, 1991), esp. the section "Interpretación lezamesca de la *Ciencia Nueva* de Vico", 155–76.

24. Despite the Viconian spirit of the analysis of antique civilizations in "Las imágenes posibles" (1948), there are few explicit references to the *Scienza nuova* or to the rest of Vico's work in Lezama's early essays. It is only after *La cantidad hechizada* (1970) that Lezama discusses Vico openly and in depth. Lezama's systematic study of Vico comes late in his career.

25. For an examination of the problematic nature of Joyce's use of Vico in *Finnegans Wake*, see Peter Munz, "James Joyce, Myth-Maker at the End of Time," and Bernard Benstock, "Vico . . . Joyce. Triv . . . Quad," published in Donald Phillip Verene, ed., *Vico and Joyce* (Albany: State University of New York Press, Bloomsday 1987), 48–56, 59–67.

26. José Lezama Lima, *La expresión americana* (Havana: Instituto Nacional de Cultura, 1957). See also Irlemar Chiampi's useful critical edition of the essay (Mexico: Fondo de Cultura Económica, 1993). For a penetrating deconstructive analysis of Lezama's theory of Western culture as expressed by this essay, see Brett Levinson, *Secondary Moderns. Mimesis, History, and Revolution in Lezama Lima's "American Expression"* (Lewisburg: Bucknell University Press, 1996). For a discussion of Lezama's visualization of hybridity in New World baroque art as expressed in this essay, see César A. Salgado, "Hybridity in New World Baroque Theory," *Journal of American Folklore* 122 (445): 316–331.

27. According to legend, *Finnegans Wake* features the names of all the world's rivers. See Campbell and Robinson, 243.

28. On the critical structural role of the *Book of the Dead* in *Finnegans Wake*, see pages 191–201 of James S. Atherton, *The Books at the Wake: A Study of Literary Allusions in James Joyce's Finnegans Wake* (London: Faber & Faber, 1959) and Mark L. Troy, *Mummeries of Resurrection: The Cycle of Osiris in Finnegans Wake* (Stockholm: Upsala, 1976). See also the chapter titled "Inside the Coffin: *Finnegans Wake* and the Egyptian Book of the Dead," in John Bishop, *Finnegans Wake: Joyce's Book of the Dark* (Lincoln: University of Nebraska Press, 1988), 86–125. The importance of sacred books—of the *scriptural*—in *Paradiso* and *Oppiano Licario* is comparable to that in *Finnegans Wake*. A reading of Lezama's novels in the light (or shadow) of the *Book of the Dead* is yet to be written.

29. Concerning Vico's long travails in generating and revising the central ideas of the *Scienza nuova*, consult *The Autobiography of Giambattista Vico*, trans. Max Harold Fisch and Thomas Goddard Bergin (Ithaca: Cornell University Press, 1944).

30. Gino Bedani makes a compelling argument about the heretical implications of Vico's account of gentile history. Bedani interprets the rhetorical abstruseness of *La Scienza nuova* as a tactic to dodge the censors and the Inquisition. See "Part I (The Problem of Orthodoxy)" of *Vico Revisited* (Oxford: Berd, 1989). Bedani's argument brings up an equivalent issue regarding Lezama's writing: to what extent did Lezama's strategy of textual obscurity have to do with his religious, sexual, and political heterodoxy?

31. Statements about the Jews' privileged "exclusion" from the general patterns of human history are common in *La Scienza nuova*: "The Hebrew religion was founded by the true God on the prohibition of the divination on which all the gentile nations arose. This axiom is one of the principal reasons for the division of the entire world of the ancient nations into Hebrews and gentiles," 68. "[T]he entire first world of men must be divided into two kinds: the first, men of normal size, which includes Hebrews only; the second, giants, who where the founders of the gentile nations," 115. I quote from Thomas Goodard Bergin and Max Harold Fisch's unabridged translation of the 1744 edition, *The New Science of Giambattista Vico* (Ithaca: Cornell University Press, rev. ed. 1968).

32. The notion of poetic experience as the instantaneous recognition of an invisible realm is everywhere in Lezama's writing. Bejel argues convincingly that this is, among other things, the legacy of French symbolism in Lezama's writing (*Poet of the Image*, "Introduction"). Lezama's idea of *confluencia* is affiliated with Baudelaire's *correspondance*.

33. For an excellent exploration of the function of imagination and *fantasia* in Vico's thought, see Donald Phillip Verene, *Vico's Science of Imagination* (Ithaca: Cornell University Press, 1981).

34. In *Vico Revisited*, Bedani refutes the many readers who take Vico's discussion of "poetic wisdom" as an aesthetic theory or as a creative program. "Vico did not conceive of 'poetic' language as a 'higher,' aesthetic form of expression. Its figurative forms . . . are not artistic creations," 52. Lezama commits the same misreadings Bedani wants to rectify.

35. On Lezama's and Heidegger's visions of poetry, see Bejel, *Poet of the Image*, 47–48, 52–56.

36. On the tactical, aesthetic purpose of the "difficult" in Lezama, consult Julio Ortega's prologue to his selection of Lezamian writings, *El reino de la imagen* (Caracas: Ayacucho, 1988), ix–xxviii.

37. See Erich Auerbach, "Figura," *Scenes from the Drama of European Literature* (Minnesota: University of Minnesota Press, 1984), 11–78. This edition is a facsimile of the 1959 English text. This text also includes an illuminating essay on Vico, "Vico and Aesthetic Historism," 183–200. Given that Lezama was an avid reader of Auerbach (an annotated copy of the Spanish edition of *Mimesis* is still part of his library), we might speculate that Auerbach's article motivated Lezama's rereading of Vico late in his career. It could have inspired Lezama's conceptualization of the *imagen histórica* notion in *Las eras imaginarias*.

38. Vico: "That such was the origin of poetry is finally confirmed by this eternal property of it: that its proper material is the credible impossibility. It is impossible that bodies should be minds, but it was believed that the thundering sky was Jove. And nothing is dearer to poets than singing the marvels wrought by sorceresses by means of incantations. . . . In this manner the poets founded religions among the gentiles." *The New Science*, 120. In "La imagen histórica" Lezama writes: "Tres frases colocaría yo en el umbral de esta nueva vicisitud de la imagen en la historia. Primera: 'Lo imposible creíble', de Vico. Es decir, el que cree vive ya en

un mundo sobrenatural, cualquier participación en lo imposible convierte al hombre en un ser imposible, pero táctil en esa dimensión" (*OC* 2: 848) [I'd place three phrases on the brink of this new phase of the *imagen* in history. The first would be: The impossible-believable. In other words, he who believes already lives in a supernatural world; any participation within the impossible transforms man into an impossible being himself, and makes him tactile in this dimension]. Note Lezama's "supernatural" reformulation of Vico's secular concept. That Lezama was more of a creative "compiler of aphorisms" rather than an analytical reader of arguments can be surmised by the nature of his notetaking in some of his surviving notebooks. In them Lezama often does not summarize points or recapitulate arguments, but writes down verbatim the sentences that stimulate him the most.

39. "Among the gentiles the fathers were sages in auspicial divinity, priests who sacrificed to take the auspices or make sure of their meaning, and certainly monarchs who commanded what they believed to be the will of the gods as shown in the auspices, and consequently were subject to no one but God," *New Science*, 15.

40. The idea of a "choral," egalitarian social system appears frequently in Lezama's writing. It would be fruitful to consider to what extent Lezama fashions this *coralidad* as a coded, classical equivalent to Cuban nationalism or Marxist socialism. Lezama did read Marx critically; his extensive notes on the young Marx's concept of "alienation" in the *Carpeta VII* at the Fondo Lezama in Havana are evidence of this. There are thus attempts in Lezama's writings after April 1961 (when Fidel Castro declared the Cuban Revolution a socialist revolution) to reconcile his "poetic system of the world" with a socialist outlook. The results, judging from his discussion of the Etruscans, were extremely eccentric and anti-ideological, and no doubt were unpalatable to the Cuban cultural apparatchiks of the sixties and seventies.

There is, however, throughout Lezama's work (even within *Paradiso* itself) a complex use of the concept of the chorus that is frought with contradictions and ambiguities. Arnaldo Cruz-Malavé's keen analysis of the image of the crowd-like or mob-like "coro" as a "dragón devorador" [devouring dragon] in chapter 11 of *Paradiso* proves that Lezama also had a Ortegian aversion to "choral" or massive popular action when this action responded either passively or mechanically to mediocre or destructive drives, like consumerism or war. See the chapter titled "El dragón devorador, o el espectador moderno" in Cruz-Malavé, *El primitivo implorante*, 117–32.

41. "Otra de las más significativas eras imaginarias es la etapa de los reyes como metáforas. El período cesáreo, el merovingio. Los reyes confesores (Eduardo el Confesor, entre los ingleses, y San Luis, rey de todos los franceses). Los reyes perseguidos: Fernando III el Santo, Alfonso X el Sabio, Sancho IV el Bravo, Alfonso XI" (*OC* 2: 837) [Another of the most significant imaginary eras is the stage of kingship as metaphor. The Cesarean period, the Merovingian. The confessor kings—Edward the Confessor among the English and Saint Louis, king of all the French. The persecuted kings: Saint Ferdinand the Third, Alfonse X the Wise, Sancho IV the Brave, Alfonse XI].

42. Lezama does not renounce his belief in spiritual aristocracy (required by the principle of *areté* so essential to *Paradiso*) when he postulates a social order founded on *coralidad*. This "egalitarian" *polis* has need for a nobility, but the status of this "high class" (ideally constituted, according to Lezama, by the poets) is determined not by economic factors but by its disposition to be sacrificed for

the common good. Thus, in "La dignidad de la poesía" (1956) Lezama writes: "la idea de que los dioses sólo se calman por el sacrificio de los mejores, de que es necesario alimentar la *némesis* de los dioses con los manjares humanos más misteriosos, fue lo que mantuvo a esa nobleza en el sentido de los escogidos para el sacrificio. . . . La relación de la verdadera aristocracia en la *polis* [es] el convencimiento de que el error de cualquiera obliga al sacrificio de uno de los mejores" (*OC 2:* 779) [The idea that only the sacrifice of the best appeases the gods, that it is necessary to feed the god's *nemesis* with the most mysterious human morsels, was what sustained this nobility in the sense of those chosen for sacrifice. . . . The situation of the true aristocracy in the polis (is) the belief that anybody's mistake obliges the sacrifice of one of the best].

43. "La entrada del campesinado en lo irreal" [the entrance of the peasantry into the unreal] and the theme of the siege of the city are two very enigmatic and highly developed topics in Lezama's later writing. They can be read as Lezama's projection into his poetic system of the historical event that culminates in the Cuban Revolution: the entrance of the Sierra Maestra guerillas—made up by revolutionaries, peasants, and squatters coming from the countryside—into Havana after Batista's abdication. When, in "A partir de la poesía," Lezama writes that "Vico no pudo conocer esa otra naturaleza del pueblo como penetración de un coro en los designios [de la historia]" [Vico did not get to know that state of the people penetrating like a choir into the designs of history] (*OC 2:* 832), he implies that he (Lezama) can, since he has witnessed such a historic entrance.

44. On Vico's trenchant opposition to Cartesian rationalism, see *The Autobiography of Giambattista Vico*, trans. Max Harold Fish and Tomas Goddard Bergin (Ithaca: Cornell University Press, 1944): "We shall not here feign what René Descartes craftily feigned as to the method of his studies simply in order to exalt his own philosophy and mathematics and degrade all the other studies included in divine and human erudition," 113. (This is one of many disparagements). In *La cantidad hechizada*, Lezama follows Vico's systematic refutation of Cartesian postulates. By doing this, Lezama revises his own intellectual biography; the *Diario* shows that as a young man he pondered Descartes's writings obsessively.

45. On Vico's *vera narratio*, see Bedani, "The 'Vera Narratio' as Historical Method,' *Vico Revisited*, 52–60.

46. The Immaculate Conception thus appears as the defining *imagen* of the ninth *era imaginaria*, representing the Catholic concepts of grace, charity, and resurrection. In this era, "sanctity is achieved," "A partir de la poesía," *OC* 838. To Lezama, the Virgin Mary is the most radiant *imagen*, since she—*deípara, paridora de dios* (begetter of god)—incarnates the impossible possibility of the human to "contain" the divine. This is why Lezama reveres the myth of the Virgin more than the figure of Christ. On page 137 of the *Carpeta II* in the Lezama Manuscript Collection he writes: "La resurrección de Cristo es tan sólo, a pesar de su enorme importancia, la resurrección de un dios. La resurrección de María es como el símbolo de la resurrección de todos los hombres" [In spite of its importance, Christ's resurrection is only the resurrection of a god. Mary's resurrection is like the symbol of the resurrection of all people].

47. See Bedani, "Conclusion," 275–88.

48. In the tradition of *Ulysses'* careful patterning of Stephen and Bloom's crossovers and postponed encounters (which Lezama examined in "Joyce and Proteus"), wakes and death scenes in *Paradiso* are arranged to prefigure the funeral at the end, where all the visions of the dead converge into that of Oppiano Licario.

49. On the funereal and "funferall" bric-a-brac in *Finnegans Wake,* see John Bishop's introduction to his *Joyce's Book of the Dark.*

50. The 1725 edition of the *Scienza nuova* discusses the three basic institutions of society more emphatically than the 1744 edition. I quote from José Carner's translation: "La Humanidad . . . siempre rigió sus prácticas de acuerdo con estos tres sentidos comunes del Género Humano: primero que existe una Providencia; segundo, que se tengan ciertos hijos con ciertas mujeres, con las cuales anden compartidos siquiera los principios de una religión civil . . . ; tercero, que se entierren a los muertos" (*Principios de una ciencia nueva,* 5) [Humankind . . . always rules its practices following three common sense principles of the species: first, that there is a Providence; two, that humans may multiply within sexual arrangements more or less dictated by the principles of a civil religion . . . ; third, that the dead be buried].

51. The twelve mourners persuade Finnegan to lie down in his grave again: "Now be aisy, good Mr Finnimore, sir. And take your laysure like a god on pension and don't be walking abroad. Sure you'd only lose yourself in Healiopolis now the way your roads in Kapelavaster are" "Drop in your tracks, babe! Be not unrested!" "Repose you now! Finn no more!" *Finnegans Wake,* 24, 26, 28.

52. "In Joyce's composition, the comical Finnegan episode is only the prologue to the major action. It is related to the later episodes as prehistory is related to history; or (to use a Viconian image) as the giants of the dawn-chaos are related to the patriarch of orderly history," Joseph Campbell and Henry Morton Robinson, "Foreword," *A Skeleton Key,* 5–6.

53. Ynaca Eco Licario verbalizes this succession—Cemí's replacement of Licario—in the conversation she holds with Cemí when she meets him by chance on the bridge of the Castillo de la Fuerza in chapter 4 of *Oppiano Licario*: "Licario me decía con frecuencia: él tiene lo que a nosotros nos falta. . . . Conocerlo a él, será tu mejor fuente de conocimiento" (*OP* 148–52) [Licario used to often tell me: he has what we are missing. Knowing him will be your best source of knowledge".

54. HCE's interment occurs in *Finnegans Wake* 75–79: "Any number of conservative public bodies, through a number of select and other committees . . . following a koorts order of the groundwer . . . made him, while his body still persisted, their present of a protem grave in Moyelta of the best Lough Negh pattern" *Finnegans Wake,* 26. See *A Skeleton Key to Finnegans Wake,* 81–84, for an *explication du texte.*

55. Reports of HCE's resurrection are "detailed" in *Finnegans Wake,* 96–100: "[A]ll the soundest sense to be found immense our special mentalists now holds that by such playing possum our hagious curious encestor bestly saved his brush with his posterity . . . a dead fuchser's volponism hid him close in covert, miraculously ravenfed and buoyed up, in rumer, ricule, onasum and abomasum. . . . Mikkelraved, Nikkelsaved." (96, 97) For an explication, see *A Key,* 92–94.

56. Licario's apparitions all take place in chapter 4 of the novel, "Otra visita de Oppiano Licario" [Another Visit by Oppiano Licario], the only one with a title: "Eran las dos de la mañana. Cemí y Licario volvían a encontrarse, lo mismo en la cabeza de fósforo del sueño que en la fundamentación sin bordes de las aguas centrales. Con pantalón citrón y camisa de mangas de campana, con pequeños puntos rojos, se mecía en un trapecio." (*OP* 119) [At two o'clock in the morning, Cemí and Oppiano met again, either in the phosphorus of sleep or in the borderless realm of converging waters. With citron pants and a shirt with bell sleeves, (Oppiano) swung himself on a trapeze.]

57. See Enrico Mario Santí, " 'Oppiano Licario', la poética del fragmento," in

Coloquio Internacional sobre la obra de José Lezama Lima (Madrid: Editorial Fundamentos, 1984), 135–51. César López also discusses "Esbozo para el *Infierno*"—Lezama's preliminary plan for *Oppiano Licario*—in his introduction to his critical edition *Oppiano Licario* (Madrid: Cátedra, 1989), 95–98. I consulted this plan in my visit to the Lezama Manuscript Collection in July 1993. In an interview, César López claims to have found the missing chapters of *Oppiano Licario*. He is editing them for publication. Interview with César López, 8 July 1993, unpublished.

58. On the paleographic reconstruction and interpretation of the ancient manuscript in *Finnegans Wake*, see Campbell and Robinson, "The Manifesto of ALP," 96–123.

59. " 'The fall,' and the strange polysyllable following it, introduce us to the propelling impulse of *Finnegans Wake*. The thumping of Finnegan's body tumbling down the ladder is identical with the Viconian thunderclap, the voice of God's wrath, which terminates the old aeon and starts the cycle of history anew," *A Skeleton Key*, 31.

60. For example: "Bladyughfoulmoecklenburgwhurawhorascortastrumpapor nannennykocksapastippatappatupperstrippuckputtnach." *Finnegans Wake*, 90.

61. "Ayuda al ciclón en sus furias pavorosas el agua que lo acompaña. . . . Estas son las terribles invasiones de las costas por el mar, motivadas por causas metereológicas, las *storm-lides*, las *storm-waves*, las llamadas por los franceses *raz de marée*, que en Cuba decimos "ras de mar" ' [The ciclone's fury is incremented by the water that follows it. . . . These are the terrible invasions into the coastlands by the sea for meteorological reasons, the *storm-lides*, storm-waves, which the French call *raz de marée* and the Cubans *ras de mar*]. Fernando Ortiz, *El Huracán: Su mitología y sus símbolos* (Mexico: Fondo de Cultura Económica, 1947), 52. All further quotations in this chapter come from this edition. The *ras de mar* is what destroys Licario's manuscript, *OP* 194.

62. The impact of the reading of Sir James Frazer's study among Cuban intellectuals of the first half of the century has not been fathomed yet. Frazer's work informs the range and method of Fernando Ortiz's, Lydia Cabrera's and Samuel Feijóo's ethnological research, among others. "La rama dorada" (the golden bough) is one of the most striking and baffling recurrent images in Lezama's fictions and essays. "El ladronzuelo. . . . adelantó la mano y empuñó la rama que él creía era de oro. . . . Se detuvo cuando la rama, deshaciéndose, comenzó a gotear" (*OP* 136) [The young thief . . . moved forward his hand and wield the branch he thought of gold . . . he stopped when the dissolving branch began leaking]. In "La imagen histórica," Lezama writes: "Una rama puede ser un símbolo de la fertilidad, si con esa rama penetramos en los infiernos, como en *La Eneida*, quien la porta la trueca en imagen" (*OC 2*: 847–48) [A bough can be a symbol for eternity: if we enter with this bough into Hell as in the *Aeneid*, we will transform it into an *imagen*].

63. In his essays of *Las eras imaginarias*, Lezama pays scant attention to Vico's most noted thesis, the *corsi-recorsi* or cyclical vision of history, so important in the textual riverlike recirculation of *Finnegans Wake*'s design. We could speculate that Lezama only knew of Carner's translation of the 1725 edition of the *Scienza nuova* (see note 18). The evident answer is that Lezama had a Christian-eschatological vision of history (see chapter 1); its end is Paradise, not Joyce's "commodius vicus of recirculation," *Finnegans Wake*, 3.

64. The best example of Fernando Ortiz's aesthetization of the discourse of the social sciences is his ethnohistorical study *Contrapunteo del tabaco y el azúcar*:

Advertencia de sus contrastes agrarios, económicos, históricos y sociales (Havana: 1940). Though this essay introduces some of the most innovative and complex sociological concepts in the study of Latin American culture (i.e., transculturation), Ortiz uses the Arcipreste de Hita's medieval poem *El libro del buen amor* as a rhetorical model for his scientific tract.

65. The *malecón* is always a magical region of encounters in Lezama's fiction. It is where Fronesis has his vision of the *Moloch horridus* in *Paradiso*'s chapter 10 (*P* 294–98/*R* 295–99). In *Oppiano Licario*'s chapter 9, Foción dives from the *malecón* into the sea with the mad intention of swimming to Europe to see Fronesis. In this episode, he struggles with a god-shark that severely wounds him.

66. In *The Anxiety of Influence* (Oxford: Oxford University Press, 1970), Bloom calls this particular form of misreading a clinamen. I have not adopted Bloom's terminology here since I do not believe the relation between Joyce and Lezama to be strictly one of "influence." My theoretical use of the term "refraction" might be thought of as another form of Bloom's clinamen, but in Bloom's analysis this "deflection or distortion" of the source constitutes a Freudian mechanism of defense in the poet's psyche. Bloom does not factor into his method the complexities of marginal or peripheric literature. The cultural margin does not reject influences; it demands and devours them. In its avid thirst for new techniques and themes, it often distorts them. Moreover, refraction is not a tactic necessarily deployed by a will to originality. Refraction occurs through the inevitable accidents that accompany the transmission or communication of literature from one language system to another. "Refraction" is a better operative term because of its reflexive rather than transitive nature.

67. Vico regards Juno as the divine principle that follows Jove in the nascent human imagination. In the section titled "Divine Principles of All Gentile Nations" of the 1725 edition, June appears as the female counterpart of Jove-sky; an emanation of the primordial god, she is the "air where Jove's signs are written": "Juno es el Principio de las Nupcias solemnes, o bodas celebradas bajo los auspicios de Jove y por ello denominadas de Yugal, por el yugo del matrimonio, . . . [fue] hermana y mujer de Jove." (*Principios de una ciencia nueva,* 152–53) [Juno is the Principle of the Solemn Weddings, or Marriages celebrated under the auspices of Jove and thus called conjugal for Yugal, the link of marriage. . . . (Juno) was Jove's sister and wife.]

68. A complete list of Lezama's neologisms still needs to be compiled. Much of his theoretical vocabulary should figure in it: *hipertelia, potens, súbito, perplejo,* and so on.

69. In some annotations to his critical edition of *Paradiso,* Vitier observes: "Lezama suele atribuir a 'ingurgite' (derivado de ingurgitar, engullir) una acepción opuesta, más bien la de regurgitar. Modalidad típica del habla-escritura lezamiana: uno de sus modos más frecuentes de desestabilización y reconstrucción del lenguaje" (*P* 21n) [Lezama tends to attribute to 'ingurgite' (derived from ingurgitation, gulping down) a contrary meaning, more like regurgitating. Typical modality of the speech-like writing of Lezama, this is one of the ways in which he most often destabilizes and reconstructs language]. Discussing expressions like "el perplejo" ["the perplexing"] and other constructions in which adjectives are made into nouns, Vitier writes: "[Lezama está] siempre a favor de una gramática desinstitucionalizada, original, en estado naciente (no si un *plus* de sorpresa para el lector . . .). No se trata de la 'evolución' de la lengua a través de los siglos sino del *súbito*—estabilizado—de una apropiación, o re-creación, personal" (*P* 29n) [(Lezama) always favor a counter-institutional, original grammar that seems to be

in a nascent state (and furnishing many surprises for his reader . . .). It is not the reflection of the "evolution" of language throughout the ages, but of a "sudden"—yet stabilized—personal appropriation or recreation.]

70. "Now these are the same three languages that the Egyptians claimed had been spoken before in their world, corresponding exactly both in number and in sequence to the three ages that had run their course before them. (1) The hieroglyphic or sacred or secret language, by means of mute acts. This is suited to the uses of religion, for which observance is more important than discussion. (2) The symbolic, by means of similitudes, such as we have just seen the heroic language to have been. (3) The epistolary or vulgar, which served the common uses of life." Giambattista Vico, *New Science*, 21.

71. Lezama was an avid reader of Baltasar Gracián's *Agudeza y arte de ingenio.* The edition kept in the Lezama Manuscript Collection (Madrid: Imprenta La Rafa, 1929) is well annotated and underlined, a rare example in Lezama's library since he did this in very few of his books. Lezama avoided writing on the pages of the books he read by jotting down the sentences he liked in his notebooks.

5: Joyce Wars, Lezama Wars: The Scandals of *Ulysses* and *Paradiso* as "Corrected" Texts

Cortázar's letter (in which he informs Lezama that he is writing an "aproximation" to *Paradiso* that eventually was published under the title "Para llegar a Lezama Lima") is reproduced in Cintio Vitier's critical edition of *Paradiso* (Paris: ALLCA/ UNESCO, 1988), 715–17. The quotation is from p. 717.

1. On the history of the emergence of the "Joyce industry" in the United States see Jeffrey Segal, *Joyce in America: Cultural Politics and the Trials of Ulysses* (Berkeley: California University Press, 1993).

2. For an academic history of the "Joyce Wars," see Charles Rossman, "The Critical Reception of the 'Gabler *Ulysses*': Or, Gabler's *Ulysses* Kidd-napped," *Studies in the Novel* 21 (1989): 154–81. For a layman's account, see Bruce Arnold, *The Scandal of Ulysses* (London: Sinclair-Stevenson, 1991). Also of great use is the "Special Issue on Editing *Ulysses*" of *Studies in the Novel* 22 (1990), edited and introduced by Charles Rossman, with articles by journalist Robin Bates and Joycean critics Eyal Amiran, Patrick McGee, Ira B. Nadel, Fritz Senn, David Hayman, Thomas A. Vogler, and Michael Patrick Gillespie; a "Historical Record" featuring the exchange between Gabler and Kidd at the Society for Textual Scholarship in April 1985; and an encompassing bibliography.

3. Brett Levinson, "Summas Críticas/Restas Erratas": Strange Notes on Lezama's Miscues," *Cuban Studies Annual* 22 (1992): 195–215; Enrico Mario Santí, "*Paradiso* de José Lezama Lima (ed. de Cintio Vitier)" *Vuelta* 187 (1992): 45–48; Bernardo Teuber, "¡O feliz lapsus! Autobiografía, crítica genética y genealogía del sujeto en *Paradiso* de José Lezama Lima," *MLN* 108 (1993): 314–30.

4. For information and discussion of the technological and financial aspects of Gabler's edition, see Hugh Kenner, "The Computerized *Ulysses*," *Harper's* (April 1980): 89–95; Hans Walter Gabler's "Afterword" to his edition, *Ulysses: A Critical and Synoptic Edition* (New York and London: Garland Publishing, 1984), vol. 3: 1859–1907; also by Gabler, "Computer-Aided Critical Edition of *Ulysses*," ALLC Bulletin 8 (1981): 232–48. On the issue of copyright extension and the role of the Joyce state, see Charles Rossman, "The New *Ulysses*: The Hidden Contro-

versy," *The New York Review of Books* (8 December 1988): 53–58; Peter du Sautoy, "Editing *Ulysses*: A Personal Account," *James Joyce Quarterly* 27 (1989): 69–76.

5. Proceedings were published for each of these conferences: G. George Sandulescu and Clive Hard, *Assessing the 1984 ULYSSES* (Garrands and Totowa: Colin Smythe and Barnes & Noble, 1986); Bernard Benstock, ed. *"Ulysses*: The Text," *James Joyce Literary Supplement* 3 (1989).

6. Cintio Vitier, Responses to a Questionnaire by César A. Salgado, 18 September 1996. Unpublished.

7. Like Don Gifford, with Robert Seidman, *Ulysses Annotated: Notes for Joyce's Ulysses* (Berkeley: University of California Press, 1988) and Weldon Thornton, *Allusions in Ulysses* (Chapel Hill: University of North Carolina Press), the Archivos *Paradiso* includes an extensive (but not exhaustive) selection of notes organized by chapter that substantially explain many of the dense, encyclopedic cultural, literary, historical, local, and idiomatic allusions in the novel. Like Clive Hart and David Hayman, *James Joyce's Ulysses: Critical Essays* (Berkeley: University of California Press, 1974) the edition has a section of "lecturas concurrentes" [concurrent readings] where a number of Cuban Lezama scholars each write critical summaries and appreciations for each of the chapters of *Paradiso*.

8. Julio Ortega in a letter to César A. Salgado, 27 December l996.

9. About the quinquenio see Eliseo Alberto, "Los años grises," *Revista Encuentro de la Cultura Cubana* 1 (1996): 35–57; also see some of the interviews with Cuban writers in Emilio Bejel, *Escribir en Cuba* (Río Piedras: University of Puerto Rico Press, 1991), sp. Pablo Armando Fernández (88–89) and César López (222–23).

10. Vitier summarizes Lezama's career with the Revolution's cultural agencies in an interview in Emilio Bejel, *Escribir en Cuba*, 381–2.

11. See the text of Padilla's "self-criticism" in *Casa de las Américas* 11, no. 65–66 (marzo–junio 1971): 191–203; reprinted in Lourdes Casal, ed., *El caso Padilla: Literatura y Revolución en Cuba. Documentos* (Miami: Ediciones Universal, 1976), 77–104. Padilla attacks Lezama in pages 100–101; he also denounced the counterrevolutionary attitudes of other writers, César López and Manuel Díaz Martínez among them. For Padilla's own recollections about the "Padilla Affair," see *Self-Portrait of the Other* (New York: Farrar, Straus and Giroux, 1990), 167–77.

12. Although there is fierce disagreement about the extent to which Lezama was harassed or marginalized by the regime at this time (critics like Armando Alvárez Bravo argue that Lezama was kept in the country against his wishes), it is generally acknowledged that there was an "enfriamiento" [cooling down]—the term is Cintio Vitier's—between Lezama and Cuban cultural agencies in the seventies. Lezama's creative and scholarly work was not as sought after in Cuba as it had been before the "affair." Vitier considers this was a problem with "funcionarios intermedios" [bureaucratic middlemen] that did not recognize Lezama's importance. He speaks that a "rectification" of this mistake was put in motion by "personas de alto nivel" [people in high posts] right before Lezama's death occurred in 1976. See Bejel's interview with Vitier in *Escribir en Cuba*, sp. 379–87, and Vitier's response to Armando Alvarez Bravo in Cristina Vizcaino, *Coloquio Internacional sobre la obra de José Lezama Lima* (Madrid: Fundamentos, 1984), 99–101.

13. See Bejel, *Escribir en Cuba*, 387.

14. "*Paradiso*: Treinta años de un mito," Havana, 25–28 June 1996. Vitier's inaugural address—published with the above title in the Mexican journal *Crítica*

12 (Dec.–Jan. 1996–97): 27–34—situates Lezama's novel and artistic philosophy in a line of the *patrística*-inspired tradition of nineteenth-century Christian illuminism that included clergymen like Félix Varela, Caballero, and José de la Luz. With important references to Justinian, Tertullian, Saint Augustine, and Thomas of Aquinas, Vitier declares Lezama a key part of the "linaje fundador del catolicismo cubano" [founding linage of Cuban Catholicism]. This "patristic" reading makes this document the most militantly religious among all of Vitier's interpretations of *Paradiso*'s "Catholicism."

15. *Fresa y chocolate*. A film directed by Tomás Gutierrez Alea and Paco Tabío; screenplay by Senel Paz (Cuba: ICAIC, 1993). For English translation of the screenplay and the short story that inspired the film, see Senel Paz, *Strawberry and Chocolate*, trans. Peter Bush (London: Bloomsbury, 1995). For a comprehensive review and bibliography of articles on the film and its makers, see Enrico Mario Santí, "*Fresa y chocolate*: The Rhetoric of Cuban Reconciliation," *MLA* 113, no. 2 (407–25).

16. For another discussion of the politics behind the current "Lezama vogue" in Cuba today, see my essay "Las mutaciones del escándalo: *Paradiso* hoy," *Revista Encuentro de la Cultura Cubana*.1, no. 4–5 (Spring 96/Summer 1997): 175–78.

17. For the compositional history of *Ulysses* see, for starters, Frank Budgen, *James Joyce and the Making of Ulysses* (London: Oxford University Press 1972; 1st ed. 1934); Sylvia Beach, *Shakespeare & Company* (Lincoln: University of Nebraska Press, 1991; 1st ed. 1956); Michael Groden, *Ulysses in Progress* (Princeton: Princeton University Press, 1977); and Hans Walter Gabler, "Afterword."

18. See Jack B. Dalton, "The Text of *Ulysses*," in *New Light on Ulysses from the Dublin Symposium*, ed. Fritz Senn (Bloomington: Indiana University Press, 1972), 99–119.

19. For details about Joyce's "loss of interest" in the novel as the fires of scandal died down and he prepared to launch the writing of *Finnegans Wake*, see Richard Ellmann's classic biography, *James Joyce* (Oxford: Oxford University Press, 1983; 1st ed. 1959), 471–72, 477–79.

20. That censorship heightens an author's drive to make a text more polished, technically experimental, and "literary" is Paul Vanderham's argument in *James Joyce and Censorship: The Trials of Ulysses* (New York: New York University Press, 1998). In the chapter dedicated to analyzing Joyce's own creative response to censorship in his writing ("Making Obscenity Safe for Literature," 57–86), Vanderham argues that "while Joyce's confrontations with the censor undoubtedly influenced his development as an artist, they never made him abandon his holy office of mentioning the unmentionable" (58). A similar claim could be made about Lezama's treatment in *Paradiso* of middle-class life, polysexuality, and religiosity, unmentionable topics within the esthetico-ideological program that the Cuban Revolution began assuming in the sixties. Vanderham believes that Joyce worked to avoid censorship by "writing in a language foreign enough to baffle any authorities inclined to ascertain where they should be banned as obscene," thus leading to the cryptographical, neologistic style of *Finnegans Wake* (59). The foreignness of Lezama's poetic and allusive style in *Paradiso* could be analyzed along this line of interpretation. Later Vanderham argues that, in *Ulysses'* most experimental chapters (undertaken after the censorship of The Little Review began in the United States), "the shift . . . from character to style, from story to structure, effects a transfer of the reader's attention away from the controversial action of the story to its artifice" (72). These points are just as applicable to the

textual dynamics operating within the most controversial or "scandalous" episodes in *Paradiso*.

21. See letters included in Pedro Simón, ed. *Recopilación de textos sobre José Lezama Lima* (Havana: Casa de las Américas, 1970): 308, 310–13, 316.

22. After the demise of *Orígenes* in 1956, Lezama's involvement in other essayistic and poetic projects (*La expresión americana*, 1957; *Dador*, 1960) delayed his work on the novel, which he seems to have retaken between 1962 and 1964.

23. Manuel Díaz Martínez, "Lezama, crítico de nuestra poesía," *Bohemia* 58 (14 January 1966): 26–27.

24. On *Lunes de Revolucion*'s attacks against Lezama and the *Orígenes* group, see Heberto Padilla, "La poesía en su lugar," *LR* (7 December 1959): 5–6; Virgilio Piñera, "Cada cosa en su lugar," *LR* (14 December 1959): 11–12; Guillermo Cabrera Infante, *Mea Cuba* (Madrid: Plaza Janés, 1992), 327–28, 330–33.

25. I found this document working in the "Fondo Lezama" at the Biblioteca Nacional José Martí during a visit to Havana in June 1993.

26. Salvador Bueno, "Sobre *Paradiso*," *Bohemia* 23 (10 June 1966): 17.

27. For these and other illuminating selections of early damning and admiring reviews of *Ulysses*, see Robert H. Deming, ed. *James Joyce: The Critical Heritage Vol. 1 1902–1927* (London: Routledge & Kegan Paul, 1970).

28. Loló de la Torriente, "Paradiso," *Bohemia* (8 July 1966): 38–39; Juliosvaldo, "El infierno de Paradiso," *Bohemia* (8 July 1966): 40.

29. Nothing has been written about the possible connection between the regime's UMAP project during the sixties and Lezama's decision to openly address issues of homosexuality in *Paradiso*.

30. Emir Rodríguez Monegal and Mario Vargas Llosa, "Sobre el 'Paradiso' de Lezama," *Mundo Nuevo* 16 (October 1967): 89–95. Rodríguez Monegal responds, in a letter dated "Paris, July 6, 1967" to a letter from Vargas Llosa dated "London, June 12, 1967." The article that initiated this debate—Mario Vargas Llosa's "*Paradiso*: una summa poética, una tentativa imposible"—is reprinted in *Recopilación de textos sobre José Lezama Lima* (Havana: Casa de las Américas, Serie Valoración Múltiple, 1970).

31. Julio Cortázar, "Para llegar a Lezama Lima," *La vuelta al día en ochenta mundos* (México: Siglo Veintiuno, 1967): 40–81. First published in *Unión* 4 (1966): 36–60. I quote the English text from Thomas Christensen's translation, "To Reach Lezama Lima," included in Julio Cortázar, *Around the Day in Eighty Worlds* (San Francisco: North Point Press, 1986), 82–108

32. In *James Joyce and Censorship*, Paul Verderham studies how critics sympathetic to Joyce's creative enterprise such as Valery Larbaud and Ezra Pound used their essays to deflect reading away from the controversial zones of the text and thus suppress scandal and the text itself, just in the fashion I argue Vargas Llosa and Cortázar's analysis of *Paradiso* operated. "Larbaud's talk 'set the key for the critical reception' [of *Ulysses*] by shifting attention from the provocative content of the novel to its elaborate form, its schematic complexity. It thus occupies a prominent place in what may be loosely call the tradition of critical (as opposed to legal or editorial) censorship of *Ulysses*. That tradition . . . is characterized by the critic's strategic suppression or avoidance of the controversial elements of Joyce's novel" (14). See the chapter titled, coincidentially, "*Ulysses* at War," 16–36.

33. Severo Sarduy, "Dispersión/Falsas notas: Homenaje a Lezama," *Mundo Nuevo* 24 (June 1968): 7.

34. "The situation, I found, was this: the old edition had been, of course, an

early collateral descendant of the first edition, whereas the new edition was a lineal descendant. The new edition, far from being 'scrupulously corrected,' was merely a reprint, with some new errors, of the 1960 English resetting. It was the fifth successive resetting of type since the first edition; each edition had been copied from the one preceding. Some 1,700 errors had accumulated in thirtyfive years of resetting, and most of these errors were, in 1961, already at least twentyfive years old and had appeared in at least three successive settings. And then there were well over 2,000 corruptions which went back to the manuscripts, things which had *never* been printed correctly," "The Text of *Ulysses*," 102.

35. Lezama, in fact, wrote Emmanuel Carballo in September 1968 about his satisfaction with the "correctness" of the "impeccable" Editorial Era 1968 edition of *Paradiso*, published now "sin el sobresalto de las erratas, esos piojos de la palabra, como decía Flaubert" [without the commotion of errata, those lices of words, as Flaubert used to say]. *Paradiso*, Archivos edition, 719.

36. Gabler writes in his "Afterword': "The text of highest overall authority on which to base a critical edition of *Ulysses* resides in Joyce's autograph notation. This, it is true, is not assembled in a unified holograph manuscript at a state of development corresponding to the first-edition text. The one comprehensive holograph that exists of *Ulysses*, the Rosenbach Manuscript, represents the work only at the point of culmination of the draft composition of its successive chapters. But the autograph notation—or the revisional overlay of lost final working drafts inferred from their collateral descendants—that carries the text forward beyond its final-working-draft/fair copy state and towards its ultimate stage of compositional development for book publication is present in the typescript and proofs. . . . Thus, one may define a continuous manuscript text for *Ulysses*, extending over a sequence of actual documents," p. 1895.

37. The most famous of these "restitutions" of error in Gabler's edition is the misspelled telegraph Stephen receives from his father telling him of his mother's worsening health: "Nother dying. Please come. Father." In his stream-of-consciousness, Stephen considers the note "a curiosity to show;" thus, many editions had before corrected a typo Joyce intended to retain on the page. There are numerous cases of these "strategic errors" throughout *Ulysses*.

38. Besides Cintio Vitier, the other contributing essayists and critics in the Archivos edition were Cuban island scholars Ciro Bianchi Ross, Raquel Carrió Mendía, Roberto Friol, Manuel Pereira, José Prats Sariol. Except for Severo Sarduy, no Cuban exile scholars of Lezama, such as Enrico Mario Santí or Roberto González-Echevarría, were invited to participate.

39. "Como casi todos los autores, Lezama era mal corrector, quizás peor que la mayoría" [Like almost all writers, Lezama was a lousy proofreader, maybe worse than most]. Cintio Vitier, Responses to a Questionnaire by César A. Salgado.

40. See Walter Hans Gabler, "James Joyce as Author and Scribe: A Problem in Editing 'Eumaeus,' " in *Nordic Rejoycings 1982—In Commemoration of the Centennary of the Birth of James Joyce* (James Joyce Society of Sweden and Finland). 98–105

41. Clive Hart, "Are Thou Real, My Ideal," in *Assessing the 1984 Ulysses*, 58–65.

42. See, by John Kidd, "Errors of Execution in the 1984 *Ulysses*," *Studies in the Novel* special issue: 243–49; "The Scandal of *Ulysses*," *The New York Times Review of Books* (June 30, l988): 32–39; "An Inquiry into *Ulysses: The Corrected Text*," *The Papers of the Bibliographical Society of America* 82 (1988): 411–584.

43. Enrico Mario Santí, "Parridiso," *MLN* 94 (1979): 355.

44. In his reading of Oppiano Licario's deathbed scene, Santí demonstrates how systematic is *Paradiso*'s practice of misquoting and miswriting: the text attributes to Descartes a phrase in fact used by one of Descartes's opponents. Such distortion subverts the visible anti-Freudianism and affirmative Catholicism of this phrase, "Davum esse, non Oedipum" (Licario's last words, which could be superficially paraphrased as "I have been a servant to the Father, not an aggressor"), thus allowing a heretic, "parricidal" element to subsist despite the piety of the scene. "Parridiso," 357–59.

45. See Brett Levinson, "Translating Erasures: The True Story of Lezama's 'Eras imaginarias,' " *Translation Perspectives* 6 (1991): 79–86.

46. Irlemar Chiampi, "Hacia una lectura irrerupta de *Paradiso*," *Revista Iberoamericana* 75 (1991): 65–76. "Cabe examinar, desde la perspectiva funcionalista-pragmática cómo este texto recorre ciertos dispositivos para arriesgar la constitución del sentido y provocar el efecto de ilegibilidad. . . . Con ello pretendemos considerar que los problemas de percepción en *Paradiso* no son meros 'ruidos' o accidentes (imputables al autor o al lector), sino un hecho textual, agenciado y programado para generar lo que designaremos como lectura interrupta" (68) [We should examine, from a functionalist-pragmatic perspective, how this text activates certain mechanisms that put in risk the constitution of meaning and provoke an effect of illegibility. . . . With this we intend to consider that the problems of interpretation in *Paradiso* are not just 'noises' or 'accidents' but textual facts, orchestrated and programmed to generate what we will call an interrupted reading.] In a paper read in the panel "Textual and Sexual Errancy: The Scandals of *Paradiso*" held at the Modern Language Association Convention on December 1996, Chiampi used Theodor Adorno's notion of "skoteino" to describe this type of programmatic error or deliberate effect of the illegible as a key textual mechanism in Lezama. Curiously, Chiampi dissassociates the intentional errancy in Lezama's textuality from that of Joyce (69), since Lezama's "skoteinos," according to Chiampi, do not have the translinguistic o neologistic constitution of Joyce's. Here she fails to bear in mind some textual instances of neologistic word play in *Paradiso* such as Uncle Alberto's letter or the Joyce-like verbal transmogrification in episodes such as Elpidio Michelena's bewildering encounter with the Siren-Manatee in chapter 3. (*P* 47–54)

47. Cintio Vitier comments on this exchange between Lezama and Didier Coste in footnote 'j of the sixth chapter of his edition of *Paradiso*, 146.

48. Sarduy, "Dispersión/falsas notas," *Mundo Nuevo* 24 (June 1968): 6.

Bibliography

Adams, Robert Martin. *Afterjoyce: Studies in Fiction After Ulysses*. New York: Oxford University Press, 1977.

Alberto, Eliseo. "Los años grises." *Revista Encuentro de la Cultura Cubana* 1 (1996): 35–57.

Alonso, Carlos J. *The Latin American Regionalist Novel*. Cambridge: Cambridge University Press, 1989.

Alonso, Dámaso. *Obras Completas: Góngora y el gongorismo*. Madrid: Editorial Gredos, 1978.

Anderson, C. G. "The Sacrificial Butter." *Accent* 12, no. 1 (1952): 3–13.

Aparicio, Frances. *Imitación, interpretación y creación: el arte moderno de la traducción en Hispanoamérica*. Dissertation, Harvard University, 1983.

Arcos, Jorge Luis. *La solución unitiva: Sobre el pensamiento poético de Lezama Lima*. Havana: Editorial Academia, 1990.

Arnold, Bruce. *The Scandal of Ulysses*. London: Sinclair-Stevenson, 1991.

Arrom, José Juan. "Lo tradicional cubano en el mundo novelístico de José Lezama Lima." *Revista Iberoamericana* 92–93 (1975): 470–77.

Asturias, Miguel Angel. *Periodismo y creación literaria (París 1924–1933)*. Edited by Amos Segala. París: Ediciones Archivos,1990.

Atherton, James S. *The Books at the Wake: A Study of Literary Allusions in James Joyce's Finnegans Wake*. London: Faber & Faber, 1959.

Auerbach, Erich. *Scenes from the Drama of European Literature*. Minnesota: University of Minnesota Press, 1984.

Austin, J. C. *How To Do Things With Words*. Cambridge: Harvard University Press, 1975.

Bajarlía, Juan Jacobo. *Literatura de vanguardia de Ulises de Joyce y las escuelas poéticas*. Buenos Aires: Editorial Araujo, 1946.

Barth, John. *The Friday Book*. New York: G. P. Putnam's Sons, 1984.

Beach, Sylvia. *Shakespeare & Company*. Lincoln: University of Nebraska Press, 1991. [First edition: 1951.]

Beckett, Samuel et al. *Our Exagmination Round his Factification for Incamination of Work in Progress*. London: Faber & Faber, 1929.

———. "Dante . . . Bruno. Vico . . . Joyce." *transition* 13 (1928): 242–53.

Bedani, Gino. *Vico Revisited*. Oxford: Berd, 1989.

Bejel, Emilio. *Escribir en Cuba. Entrevistas con escritores cubanos: 1979–1989*. Rio Piedras: Editorial de la Universidad de Puerto Rico, 1991.

———. *José Lezama Lima: Poet of the Image*. Gainesville: University of Florida Press, 1990.

Bell, Ian F. A. *The Critic As Scientist: The Modernist Poetic of Ezra Pound*. London: Methuen, 1981.

Benjamin, Walter. *The Origin of German Tragic Drama*. Translated by John Osborne. London: NLB, 1977.

Benstock, Bernard, ed. *James Joyce: The Augmented Ninth. Proceedings of the Ninth International James Joyce Symposum*. Syracuse: Syracuse University Press, 1988.

———, ed. *The Seventh of Joyce*. Bloomington: Indiana University Press, 1982.

———. "The Temptation of St. Stephen: A View of the Villanelle." *James Joyce Quarterly* (1976): 31–38.

Bérard, Victor. *Did Homer Live?* Translated by Brian Thys. New York: E. P. Dutton, 1931. [Spanish version: *Resurrección de Homero*. Trans. Alfonso Alemán. Mexico: Editorial Jus, 1945.]

———. *Les Pheniciens et l'Odyssée*. 3 vol. Paris: Armand Colin, 1902–1903.

Bishop, John. *Finnegans Wake: Joyce's Book of the Dark*. Lincoln: University of Nebraska Press, 1988.

Bloom, Harold. *The Anxiety of Influence*. Oxford: Oxford University Press, 1970.

Booth, Wayne. *The Rhetoric of Fiction*. Chicago: Chicago University Press, 1960.

Borges, Jorge Luis. *Borges: A Reader*, ed. E. Rodríguez Monegal and Alistair Reed. New York: Dutton, 1981.

———. *Discusión*. Buenos Aires: Gleiser Editor,1932.

———. *Discusión*. Madrid: Alianza Editorial, 1983. [Edition of 1957.]

———. *El idioma de los argentinos*. Buenos Aires: M. Gleizer Editor, 1928.

———. *Ficciones*. Buenos Aires: Emecé, 1956.

———. *Historia de la eternidad*. Buenos Aires: Emecé, 1953.

———. *Inquisiciones*. Buenos Aires: M. Gleizer, 1925.

———. *An Introduction to English Literature*. Translated by L. Clark Keating and Robert O. Evans. Lexington: The University of Kentucky Press, 1974.

———. *Labyrinths*. Edited and translated by Donald A. Yates and James E. Irby. New York: New Directions, 1964.

———. "Nota sobre el Ulíses en español," *Los anales de Buenos Aires* 1, no. 1 (1946).

———. *Obra poética*. Madrid: Alianza Editorial, 1972.

———. *Obras completas*. Alianza/Emecé: 1960.

———. *Páginas de Jorge Luis Borges escogidas por el autor*. Buenos Aires: Editorial Celtia, 1982.

———. *Prólogos con un prólogo de prólogos*. Buenos Aires: Torres Agüero, 1975.

———. *Seven Nights*. Translated by Eliot Weinberger. New York: New Directions, 1984.

———. *Siete noches*. Buenos Aires: Emecé Editores, 1979.

———. *Textos cautivos: Ensayos y reseñas en "El Hogar" (1936–1939)*. Edited by Enrique Sacerio-Garí and Emir Rodríguez Monegal. Barcelona: Tusquets Editores, 1986.

Bravo, Víctor. *El secreto en geranio convertido. Una lectura de Paradiso*. Caracas: Monte Avila Editores, 1991.

Brown, John Lackey. *Valery Larbaud*. Boston: Twayne, 1981.

Buckley, Jerome Hamilton. *Season of Youth: The Bildungsroman from Dickens to Golding*. Cambridge: Harvard University Press, 1974.

Budgen, Frank. *James Joyce and the Making of Ulysses*. Bloomington: Indiana University Press, 1960.

Bueno, Salvador. "Sobre *Paradiso*." *Bohemia* 23 (10 June 1966): 17.

Burke, Kenneth. *Terms for Order*. Edited by Stanley Edgar Hyman. Bloomington: Indiana University Press, 1964.

———. *The Philosophy of Literary Form*. Berkeley: University of California Press, 1973.

Cabrera Infante, Guillermo. *Mea Cuba*. Madrid: Plaza Janés, 1992.

Cairns, Helen. *Psycholinguistics: A Cognitive View of Language*. New York : Holt, Rinehart & Winston, 1976.

Camacho-Gingerich, Alina L. *La cosmovisión poética de José Lezama Lima en Paradiso y Oppiano Licario*. Miami: Ediciones Universal, 1990.

Campbell, Joseph, and Henry Morton Robinson. *A Skeleton Key to Finnegans Wake*. New York: The Viking Press, 1961.

Carpentier, Alejo. *Crónicas del regreso*. Salvador Arias, ed. Havana: Ediciones Unión, 1991.

———. *Guerra del Tiempo*. Mexico: Compañía General de Ediciones, 1958.

———. *Tientos y diferencias: Ensayos*. Montevideo: Arca, 1967.

Casal, Lourdes, ed. *El caso Padilla: Literatura y Revolución en Cuba. Documentos*. Miami: Ediciones Universal, 1976.

Chiampi, Irlemar. "*La expresión americana* de José Lezama Lima: la dificultad y el diabolismo del caníbal," *Escritura*, 10 (1985) 19–20: 103–15.

———. "Sobre la lectura interrupta de *Paradiso*." *Revista Iberoamericana* 54, no. 154 (1991): 65–76.

———. "Skoteinos: El escándalo de la dificultad en *Paradiso*." Paper read at the Modern Language Association Convention, San Francisco, 28 December l996.

Chomsky, Noam. *Reflections on Language*. New York: Pantheon, 1975.

Clark, Herbert C. *Psychology and Language: An Introduction to Psycholinguistics*. New York: Harcourt, Brace, 1977.

Connoly, Thomas E. "Kinesis and Stasis: Structural Rhythm in Joyces's *Portrait*." *University Review* (Dublin) 3 (1966): 21–30.

Cortázar, Julio. *Final del juego*. Buenos Aires: Sudamericana, 1964.

———. "Para llegar a Lezama Lima." In *La vuelta al día en ochenta mundos*. Mexico: Siglo XXI, 1967, 40–81.

———. "To reach Lezama Lima." Translated by Thomas Christensen. In *Around the Day in Eighty Worlds*. San Francisco: North Point Press, 1986: 82–108.

———. *Los reyes*. Buenos Aires: Gulab y Aldabahor, 1949.

———. *Rayuela*. Buenos Aires: Editorial Sudamericana, 1963.

———. *Todos los fuegos el fuego*. Buenos Aires: Sudamericana, 1966.

Corvasi, J. *Indice de la Revista de Occidente*. Madrid: 1952.

Croce, Benedetto. *The Philosophy of Giambattista Vico*. Translated by R. G. Collingwood. New York: Russell and Russell, 1964.

Cruz-Malavé, Arnaldo. *El primitivo implorante. El "sistema poético del mundo" de José Lezama Lima.* Amsterdam-Atlanta, GA: Rodopi, 1994.

Curtius, E. R. *Essays on European Literature.* New Jersey: Princeton University Press, 1973.

de Campos, Augusto and Haroldo. *Panorama do Finnegans Wake.* Sao Paulo: Conselho Estadual de Cultura, 1962.

de Grazia, Edward. *Girls Lean Back Everywhere: The Law of Obscenity and the Assault on Genius.* New York: Random House, 1992.

de la Torriente, Loló. "Paradiso." *Bohemia* (8 July 1966): 38–39.

Dalton, Jack B. "The Text of *Ulysses.*" In Fritz Senn, ed. *New Light on Ulysses from the Dublin Symposium.* Bloomington: Indiana University Press, 1972.

de Torre, Guillermo. *Historia de las literaturas de vanguardia.* Madrid: 1967.

———. *Ultraísmo, existencialismo y objetivismo en literatura.* Buenos Aires: Alfaguarra, 1948.

Deming, Robert H., ed. *James Joyce: The Critical Heritage (1902–1927).* New York: Barnes & Noble, 1970.

Derrida, Jacques. *Dissemination.* Translated by Barbara Johnson. Chicago: University of Chicago Press, 1981.

Díaz Quiñones, Arcadio. *Cintio Vitier: La memoria integradora.* San Juan: Editorial Sin Nombre, 1987.

Diego, Gerardo, ed. *Antología poética en honor de Góngora.* Madrid: Alianza Editorial, 1979.

du Sautoy, Peter. "Editing *Ulysses*: A Personal Account." *James Joyce Quarterly* 27 (1989): 69–76.

During, Ingemar. *Alfonso Reyes, helenista. Homenaje del Instituto Ibero-americano de Gotemburgo a Alfonso Reyes.* Madrid: Insula, 1955.

Eco, Umberto. *The Aesthetics of Chaosmos. The Middle Ages of James Joyce.* Translated from the Italian by Ellen Esrock. Cambridge: Harvard University Press, 1982.

Elizondo, Salvador. *Teoría del Infierno y otros ensayos.* Mexico: El Colegio Nacional/Ediciones del Equilibrista, 1992.

Ellmann, Richard. *James Joyce.* Rev. ed. Oxford: Oxford University Press, 1983.

———. *Ulysses on the Liffey.* London: Faber & Faber, 1972.

Erickson, Eric. *Life History and the Historical Moment.* New York: Norton, 1975.

Erlich, Heyward, ed. *Light Rays. James Joyce and Modernism.* New York: New Horizon Press Publishers, 1984.

Espinosa, Carlos. *Cercanía de Lezama Lima.* Havana: Editorial Letras Cubanas, 1986.

Farris, Wendy. *Labyrinths of Language: Symbolic Landscape and Narrative Design in Modern Fiction.* Baltimore: Johns Hopkins University Press, 1988.

Fernández Moreno, César, ed. *América Latina en su literatura.* Mexico: Siglo Veintiuno Editores, 1972.

Fernández, Luis F. *José Lezama Lima y la crítica anagógica.* Miami: Ediciones Universal, 1976.

Ferré, Rosario. "*Oppiano Licario* o la resurrección en la imagen." *Escritura* 2 (1976): 319–26.

Fitch, Noel Riley. *Sylvia Beach and the Lost Generation: A History of Literary Paris in the Twenties and Thirties*. New York: Norton, 1983.

Fresa y chocolate. A film directed by Tomás Gutierrez Alea and Paco Tabío; screenplay by Senel Paz (Cuba: ICAIC, 1993).

Frobenius, Leo. *La cultura como ser viviente: contorno de una doctrina cultural y psicológica*. Translated by Máximo Jose Kahn. Madrid: Espasa-Calpe, 1934.

Frazer, James George. *The Golden Bough*. New York: Macmillan Publishing Company, 1922.

Fuentes, Carlos. *La nueva novela latinoamericana*. Mexico: Joaquín Mortiz, 1970.

Gabler, Walter Hans. "James Joyce as Author and Scribe: A Problem in Editing 'Eumaeus.'" In *Nordic Rejoycings 1982—In Commemoration of the Centenary of the Birth of James Joyce*. James Joyce Society of Sweden and Finland: 98–105.

García Vega, Lorenzo. *Los años de Orígenes*. Caracas: Monte Avila, 1978.

Gardner, Howard et al. *Language and Learning: The Debate between Jean Piaget and Noam Chomsky*. Edited by Massimo Pietlli-Palmari. Cambridge: Harvard University Press, 1980.

Gifford, Don (with Robert S. Seidman). *Ulysses Annotated. Notes for James Joyce's Ulysses*. Berkeley: University of California Press, 1988.

Gilbert, Stuart. "A Prolegomenon to Work in Progress." *transition* 13 (1928): 265–70.

———. *James Joyce's Ulysses: A Study*. New York: Vintage Books, 1955.

———. "Thesaurus Minusculus: A Short Commentary on a Paragraph of Work in Progress." *transition* 16–17 (1928):15–24.

Givens, Seon, ed. *James Joyce: Two Decades of Criticism*. New York: Vanguard Press, 1948.

Góngora, Luis de. *Las Soledades*. Edited and commented by Dámaso Alonso. Madrid: Sociedad de Estudios y Publicaciones, 1956.

González Echevarría, Roberto. *Alejo Carpentier: The Pilgrim At Home*. Ithaca: Cornell University Press, 1978.

———. "Borges, Carpentier y Ortega: dos textos olvidados." *Revista Iberoamericana* no. 100–101 (1977): 697–704.

———. "The Humanities and Cuban Studies, 1959–1989." In Damián J. Fernández, ed., *Cuban Studies Since the Revolution*. Gainesville: University Press of Florida, 1990.

———. *Isla a su vuelo fugitiva*. Madrid: José Porrúa Turranzas, 1983.

———. *Relecturas: Estudios de Literatura Cubana*. Caracas: Monte Avila Editores, 1976.

González Lanuza, Eduardo. "Adán Buenosayres." *Sur* 16, no. 169 (1948): 87–93.

González, Reynaldo. *Lezama Lima, el ingenuo culpable*. Havana: Editorial Letras Cubanas, 1988.

González-Millán, Juan. "La odisea de traducir el *Ulysses* al gallego (1926)." *La Torre* 16, no. 4 (1990): 489–509.

Gordon, Ambrose. "Dublin and Buenos Aires, Joyce and Marechal." *Comparative Literature Studies*, 19, no. 2 (1982): 208–19.

Gorman, Herbert. *James Joyce: El hombre que escribió Ulises*. Translated by Máximo Siminovich. Buenos Aires: Santiago Rueda, 1945.

———. *James Joyce: His First Forty Years*. New York: Viking Press, 1925.

Gracián, Baltasar. *Agudeza y arte de ingenio*. Madrid: Imprenta La Rafa, 1929.

Grey, Rockwell. *The Imperative of Modernity. An Intellectual Biography of José Ortega y Gasset*. Berkeley: University of California Press, 1989.

Grimal, Pierre, ed. *Larouse World Mythology*. London: Hamlyn, 1965.

Groden, Michael. *Ulysses in Progress*. Princeton: Princeton University Press, 1977.

Gullón, Ricardo. "Ortega y la teoría de la novela." *Letras de Deusto* 19 (1989): 105–21.

Halperin, John, ed. *The Theory of the Novel*. New York: Oxford University Press, 1974.

Hart, Clive and David Hayman. *James Joyce's Ulysses: Critical Essays*. Berkeley: University of California Press, 1974.

Hartman, Geoffrey. *Beyond Formalism: Literary Essay 1958–1970*. New Haven: Yale University Press, 1970.

———. *Saving the Text*. Baltimore: Johns Hopkins, 1981.

Hayes, John R. *Cognition and the Development of Language*. New York: John Willis, 1970.

Hayman, David. *Joyce and Mallarmé*. Paris: Lettres Modernes, 1956.

Heller, Ben A. *Assimilation/Generation/Resurrection: Contrapuntal Readings in the Poetry of José Lezama Lima*. Lewisburg: Bucknell University Press, 1997.

Henríquez Ureña, Pedro. *Estudios mexicanos*. Mexico: Fondo de Cultura Económica, 1984.

Hirshbein, Cesia Zionia. *Las eras imaginarias*. Caracas: Biblioteca de la Academia Nacional de la Historia, 1984.

Homer, *The Odyssey*. Translated by Rodert Fitzgerald. New York: Vintage Classic, 1990.

Instituto de Filosofía de la Universidad de Buenos Aires. *Vico and Herder. Ensayos conmemorativos del segundo centenario de la muerte de Vico y el nacimiento de Herder*. Buenos Aires: Universidad Nacional, 1948.

Jaeger, Werner Wilheim. *Paideia, los ideales de la cultura griega*. Translated by Joaquín Xirau and Wenceslao Roces. Mexico: Fondo de Cultura Económica, 1942, 1945. 4 vols.

———. *Paideia: The Ideals of Greek Culture*. 3 vols. New York: Oxford University Press, 1945.

Janusko, Robert. *The Sources and Structures of James Joyce's "Oxen."* Ann Arbor: UMI Research Press, 1963.

Jarnés, Benjamín. "James Joyce: El artista adolescente." *Revista de Occidente* 13 (1926): 382–86.

Jitrik, Noé. "*Adán Buenosayres*: La novela de Marechal." *Contorno* (1955).

———. "*Paradiso* entre desborde y ruptura." *Texto Crítico* 5, no. 13 (1979): 71–145.

Joyce, James. *A Portrait of the Artist as a Young Man*. Middlesex: Penguin Books, 1976.

———. *El artista adolescente (retrato)*. Translated by Dámaso Alonso. Prologue by Antonio Marichalar. Madrid: Biblioteca Nueva, 1926.

———. *Finnegans Wake*. New York: Viking Press, 1968.

———. *James Joyce: The Critical Writings*. Edited by Ellsworth Mason and Richard Ellmann. New York: The Viking Press, 1964).

———. *Letters*, vol. 1. Edited by Stuart Gilbert. New York: The Viking Press, 1957.

———. *Letters*, vols. 2 & 3. Edited by Richard Ellmann. New York: The Viking Press, 1966.

———. *Stephen Hero: A Part of the First Draft of A Portrait of the Artist as a Young Man*. Introduction by Theodore Spender. Binghamton: New Directions, 1944.

———. *The Workshop of Daedalus: James Joyce and the Raw Materials for A Portrait of the Artist as a Young Man*. Collected and edited by Robert Scholes and Richard M. Kain. Evanston: Northwestern University Press, 1965.

———. "Proteo." Translated by Oscar Rodríguez Feliú. *Espuela de Plata*, no. E–F (1940), 22–27; no. G (1941), 3–7.

———. *Ulises*. Translated by J. Salas Subirat. Prologue by Jacques Mercaton. Buenos Aires: Santiago Rueda, 1959. [First editon 1945.]

———. *Ulysse*. Traduit de l'anglais par M. Auguste Morel, assisté par M. Stuart Gilbert; traduction entièrement revue par M. Valery Larbaud, avec la collaboration de l'auteur Paris: Achienne Monnier, 1929.

———. *Ulysses. The Corrected Text*. Edited by Hans Walter Gabler. New York: Random House, 1986.

Juliosvaldo. "El infierno de Paradiso." *Bohemia* (8 July 1966): 40.

Junco Fazzolari, Margarita. *Paradiso y el sistema poético de Lezama Lima*. Buenos Aires: Editorial García Gamberio, 1979.

Jung, C. L. *Wirklichkeit der Seel*. Zurich, Rascher 1934. English translation in *Complete Works*, vol. 10. Princeton: Bollingen Press, 1960.

———. *¿Quién es Ulises?* Buenos Aires: Santiago Rueda, 1945.

———. "*Ulises* ." *Revista de Occidente* 39 (1933): 133–49.

Kenner, Hugh. *Dublin's Joyce*. Bloomington: Indiana University Press, 1956.

———. "The Computerized *Ulysses*." *Harper's* (April 1980): 89–95.

———. *The Pound Era*. Berkeley: Berkeley University Press, 1971.

———. *Ulysses*. Baltimore: The Johns Hopkins University Press, 1987.

Kidd, John. "The Scandal of *Ulysses*." *The New York Times Review of Books* (30 June l988): 32–39.

———. "An Inquiry into *Ulysses: The Corrected Text*." *The Papers of the Bibliographical Society of America* 82 (1988); 411–584.

Larbaud, Valery-Alfonso Reyes. *Correspondance, 1923–1952*. Avant-propos de Marcel Bataillon. Paris: Edidier, 1972.

Larbaud, Valery. "James Joyce." *Nouvelle Revue Française* 18 (1922): 385–405.

———. "The *Ulysses* of James Joyce." *Criterion* 1, no. 1. (1922): 84–103

———. "*Ulises*." Translated by J. M. Guarnido, *Alfar* 23, no. 85 (1945).

Leal, Luis. "Borges y la novela." *Revista Iberoamericana* 36, no. 70 (1970): 11–23.

Lermout, Geert. *The French Joyce*. Ann Arbor: The University of Michigan Press, 1990.

Levin, Harry. *James Joyce: A Critical Introduction*. Norfolk: New Directions, 1941.

Levinson, Brett. *Secondary Moderns. Mimesis, History, and Revolution in Lezama Lima's "American Expression."* Lewisburg: Bucknell University Press, 1996.

———. " 'Summas Críticas/Restas Erratas': Strange Notes on Lezama's Miscues."
Cuban Studies Annual 22 (1992): 195–215.

———. "Translating Erasures: The True Story of Lezama's 'Eras imaginarias,' "
Translation Perspectives 6 (1991): 79–86.

Lezama Lima, José. *Analecta del reloj.* Havana: Orígenes, 1953.

———. Fondo de Manuscritos de José Lezama Lima. [Fondo Lezama.] Biblioteca
Nacional José Martí, Havana.

———. *Cartas (1939–1976).* Edited with an introduction by Eloísa Lezama Lima.
Madrid: Editorial Orígenes, 1979.

———. *Confluencias.* Edited with an introduction by Abel Prieto. Havana: Letras
Cubanas, 1988.

———. *Diarios [1939–49/1956–58].* Edited by Ciro Bianchi Ross. Mexico: Ediciones Era, 1994.

———. *El reino de la imagen.* Edited with an introduction by Julio Ortega. Caracas: Ayacucho, 1988.

———. *Imagen y posibilidad.* Edited by Ciro Bianchi Ross. Letras cubanas: 1981.

——— *Fascinación de la memoria. Textos inéditos de José Lezama Lima.* Edited by
Iván González Cruz. Havana: Editorial Letras Cubanas, 1994.

———. *La cantidad hechizada.* Havana: UNEAC, 1970.

———. *La expresión americana.* Havana: Instituto Nacional de Cultura, 1957.

———. *La expresión americana.* Critical edition by Irlemar Chiampi. Mexico:
Fondo de Cultura Económica, 1993.

———. *La Habana.* Edited by José Prats Sariol. Madrid: Editorial Verbum, 1991.

———. *Las eras imaginarias.* Madrid: Editorial Fundamentos, 1971.

———. *Obras completas.* 2 vols. Prologue by Cintio Vitier. Mexico: Aguilar, 1975.

———. *Oppiano Licario.* Madrid: Alianza/Era, 1983.

———. *Orbita de Lezama Lima.* Edited by Armando Alvarez Bravo. Havana:
Unión, 1966.

———. *Paradiso.* Havana: Ediciones Unión, 1966.

———. *Paradiso.* Edition revised by Julio Cortázar y Carlos Monsiváis. México:
Ediciones Era, 1968.

———. *Paradiso.* Translated by Gregory Rabassa. New York: Farrar, Strauss and
Giroux, 1974.

———. *Paradiso.* Critical edition coordinated by Cintio Vitier. Paris: ALLCA/
UNESCO, 1988.

———. *Paradiso.* Introduction by Cintio Vitier. Havana: Letras Cubanas, 1991.

———. *Poesía completa.* Havana: Editorial Letras cubanas, 1985.

Lezama Lima, José "Summa Critica of American Culture." Trns. Mark Shafer. In
Ilan Stavans, ed., *The Oxford Book of Latin American Essays.* Oxford: Oxford
University Press, 1997: 244–59.

Lihn, Enrique et al. *Paradiso: Lectura de conjunto.* Mexico: Universidad Autónoma de México, 1984.

Litz, Walton A. "Pound and Eliot on *Ulysses*: The Critical Tradition." In *Ulysses:
Fifty Years.* Bloomington: Indiana University Press, 1974: 5–17.

López Campillo, Evelyn. *La "Revista de Occidente" y la formación de minorías.* Madrid: Taurus, 1972.

Marechal, Leopoldo. *Adán Buenosayres*. Buenos Aires: Editorial Sudamericana, 1976.

———. "James Joyce." *Macedonio* 1, no. 3 (1969): 31–37.

Marichalar, Antonio. "James Joyce en su laberinto." *Revista de Occidente* 6 (1924): 177–202.

Márquez, Enrique. *José Lezama Lima: Bases y génesis de un sistema poético*. New York: Peter Lang, 1991.

Martin, Gerald. *Journeys through the Labyrinth. Latin American Fiction in the Twentieth Century*. London: New York, 1989.

Martínez, Manuel Díaz. "Lezama, crítico de nuestra poesía." *Bohemia* 58 (14 January 1966): 26–27.

Mercanton, Jacques. "James Joyce." Translated by J. M. Guarnido. *Contrapunto* 4 and 5 (1945).

Merleau Ponty, Maurice. *Consciousness and the Acquisition of Language*. Evanston: Northwestern University Press, 1973.

Molinero, Rita. *José Lezama Lima o el hechizo de la búsqueda* Madrid: Playor, 1989.

Molloy, Sylvia. *La Diffusion de la littérature latinoaméricaine en France au XXeme siècle*. Paris: Presse Universitaire de France, 1972.

Moris, Beja et al., ed. *James Joyce: The Centennial Symposium*. Urbana: University of Illinois Press, 1986.

Newby, Elizabeth A. *A Portrait of the Artist: The Legends of Orpheus and Their Use in Medieval and Renaissance Aesthetics*. New York: Garland Publishing, 1987.

Nietzsche, Friedrich. *The Use and Abuse of History*. Translated by Adrian Collins. New York: Liberal Arts Press, 1977.

Noon, William T. *Joyce and Aquinas*. New Haven: Yale University Press, 1971.

———. "*A Portrait*: After Fifty Years." *James Joyce Today*. Bloomington: Indiana University Press, 1966.

Novás Calvo, Luis. *Obra narrativa*. Havana: Letras Cubanas, 1990.

Orringer, Nelson R. *Ortega y sus fuentes germánicas*. Madrid: Gredos, 1979.

Ortega y Gasset, José. *Ideas sobre el teatro y la novela*. Madrid: Alianza Editorial, 1975.

———. *La deshumanización del arte y otros ensayos de estética*. Madrid: Alianza Editorial, 1981.

———. *Meditaciones sobre la literatura y el arte*. Edited by E. Inman Fox. Madrid: Clásicos Castilia, 1987

———. *The Dehumanization of Art and Other Writings on Art and Culture*. Garden City: Doubleday & Co., 1958.

———. "Tiempo, distancia y forma en el arte de Proust." *Obras completas* (Madrid: Ediciones Revista de Occidente, 1960): 695–703.

Ortiz, Fernando. *Contrapunteo del tabaco y el azúcar: Advertencia de sus contrastes agrarios, económicos, históricos y sociales*. Havana: 1940.

———. *El Huracán: Su mitología y sus símbolos*. Mexico: Fondo de Cultura Económica, 1947.

Padilla, Heberto. "La poesía en su lugar," *Lunes de Revolución* (Havana, 7 December 1959): 5–6.

———. *Self-Portrait of the Other*, New York: Farrar, Straus and Giroux, 1990.

Paz, Octavio. *Corriente alterna*. Mexico: Siglo Veintiuno, 1967.

Pellón, Gustavo. *José Lezama Lima's Joyful Vision. A Study of Paradiso and Other Prose Works*. Austin: University of Texas Press, 1990.

Perez, Louis A. *Cuba under the Platt Ammendment: 1902–1934*. Pittsburgh: University of Pittsburgh, 1986.

Philip, J. A. *Pythagoras and Early Pythagoreanism*. Phoenix: University of Toronto Press, 1966.

Piaget, Jean. *The Language and Thought of The Child*. Translated by Margaret Gabain. New York: Meridian Books, 1955.

Piñera, Virgilio. "Cada cosa en su lugar." *Lunes de Revolución* (Havana: 14 December 1959): 11–12.

Pound, Ezra. *Literary Essays of Ezra Pound*. Edited with an introduction by T. S. Eliot. London: Faber & Faber, 1954.

Pound/Joyce. The Letters of Ezra Pound to James Joyce. Edited by Forrest Read. New York: New Directions, 1970.

Prieto, Adolfo. et al. *Las claves de Adán Buenosayres*. Mendoza: Azar, 1966.

Pucinni, Darío. "Borges como crítico literario y el problema de la novela." In *El ensayo y la crítica literaria en Iberoamérica*, Kurt L. Levy and Keith Ellis, ed. Toronto: University of Toronto Press, 1970, pp. 145–54.

Reyes, Alfonso. *Cuestiones estéticas* Paris: Paul Ollendorff, 1910.

———. *Cuestiones gongorinas*. Madrid: Espasa Calpe, 1927.

———. *Junta de sombras: estudios helénicos*. Mexico: Edición del Colegio Nacional, 1949.

———. *La afición a Grecia*. Mexico: Editorial del Colegio Nacional, 1960.

———. *Mallarmé entre nosotros*. Ediciones Tezontle, 1955.

———. *Obra completas*. Edited and commented by Ernesto Mejía Sánchez. Mexico: Fondo de Cultural Económica, 1958–1985.

Ricard, Alain, ed. *Coloquio Internacional sobre la obra de José Lezama Lima*. Madrid: Editorial Fundamentos, 1984. 2 vols.

Ríos Avila, Rubén. "A Theology of Absence: The Poetic System of José Lezama Lima." Dissertation, Cornell University, 1983.

———. "The Origin and the Island: Lezama and Mallarmé." *Latin American Literary Review* 8, no. 16 (1980): 242–55.

Rodríguez Feo, José. *Mi correspondencia con Lezama Lima*. Havana: Ediciones Unión, 1989.

Rodríguez Feo, José and Wallace Stevens. *Secretaries of the Moon: The Letters of Wallace Stevens & José Rodríguez Feo*. Edited by Beverly Coyle and Alan Filreis. Durham: Duke University Press, 1986.

Rodríguez Monegal, Emir. *Jorge Luis Borges: A Literary Biography*. New York: E. P. Dutton, 1978.

Rodríguez Monegal, Emir, and Mario Vargas Llosa. "Sobre el 'Paradiso' de Lezama." *Mundo Nuevo* 16 (October 1967): 89–95.

Rossman, Charles. "The Critical Reception of the 'Gabler *Ulysses*;' Or, Gabler's *Ulysses* Kidd-napped." *Studies in the Novel* 21 (1989): 154–81.

———. "The Hidden Controversy." *The New York Review of Books* (8 December 1988): 53–58.

———, ed. "Special Issue on Editing *Ulysses*." *Studies of the Novel* 22 (1990).

———. "Stephen Dedalus' Villanelle." *James Joyce Quarterly* (1976): 292–93.

Ruiz Barrionuevo, Carmen. *El Paradiso de Lezama Lima: Elucidación crítica*. Madrid: Insula, 1980.

Running, Thorpe. *Borges' Ultraist Movement*. Michigan: International Book Publishers, 1981.

Salas Subirat, J. "La experiencia de traducir el *Ulises*." *Contrapunto* 1, no. 4 (1945): 12.

Salgado, César A. "*Barroco* Joyce: Jorge Luis Borges' and José Lezama Lima's Antagonistic Readings." In Karen Lawrence, ed. *Transcultural Joyce*. Cambridge: Cambridge University Press, 1998: 63–92.

———. "Hybridity in New World Baroque Theory." *Journal of American Folklore*, 112 (445): 316–331.

———. "Finezas de Sor Juana y Lezama Lima." *Actual: Revista de la Universidad de los Andes*, 37 (September–December 1997): 75–102.

———. "Lezama y Joyce." *La Torre* 2, no. 6 (1997): 475–96.

———. "Las mutaciones del escándalo: *Paradiso* hoy." 1, no. 4–5 (Spring 96/Summer 1997): 175–78.

———. "*Ulysses* en *Paradiso*: Joyce, Lezama, Eliot, y el método mítico." *Inti: Revista de Literatura Hispánica* 45 (Spring 1997): 223–33.

Sandulescu, George, and Cliff Hart. *Assessing the 1984 Ulysses*. Garrands and Totowa: Colin Smythe and Barnes & Noble, 1986.

Sánchez Cámara, Ignacio. *La teoría de la minoría selecta en el pensamiento de Ortega y Gasset*. Madrid: Editorial Tecnos, 1984.

Sánchez Robayna, Andrés. "Borges y Joyce." *Insula* 38, no. 437 (1983): 1,12.

Sandulescu, C. George, and Cliff Hart, ed. *Assessing the 1984 Ulysses*. Totowa, N.J.: Barnes & Noble, 1986.

Santa Cecilia, Carlos G. *La recepción de James Joyce en la prensa española (1921–1976)* Sevilla: Universidad de Sevilla, 1997.

Santí, Enrico Mario. *Escritura y tradición: Texto, crítica y poética en la literatura hispanoamericana*. Barcelona: Editorial Laia, 1987.

———. "*Fresa y chocolate*: The Rhetoric of Cuban Reconciliation," *MLA* 113, no. 2 (1998): 407–25.

———. "*Paradiso* de José Lezama Lima" (ed. de Cintio Vitier). *Vuelta* 187 (1992): 45–48.

———. "Parridiso," *MLN* 94 (1979): 355

Sarduy, Severo. "Dispersión/falsa notas: Homenaje a Lezama." *Mundo nuevo* 24 (June) 1968: 5–17.

———. *Ensayos generales sobre el barroco*. Mexico: Fondo de Cultural Económica, 1987.

———. *La simulación*. Caracas: Monte Avila, 1982.

———. "Un Proust Cubain." *La Quinzaine Littéraire* 15, 1971: 3–4.

Scholes, Robert. "Stephen Dedalus, Poet or Esthete?." *PMLA*, 84 (1964): 484–89.

Schwartz, Jorge. "La última página del Ulises." *Revista Iberoamericana* 100–101 (1967): 721–23.

———. *Las vanguardias latinoamericanas: Textos pragmáticos y críticos*. Madrid: Cátedra, 1991.

Scott, Boni Kime, ed. *New Alliances in Joyce Studies: When Its Aped To Foul a Delfian*. Newark: University of Delaware Press, 1988.

Scrimaglio, Marta. *Literatura argentina de vanguardia, 1920–1930*. Rosario: Editorial Biblioteca, 1974.

Searle, John. *Speech Acts: An Essay in the Philosophy of Language*. London: Cambridge University Press, 1969.

Seidel, Michael. *Epic Geography: James Joyce's Ulysses*. Princeton: Princeton University Press, 1976.

Segal, Jeffrey. *Joyce in America: Cultural Politics and the Trials of Ulysses*. Berkeley: California University Press, 1993.

Shaw, George Bernard. "Literatura y erotismo." *Revista de Occidente* 7, no. 21 (1925): 302–32.

Shumway, Nicholas, and Thomas Sant. "Literary Theory in Borges." *Latin American Literary Review* 9.17 (1980): 41–.

Simo, Ana María. et al. *Cinco miradas sobre Cortázar*. Buenos Aires: Editorial Tiempo Contemporáneo, 1968.

Simón, Pedro, ed. *Recopilación de textos sobre José Lezama Lima*. Havana: Casa de las Américas, 1970.

Souza, Raymond D. *Major Cuban Novelists*. Columbia: University of Missouri Press, 1976.

———. *The Poetic Fiction of José Lezama Lima*. Columbia: University of Missouri Press, 1983.

Splitter, Randolph. "Watery Words: Language, Sexuality, and Motherhood in Joyce's Fiction." *ELH* 49, no. 1 (1982): 190–213.

Staley, Thomas F., and Bernard Benstock, ed. *Approaches to Joyce's Portrait: Ten Essays*. Thomas, F. Pittsburgh: University of Pittsburgh Press, 1976.

Staley, Thomas F., and Bernard Benstock, ed. *Approaches to Ulysses: 10 essays*. Pittsburgh: University of Pittsburgh Press, 1970.

Staley, Thomas F., ed, *Ulysses: Fifty Years*. Bloomington: Indiana University Press, 1974.

Stark, John O. *The Literature of Exhaustion: Borges, Nabokov and Barth*. Durham: Duke University Press, 1974.

Teuber, Bernardo. "¡O feliz lapsus! Autobiografía, crítica genética y genealogía del sujeto en *Paradiso* de José Lezama Lima." *MLN* 108 (1993): 314–30.

Thibaudet, Albert. *La poésie de Stephane Mallarmé*. Paris: Editions de la NRF, 1912.

Thorton, Weldon. *Allusions in Ulysses: An Annotated List*. Chapel Hill: University of North Carolina Press, 1968.

Troy, Mark L. *Mummeries of Resurrection: The Cycle of Osiris in Finnegans Wake*. Stockholm: Upsala, 1976.

Ulloa, Justo C. *Sobre José Lezama Lima y sus lectores. Guía y compendio bibliográfico*. Boulder: Society of Spanish and Spanish-American Studies, 1987.

Valdievieso, Jaime. *Bajo el signo de Orfeo: Lezama Lima y Proust*. Madrid: Orígenes, 1980.

Vanderham, Paul. *James Joyce and Censorship: The Trials of Ulysses*. New York: New York University Press, 1998.

Vasconcelos, José. *Pitágoras, una teoría del ritmo*. [Mexico]:Tip. Murgia, 1921.

Vera Cuspinera, Margarita, ed. *Alfonso Reyes. Homenaje de la Facultad de Filosofía y Letras*. México: Universidad Autónoma, 1981.

Verani, Hugo. *Las vanguardias literarias en Hispanoamérica*. Roma: Editores, 1986.

Verene, Donald Phillip, ed. *Vico and Joyce*. Albany: State University of New York Press, 1987.

———. *Vico's Science of Imagination*. Ithaca: Cornell University Press, 1981.

Vickery, John. *The Literary Impact of The Golden Bough*. Princeton: Princeton University Pres, 1973.

Vico, Giambattista. *Autobiografía*. Buenos Aires: Espasa-Calpe Argentina, 1948.

———. *The Autobiography of Giambattista Vico*. Translated with an introduction by Max Harold Fisch and Thomas Goddard Bergin. Ithaca: Cornell University Press, 1944.

———. *The New Science*. Translated with an introduction by Max Harold Fisch and Thomas Goddard Bergin. Ithaca: Cornell University Press, rev. ed. 1968.

———. *Principios de una Ciencia Nueva en Torno a la Naturaleza Común de las Naciones*. Translated by José Carner. Mexico: El Colegio de Mexico, 1941.

———. *Principj di una Scienza nuova d'intorno alla comune natura delle nazioni*. Edited by Giuseppe Ferrari. Napoli: Stamperia de Classici Latini, 1859.

———. *Sabiduría primitiva de los italianos*. Buenos Aires: Instituto de Filosofia, 1939.

Vitier, Cintio. "*Paradiso*: Treinta años de un mito." *Crítica* 12 (Dec.–Jan 1996–7): 27–34.

Wellek, René. *Concepts of Criticism*. New Haven: Yale University Press, 1963.

Wheelock, Carter. "Borges' New Prose." In Harold Bloom, ed. *Jorge Luis Borges*. New Haven : Chelsea House Publishers, 1986.

Whitman, Walt. *Hojas de hierba*. Selected and translated with an prologue by Jorge Luis Borges. Buenos Aires: Juárez, 1969.

Will, Frederick, ed. *Hereditas: Seven Essays on the Modern Expression of the Classical*. Austin: Univeristy of Texas Press, 1969.

Wilson, Edmund. *Axel's Castle. A Study on the Imaginative Literature of 1870 to 1930*. New York: Charles Scribner's Sons, 1947.

Wilson, Edmund. "James Joyce y el '*Ulises*'." Translated by J. Salas Subirat, *Davar* 1 and 2 (1945).

Zambrano, María. *María Zambrano en "Orígenes"*. Mexico: Ediciones del Equilibrista, 1987.

Index

Adams, Robert Martin, 21–22
Aldington, Richard, 95, 227n. 20
Aleixandre, Vicente, 189
Alonso, Carlos J., 224n4,
Alonso, Dámaso, 79–83, 88, 219n. 46, 220nn. 55, 58, and 59, 221nn. 60 and 61; *El artista adolescente Retrato*, 79–80, 82–83, 219n. 46, 220n. 59, 60, 61, and 62
Alvárez Bravo, Armando, 244n. 14
anagnorisis, 27–28
Anderson, C. G., 213n. 4
Aquinas, Saint Thomas of, 21, 26, 52, 73–74, 76–78, 219nn. 44 and 45
Arenas, Reinaldo, 17
Aristotle, 148
Arrom, José Juan, 213n. 4
Artaud, Antonin, 27
Asturias, Miguel Angel, 89
Ateneo de la Juventud, 107, 111
Auerbach, Erich, 152, 237n. 37
Augustine, Saint, 21, 163

Bajarlía, Juan Jacobo, 31, 89, 96, 225n. 8
Barth, John, 209n. 3
Bataille, Georges, 120
Beach, Sylvia, 189
Beckett, Samuel, 140–43, 145–46, 176
Bedani, Gino, 237n. 30
Bejel, Emilio, 16, 212n. 3, 214n. 10, 236n. 23, 237n. 34
Benjamin, Walter, 79
Bérard, Victor, 39, 106, 109–10
Berlin, Isaiah, 147
Benstock, Bernard, 217n. 41
Bishop, John, 212n. 30
Bloom, Harold, 175, 242n. 66
Boas, Franz, 24, 27
Book of the Dead, The, 45
Booth, Wayne, 84, 221n. 66

Borges, Jorge Luis, 15, 16, 29, 31, 32, 33–42, 45, 82, 87, 89, 91, 97, 99, 120, 130, 132, 139, 208n. 1, 210nn. 6, 9, and 15, 211nn. 21 and 24, 223n. 1, 224n. 6, 232n. 3, 235n. 15; *Discusión,* 89; *Elogio de la sombra,* 39; "Fragmento sobre Joyce," 39–41; "Funes el memorioso," 45; *El idioma de los argentinos,* 37; *Introducción a la literatura inglesa,* 41; "Joyce y los neologismos," 38, 132; "Los teólogos," 32; "El *Ulises* de Joyce," 36–37; "El último libro de Joyce," 38; "Vindicación de *Bouvard et Pécuchet,*" 35
Breton, André, 26
Bruno, Giordano, 26, 49, 71, 142, 188
Buckley, Jerome Hamilton, 221n. 64, 222n. 68
Bueno, Salvador, 191–93, 212n. 28
Burke, Kenneth, 56, 59, 217n. 28
Burroughs, William, 296

Cabrera, Lydia, 241n. 62
Cabrera Infante, Guillermo, 17, 20, 104
Campbell, Joseph, and Henry Morton Robinson, 146, 240n. 52
Campos, Augusto and Haroldo de, 146
cantidad hechizada, La, 33, 135–39, 142–43, 147–49, 179
Carner, José, 146, 235n. 15
Carpentier, Alejo, 15, 16, 89, 120, 130, 185, 224n. 5
Cervantes, Miguel de, 40, 44
Chiampi, Irlemar, 20, 205, 248n. 46
Chomsky, Noam, 54–55
"Conversación con Juan Ramón Jiménez," 229n. 46
"Cortázar y el comienzo de la nueva novela," 137–39, 233n. 11
Cortázar, Julio, 15, 17, 23, 26, 50, 104,

120–21, 130, 135, 144–45, 164, 181, 189, 195–99, 213 n. 5, 227 n. 28, 233 nn. 10–11, 243
Croce, Benedetto, 146–47
Cruz, Sor Juana Inés de la, 17, 148
Cruz Malavé, Arnaldo, 215 n. 12, 219 n. 44, 299 n. 46, 238 n. 40
Curtius, E. R., 43, 91
Cusa, Nicholas of, 26, 71

Dalton, John, 198, 246 n. 34
Dante Alighieri, 17, 46
Darantiere, Maurice, 189
Darío, Rubén, 17, 81
Derrida, Jacques, 63, 217 n. 28
Diario (1939–49), 51, 86
Diego, Eliseo, 221 n. 62
Dodds, E. R., 120
Dostoevsky, Fyodor, 35

Eastman, Max, 44
Eliot, T. S., 18, 25, 31, 33, 39, 43, 92, 95–97, 99, 105, 107, 110, 139, 192
Elizondo, Salvador, 235 n. 17
Ellmann, Richard, 131, 226 n. 17, 232 n. 74, 234 n. 13
epiphany, 20–21, 55–65, 216 n.17
eras imaginarias, 151–55, 159–60, 162, 164–65
Ernst, Morris L., 192
Espuela de Plata, 89
expresión americana, La, 22–23, 33, 148, 171

Faulkner, William, 24, 26, 27, 35
Feijóo, Samuel, 241 n. 62
Fernández Retamar, Roberto, 23, 208 n. 9, 234 n. 11
fijeza, La, 75–76
Flaubert, Gustave, 92–94, 97
Fresa y chocolate, 185
Frazer, Sir James, 106, 110, 170, 241 n. 62
Freud, Sigmund, 204–5
Frobenius, Leo, 215 n. 12
Fuentes, Carlos, 24, 104

Gabbler, Hans Walter, 181–83, 185, 198–204, 247 n. 36
García Carranza, Araceli, 208 n. 2
García Márquez, Gabriel, 16, 24, 26, 27

García Vega, Lorenzo, 217 n. 25
Generación del 27, 36, 79–82, 86
Gide, André, 17
Gifford, Don, 183
Gilbert, Stuart, 31, 38, 42, 43, 79, 90–92, 94, 97–98, 102, 105–7, 134, 139–46, 176, 189, 197, 211 n.19, 230 n. 57; *James Joyce's Ulysses*, 105–8
Goddard Bergin, Thomas, and Max Harold Tish, 146
Goethe, Johann Wolgang Von, 17, 20, 40, 52, 83–85; *Wilhelm Meister*, 20, 52, 83–85
Góngora, Luis de, 17, 36–38, 44, 47, 75, 79; *Las Soledades*, 37, 80–82
González-Echevarría, Roberto, 207 n. 2, 223 n. 4
González Lanuza, Eduardo, 100
Gordon, Samuel, 185
Gorman, Herbert, 42, 43
Gracián, Baltasar, 133, 178, 206, 243 n. 71
Groden, Michael, 185
Guillén, Jorge, 78
Guillén, Nicolás, 15

Harrison, Jane, 106, 110
Hart, Clive, 200
Hartman, Geoffrey, 59, 217 n. 28
Heidegger, Martin, 152
Heller, Ben A., 16, 18
Hemingway, Ernest, 189
Henríquez Ureña, Pedro, 108–9
Heredia, José María, 172
Hesse, Herman, 17
Homer, 26, 124

imagen (or imago), 74–75, 78, 135–39
"Introducción a los vasos órficos," 122–23

Jaeger, Werner, 109–15, 127, 230 nn. 52, 54, and 55; *Paideia: The Ideals of Greek Culture*, 110, 112–15, 127
Jarnés, Benjamín, 209 n. 5
Jitrik, Noé, 100, 216 n. 20,
Jolas, Eugene, 38
Joyce, James, compared to Lezama Lima, 18–22, 45–47, 187–88; critical reception of *Ulysses* in Latin America, 88–92, 96–97; errors in

Ulysses, 188–89; Ezra Pound and T. S. Eliot on *Ulysses,* 92–96; the "Joyce Wars," 181–87; Lezama on, 22–24, 41–51, 97–99, 116–18, 135; *A Portrait of the Artist as a Young Man,* 48–87; *Chamber Music,* 42; *Finnegans Wake,* 38, 132–147, 165–170, 174, 176–177, 179–180; *Stephen Hero,* 74, 86, 90; *Ulysses,* 88–108, 110, 115–19,121,128, 130–31, 181–89; *Work in Progress,* 37, 132 "Joyce y Proteo," 117–18

Juliosvaldo, 193–196

Jung, Carl G, 89, 91, 96–97, 159

Kafka, Franz, 24

Kenner, Hugh, 84, 119, 216n. 22, 221n. 66

Kidd, John, 181–83, 185–87, 201–4

Larbaud, Valery, 31, 43, 79, 91–92

Lautréamont, comte de 79

Lawrence, D. H., 27, 110

Levin, Harry, 56, 90, 146, 212n. 2, 216n. 21, 234n. 13

Levinson, Brett, 16, 18, 20, 182, 187, 199–202, 205

Lévi-Strauss, Claude, 159

Lewis, Wyndham, 43

Lezama Lima, José: current criticism on, 15–18; and high modernism, 24–29; and James Joyce, 18–21, 45–47; Jorge Luis Borges and, 33–34; on neologism, 176–80; writings on Joyce, 22–24; on *A Portrait,* 41–45, 48–52; on *Ulysses,* 91–92, 97–100; on *Finnegans Wake,* 135–39, 144–46; *La cantidad hechizada,* 33, 135–39, 142–43, 147–49, 179; "Conversación con Juan Ramón Jiménez," 229n. 46; "Cortázar y el comienzo de la nueva novela," 233n. 11; *Diario (1939–49),* 51, 86; *La expresión americana,* 22–23, 33, 148, 171; *La fijeza,* 75–6; "Joyce y Proteo," 117–118; "Muerte de Joyce," 41–46, 48–51, 97–99, 116, 135; *Muerte de Narciso,* 17; *Paradiso,* 52–69, 83–86, 116–19, 124–26, 130–31, 181–83, 189–97, 124–28,

147–65; *Oppiano Licario,* 165–76; *Sonetos a la Virgen,* 55

Litz, A. Walton, 226n. 15

Lopez, César, 241n. 57

Loyola, Saint Ignatius of, 49, 99

Lunes de Revolución, 190

Mahaffey, Vicki, 185

Mallarmé, Stéphane, 18, 80–81, 91

Mann, Thomas, 17, 22, 24, 116,

Marechal, Leopoldo, 31, 89, 100–104, 224n. 5; *Adán Buenosayres,* 100–104

Marichalar, Antonio, 31, 91, 98, 209n. 5

Márquez, Enrique, 236n. 23

Martí, José, 57, 148

Martin, Gerald, 90, 225n. 11,

Marx, Karl, 238n. 40

Mazo, Marcelino del, 133

Menéndez Pelayo, Marcelino, 81

Merleau-Ponty, Marcel, 69, 217n. 37

Mier, Fray Servando Teresa de, 148

Milton, John, 133

Miranda, Francisco de, 148

Mirandola, Pico della, 188

Monsiváis, Carlos, 197–198

"Muerte de Joyce," 41–46, 48–51, 97–99, 116, 135

Muerte de Narciso, 17

Murray, Gilbert, 106, 109, 110

Newby, Elizabeth A., 231n. 67

Nietzsche, Friedrich, 120

Noon, William T., 217n. 39, 219n. 44

Novas Calvo, Lino, 172

Oppiano Licario: compared to *Finnegans Wake,* 165–70, Viconean notions in, 169–76

Orígenes, 17–18, 86, 89, 184, 190

Orphism, 122–25

Orr, Leonard, 20

Ortega, Julio, 200

Ortega y Gasset, José, 31, 33, 79–80, 146, 209nn. 4 and 5; "Ideas sobre la novela," 34

Ortiz, Fernando, 170–75, 241nn. 61, 62, and 64

Padilla, Heberto, 184, 244n. 11

paideuma, 53, 215n. 12

Paradiso: compared with *A Portrait of*

the Artist as a Young Man, 52–69; as bildungsroman, 26, 51–52, 83–86; aesthetic theory in, 83–86; compared with *Ulysses*, 116–19, 130–31; neohellenism in 119–30; editorial history, 181–83; polemic on sexual corruption in, 189–97; "Retrato de José Cemí," 124–26; Orphism and Pythagoreanism in, 124–28
Parnell, Charles Stewart, 57, 63
Paso, Fernando del, 104
Paz, Octavio, 15, 27, 75, 189, 217 n. 43
Paz, Senel, 185
Pellón, Gustavo, 16, 18, 20, 28, 32, 214 n. 5, 215 n. 11
Piaget, Jean, 54–55
Picasso, Pablo, 22
polemic on the "death" of the novel, 34–36
Pound, Ezra, 18, 31, 43, 55, 91–94, 92–97, 99, 192, 216 n. 19
Prats Sariol, José, 185, 200
Prieto, Adolfo, 100, 102
Proust, Marcel, 7, 18, 22, 24, 35, 116
Puccini, Darío, 210 n. 7
Pynchon, Thomas, 21
Pythagoras, 119, 126–28, 178

Quevedo, Francisco de, 40

Rabassa, Gregory, 16, 183
Revista de Occidente, 35–36, 79–80, 86, 89, 91, 209 n. 5
Reyes, Alfonso, 80–82, 108–12, 120, 124–125, 130, 220 n. 55, 229 nn. 41 and 42, 231 n. 61; *La afición a Grecia*, 120; *Junta de sombras*, 109–11, 113, 120, 231 n. 63
Rilke, Rainer Maria, 22
Ríos, Julián, 104
Ríos-Avila, Rubén, 230 n, 56
Roces, Wenceslao, and Joaquín Xirau, 112
Rodríguez Feliú, Oscar, 89, 230 n. 59
Rodríguez Feo, José, 89
Rodríguez Monegal, Emir, 184, 194–97, 246 n. 30
Rossman, Charles, 217 n. 40, 243 n. 2

Salas Subirat, J., 90, 96, 224 n. 6
Sánchez Robayna, Andrés, 36, 210 n. 16

Santí, Enrico Mario, 20, 182, 187, 197, 201–4, 240 n. 57, 248 n. 44
Sarduy, Severo, 17, 75, 184, 200, 206, 217 n. 43, 220 n. 54
Saussure, Ferdinand de, 54, 178
Scholes, Robert, 84, 222 n. 66
Schwartz, Jorge, 210 n. 12, 211 n. 18
Shakespeare, William, 133
Sigüenza y Góngora, Carlos de, 148
Sola, Graciela de, 100
Sonetos a la Virgen, 55
Souza, Raymond, 16, 18–19, 21, 216 n. 21
Spencer, Theodore, 222 n. 68
Spender, Stephen, 18, 90
Stevens, Wallace, 18
Stravinsky, Igor, 22
súbito, 177–80, 205–6

Teuber, Bernardo, 182, 187
Thibaudet, Albert, 81, 91, 220 n. 53, 226 n. 13
Thorton, Weldon, 183
Torre, Guillermo de, 89
Torriente, Loló de la, 192–93, 196

ultraísmo, 36–37
Unamuno, Miguel de, 40

Valéry, Paul, 91
Vanderham, Paul, 245 n. 20, 246 n. 32
Vargas Llosa, Mario, 194–95, 246 n. 30
Vasconcelos, José, 108
Vega, Lope de, 37
Vico, Giambattista, 26, 29, 47, 139–79, 205, 235 nn. 15 and 19, 237 n. 38, 240 n. 44
Vitier, Cintio, 112, 125, 177, 182–87, 197–204, 242 n. 69, 244 n. 10, 244 nn. 12 and 14; 248 n. 47

Wells, H. G., 55, 216 n. 19
Whitman, Walt, 37
Woolf, Virginia, 24, 41
Woolsey, John W., 88

Yeats, William Butler, 189

Zambrano, María, 124–25